EDWARD CONZE'S THE PSYCHOLOGY OF MASS PROPAGANDA

Edward Conze's *The Psychology of Mass Propaganda* presents a commentary on the psychology of propaganda during the rise of fascism in Europe in the 1930s. It discusses the conditions which generate vulnerability to misinformation in human societies, and thus offers insight into how propaganda may be "withstood." Completed in 1939, during the period of Conze's own inflection from Marxist philosophy to Buddhist studies, the original manuscript was never published and is now in print for the first time.

Presenting a unique historical perspective, while also appealing to an acutely topical interest in the conditions under which autocracy and fascism arise, the book examines the psychology of mass propaganda through copious contemporary and historical examples. Conze focuses especially on recent news articles and the statements of the propagandists of many of the governments that would go on to participate in the Second World War, including Germany, Italy, the USSR, USA, and UK, all of which he interprets through the lens of recent psychological and historical research. The book has been edited and includes a new introduction by Richard N. Levine and Nathan H. Levine, also featuring a foreword by American legal scholar Laurence H. Tribe, and an afterword by actor, director, writer, and Buddhist priest Peter Coyote.

This is a fascinating opportunity for scholars across several disciplines, including political scientists and psychologists, historians, and sociologists, to access one of Conze's previously unpublished works. It will also be of importance to those interested in Conze's work on Buddhist philosophy and in the psychology of propaganda more broadly.

Edward Conze (1904–1979) was a pioneering scholar of Buddhism in the West. Prior to that career, he had been a Marxist philosopher and political activist. He authored several works in political psychology during the 1930s, and today he is best known for his translations and commentaries on the *Prajñāpāramitā* literature and for several other books on Buddhism.

Richard N. Levine is a former student and personal secretary to Dr. Edward Conze. He is a medical doctor and retired Associate Clinical Professor of Medicine at UCSF School of Medicine.

Nathan H. Levine is currently studying for a PhD in Ancient Greek and Roman Studies at the University of California, Berkeley.

EDWARD CONZE'S THE PSYCHOLOGY OF MASS PROPAGANDA

Richard N. Levine and Nathan H. Levine

Routledge
Taylor & Francis Group
NEW YORK AND LONDON

Cover image: © Getty Images

First published 2023
by Routledge
605 Third Avenue, New York, NY 10158

and by Routledge
4 Park Square, Milton Park, Abingdon, Oxon, OX14 4RN

Routledge is an imprint of the Taylor & Francis Group, an informa business

ISBN: 978-1-032-42597-9 (hbk)
ISBN: 978-1-032-42594-8 (pbk)
ISBN: 978-1-003-36340-8 (ebk)

DOI: 10.4324/9781003363408

Typeset in Bembo
by Newgen Publishing UK

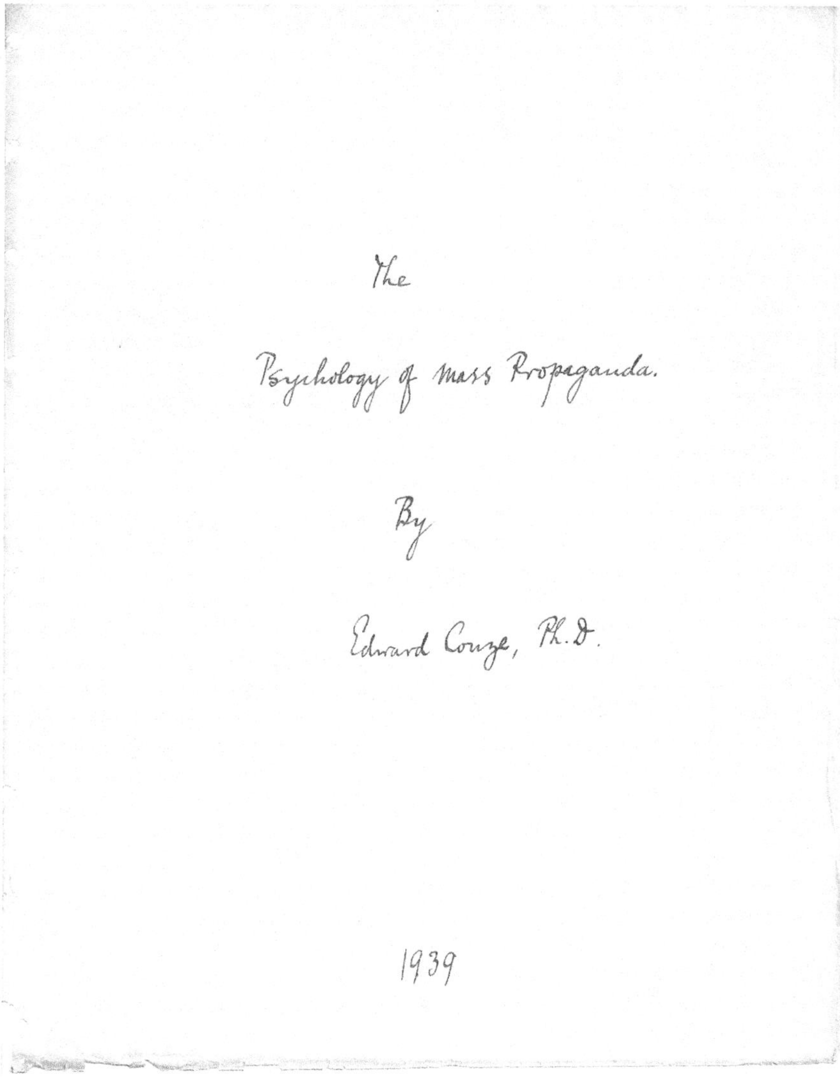
The

Psychology of mass Propaganda.

By

Edward Conze, Ph.D.

1939

Title page of the original typescript

The editors dedicate this volume
to the memory of Dr. Alexander Tribe
Psychiatrist and Zen Buddhist priest
(May 18, 1946–November 27, 2017)

CONTENTS

Title calligraphy on facing page by Richard N. Levine and Nathan H. Levine

Edward Conze's

The Psychology of Mass Propaganda

FOREWORD

Richard and Nathan Levine, the editors of this magnificent volume, were good enough to invite me to write this Foreword. They had me at "Dedicated to the memory of Dr. Alexander Tribe, Psychiatrist and Zen Buddhist priest." Dr. Tribe is my late brother. He was also my best friend.

It also helped that the afterword to this book by the enormously learned and prolific Edward Conze, Richard and Nathan explained, was to be written by someone who knew my brother well. He is the talented writer/actor Peter Coyote, whose voice the world has heard and come to love as the mellifluent narrator of virtually every documentary by Ken Burns. Peter was ordained a Zen Buddhist priest the same day as my brother, was a close friend and "dharma brother" to my brother, and … wait for it, was born the same day as I was: October 10, 1941, although thousands of miles from where I entered the picture. Kismet.

Let me back up a bit. I was a few months short of five years old when Shurka—that's the only name I ever knew my brother by, and the only name I ever called him—was born on May 18, 1946. I had turned 76 a little over a month before he died—very suddenly, of causes still unclear, on November 27, 2017. He wasn't yet 72. Much too young to die, leaving behind two wonderful adult children, Jessica and Joshua, and two delightful grandchildren, who of course have never stopped missing their great dad and loving granddad.

When Shurka—whom everyone came to call "Al" or "Doctor Al"—was born, we were living in cramped, dusty quarters in war-torn Shanghai, in the French Concession where I too had been born, just months before Japanese troops took over the city. It was the day their air forces conducted the infamous sneak attack on Pearl Harbor. Our modest home—we weren't among the Tandoori Jews of that great city, the ones depicted in "Empire of the Sun," but among the humblest—was nearly destroyed when the U.S. Air Force bombed Shanghai in order to liberate it from the Japanese at the war's end.

We had the great good fortune not to be killed in the American air raids that ensued, just as we'd narrowly escaped being exterminated by the Butcher of Warsaw, Josef Meisinger, who all but persuaded the Third Reich's ally, the Empire of Japan, to pack all the Jews being sheltered in Shanghai in wooden boats and then send the boats out to sea to drown us all in what many came to call the Passover Plot.

Our father, George Israel Tribuch, came from a little town called Luninetz near Minsk. He was born there in 1905, the year after both Conze, this book's author and the great European expert in Buddhism, and Suzuki-roshi, leader of the branch of Zen my brother followed, were born. Our father had traveled across many time zones with his parents, traversing Russia to escape the pogroms and ending up in Harbin, Manchuria, where he met our mother, Paulina Diatlovitsky, born in Harbin in 1915.

Our father had changed his last name to Tribe at the insistence of immigration authorities in San Francisco, the port to which he traveled in the 1920s, determined to become the first in his family ever to attend college. Unfortunately persuaded by a well-meaning friend to seek employment instead, he became a short-order cook and eventually a car salesman before, having become a U.S. citizen, he returned to Harbin, from which he and his family, and my mother and her parents and sisters, were forced to emigrate to the only place where Jews were then welcomed, Shanghai. It is a story shared by many in the Jewish diaspora. Because he had become an American citizen long before the Japanese Empire made war on the United States, our father was interned in a Japanese prison camp across the river from Shanghai from February 1943 to August 1945. Shurka—Al, to most of you—must have been conceived within days of our father's reunion with his family upon his release from the concentration camp. Fearing what the impending advent of Communism would mean, our parents were desperate to leave China and managed to bring me and Shurka to San Francisco, where we spent our childhoods.

Our paths diverged when, not yet 17, I left home to attend Harvard, an institution I'd never even heard of before a good friend asked me why I'd not considered applying. Shurka stayed back in the Bay Area, earning his MD degree and becoming a beloved psychiatrist, recognized at one point as the best-liked physician in Northern California. It's no wonder. He was open, generous, kind, insightful, caring, brilliant, funny. Everything a doctor should be. He once joked to me that it had been so long since he had practiced regular medicine that he no longer remembered which end of the stethoscope to put in his mouth. In the meantime, I took up mathematics, then became a lawyer. Every Jewish mother's dream: my sons, the doctor and the lawyer. Not exactly her dream for him to become a Zen Buddhist priest, but you can't have everything. As one humorist wisecracked, where would you put it all?

But I digress. The reason I was asked to write this Foreword, apart from all the serendipity and synchronicity I've recounted here, is no doubt that the tyrannical regimes from which my family fled—the authoritarianism and oppression both my brother and I felt so fortunate to escape by being brought up in sunny California, breathing the (somewhat polluted but, as I said, you can't have everything) air of freedom, has for some time now come back to darken the skies overhead. It's tempting to blame much of it on the megalomaniacal madman who managed, with Russia's not-so-kosher help, to win the presidency in 2016 and who claims, in just another example of the Big Lie that is his specialty, to have been robbed of that office in 2020. That's tempting because it paints the comforting picture of Donald J. Trump as a one-off, an aberration in an otherwise hopeful trajectory.

Alas, that temptation is out of joint with reality. As many who have carefully studied the death of democracies and the rise of tyrannies have concluded, the cult leaders who manage to mesmerize large enough swaths of the populace to sweep aside the institutional and traditional guardrails of the rule of law, including orderly elections, peaceful transitions from one regime to the next, and informal norms of mutual forbearance, are more often symptoms than causes of the cancer they inject into the body politic.

For the several years leading up to my taking emeritus status—the last several years of my tenure as the Carl M. Loeb University Professor and Professor of Constitutional Law at Harvard University—I created and taught an advanced constitutional law seminar called "Strategies for Defending Constitutional Democracy Under Stress." We explored a broad range of options from impeachment to civil and criminal litigation to grassroots activism to civil disobedience—doing so in real time. For instance, while I was teaching the seminar, I was simultaneously advising such former students of mine as Representatives Adam Schiff and Jamie Raskin, each of whom served essentially as chief prosecutor pressing one of the two historic impeachments of President Trump, the first for his abuse of power in seeking to extort the president of Ukraine in order to promote the lie that his principal opponent's son, Hunter Biden, was under investigation for corruption; and the second for his even more dangerous abuse in inciting the insurrection of January 6, 2021, in an attempted coup that many, including me, believe he is planning to repeat should the Republican Party's legislative machinations of vote suppression and manipulation, coupled with ongoing propaganda, not suffice to sweep Trump back into power, this time perhaps to remain indefinitely.

This is hardly the place to elaborate on all the reasons I have for sounding so fearful. Suffice it to say that the psychology of mass propaganda, the topic of Conze's fine book, could hardly be more timely. The fact that it was written decades ago, at the dawn of the Second World War, makes its dazzling and still fresh insights all the more impressive and none the less illuminating.

It may seem Panglossian to view Truth—yes, I write it with a capital "T" as a believer that there is indeed such a thing, perhaps a Platonic hangover from my days as a budding mathematician—as the ultimate antidote to the forces of deception that threaten the survival of liberty, of respect for human dignity, and of government of the people, by the people, for the people. But if my belief in the cleansing power of Truth makes me naïve, then so be it. Despair, like deceit, are the enemies of decency and democracy. So let us not despair. Books like this one—so suitably dedicated to my always hopeful brother Shurka, and so deeply undergirded by the equanimity that he found in Zen Buddhist practice—may be our last best hope.

Laurence H. Tribe
Carl M. Loeb University Professor
Professor of Constitutional Law *Emeritus*
Harvard Law School

EDITORS' INTRODUCTION

Richard N. Levine and Nathan H. Levine

Dr. Conze's text stands on its own and speaks best for itself. Even so, we offer a little background for those who may be interested.[1]

I first met Dr. Conze while auditing his class on the *Madhyamaka* school of Buddhism at UC Berkeley in the fall semester of 1971, and again during a biweekly seminar at the San Francisco Zen Center in the spring of 1973. When he was then invited to be visiting professor at UC Santa Barbara in the summer of 1973, it was arranged that I would be his personal secretary there, in exchange for permission to attend his seminar on *Abhidharma* as well as a more general survey course on Buddhism.[2] I knew him as a brilliant, exhilarating teacher, immersed in the study and practice of Buddhism. He ended his last lecture at Santa Barbara by invoking a sutra-ending trope of Śakyamuni Buddha, "I have spoken," and there followed a prolonged standing ovation from a full auditorium.[3]

One day in his office at Santa Barbara he gave me a bound typescript, dated 1939, entitled *The Psychology of Mass Propaganda* (hereafter, "PMP"). I later became aware of his comment that "This book was, on ideological grounds, never brought out by the publisher who had commissioned it, and it will probably be found among my posthumous papers."[4] I also knew that he had always wanted it published, and vaguely hoped to facilitate that some day.

---

1 The editors' introduction is co-authored by Richard N. Levine and Nathan H. Levine. First-person references and "private conversations" are attributable to Richard Levine; the section "Propaganda Studies" is primarily written by Nathan Levine.

2 For Conze's own comments about this arrangement, see Conze, *The Memoirs of a Modern Gnostic*, vol. 1 (Manchester: Frederick Law & Co., Ltd., 1979), p. 143.

3 See, for example, Conze's translation of the *Diamond Sutra*, which concludes, "Thus spoke the Lord." *Buddhist Wisdom Books: Containing the Diamond Sutra and the Heart Sutra* (London: Allen & Unwin, Ltd., 1958), p. 71.

4 Conze, *Further Buddhist Studies* (Oxford: Bruno Cassirer, Ltd., 1975), p. x.

Four decades passed, and the American elections of 2016 prompted me to re-read the book. I found it freshly topical and remarkably illuminating in several ways, but particularly with respect to shining a light on the flagrant and malign use of propaganda by the new American administration. As a further resonance with contemporary American politics, I was aware that Conze had "formulated a theory of Social Blindness to indicate that one class of the population has not the remotest idea of how the other lives, thinks, or feels, and fills the vacuum with totally unfounded imaginations." He goes on to say, "I regarded this as an important contribution, not only to sociology, but also to the elucidation of the Buddhist concept of ignorance, and I regret that so far it seems to have passed unnoticed."[5] The current edition is offered with the wish that Conze's writing on propaganda may yet be noticed while it remains especially pertinent, and not merely as an artifact of intellectual history.

Early Years

Eberhard[6] Julius Dietrich Conze was born in London to German parents in 1904. His father was the German Vice-Consul at the time, and the scion of a long-established affluent family whose money came from the silk industry. Conze himself was the product of a merger of business interests: his father's family owned a silk-spinning factory in Langenberg, Germany, while his mother's owned the silk-dyeing factory. (His father's brother was married to his mother's sister, and all concerned appear to have been more or less symmetrically unhappy about the arrangement.)

About six months after his birth the family returned to Germany where Conze was raised and educated. As he says in his memoir, it was at "gymnasium" (akin to American "prep" or academic high school) that he was attracted to Marxism "at a time when it was a fashionable thing to do."[7] This would be around the same time he first remembers encountering Buddhism, during his early teens, through a copy of Lafcadio Hearn's *Gleanings in Buddha-Fields* found in his father's library.[8] He remained an "ardent young communist,"[9] and party member, until he left Germany in 1933, and although ruptures occurred along the way, it wasn't until

5 Conze, *The Memoirs of a Modern Gnostic*, vol. 2 (Manchester: Frederick Law & Co., Ltd., 1979), p. 17 fn., citing his own comment from his book *Der Satz vom Widerspruch: Zur Theorie des dialektischen Materialismus* (Hamburg: Self-published, 1932; reprint Verlag Neue Kritik, 1976); English trans. Holger R. Heine, *The Principle of Contradiction: On the Theory of Dialectical Materialism* by Edward Conze (Maryland: Lexington Books, 2016).

6 Eberhard later changes to Edward "because I couldn't do that to the British" (private conversation).

7 Conze, *Memoirs* 2, p. 19.

8 Conze, *Memoirs* 1, p. 6 (Lafcadio Hearn, *Gleanings in Buddha-Fields: Studies of Hand and Soul in the Far East* [London: Kegan Paul, Trench, Trübner, 1897]).

9 Conze, *Memoirs* 1, p. 11.

FIGURE 0.1 Conze's parents.

Source: Photo courtesy of Eric Zsebenyi.

1960, during a visit to the Soviet Union, that Conze realized a "final parting" from Communism.[10]

At age 24, in 1928, Conze received a PhD in Philosophy from the University of Cologne, with a study of Francisco Suarez, the Jesuit scholastic philosopher. Completing this, he turned immediately to his preferred and central work in philosophy, a Marxist analysis of Aristotle's "Principle of Contradiction" (originally titled *Der Satz vom Widerspruch*, 1932). But the timing was poor. "Most of my time between 1928 and 1932 was spent working on my large book about 'The Principle of Contradiction' which came out a few months before the Nazi flood engulfed Germany."[11]

On January 27, 1932, Conze and his father attended a meeting in Dussdeldorf at which Hitler appeared. Conze remembered his father commenting, "This fellow looks just like a seedy waiter."[12] He cites Albert Speer, in agreement, that because Hitler "himself was nothing, he provided ample room for demonic forces to operate in him."[13] He was "a low-born part-German clown from Braunau in Austria."[14]

As for the book, it was "a catastrophic failure," says Conze. "500 copies had been printed and most of these were lost, some on the bonfire by which the S. A. in Hamburg testified to their devotion to German culture."[15] By early 1933

10 Conze, *Memoirs* 2, p. 30.

11 Conze, *Memoirs* 1, p. 9.

12 Ibid., p. 11.

13 Ibid., pp. 10–11. Conze is paraphrasing Speer's view here.

14 Ibid., pp. 36–37.

15 Ibid., p. 35.

FIGURE 0.2 Edward Conze ca. 1935.

Source: Photo courtesy of Herbert Elbrecht.

the Nazis had assumed power in Germany. Conze's safety was in jeopardy, his magnum opus had been burned, and with it had perished the previously bright prospect of a German academic career. He emigrated urgently to London, his birthplace, starting out by teaching tutorial classes in psychology at the University of London.[16]

To be clear about his own political commitments, Conze describes himself as an ardent communist "Agit Prop"[17] during his last years in Germany, and Holger Heine writes that he combined a conventional position teaching classroom philosophy by day "with a militant activism in the desperate struggle against the rising tide of Fascism in Germany."[18] He adds,

> At night, [Conze] taught clandestine courses on dialectical materialism at the Communist-run Marxist Workers School and organized the deployment of militant ANTIFA (Anti-Fascist Action) cadres to defend against the increasingly frequent and often deadly assaults by Nazi SA troops on workers and union organizers.[19]

16 "What in my first years in England I taught as 'Psychology' was largely Freud, Oedipus complex and all" (Ibid., p. 29).

17 See Conze, *Memoirs* 2, p. 25 as to his personal involvement with agitprop in Germany. Agitprop being shorthand for "agitation and propaganda."

18 Heine, *The Principle of Contradiction*, p, xxvii (translator's introduction).

19 Ibid., p. xxiv. See Conze, *The Scientific Method of Thinking* (London: Chapman & Hall, Ltd., 1935) and *An Introduction to Dialectical Materialism* (London: NCLC Publishing Society, Ltd., 1936).

In May 1936, after re-establishing himself in London, he went to Spain "because I felt that the situation there was on the point of boiling up."[20] The Spanish Civil War was to erupt in July. He went with passionate partisan sympathies, identifying with the "anarcho-syndicalists,"[21] and the result of his trip, the book *Spain Today*, was published in 1936 under contract with the publishers Secker & Warburg.[22] At the same time he was actively recreating an English version of his magnum opus, *Der Satz vom Widerspruch* (more on this under "Red Threads" below). And this was the period when he began work on *The Psychology of Mass Propaganda* (PMP).[23]

Publication History

The typescript of PMP which is the basis for the present volume has an original, pen-and-ink title page on yellowing, edge-worn paper with Conze's signature, dated 1939 (see front matter). He was living in London that year. Hitler was in Berlin, Mussolini in Rome, Stalin in Moscow, and Franco in Madrid.

Most of what we know about the typescript comes from the author's *Memoirs*, where he comments:

> [The] madmen could do their work only if they had the willing collaboration of their victims, and so I wrote a book on the 'The Psychology of Mass Propaganda.' It was commissioned by Secker & Warburg, but in the end the manuscript was never published. Mr. Warburg objected chiefly to my thesis that psychologically speaking the appeal of Russian communism was no different from that of German Nazism or Italian Fascism. So we agreed that I could keep my advance and he could keep the book off his List. The manuscript I submitted to him seems to have been lost. All I appear to have

20 Conze, *Memoirs* 1, p. 18.

21 Conze, *Memoirs* 2, p. 48.

22 Conze, *Spain Today: Revolution and Counter-Revolution* (London: Secker & Warburg, Ltd., 1936). For an additional vivid evocation of Spain during that same year, 1936, the reader is referred to George Orwell's "Homage to Catalonia," also published by Secker & Warburg (1938).

23 As Herbert Elbrecht suggests, PMP "was underway as early as 1935" (private correspondence, August 24, 2017). Elbrecht refers specifically to Conze's "'Fascist and Tribal Mentality,' a summary of points made in his lecture at the Summer School of the F. P. S. I." Also pertinent are four articles by Conze which appeared in the journal *The Plebs: Organ of the National Council of Labour Colleges*: "The Psychology of Imperialism" in *Plebs* 27.12 (December, 1935): 280–83; "The Psychology of Imperialism II.—On Camouflage" in *Plebs* 28.1 (January, 1936): 41–44; "The Psychology of Imperialism III.—The Empire's Appeal to the Mind" in *Plebs* 28.3 (March, 1936): 57–60; and "The Psychology of Imperialism IV. Internationalism" in *Plebs* 28.4 (April, 1936): 85–91. Written during the same period, although the precise date is not known, is an unpublished essay in seventeen typewritten pages entitled "How to sell goods," with the note "in collaboration with A. and D. Deys." We have not been able to learn anything further about the identity of these co-authors. As Elbrecht reports, the essay was included in the photocopy of PMP which he received from Conze in the 1970s ("diese Seiten lagen in losem Durchschlagpapier dem 'PSYCHOLOGY OF MASS PROPAGANDA' bei").

> left is a copy in 322 pages which Mrs. Hunt of Woodstock... typed in the Fifties of the 1939 version.[24]

Later, when I read the *Memoirs*, I realized that this was the typescript Dr. Conze had given me in Santa Barbara. According to Herbert Elbrecht, a friend of Conze during his last years, the typing was done in 1951.[25]

As to why Fredric Warburg forfeited an author's advance and declined to publish the book, his own autobiography seems discordant with Conze's version of the story.[26] First Warburg acknowledges the success of his prior collaboration with Conze:

> *Spain Today* by Edward Conze appeared on 17 August [1936]. The Spanish affair had started only thirty days before, and interest was intense. Congratulating myself on my foresight in having commissioned so topical a book, I was delighted when it went into a second impression.[27]

Warburg goes on to describe the political and business climate he was facing during the years 1936–1939. Conditions were desperate on both fronts. Franco's war against the republican Spanish government broke out within months of the establishment of his firm, Secker & Warburg. Financial prospects for the new publishing house were tenuous at best, in grave jeopardy really, and in language that may resonate with some readers today, he writes that the revolt in Spain, and the attendant international political climate, "roused me and many of my generation to a frenzy of indignation."

> The period from the German occupation of the Rhineland in March 1936 to the betrayal of Czechoslovakia in September 1938 was a nightmare.... No longer was our interest centred in what appeared to be the stale old struggle in the House of Commons between two venerable, if slightly corrupt, political caucuses.... Through the Western world travelled the deadly international viruses of Hitlerism and Stalinism.... Nazi seeds appeared to be sprouting in the ranks of the Conservatives.... But when I turned to the Left I surveyed a movement where Stalinism seemed welcome as the next step in democratic development. These issues were inflamed by the Spanish political influenza.... Into this political maelstrom I rushed naively, like a man chased by a bull.... In fact I had no choice.... Against the ideas of evil and madness we must mobilize, I thought, the counter-ideas of sanity and health. They would have to be hammered out in words by the finest minds

24 Conze, *Memoirs* 1, pp. 33–34.

25 See Elbrecht's illuminating website celebrating Conze: http://conze.eu/.

26 Fredric Warburg, *An Occupation for Gentlemen* (Boston: Houghton Mifflin Company, 1960).

27 Warburg, *An Occupation for Gentlemen*, p. 192.

> of our generation.... My firm...must play its part in the war of words and the clash of ideas.[28]

Totalitarianism was anathema, but its worst face was Nazism. Thus, if compelled to make alliances, as he perceived himself to be, Warburg leaned toward the Socialists, and even considered aligning with the Communists. One day in 1936 Warburg met for lunch with his friend H. N. Brailsford, a prolific Socialist journalist associated with the Left Book Club.

> Forcibly I put my doubts to [Brailsford], and his answer was clear. 'We can't altogether approve of much that is done by the Soviet Union,' he told me, 'it's a young and raw system, and at present certainly totalitarian. But...if we are forced to choose between two totalitarian systems, Nazi and Communist, we must choose the Communist.... Nazism is the apotheosis of lunacy, anti-semitism and brutality.'[29]

Warburg goes on to list Conze as a member of the Independent Labour Party (ILP), one among a number of "promising writers" including George Orwell, Jomo Kenyatta, and a few others. These were commended to Warburg by Fenner Brockway, secretary of the ILP, who suggested that these writers would bring him their books to publish. "But," writes Warburg,

> were these the ones to support, politically or commercially? Certainly the communists would review them without enthusiasm in the literary and political magazines. The I.L.P. writers were not communists, but socialists, and socialists of a peculiar brand, libertarian socialists, anarchists even, whose attitude to the USSR was at best ambivalent, at worst plain hostile.... Their books might or might not be good books, but if they sold it would be without benefit of communist clergy.[30]

Uncertain how to balance this opportunity to publish the ILP authors against his reluctance to offend the "communist clergy," he brought his concerns to his wife Pamela.

> 'The Liberals and the independent socialists have no love for communists,' I said. 'Yet is it wise to attack the communists when they seem to be our only reliable allies?' 'The Soviet Union is quite big enough to stand a little criticism,' my wife said. 'And obviously you need these books for your list. Don't you think yourself it's the right thing for you to do?'[31]

28 Ibid., pp. 196–199.
29 Ibid., p. 205.
30 Ibid., p. 206.
31 Ibid., p. 209.

This conversation appears to have marked the end of any tenuous sympathies Warburg harbored toward Communism, and the vehemence of his wife's arguments must have helped. As he quotes her, "I'd rather be married to a miser than to an English communist."[32] By the end of 1936, he writes, "I had embarked on a policy of anti-fascist publishing which paid no heed to communist susceptibilities."[33]

Conze apparently thought, and wrote, that Warburg declined to publish PMP because of an unwillingness to insinuate even the slightest disparagement of Communism (see above, p. xx: "Mr. Warburg objected chiefly to my thesis that psychologically speaking the appeal of Russian communism was no different from that of German Nazism or Italian Fascism"). But this view is not easy to reconcile with Warburg's avowed anti-Communism from 1936 onwards, especially given that most of Conze's work on PMP, as inferred from the dates of references and citations within the text, seems to have taken place during the years 1937 and 1938. Warburg's reasons for ultimately declining to publish PMP are not entirely clear. While the two men would have shared an array of political sympathies, it may be that Conze's assessment of the matter reflects a projection of his own attitude toward the book as a step in his arduous withdrawal from communist orthodoxy. As he wrote in a letter of 1978 to Herbert Elbrecht, "If they want to know why I moved from communism to Buddhism they may be interested in *The Psychology of Mass Propaganda* which gives the reasons."[34]

All the same Conze continued to pursue publication:

> My Socialist friends basically agreed with Mr. Warburg. In 1937 and 1938 G. D. H. Cole and Raymond Postgate were editing a series of Socialist pamphlets called 'Fact' and were willing to include a summary of 'Mass Propaganda'. I still remember being invited by Postgate to an extremely opulent lunch where his rubicund hedonism foreshadowed his later career as a compiler of Good Food Guides. He was willing to take my typescript, provided I removed all references to the Soviet Union which implied that Soviet man was essentially the same as Nazi man, and democratic man for that matter. Nothing could shake him, and he gave as his reason for his inflexibility that his sister, Margaret Cole, would never stand for any even apparently unfavourable comment on the Soviet Union, which had just been praised by her mentors, the Webbs, in two fat volumes (1935) as the society for which they had always longed.[35]

32 Ibid., p. 208.

33 Ibid., p. 221.

34 Excerpt from private letter, dated January 2, 1978 (Edward Conze to Herbert Elbrecht), kindly made available by Elbrecht.

35 Conze, *Memoirs* 1, p. 34.

PMP was clearly not purged of reference to Soviet man as being the same as other men, and it is not likely to have been significantly revised for Mr. Warburg, for Conze's own Socialist friends, or for anyone else. See, for example, PMP, p. 156: "The propaganda for communism in Russia led to the establishment of a ruthless state capitalism."

Warburg's copy of the manuscript, which he had declined to publish, may have been lost when the publisher's stock was destroyed in 1940 during the Battle of Britain.[36] In any case, with or without revisions, the projected "summary" version of the book, discussed with the "Socialist friends" mentioned above, failed to materialize. And there the matter lay until 1951 when the textual basis for the current edition was typed out by the aforementioned Mrs. Hunt of Woodstock, carrying Dr. Conze's signature and the 1939 date.

As late as 1978, Herbert Elbrecht, who had a photocopy version of the book, was endeavoring to have it published through Suhrkamp-Insel. On February 23, 1978, Conze writes to Elbrecht: "The book itself has lost much of its lustre through the passage of time. All the illustrations are at least forty years old. But the theoretical analysis is, I think, still basically valid." On July 2, 1978, he writes again, "A few weeks ago Suhrkamp-Insel have suddenly come to life.... They have received the typescript of 'The Psychology of Mass Propaganda' which they seem to find interesting." Finally, on August 15, 1978, "Dr. Unseld is not interested in 'The Psychology of Mass Propaganda', but Herr Werner Berthel wrote that 'in my opinion the book is—after forty years—still suitable for publication.'"[37]

Edward Conze died in an ambulance after an apparent heart attack, on Monday, September 24, 1979. His wife Muriel was beside him. As she later told me, "He looked up and said, 'I can't hold on anymore, goodbye.'" To the best of our knowledge, until the present volume, no further efforts were made with regard to the publication of PMP during the four decades following the author's death.

Red Threads: Marxism and Buddhism

In Conze's introduction to the current volume he summarizes one of its sustained arguments, namely that propaganda creates an artificial sense of social unity, and calls it a "red thread."[38] It would not have been lost on Conze that the canonical Buddhist texts, the *Sutras* (literally "threads" in Sanskrit), represent the unifying coherence of central core traditions underlying what might otherwise appear to

---

36 Warburg, *All Authors Are Equal: The Publishing Life of Fredric Warburg, 1936–1971* (London: Hutchinson & Co., 1973), p. 23: "We lost about 150,000 bound books and half that number of unbound.... We actually lost manuscripts of new books [and] we lost the whole of our stock of unused paper." Recall Conze saying "the manuscript I submitted to [Warburg] seems to have been lost" (*Memoirs* 1, pp. 33–34).

37 Excerpts from private letters (Edward Conze to Herbert Elbrecht), kindly made available by Elbrecht.

38 Conze, PMP, p. 13.

be a disparate sectarianism. It is easy enough to see why these suturing threads, applied to his own intellectual and spiritual life, would be "red." Blood red is the emblematic flag symbol for social resistance, a usage which pre-dates the advent of Communism. We will therefore borrow the metaphor in order to situate PMP among the red threads which give coherence to Conze's work and life. First, his engagement with Marxism and Marxist dialectics, which found expression, over more than three decades, in several iterations of books and papers on Aristotle's "Principle of Contradiction." And second, his engagement with Buddhism.

At the time of Conze's birth in 1904, tempestuous cultural changes were sweeping across Europe. It was the "Belle Époque," the late Victorian period. Aristocracies and monarchies, and their attendant social hierarchies, were unraveling. Post-Impressionism and Modernism were ascendant movements in the arts. It was the year of Bloomsday (June 16, 1904), when James Joyce situates Leopold Bloom's epic day in *Ulysses*. And in the only known film clip of Marcel Proust, we see him at the 1904 wedding for the daughter of his thinly fictionalized characters the Duc and Duchesse de Guermantes. In this early version of a home movie, Proust is seen sinuously walking down a grand outdoor stone stairway beside the gathering members of an elaborate wedding procession. His descent contrasts with the cinematic background of the crowd around him, its Chaplinesque herky-jerky movement.

Like any historical moment, Conze's birth year may be viewed with respect to its antecedent causes and conditions, or to its unfolding consequences. For a singular example, Conze might have appreciated the synchronicity that Lafcadio Hearn, whose book *Gleanings in Buddha-Fields* introduced him to Buddhism, died that year. Shunryu Suzuki Roshi, a carrier of Buddhism to the West, who was later to advise his students to attend Conze's Berkeley classes, was born.[39]

In Edmund de Waal's memoir of the history of his own family, the Ephrussi dynasty, he depicts the European fin-de-siècle fascination with "orientalism," more specifically "Japonisme."[40] Among his forebears is de Waal's great uncle Charles Ephrussi, a renowned collector and connoisseur of Japanese art. Ephrussi is thought to be one of the principal models for Proust's central character Charles Swann. And he collected "netsuke," the miniature sculptures, both useful and beautiful, made by Japanese craftsmen. Mr. de Waal takes his ancestor's precious netsuke collection as the standpoint from which to view the sweep of history, that of his family, and of society more broadly.

It is also Conze's history. In June of 1933, after the catastrophic rise of the Nazis, after the book-burning, Conze sent his private library to his father's house in Dusseldorf for safekeeping.

---

39 See San Francisco Zen Center, "News," *Wind Bell: Publication of Zen Center* 12 (1973): 15–31 at 16.

40 Edmund de Waal, *The Hare with Amber Eyes: A Family's Century of Art and Loss* (New York: Farrar, Straus and Giroux, 2010).

> When unloaded one of the boxes burst open and revealed various items then forbidden, i.e. books by Marx, Lenin and Rosa Luxemburg. In sheer self-defense, he [my father] disposed of the entire library. If he had not done so the RAF would in any case have disposed of it later on, as it did of his fine collection of netsuke and Japanese woodcuts.[41]

Conze had used those books, the forbidden books of Marxist philosophy, to write his central work on the "Principle of Contradiction," *Der Satz vom Widerspruch*. The netsuke, along with the book by Lafcadio Hearn that Conze had discovered as a boy in his father's library, constituted his first introductions to Buddhism. Each is a node along the "red threads" that animated Conze's intellectual life during the gestation period of PMP and beyond.

Der Satz vom Widerspruch is the large book that Conze wrote from 1928–1932, the burned book. His 1928 doctoral dissertation had been more or less assigned to him after his own proposal for a study of either Schopenhauer or Spinoza was rejected. Instead he was consigned a "dusty and mildewed old folio volume which turned out to be the *Disputationes Metaphysicae* of Franciscus Suarez," the medieval Scholastic Philosopher.[42] He completed the dissertation and then turned immediately to his work on the Principle of Contradiction, an ambitious labor of love, which he refers to as "my Hauptwerk. In fact it contains all my later ideas without exception."[43] After emigrating to England, Conze began to revise and expand *Der Satz vom Widerspruch* into English, working presumably from one of the few copies he had been able to smuggle out of Germany. "When in 1933 I removed myself to England I regarded this book as my greatest, and in fact only, asset, and started to decant it into the English language."[44]

Something is clearly afoot if he viewed the job as "decanting" rather than "translating."[45] He prided himself on "a special gift for learning languages," professing that "when I was twenty-four I knew fourteen."[46] When, as a teenager, he first encountered the *Diamond Sutra*, he was aware that the text he was reading was "a German translation of an English translation of a Japanese translation of a Chinese translation of a Sanskrit original."[47] In short, Conze had a philologist's unusually keen sensibility toward language. As to why he chose to produce his scholarship after 1933 in English rather than in his native German, we offer a few anecdotes.

During his 1971 seminar on *Madhyamaka* at UC Berkeley, a person sitting near me asked him, "Why did you write your books and translate the *Prajñāpāramitā* into English, when German is both your native language, and the scholarly

41 Conze, *Memoirs* 2, p. 53.
42 Conze, *Memoirs* 1, p. 8.
43 Conze, *Further Buddhist Studies*, p. ix.
44 Ibid., p. ix.
45 Conze, *Memoirs* 1, p. 7.
46 Ibid., p. 4.
47 Ibid., p. 7.

language of Europe?" He paused before responding, "because the Germans have misconducted themselves to such an extent..." and his voice trailed off. In his *Memoirs* he amplifies this sentiment, writing,

> I...had become thoroughly disgusted by the way in which both the legal colleagues of my father in Dusseldorf and the Professors in Hamburg had reacted to the victory of the Nazis, revealing an abject cowardice and slimy duplicity which I would not have believed possible. In consequence I decided that I would no longer wish to use a language degraded so much by this contemptible rabble.... We would therefore speak only English at home and my daughter Jane would learn no German at all.[48]

He comments further,

> One of the greatest benefits of my return to England has been that I have been able to do my Buddhist work in English and not in German, a language scarcely worth writing in any longer on scholarly matters concerning the East.[49]

After leaving Germany, having found employment teaching psychology at the University of London, Conze immediately got back to work on *Der Satz vom Widerspruch* (1932). As he puts it, "When you destroy a spider's web it will soon build a new one."[50] And so he did. He first created a greatly expanded version in English, some one thousand pages long, and later distilled it into a 32-page pamphlet summary which he entitled "Contradiction and Reality," and which he viewed as containing the heart of the subject. Then, after the Second World War, there was a re-expanded 117-page version dated 1960.[51] The Principle of

48 Conze, *Memoirs* 2, p. 2.

49 Conze, *Memoirs* 1, p. 12.

50 Ibid., p. 35.

51 This exists in the form of a partial photocopy of the original 32-page pamphlet interspersed with typed pages and handwritten notes, bearing the handwritten heading, "Carbon copy of revised version typed by author, sent in Dec. 1960 to Mrs. Zafiropulo." In *Memoirs* 1, p. 38, Conze writes, "After the war I produced a greatly expanded version, though only one other person, in Woking, has seen it and he is dead." This final iteration opens with a summary of its contents, beginning with Book I, which will discuss "problems and definitions." In particular it opens with a distinctly Buddhist-sounding, virtuosic riff on the subject of the "self," its nature, its structure, its relative reality, and so on. Then there is a kind of telegraphic "note-to-self" which epitomizes Conze's attitude toward translation as a "decanting" of one language into another. He proposes the playful idea that the foregoing map of the territory covered by *selfhood* might be subject

> to correction by translation into Latin, Latin as a language in which the English use of 'self' is not natural. Get over [the] solution of problems by thoughtless use of [a] ready-made word, or racial idiom, and see traditional background by expressing ideas in another tradition, [as a] way of minimising historical and tribal conditions.

Contradiction was central to his work and would occupy his attention from 1928 to 1960.

The original German-language *Der Satz* was favorably reviewed by Herbert Marcuse in 1934 ("The uncertainties of a first step into a new territory of materialism find clear expression in Conze's book").[52] It served as the basis for three English-language articles composed during the 1930s, which were ultimately reprinted in *Further Buddhist Studies* (1975). It was also the source for two books for the general public: *The Scientific Method of Thinking* (1935) and *An Introduction to Dialectical Materialism* (1936). The original 1932 version of *Der Satz* was reprinted in 1976 (Verlag Neue Kritik). Most recently, in 2016, it has been translated into English and elegantly re-introduced by Holger Heine.[53]

In *Der Satz* Conze takes on Aristotle's Principle of Contradiction, a fundamental tenet of European philosophy. He does so in the light of "dialectics," that is to say, a way of reasoning and of apprehending reality rooted in ancient Greece, later elaborated by Hegel (the Idealist) and then adapted by Marx and Engels (the Materialists) to an analysis of capitalist economics. Heine offers that "the conceptual foundations for an analysis of dialectic thought are descendants—in one form or another—of Aristotle's...science of metaphysics [and of his] defense of the non-contradictory nature of all being *qua* being."[54]

Without aspiring to unravel these and several other abiding problems in philosophy, for our current purpose we'll just say that dialectical materialism, most certainly Conze's version of it, accommodates contradictions in a way that Aristotle's approach to logic does not. It is characterized by the familiar formula for dialectics, consisting of a thesis, an antithesis, and a synthesis. It says, in small part, that contradictions are not mutually canceling in all circumstances. Further, a fundamental quality of the Principle of Contradiction, especially as Conze approaches it as a Marxist, is that it is not an abstract metaphysical theory. It is grounded in concrete human social contexts, and particularly in the human practice of communication through language[55]:

> In Der Satz vom Widerspruch I had preached the primacy of practice over mere facts and concluded that the question 'What is the Truth?' could be resolved by finding out what kind of people were able to get at the truth. In other words what had to be done was to discover a disinterested truth-bearing section in Society. This was, as I said then, the revolutionary

---

There follow five pages of Latin, comprising a literal translation of the English riff on selfhood. The book closes with a table showing simple uses of the word "self" comparing the English, Sanskrit, Greek, Latin, and German.

52 Herbert Marcuse, "Review of *Der Satz vom Widerspruch* by Edward Conze," *Zeitschrift für Sozialforschung* 3 (1934): 266–267, trans. Holger Heine, 2011.

53 Heine, *The Principle of Contradiction*.

54 Ibid., p. xxvii.

55 Ibid., p. xxxi.

> proletariat represented by the C.P. [Communist Party] trained in Scientific Socialism. In retrospect this seems an extraordinary statement to make.[56]

By 1933 his confidence in that statement was coming undone, along with other dimensions of his world view. In fact, Conze describes PMP, as well as the other political books he produced in the mid- to late-1930s, as endeavors "to neutralize the Marxist virus in my system."[57] What he regarded as the "scientific" insights of Marx's dialectical materialism endured, however, even though Stalin was making Communism untenable. They were re-situated in Buddhism, specifically in the dialectical approach of Nāgārjuna and the school of *Madhyamaka* as elaborated in the *Prajñāpāramitā* literature.

Nāgārjuna's attitude is expressed in his statement,

> There is the teaching of "individual self" (*ātma*) and the teaching of "non-individual self" (*anātma*); But neither "individual self" nor "non-individual self" whatever has been taught by the Buddhas. When the domain of thought has been dissipated, "that which can be stated" is dissipated.[58]

The view of *Madhyamaka* is that thought does not meaningfully apprehend reality. Within the domain of thought mutually contradictory statements are often found to be equally tenable, and in any case, ultimately untenable. Nāgārjuna uses *reductio ad absurdum* arguments that bear a striking resemblance to the Western tradition of dialectical criticism. Consider the above quotation from the *Kārikās* showing the three phases of the dialectic. There is the "dogma" (thesis) of *ātmavāda*, the doctrine of an enduring self or soul, and of *anātmavāda*, the doctrine of no-self (antithesis). Their contradictory co-existence comprises an impetus to "criticism," which engenders "intuition" (synthesis), a "dissipation of what can be stated." The structural necessity of the dialectical process corresponds intrinsically, in the view of *Madhyamaka*, to the "total and interminable conflict in reason."[59]

Despite a succession of political disenchantments, Conze retained explicit affinities with dialectical materialism throughout his life. "My allegiance is to the scientific studies alone which have become part of the knowledge accepted by all educated people everywhere."[60]

What sutured the apparent chasm between Marxism and Buddhism were a number of compelling commonalities. For one,

---

56 Conze, *Memoirs* 1, p. 36.

57 Conze, *Further Buddhist Studies*, p. x.

58 Nāgārjuna, *Mūlamadhyamakakārikā* 18.6–7, trans. Frederick J. Streng in *Emptiness: A Study in Religious Meaning* (New York: Abingdon Press, 1967).

59 T. R.V. Murti, *The Central Philosophy of Buddhism* (London: G. Allen & Unwin, Ltd., 1960), p. 9.

60 Conze, *Memoirs* 2, p. 18.

> What had attracted me, as well as many of the German young men of my generation, to the collectivist tenets of Communism (or of National Socialism for that matter), had been the hope that in this way we would manage to get rid of the intolerable burden of our individuality, of our ridiculously insistent claims to self-importance, and of the necessity to constantly make personal decisions on matters about which we knew next to nothing. To merge into the anonymous mass was to us the equivalent of the Nirvana which a poet once described by saying that 'the dewdrop slips into the shining sea'. Buddhism is as insistent as Marxism about combating the illusions of individuality, and the doctrine of 'not-self' as well as the goal of self-extinction lie within its very core.[61]

Beyond "not-self," Conze found some compatibility with Buddhism because "I would in Bolshevism have found a movement very much akin to the Mahayana—in its concern for the masses, in the dialectical nature of its thinking and in its desire to perform heroic deeds which have miraculous results."[62]

To augment this argument, particularly with respect to dialectical thinking, and their respective attitudes toward contradictions, Conze observed that the Buddhists go beyond the binaries of Aristotelian thought in a way that is quite similar to the Marxists. For example, in a discussion of how the *bodhisattva* combines "wisdom" and "compassion," he writes that wisdom perceives people's individuality (which is actually a composite of impersonal elemental *dharmas*) as fundamentally illusory; compassion nevertheless cultivates lovingkindness toward these non-existent people. He concludes, "The Buddhist philosophers differ from philosophers bred in the Aristotelian tradition in that they are not frightened but delighted by a contradiction."[63]

PMP is rife with more or less apparent references to Buddhist thought. For example, when Conze opens Chapter 1.3 with a statement concerning the "mental concomitants" of oppression, he is invoking Buddhist terminology. The Sanskrit term *caitta dharma* (Pali: *cetasika dhamma*), fundamental to *Abhidharma* psychology, is commonly translated as "mental concomitants." In this instance he is using the term to elucidate the complex psychology of oppression. Part 2 of PMP is entitled "The Veils Which Hide the Truth," to which he refers in the *Memoirs* as "a long meditation on the Buddhist theory of self-deception (Moha)."[64] Elsewhere he writes that "*The Psychology of Mass Propaganda*...argued for the futility of all political action on the ground that mass activities must necessarily be permeated and vitiated by self-deception, as well as by greed and hatred."[65] The reference to the "three poisons" of Buddhism, greed, hatred, and delusion, is explicit.

---

61 Ibid., p. 133.

62 Ibid., p. 19.

63 Conze, *Buddhism: Its Essence and Development* (Oxford: Bruno Cassirer, Ltd., 1951), p. 129.

64 Conze, *Memoirs* 1, p. 34.

65 Conze, *Further Buddhist Studies*, p. x.

In the 1930s, when Conze was starting out in Buddhist Studies, it wasn't difficult to sort out who was who in the field, and what was what, at least in the western hemisphere. The discipline was young, its ranks sparse, and the taxonomy fairly simple. "Up to about 1935," he writes, "Buddhist research was divided into three distinct schools."[66] First there was an "Older Anglo-German school," with a moralistic bias, in the persons of T. W. Rhys Davids and Henry Oldenberg. Based on recourse to the Pali Canon, it aspired to an "original, pure, or true" Buddhism. As Conze says summarily, "its position has become untenable."[67] He was to observe later that "At this stage of human history one can not have Buddhism in a pure state. It can exist only as one component in a new synthesis."[68]

The second school is "Leningrad," led by Fyodor Stcherbatsky, Otto Rosenberg, and E. E. Obermiller. These are the scholars who asked, "Why don't we see how the Buddhists themselves interpret their doctrine?"[69] Stcherbatsky, for example, studied with a local pandit during his 1910 trip to India, and Obermiller studied texts with Mongolian monks in Buryat monasteries.

Finally, there is a "Franco-Belgian" school which included Louis de la Vallée-Poussin, Sylvain Lévi, Étienne Lamotte, and others. These scholars followed in the steps of the Leningrad school, enriching their philological work with the recent findings of sociology and other emerging disciplines. Conze quotes Constantin Regamey on them: "They have abandoned as fruitless the attempt to reconstruct a pure Buddhism, are convinced that Buddhism is as much the work of the Buddhists as of the Buddha himself."[70] Conze concludes,

> While the 'Older Anglo-German' school has died out from inanition, and the Leningrad school has perished through unfavourable social conditions, the principles of the Franco-Belgian school have now been universally adopted by all scholars working in the field, whatever the country they may live in.[71]

This is what Buddhist Studies looked like to Conze when in 1937, aged 33, "the bottom had fallen out of what I then thought was my world."

---

66 Conze, *Thirty Years of Buddhist Studies: Selected Essays* (Oxford: Bruno Cassirer, 1967), p. 1.

67 Conze, *Thirty Years of Buddhist Studies*, p. 1.

68 Conze, *Memoirs* 2, p. 38.

69 This comment is transcribed from recordings of the seminar Conze conducted in the dining room of the San Francisco Zen Center in Spring 1973. See link to recordings at Cuke.com, "Audio-Video," accessed August 23, 2022, www.cuke.com/audio%20files/av.htm#conze (courtesy of David Chadwick).

70 Conze, *Thirty Years of Buddhist Studies*, p. 2 (from Constantin Regamey, *Der Buddhismus Indiens* [1951], pp. 247–248).

71 Conze, *Thirty Years of Buddhist Studies*, p. 3.

> My political faith had collapsed under the impact of Stalinism and of what I had observed in Spain, my marriage had failed, my job seemed distinctly bleak, I had even begun consulting psychoanalysts, and there seemed nothing left that I could live for.[72]

He would add that two years later, "at 35, in the middle of my life I had, as Dante would have it, 'lost my way in the middle of a dark wood'. All my previous beliefs had collapsed and lay around me shattered to pieces."[73]

> Then one day I happened to look into the window of one of the bookshops opposite the British Museum, my curiosity was aroused and just on chance I bought the third volume of 'Essays in Zen Buddhism'.[74]

D. T. Suzuki's essays rekindled Conze's boyhood interest in Buddhism, originally sparked in his father's library. This was an epochal event in his life: it was the moment of his inflection from committed, activist Marxism to immersion in the study and practice of Buddhism.

> It was in the shadow of the great historical events of the thirties that I had my *āśrayaparavṛtti*, or spiritual rebirth. I shifted my truth-bearing section of Society from revolutionary commissars to contemplative Buddhist monks and so my later work is directly continuous with my earlier one.[75]

At the time of this emergence from Marxism toward Buddhism, Conze created the 1000-page expansion in English of *Der Satz vom Widerspruch*, and then a distillation into a short pamphlet containing the heart of the matter:

> I now re-wrote my Der Satz on the basis of these new insights. Soon my work had reached more than 1000 typed pages though it was threatened by a looming catastrophe just as the previous one was—this time by the coming War.... So I summarized my results in 1939 in a pamphlet of 32 pages called 'Contradiction and Reality'.[76]

One may be reminded of the *Prajñāpāramitā* texts, which started as a core work in 8,000 lines and expanded over time to 100,000 lines, before contracting to summary versions such as the *Heart Sutra* in some fourteen lines.

72 Conze, "A Personal Tribute," *The Eastern Buddhist* 2.1, New Series (August, 1967): 84–85 at 84.
73 Conze, *Memoirs* 1, p. 27.
74 Conze, "A Personal Tribute," p. 84.
75 Conze, *Memoirs* 1, p. 37.
76 Ibid., p. 37.

Today Conze is primarily remembered as a pre-eminent scholar, translator, and teacher of Buddhism. Sixty years after its original publication, *Buddhist Thought in India* (1962) remains a serviceable textbook on the subject. *Buddhism: Its Essence and Development* (1951), and others, stand up to the passage of time. But his major enduring contribution is his translation into English, and explanatory scholarship, of most of the roughly 42 texts comprising the *Prajñāpāramitā* literature. His translations cover the historic arc of this Mahayana literary tradition, prominently including the *Aṣṭasāhasrikā* (or *Perfection of Wisdom in 8,000 Lines*, 1958), the earliest representative of the *Prajñāpāramitā* textual tradition[77]; the later, expanded *Large Sutra on Perfect Wisdom* (1961); and finally, *Buddhist Wisdom Books* (1958), containing enduring translations of the short summary versions, the *Heart Sutra* and the *Diamond Sutra*, with commentaries on both.[78]

Propaganda Studies

Today, in the wake of the largest military operation in Europe since the Second World War, and in the third year of an ongoing pandemic which has accelerated an already growing political and social polarization worldwide, the engines of propaganda are on public display to an unprecedented degree. We are subjected to everything from personally targeted advertisements fueled by "big data" to direct communication from politicians through social media, not to mention the many unconscious forms of propaganda that have always operated but are now amplified with the aid of the internet.

In comparison to the contemporary propaganda landscape, the disturbing flows of information that Conze treats in PMP were clumsy and inefficient. The structure of our societies, the nature and efficiency of media technologies, and the discourse around these subjects, have all undergone revolutions in the eight-plus decades since Conze's completion of the volume in 1939. Moreover, some of his theoretical presumptions, both conscious and unconscious, are dated. Conze's analysis of propaganda challenges, but does not entirely escape, the conventional "top-down" model prevalent in his time, according to which, as Sahar Khamis, Paul B. Gold and Katherine Vaughn put it, "'propagandists' (or 'masters'), representing authoritarian regimes, constrain and shape how citizens think, feel, and act."[79] Conze sometimes characterizes propaganda in this traditional vein, as a conscious imposition upon naive victims. At other times, however, he offers a prescient

77 Conze, *Selected Sayings from the Perfection of Wisdom* (London: The Buddhist Society, 1955): "The oldest text is the Perfection of Wisdom in 8,000 Lines...[and some parts] date back to 100 B.C."

78 See Herbert Elbrecht, http://conze.eu/ for a more complete bibliography of Conze's works, both published and unpublished.

79 Sahar Khamis, Paul B. Gold, and Katherine Vaughn, "Propaganda in Egypt and Syria's 'Cyberwars': Contexts, Actors, Tools, and Tactics" in Jonathan Auerbach and Russ Castronovo, eds., *The Oxford Handbook of Propaganda Studies* (Oxford: Oxford University Press, 2013): 418–438 at 432. See also Auerbach and Castronovo's introduction to the volume, pp. 9–10.

critique of the "top down" approach by studying propaganda as an inherent feature of social life on a large scale. Another critique of the "top-down" approach is the still emerging model of "grassroots propaganda," a term which Khamis, Gold, and Vaughn have used of propaganda as a form of social and political resistance. This approach would surely have been of great interest to Conze.

But as intriguing as such new approaches may be, they build on the work of more than a century of earlier theorists. And simply because those theorists studied forms of propaganda embedded in different historical and institutional contexts than our own, their role in shaping the modern discipline is no less crucial. Given the difficulty, even impossibility, of finding a disinterested standpoint from which to evaluate the propaganda operating in our own lives, it is all the more essential to study the theorists of the past, for both their enduring insights and their limitations.

PMP is thus an unusual and valuable resource: precisely because Conze's work was unavailable for later thinkers to draw upon and is only now being published, it presents an opportunity to revisit the history of propaganda studies in the period after the First World War, when modern approaches to the phenomenon were still in their infancy. While we are not specialists in the history of propaganda studies, it is hoped that by citing and briefly commenting on some of the touchstones of the field, we will enable the reader to better contextualize the book. At the least, it is hoped that our discussion will both help the reader to appreciate the lay of the land and serve as a basis for further study. By examining how Conze does and does not echo other theorists, we sharpen our understanding of their work as much as his. What emerges, we contend, is that PMP offers unique and valuable perspectives on features of mass propaganda that remain pertinent today.

It was Gustav Le Bon who, in his *The Crowd: A Study of the Popular Mind* (*Psychologie des Foules*, 1895), laid the groundwork for the study of what came to be recognized as "mass psychology." Le Bon's emphasis on the vulnerability of groups to suggestion, prestige, social contagion, and the power of unconscious thinking would impact Sigmund Freud, who picks up the influence in his *Group Psychology and the Analysis of the Ego* (*Massenpsychologie und Ich-Analyse*, 1921). Though Freud takes a less contemptuous attitude toward "the masses" than Le Bon, he praises Le Bon's "brilliantly executed picture of the group mind"[80] and quotes him at length:

> We see, then, that the disappearance of the conscious personality, the predominance of the un-conscious personality, the turning by means of suggestion and contagion of feelings and ideas in an identical direction, the tendency to immediately transform the suggested ideas into acts; these, we see, are the principal characteristics of the individual forming part of

80 Sigmund Freud, *Group Psychology and the Analysis of the Ego*, trans. James Strachey (London: Hogarth Press, 1949; 1st ed. 1921, *Massenpsychologie und Ich-Analyse*), p. 22.

> a crowd. He is no longer himself, but has become an automaton who has ceased to be guided by his will.[81]

Freud elaborates: "Le Bon explains the condition of an individual in a group as being actually hypnotic."[82] Indeed, hypnosis was a common theme in these early treatments of mass psychology. Not only were large groups susceptible to falling under hypnotic spells, according to Le Bon and Freud, but their leaders were masterful hypnotists, able to use the power of suggestion to bend a group's will in whatever direction they wished. We are reminded of what the proto-fascist hypnotist Cipolla says in Thomas Mann's *Mario and the Magician* (*Mario und der Zauberer*, 1929): "Surely you will not struggle against the performance of a perfectly natural action just because somebody suggests it to you?"[83]

Popular interest in propaganda began in earnest in the wake of the First World War, which saw the emergence of political propaganda on a grand scale and gave to the term the sinister connotations it enjoys today. A foundational theorist of "international propaganda" was Walter Lippmann, who, as early as 1919, wrote that "some day the technic [*sic*] must be investigated if the judgments of the people are to escape persistent exploitation."[84] Lippmann's contributions to the study of propaganda, presented most fully in his *Public Opinion* (1922), would be taken up in Harold D. Lasswell's *Propaganda Technique in the World War* (1927) and Edward L. Bernays' *Propaganda* (1928). Both of the latter works took an "instrumentalist" attitude toward propaganda, advocating for the refinement of its techniques for the purpose of more effective social management.[85] While Lasswell, in particular, provided Conze with several examples and theoretical insights, Conze's own orientation toward the study of propaganda differs radically from these predecessors: "I must say frankly that I do not share the assumption of the majority

---

81 Gustav Le Bon, *The Crowd: A Study of the Popular Mind* (New York: The Macmillan Company, 1896; 1st ed. 1895, *Psychologie des foules*), pp. 12–13, quoted in Freud, *Group Psychology*, p. 12.

82 Freud, *Group Psychology*, p. 13; see also pp. 99–100 and 125–126.

83 Thomas Mann, *Early Sorrow and Mario and the Magician*, trans. H. T. Lowe-Porter (London: Secker & Warburg, 1953; 1st ed. 1929, *Mario und der Zauberer*), p. 159.

84 Walter Lippmann, *The Political Scene: An Essay on the Victory of 1918* (New York: H. Holt and Company, 1919), p. 38.

85 See Sue Curry Jansen, "'The World's Greatest Adventure in Advertising': Walter Lippmann's Critique of Censorship and Propaganda" in Auerbach and Castronovo, eds., *The Oxford Handbook of Propaganda Studies* (Oxford: Oxford University Press, 2013): 301–325 at 304:

> [Lippman's] propaganda critique has been inverted in ways that obscure its critical power and its continuing relevance. His near contemporaries, Bernays and political scientist Harold Lasswell, co-opted Lippmann's analysis and turned his critique of propaganda into an apology for it.

A useful discussion of Lippmann's and Lasswell's work may be found in Christopher Simpson, *Science of Coercion: Communication Research and Psychological Warfare 1945–1960* (Oxford: Oxford University Press, 1994), pp. 15–30.

of my contemporaries, that propaganda in some hands is good, and in others bad—their own hands being the good ones."[86]

Frederick E. Lumley (*The Propaganda Menace*, 1933) took a starkly critical attitude toward propaganda: "There is no such thing as 'good' propaganda."[87] Although the bulk of his work consists of a litany of examples—what Leonard W. Doob has in mind when he writes that "most authors.... have become too engrossed in their stories to explain the implications or to analyze the subtleties of the propaganda they have been describing"[88]—he nevertheless proposes some important ideas that Conze picks up in PMP. For instance, it was in part from Lumley that Conze drew his repeated metaphoric reference to propaganda as a "veil that hides the truth." According to Lumley's definition:

> Propaganda is promotion which is veiled in one way or another as to (1) its origin and sources, (2) the interests involved, (3) the methods employed, (4) the content spread, and (5) the results accruing to the victims—any one, any two, any three, any four, or all five.[89]

Compare this with Conze's "Propaganda veils the results of the actions taken in response to it, whether the propagandist is aware of his interested aim or not."[90] The first clause of Conze's statement appears to be directly derived from Lumley's definition, especially its fifth point. However, Conze's addition ("whether the propagandist is aware of his interested aim or not") represents a significant divergence. Lumley treats all propaganda as malicious and intentional, and the act of "veiling" as a conscious one. Conze emphasizes that the veil may cover both the victim and the propagandist simultaneously:

> In human life, *unconscious lying is the rule and conscious lying the exception....* Both the victims of mass propaganda, and the propagandists themselves, regularly practice self-deception, whether they know it or not.[91]

---

86 Conze, PMP, p. 16.

87 Frederick E. Lumley, *The Propaganda Menace* (London: The Century Co., 1933), p. 21.

88 Leonard William Doob, *Propaganda: Its Psychology and Technique* (New York: H. Holt and Co., 1935), p. 6.

89 Lumley, *The Propaganda Menace*, p. 44. The term "veiled propaganda" seems to have been suggested to Lumley by Edward Alsworth Ross in a private letter of 1926. See Lumley, *The Propaganda Menace*, p. 28 n. 24. The term is not unique to these men, however; see Wallace S. Wharton, "Taking the Navy to the People" in *United States Naval Institute Proceedings* 49.12 (December, 1923): 2010–2021 at 2012, under the heading "Bald Propaganda Dangerous": "An organization that is successful in keeping its name before the public through the medium of the press can be said to be using 'veiled' propaganda."

90 Conze, PMP, p. 13.

91 Conze, PMP, p. 132.

If it was Lumley who suggested to Conze the use of the term "veil" in the context of propaganda, Conze ran with it. In fact, it neatly brings together the red threads of his intellectual life as discussed above, namely his engagements with Marxist dialectics and with Buddhist philosophy. As Conze translates Engels,

> Marxists consider as ideological "all those ideas which veil to the members of social groups the real motive powers which move them to think and to act as they do."[92]

Conze was also closely familiar with Schopenhauer's "veil of Maya," an appropriation of Hindu and Buddhist conceptions of illusion—recall that a decade before PMP he had proposed writing his dissertation on Schopenhauer; see above, p. xxvi.[93] Indeed, Conze would later equate the term "veil" with the Buddhist concept of "thought-coverings," as he renders the Sanskrit *citta-āvaraṇa* in his influential translation of the *Heart Sutra*:

> 'Thought coverings' is just another term for 'ignorance', for the 'delusion' which all along had been held by Buddhist tradition to cover up the true nature of dharmic facts and to hide it from us. Ignorance throws over reality a veil of manufactured entities, all of which somehow contain the false idea of 'self'.[94]

For Conze, the veil of propaganda is both ideology and self-delusion: not "a tissue of deliberate lies,"[95] but "the involuntary result of the social conditions in which mass propaganda is generated."[96]

Lumley gives little thought to the psychological aspects of propaganda, though William W. Biddle, in 1931 and 1932, had recently offered some of the earliest studies of its psychological effects.[97] It was Leonard W. Doob who, in 1935, first

---

92 Conze, PMP, p. 179 n. 5; Engels, *Letter to Mehring*, July 14, 1893, trans. E.C.

93 Arthur Schopenhauer, *The World as Will and Representation*, trans. E. F. J. Payne (New York: Dover Publications, Inc., 1966), Book 1, §3, p. 8:

> The ancient wisdom of the Indians declares that 'it is Mâyâ, the veil of deception, which covers the eyes of mortals, and causes them to see a world of which one cannot say either that it is or that it is not; for it is like a dream, like the sunshine on the sand which the traveller from a distance takes to be water, or like the piece of rope on the ground which he regards as a snake.'

94 Conze, *Buddhist Wisdom Books*, p. 96.

95 Conze, PMP, p. 156.

96 Ibid., p. 151.

97 William W. Biddle, "A Psychological Definition of Propaganda," *The Journal of Abnormal and Social Psychology*, 26.3 (October, 1931): 283–295 and *Propaganda and Education* (New York: Teacher's College, Columbia University, 1932). See also Raymond Dodge, "The Psychology of Propaganda," *Religion Education* 15 (1920): 241–252.

took the path pointed out by Biddle and offered an in-depth survey of the psychology of mass persuasion in his *Propaganda: Its Psychology and Technique*.[98] This work, in its focus on motivations, prestige, values, and other social factors, is the closest predecessor to Conze's own. It is telling, however, that Conze offers a brief but devastating critique of the same psychological tests carried out by Biddle that Doob found so validating.[99] And while Doob's ambition to schematize and classify the principles of propaganda in the abstract went beyond Conze's efforts in the same direction, Doob's work is for that very reason more limited. In 1962, Jacques Ellul would point out this shortcoming:

> We cannot name every factor working upon an individual. It would be wrong even to attempt this, for propaganda is not an isolated phenomenon with clearly delineated boundaries; it is completely integrated and immersed in a social entity.[100]

Conze implicitly acknowledges this argument throughout PMP. Nevertheless, Doob's work influenced Conze's significantly, and it is worthwhile to mention a few specific points of convergence and divergence.

For instance, Conze recognizes the importance of Doob's distinction between "intentional" and "unintentional" propaganda. "In intentional propaganda," writes Doob, "the propagandist is aware of his interested aim; in unintentional propaganda, he does not appreciate the social effect of his own actions."[101] But unlike Doob, who employs the linear paradigm of the "stimulus-response situation," Conze theorizes the effects of propaganda—intentional or not—in terms of the more complex psychology of self-deception. The difference is illustrated by the following example, in which Doob elaborates his concept of "suggestion":

---

98 Leonard William Doob, *Propaganda: Its Psychology and Technique* (New York: H. Holt and Co., 1935). See p. 115: "Dr. Biddle has carried on ingenious and praiseworthy experiments which may serve to substantiate both the philosophy and the theory of propaganda of the present writer.... His has been the real contribution to the psychology of propaganda."

99 Conze, PMP, p. 192: "Biddle seems to have attached no importance to the fact that his students lived on the Atlantic coast, and that therefore their prejudices might be less vigorous about 'Pacific relations' than about 'Atlantic relations.'"

100 Jacques Ellul, *Propaganda: The Formation of Men's Attitudes*, trans. Konrad Kellen and Jean Lerner (New York: Alfred A. Knopf, 1965; 1st ed. 1962, *Propagandes*), p. 264. Harwood L. Childs, in a review of Doob's book, makes a similar point (*The American Political Science Review* 30.2 [1936]: 389–390):

> Dr. Doob has performed his autopsy of 'mental fields' and 'stimulus-situations' with remarkable skill. Both have been dissected and laid bare with cool precision. The remains have been labelled and arranged in their respective compartments. The only difficulty is that no method is suggested for reassembling them and resurrecting a life situation. After all, unless we know *under what conditions* certain principles should be employed, they are of little practical use.

101 Doob, *Propaganda*, p. 89.

> A lover of beer hears his companion say, "Let's go get a glass of beer," and he accepts the suggestion. It is then asserted that his attitude toward beer has been released. Actually this attitude has become dominant and it has been integrated with the perceptual data obtained from the sentence. The integration is new and, being temporary, it leads to immediate action.[102]

Doob here interprets the act of suggestion—in this case, the suggestion to drink a glass of beer—as a "stimulus" leading to "the arousal of pre-existing attitudes" and "a new integration of attitudes."[103] This accords with his more general conclusion that propaganda exploits the accumulated history of past experiences and learned responses which already form a part of the victim's personality.[104]

Now see Conze's treatment of the same example (which he clearly appears to have derived from Doob, though he does not cite the source):

> When I walk along the street and somebody suggests, "Let's have a drink," the direction of my activity is deflected if I take up that suggestion. The intruder can, however, direct my actions only on condition that I accept his suggestion as my own. The foreign will is temporarily incorporated into my own personality, and acts as a subsidiary self.[105]

For a suggestion to be effective, Conze argues, one must be willing to go along with it ("suggestibility" implies "a willingness to be led, and to surrender our will, judgement, and decision to others").[106] At the same time, one must deceive oneself into accepting the will of another as one's own ("The self could not deceive itself about itself if the personality were not split into at least two parts").[107] For Conze, suggestion does not act upon pre-existing elements of an enduring personality, but rather dissolves the boundaries of the personality itself.[108] In contrast to Doob's relatively static "stimulus-response situation," Conze's paradigm attributes greater psychological depth and complexity to the subject, and views him or her as actively participating in the process of suggestion.

Doob also makes an important contribution in his discussion of propaganda and education. Where Lumley, like most other authors, treats the two as opposite ("To the present writer *education* and *propaganda* are contradictions in terms"),[109]

---

102 Ibid., pp. 53–54.

103 Ibid., p. 52.

104 Ibid., p. 406. See also Ellul, *Propaganda*, p. 279.

105 Conze, PMP, p. 163.

106 Ibid., p. 37.

107 Ibid., p. 158.

108 See Conze, PMP, p. 9: "What we call a human personality is an incompletely unified collection of 'selves' which all inhabit the same body."

109 Lumley, *The Propaganda Menace*, p. 21. Biddle, *Propaganda and Education*, p. 8, quotes John Dewey along similar lines (Dewey, "Education as Politics," *New Republic* 32 [1922]: 139–141 at 139):

Doob collapses the distinction: "No absolute social or psychological distinction can be made between propaganda and so-called 'education.'"[110] For Doob, what other authors refer to as "education" is really just "unintentional propaganda,"[111] and therefore the attempt to eliminate all forms of propaganda would be to collapse the bonds that hold society together: "Because every social order is sustained through a continual process of propaganda, they are attempting with their theory the impossible task of lifting themselves and their students out of all social *milieux*."[112]

Like Doob, Conze acknowledges the essential role of some forms of propaganda in the functioning of any modern society. But in his characteristically Buddhist way of putting it, he suggests that it is not propaganda *per se*, but the psychological basis on which propaganda operates, that gives coherence to our social world:

> For if he purifies his mind of ideas of "mine" and "not mine," of likes and dislikes, of love and hate, if he abandons self-assertion and self-affection, the inner logic of his fight against self-deception destroys the basis of social life as we know it. Without the incentives of narcissism and self-assertion, the fields would remain untilled, the factories would close, procreation would cease, and man would disappear from the face of the Earth.[113]

> The profit of education is the ability it gives to discriminate, to make distinctions that penetrate below the surface. One may not be able to lay hold of the realities beneath the froth and foam, but at least one who is educated does not take the latter to be the realities; one knows that there is a difference between sound and sense, between what is emphatic and what is distinctive, between what is conspicuous and what is important.

110 Doob, *Propaganda*, p. 87. See also Leo P. Crespi's review of Lasswell et al., *Propaganda, Communication, and Public Opinion: A Comprehensive Reference Guide* (Princeton, 1946) in *The Public Opinion Quarterly* 10.1 (1946): 99–102 at 100:

> The distinction that Smith, Lasswell, and Casey adduce between propaganda and education is quite unacceptable to anyone with a dynamic or progressive conception of education. The authors state in characterizing propaganda, that '*Propaganda is language aimed at large masses.*' [italics theirs] And '*The intention of the propagandist is to influence mass attitudes upon controversial issues.*' [italics theirs] Education, they state in contrast, is 'primarily concerned with transmitting skill or insight, not attitude.' Then is added parenthetically, '(The definition of education may be extended to include the transmission of *noncontroversial* attitudes as well as skills.)' [italics theirs] These statements cannot be left unchallenged, even in a review which is attempting to be rather more descriptive than critical. What socially enlightened educator would agree for a moment that education is concerned only with skills and noncontroversial attitudes?

111 Doob, *Propaganda*, pp. 79–80.

112 Ibid., p. 85.

113 Conze, PMP, pp. 136–137.

It may then come as a surprise to learn that Conze, so well-attuned to the inadvertent dimensions of propaganda and the insidious operations of group ideology, would write that while "the division between the two is, of course, not quite clear-cut.... education and propaganda can be quite well treated as opposites."[114] Education "respects the dignity of the people, tries to put them on their feet, to develop their latent faculties and abilities, and to make them think for themselves." Propaganda, by contrast, "treats them as childish halfwits, as 'human material,' as dumb instruments of their masters." While this appraisal of education may sound admirable at first blush, one is hard put to define a range of human interactions within a modern, industrialized society, even between friends and close relatives, entirely devoid of "propagation" and ideology. And Conze readily admits to this elsewhere in PMP (see, e.g., Chapter 2.3). Indeed, his own definition of propaganda is studiously neutral, and overlaps with any functional definition of education: "Propaganda is an attempt to extend the influence of a social group—a nation, a class, a professional or religious group, etc.—by spreading or 'propagating' beliefs and practices."[115]

To understand what Conze means by education in this context, one must take into account his discussion of "social cells." These are defined as "small groups which allow for physical contact among its members, bring out the social instincts, give them full scope, and are the condition for man's dignity."[116] It is Conze's contention that the social cell can be cultivated more or less without the veiling hand of propaganda, and therefore that it fosters an environment in which genuine education may take place. "Small-scale training differs in many ways from large-scale *social engineering*. Within a limited circle, it can genuinely increase human cooperation."[117] As he elaborates in a footnote, "Real 'education' requires a social cell. 'Mass education' is a contradiction in terms. Where the word is used, it camouflages the drilling of machine minders."[118] While this vaguely defined vision of the social cell might seem aspirational at best, it nevertheless helps to define the frame of Conze's analysis. A discussion of a topic so vast as propaganda requires some parameters and would cease to be useful if it could not separate, at least provisionally, the "artificial" bonds forged by the propagandist from more intimate and physically proximate modes of human connection. As sweeping as Conze's definition of propaganda is, his notion of the social cell serves to calibrate the delicate scale—perhaps only useful when dealing with extremes—that holds propaganda on one side and education on the other.

Conze is not, to be sure, categorically opposed to propaganda in all its forms, as Lumley appears to be. He argues persuasively that some degree of self-deception

114 Ibid., p. 2.
115 Ibid., p. 1.
116 Ibid., p. 14.
117 Ibid., p. 16.
118 Ibid., p. 16 n. 38.

is requisite to participation in social life, and therefore Lumley's attitude would represent a futile rejection of the basic psychological conditions of our humanity. But once we leave the borders of the social cell for the wider world in which propaganda is more apt to flourish, it behooves us to consider where the "good" slips over into the "bad." All of us, as vulnerable creatures living in dysfunctional societies, are susceptible to the allure of propaganda in one way or another, and some, perhaps most, propagandists exploit this vulnerability. But if there are even a few who don't, who instead use their influence over our minds to improve social and environmental conditions, how should we recognize them? Conze makes no attempt to answer this question, and simply cautions social reformers against "adding to the flood" of propaganda.[119] It is, indeed, his stated purpose in writing PMP to help readers learn to "withstand" propaganda, and Doob, elsewhere unwilling to make such distinctions, agrees with this educational intent: "Thinking about propaganda … may lead to the destruction of some propaganda."[120]

Having sketched out some of the significant themes that Conze inherited from the work of earlier theorists like Lumley and Doob, we now turn to his affinities with the work of social psychologists and political theorists who came after him. It would be impossible to give a comprehensive list, but we offer a few breadcrumbs for those who wish to better situate PMP among works written in the first decades after the Second World War.

For instance, Conze's treatment of the idealization of leaders and father figures,[121] as well as his discussion of tribal groups,[122] looks back to Freud in language strikingly similar to that of Theodor W. Adorno, especially in his influential essay on "Freudian Theory and the Pattern of Fascist Propaganda" (1951).[123] For both Conze and Adorno, the rise of totalitarian leaders can be explained with reference to the related concepts of "narcissism" and "identification." By *identifying* with a leader, or "by making the leader his ideal," as Adorno puts it, the

119 Conze, PMP, p. 17: "I believe that reformers are more likely to reach their aims by patiently building up social cells, or genuine communities, than by adding to the flood of mass propaganda." Doob also raises the question in his final chapter on "Which Propaganda?", settling on the unsatisfactory answer that we should put our trust in "experts who understand and who are not seeking to exploit human beings" (*Propaganda*, p. 412).

120 Doob, *Propaganda*, p. 5.

121 See PMP, Chapter 1.3.

122 Ibid., Chapters 1.5, 1.6.

123 Theodor W. Adorno, "Freudian Theory and the Pattern of Fascist Propaganda" reprinted in Andrew Arato and Eike Gebhardt, eds., *The Essential Frankfurt School Reader* (New York: Urizen Books, 1978): 118–137. This essay is a continuation of ideas explored earlier in Adorno's collaboration with Max Horkheimer, *Dialectic of Enlightenment*, trans. Edmund Jephcott (Stanford: Stanford University Press, 1947; 1st ed. 1947, *Dialektik der Aufklärung*), and in Adorno, Else Frenkel-Brunswik, Daniel Levinson, and Nevitt Sanford, *The Authoritarian Personality* (New York: Harper & Brothers, 1950). Other relevant sources in this lineage include Wilhelm Reich, *The Mass Psychology of Fascism*, trans. Vincent R. Carfagno (New York: Farrar, Strauss & Giroux, 1970; 1st ed. 1933, *Die Massenpsychologie des Faschismus*), and Erich Fromm, *Escape from Freedom* (New York: Farrar & Rinehart, Inc., 1941).

average person "loves himself, as it were, but gets rid of the stains of frustration and discontent which mar his picture of his own empirical self."[124] Furthermore, both authors recognize and highlight the paradox inherent in this picture: in order for a leader to make sufficient room for a group's narcissistic fantasies, he or she must conform to a "model of perfection" while simultaneously seeming down-to-earth and relatable. "While appearing as a superman, the leader must at the same time work the miracle of appearing as an average person."[125] Thomas Mann's hypnotist Cipolla comes to mind again: "He who knew how to obey knew also how to command, and conversely; the one idea was comprehended in the other, as people and leader were comprehended in one another."[126] Finally, both Conze and Adorno suggest that by adapting itself, however unconsciously, to the tendencies of group psychology, the secret of mass propaganda is simply to "take people as they are."[127] In other words, though operating more by trial and error than by scientific analysis, effective propaganda must be acutely responsive to a group's psychological condition. But rather than using its power to cultivate more genuine social and political relationships, it offers only "the caricature of true, conscious solidarity."[128]

In the same year that Adorno's essay appeared, Hannah Arendt offered a discussion of "totalitarian propaganda" in *The Origins of Totalitarianism* (1951). This text shares fundamental insights with Conze's analysis of the propagandistic power of "myth," which had recently been exploited and epitomized by Nazi propagandist Alfred Rosenberg. Though objectively untrue, writes Conze, myth possesses an emotional power far superior to that of scientific fact ("Why object to errors and illusions? They can be true in the mythical sense, when they increase our creative power").[129] Likewise, in Arendt's analysis,

> Mass propaganda discovered that its audience was ready at all times to believe the worst, no matter how absurd, and did not particularly object to being deceived because it held every statement to be a lie anyhow. The totalitarian mass leaders based their propaganda on the correct psychological assumption that, under such conditions, one could make people believe the

124 Adorno, "Freudian Theory and the Pattern of Fascist Propaganda," p. 126.

125 Ibid., p. 127. See Conze, PMP, p. 64: "The good propagandist at one time divinises a leader and at another humanises him."

126 Mann, *Early Sorrow and Mario and the Magician*, p. 173.

127 Adorno, "Freudian Theory," p. 134 ("fascist propaganda…simply takes men for what they are") and Conze, PMP, p. 194 ("mass propaganda has to take people as they are"). See also Adorno and Horkheimer, *Dialectic of Enlightenment*, p. 212: "[Propaganda] counts on [people's] ability to be counted on."

128 Adorno, "Freudian Theory," p. 126. See Conze, PMP, p. 194: Propaganda "is not likely to genuinely develop our social instincts."

129 Conze, PMP, p. 181. See also Adorno and Horkheimer, *Dialectic of Enlightenment*, p. xvii: "False clarity is only another name for myth. Myth was always obscure and luminous at once. It has always been distinguished by its familiarity and its exemption from the work of concepts."

> most fantastic statements one day, and trust that if the next day they were given irrefutable proof of their falsehood, they would take refuge in cynicism.[130]

Both Conze and Arendt recognize that the messages of propaganda are more than "magic bullets" that take over the mental function of a passive audience.[131] Instead, propagandists require their audience to be "ready to believe," to be "obsessed by a desire to escape from reality."[132] The audience must participate in the performance willingly, even derive pleasure from the drama in which they take an active role. When propagandists collapse the distinction between truth and falsehood, they feed their alienated victims exactly what gives them the most immediate gratification.[133] And as Conze clarifies, it is not the propaganda itself, as an external agent, that stimulates desire and pleasure in its victims. Rather, the pleasure is derived from the victims' own cooperation with the propagandists, and in their willing embrace of a clouded mental state: they become "addicts" who "vegetate in the twilight of self-deception."[134] The mental states of desire and pleasure, so central to Conze's analysis, remain, as Mark Wollaeger has argued, "an understudied topic in propaganda studies."[135]

The power of mythical thinking is also central to Jacques Ellul's analysis in *Propaganda: The Formation of Men's Attitudes* (*Propagandes*, 1962). Propaganda satisfies "the need to believe and obey, to create and hear fables, to communicate in the language of myths."[136] It is the myth, for Ellul, that gives meaning to a reality made bewildering by the kaleidoscopic overload of information.[137] Ellul goes further

130 Hannah Arendt, *The Origins of Totalitarianism* (Harcourt Brace & Co., 1973; 1st ed. Schocken Books, 1951), p. 382. See also pp. 341–364, and Arendt's 1967 essay "Truth and Politics" in Arendt, *Between Past and Future: Eight Exercises in Political Thought* (New York: The Viking Press, 1968), pp. 227–264.

131 See J. Michael Sproule, "Progressive Propaganda Critics and the Magic Bullet Myth," *Critical Studies in Mass Communication* 6.3 (1989): 225–246.

132 Arendt, *The Origins of Totalitarianism*, p. 352.

133 See Conze, PMP, pp. 6–7:

> We are not passively pushed into convictions as bricks are pushed into position. If somebody wants to convince me, he requires my active cooperation. He has to make me convince myself. He has to set into motion something in me that takes up his suggestion and that is eager to follow him.

134 Conze, PMP, p. 193. See also Conze, "The Intermediary World" in *The Eastern Buddhist* 7.2, New Series (October, 1974): 22–31, esp. 31.

135 Mark Wollaeger, "Propaganda and Pleasure: From Kracauer to Joyce" in Auerbach and Castronovo, eds., *The Oxford Handbook of Propaganda Studies* (Oxford: Oxford University Press, 2013): 278–297 at 278.

136 Jacques Ellul, *Propaganda: The Formation of Men's Attitudes*, trans. Konrad Kellen and Jean Lerner (New York: Alfred A. Knopf, 1965), p. 148.

137 Ellul, *Propaganda*, p. 145:

> The average person..... finds himself in a kind of kaleidoscope in which thousands of unconnected images follow each other rapidly.... A world emerges that is astonishingly incoherent, absurd, and irrational, which changes rapidly and constantly for reasons he cannot understand.

than Conze in his analysis of this phenomenon: where Conze writes that "propaganda is, normally at least, slightly informative,"[138] Ellul counters that "information actually generates the problems that propaganda exploits and for which it pretends to offer solutions."[139] With this comment Ellul adds another dimension to the analysis of the fraught relationship between propaganda and education. One can imagine that, in retrospect, Conze might be willing to acknowledge that the relatively clear distinction he aspires to maintain between the two is more tenuous than he had proposed. As he concedes in a different context, "These issues ... are probably slightly less clear than I have made them out to be."[140] Ellul nevertheless echoes Conze in his discussion of the psychological draw of propaganda, even employing the term "veil" (French *voile*) to articulate the point: "Man...needs an ideological veil to cover the harsh reality, some consolation, a *raison d'être*, a sense of values. And only propaganda offers him a remedy for a basically intolerable situation."[141] Compare Conze's analysis of more than twenty years prior: "For most of us, life would be intolerable if we saw it as it is.... The public are ready to accept the honeyed words of the propagandist because they wish to keep distressing facts out of sight."[142]

In the overarching argument of PMP, what Conze calls the "red thread" of the book, he proposes that the primary social function of propaganda is to compensate for the weak bonds characteristic of modern communities. "Propaganda succeeds in making good a deficiency in *genuine* social unity by creating a superstructure of *artificial* social unity."[143] Not only does propaganda offer an addictive source of pleasure, but by providing a false substitute for genuine social unity, it exacerbates the loneliness and alienation that render people susceptible to its influence in the first place. Though we could suggest a multitude of further resonances between PMP and other works on propaganda, we offer this final echo from Ellul: "*Propaganda is the true remedy for loneliness*."[144] Propaganda here becomes a *need* created by the conditions of modern industrial society. As Konrad Kellen writes in his introduction to Ellul's work, "The principal difference between his thought edifice and other literature on propaganda is that Ellul regards propaganda as a sociological phenomenon rather than as something *made* by certain people for certain purposes."[145] The comment applies just as well to much of Conze's analysis.

Some readers may find it counter-intuitive to learn that, since the time of Conze's writing, the emphasis on propaganda as a framework for research in the

138 Conze, PMP, p. 2.
139 Ellul, *Propaganda*, p. 114.
140 Conze, "The Intermediary World," p. 31.
141 Ellul, *Propaganda*, p. 140.
142 Conze, PMP, p. 174.
143 Ibid., p. 13.
144 Ellul, *Propaganda*, p. 148. Ellul's italics.
145 Ibid., p. v.

social sciences has considerably diminished. In fact, Conze was writing at precisely the period of the most acute public fascination with the subject, at least in the Anglophone world. According to the Google Ngram Viewer, it was in 1940 that the word "propaganda" reached its peak frequency as a proportion of all words printed in the English language.[146]

In an excellent essay of 1987, J. Michael Sproule describes how the "propaganda paradigm" flourished in the American academy between 1919 and 1937, but by the 1950s had largely been replaced by the paradigm of "communications."[147] The ostensible reason for this paradigm-shift was that the humanistic methods of propaganda studies were deemed wishy-washy by practitioners of more "statistical-experimental" methodologies. But, as Sproule argues, the more salient cause of the decline of propaganda studies was that it had become politically dangerous in a period of increasing pressure against social criticism.[148] For instance, starting in 1939, the anti-communist House Un-American Activities Committee mounted an aggressive investigation into the work of the Institute for Propaganda Analysis, an organization dedicated to broadening public awareness of mass persuasion.[149] In 1941, the Institute was unable to find a publisher for what would have been the fourth in its series of book-length studies,[150] and in its final bulletin of January, 1942, its members expressed their opinion that the organization was no longer able to engage in "dispassionate analyses of all kinds of propaganda, 'good' and 'bad'.... If it were to continue it would have to analyze all propaganda—of this country and of Britain and Russia as well as that of Germany, Italy and Japan."[151] Conze's difficulty in finding a publisher for PMP, though in a very different ideological environment (think of Raymond Postgate's insistence that he excise all remarks critical of the Soviet Union; see above, p. xxiii), affords a parallel: the looming threat of war had significantly raised the stakes for political discourse in general, and in particular for any attempt at non-partisan propaganda analysis.

---

146 Today the word is about as frequent as it was in 1915, which is to say about a third as frequent as in 1940.

147 J. Michael Sproule, "Propaganda Studies in American Social Science: The Rise and Fall of the Critical Paradigm," *Quarterly Journal of Speech* 73.1 (1987): 60–78 at 68. For references to several other of Sproule's works on the history of propaganda studies, see the bibliography to Garth S. Jowett and Victoria O'Donnell, *Propaganda and Persuasion*, 7th ed. (SAGE Publications, Inc., 2019). While Sproule documents the decline of the propaganda paradigm in the social sciences after WWII, Christopher Simpson (*Science of Coercion*) points out the American government's continued sponsorship of clandestine propaganda research during the Cold War.

148 Sproule, "Propaganda Studies in American Social Science," p. 72.

149 See "Dies Scrutinizes Propaganda Study: Inquiry into the Institute for Analysis Follows Alleged Left-Wing Expressions," *New York Times*, Sunday, February 23, 1941, pp. 1, 21.

150 Sproule, "Propaganda Studies in American Social Science," p. 72.

151 Institute for Propaganda Analysis, "We Say Au Revoir," *Propaganda Analysis: A Bulletin to Help the Intelligent Citizen Detect and Analyze Propaganda* 4.13 (1942): 1–6 at 1. For a critique of the IPA's "rhetorical" analysis of propaganda, see Sara Guyer, "The Ends of Misreading: Propaganda, Democracy, Literature" in Auerbach and Castronovo, eds., *The Oxford Handbook of Propaganda Studies* (Oxford, 2013): 366–377 at 370–371.

While the study of propaganda has been making a contemporary resurgence, it has never regained the prominence it held between the World Wars. In the preface to the first edition of their textbook *Propaganda and Persuasion* (1986), Garth S. Jowett and Victoria O'Donnell argue that "the time has come to revive the study of propaganda as a separate topic...of great significance at this point in time."[152] But more than twenty-five years later, Jonathan Auerbach and Russ Castronovo, editors of *The Oxford Handbook of Propaganda Studies* (2013), must still argue for the "continued relevance" of the marginalized discipline.[153] The essays in the recent volume *The Propaganda Model Today: Filtering Perception and Awareness*, edited by Joan Pedro-Carañana, Daniel Broudy, and Jeffery Klaehn (2018), take a similar tone in attempting to rehabilitate the "propaganda model" proposed by Edward S. Herman and Noam Chomsky in their *Manufacturing Consent: The Political Economy of the Mass Media* (1988). The publication of Conze's work may serve at least as a small contribution to this tentative but timely resurgence of interest in the field.

Coda

In his 2011 book *Understanding World Religions*, in a chapter on Conze's life and "moral quest," Irving Hexham distills Conze's *Memoirs* as revealing "a passionate concern with the moral questions raised by war.... Again and again Conze reiterates his commitment to pacifism and his horror at the brutality of modern warfare."[154] Indeed, in July of 1934, Conze co-authored (with Ellen Wilkinson, MP) an anti-war volume entitled *Why War? A Handbook for Those who will Take Part in the Second World War*.[155] On August 6, 1945, while on the train home from his teaching appointment in Reading, he learned of the atomic bombing of Hiroshima. "I vomited straight out the window.... For at that moment human history had lost its meaning."[156]

---

152 Garth S. Jowett and Victoria O'Donnell, *Propaganda and Persuasion*, 5th ed. (SAGE Publications, Inc., 2012), p. xiv. For a survey of the field in the past thirty-five years, it is illuminating to read the prefaces to subsequent editions of the book, which are retained together up to the fifth edition (2012). The sixth (2015) and seventh (2019) editions unfortunately do not include the earlier prefaces. See also Jowett, "Propaganda and Communication: The Re-emergence of a Research Tradition," *Journal of Communication* 37.1 (1987): 97–114.

153 Jonathan Auerbach and Russ Castronovo, "Introduction: Thirteen Propositions about Propaganda" in Auerbach and Castronovo, eds., *The Oxford Handbook of Propaganda Studies* (Oxford: Oxford University Press, 2013): 1–16 at 15.

154 Irving Hexham, "The Moral Quest of Edward Conze" in Hexham, *Understanding World Religions: An Interdisciplinary Approach* (Zondervan, 2011): 213–232 at 213.

155 Conze, *Why War? A Handbook for Those who will Take Part in the Second World War* (London: NCLC Publishing Society, Ltd., 1934). It is an "anti-war" book, but not only: it is more accurately a prescient, detailed analysis of war itself, much like the current volume is an analysis of propaganda. And it anticipates that the recent "Great War" would soon be known as "World War I." Conze and Wilkinson also co-authored *Why Fascism?* (London: Selwyn & Blount, 1934).

156 Conze, *Memoirs* 1, p. 48.

Knowing that Conze was a Buddhist, in particular a Buddhist committed to the "Perfection of Wisdom" tradition (the *prajñāpāramitā*), and fervently anti-war, a reader is easily forgiven the presumption that the present volume will deliver an uncompromising repudiation of propaganda. That would not be quite correct. When Conze writes that "psychologically speaking the appeal of Russian communism was no different from that of German Nazism or Italian Fascism," he means just that. Although he had been an ardent communist "Agit Prop" just a few years previous to the composition of this book, he is here endeavoring to understand the psychology of propaganda as such, and whether "in some hands [propaganda] is good, and in others bad" is, for the moment anyway, beside the point.[157] Nor does he opine as to whose hands are more or less reprehensible.

The analysis that follows will not read as an oppositional diatribe or outraged exposé of propaganda; it is, as advertised, a theoretical analysis of the psychology of propaganda, how it works, why it works, with the primary goal that it may be recognized and "withstood." Indeed, as he puts it, one may even "find one or two useful hints" for making it.[158]

But if the philosopher of social psychology is spared the onus of judging the ethical dimensions of propaganda, the rest of us are not. Dante's *Inferno* depicts a terrifying judgment for falsifiers. They are relegated to the lowest depths of Hell. Here is an epithet for the Devil himself:

> I once heard at Bologna,
> The Devil's vices told:
> With other things,
> That he's a liar, and of lies the Father.[159]

Here is where the falsifiers reside:

> To the Last rampart we had now descended
> From the long bridge, still bearing to the left:
> Now I could see the bottom more distinctly
> Where that unerring Justice minister
> Of the Omnipotent doth penalize
> The falsifiers she has there condemned.[160]

Who has Dante condemned to this special place? They are the lying slanderers, those who would counterfeit gold florins, who would "lick the mirror of Narcissus."[161] They are the falsifiers, the narcissists and sociopaths who disdain

157 Conze, PMP, p. 16.
158 Ibid.
159 Dante, *Inferno* 23, trans. Lawrence Grant White (New York: Pantheon Books, 1948).
160 Ibid., 29.
161 Ibid., 30.

Truth, who would ruin the earth's household and its economy, who are impervious to the universal censure of society, who would soil the public commons.

Conze accused his professors and the colleagues of his father of "abject cowardice and slimy duplicity" in accommodating the rise of Nazism. He was so disgusted at their behavior that he renounced the use of his mother tongue. Although in the present book Conze keeps his personal credo in the background, it does not follow that he is neutral to the malign uses of propaganda. As a Buddhist philosopher, he regarded *truth* as a mental condition analogous to the *health* of the physical body. There is no question how he felt toward those who willfully ignore the veils of deception, or worse yet, whose apparently benign indifference renders them complicit with those who would exercise power in thrall to falsehood. Today's array of damnable authoritarian madmen bears responsibility. In Dante's harshest judgment of all, "Heaven rejects them and Hell won't have them."

A Note on the Present Edition

The original typescript of PMP, as prepared by Mrs. Hunt of Woodstock in 1951, could not simply be dusted off and dropped onto the publisher's desk. We have considered every phrase in the original typescript as to its intended sense and have, for the most part, left them as they stand. However, we have had to make some modifications and emendations.

Our practice throughout has been to present Conze's prose, which was left without final revisions, in the form which is closest to what we believe he intended. For the most part, this has meant revising punctuation, standardizing spelling, reformatting and adding footnotes, and puzzling the meaning out of phrases that either lacked grammatical sense or were apparently mistranscribed. In rare cases we have changed the order of paragraphs in order to assist the flow of thought.

Our compass in the thorniest of these questions has been a personal memory of Dr. Conze's peculiar style of expression both in lecture and in private conversation, a familiarity with his published writings on many subjects, and a commitment to reading closely for context to understand the intended sense. We have often discussed how to approach material that is classist, elitist, or otherwise likely to sound objectionable to a contemporary ear. However, we are mindful of Conze's animus toward those who have "wilfully chiselled away at the pure marble of my prose,"[162] and our bias has always been to conserve rather than to revise. The present volume presents Conze's thought in Conze's words, and while we have made some minor subtractions and rearrangements, we have made no additions that were not essential to the reader's comprehension. Conze's text conforms to the conventions of British English style, while the editors' introduction and notes, as well as the foreword and afterword, conform to American conventions.

162 Conze, *Memoirs* 1, p. 130. He refers here to Christmas Humphreys, founder of the London Buddhist Society.

Works Cited in the Editors' Introduction

**Asterisks indicate works also listed in the general bibliography.*

Adorno, Theodor W. "Freudian Theory and the Pattern of Fascist Propaganda." Reprinted in Andrew Arato and Eike Gebhardt, eds., *The Essential Frankfurt School Reader.* New York: Urizen Books, 1978: 118–137.

Adorno, Theodor W., Else Frenkel-Brunswik, Daniel Levinson, and Nevitt Sanford. *The Authoritarian Personality.* New York: Harper & Brothers, 1950.

Adorno, Theodor W. and Max Horkheimer. *Dialectic of Enlightenment,* trans. Edmund Jephcott. Stanford: Stanford University Press, 1947 (1st ed. 1947, *Dialektik der Aufklärung*).

Arendt, Hannah. *The Origins of Totalitarianism.* San Diego: Harcourt Brace & Co., 1973 (1st ed. Schocken Books, 1951).

———. "Truth and Politics." In Hannah Arendt, *Between Past and Future: Eight Exercises in Political Thought.* New York: The Viking Press, 1968: 227–264.

Auerbach, Jonathan and Russ Castronovo, eds. *The Oxford Handbook of Propaganda Studies.* Oxford: Oxford University Press, 2013.

———. "Introduction: Thirteen Propositions about Propaganda." In Jonathan Auerbach and Russ Castronovo, eds., *The Oxford Handbook of Propaganda Studies.* Oxford: Oxford University Press, 2013:1–16.

Bernays, Edward L. *Propaganda.* New York: Horace Liveright Inc., 1928.

*Biddle, William W. "A Psychological Definition of Propaganda." *The Journal of Abnormal and Social Psychology,* 26.3 (October, 1931): 283–295.

———. *Propaganda and Education.* New York: Teacher's College, Columbia University, 1932.

Childs, Harwood L. "Review of *Propaganda: Its Psychology and Technique* by Leonard William Doob." *The American Political Science Review* 30.2 (1936): 389–390.

Conze, Edward. "The Psychology of Imperialism." *Plebs* 27.12 (December, 1935): 280–283.

*———. *The Scientific Method of Thinking.* London: Chapman & Hall, Ltd., 1935.

———. "The Psychology of Imperialism II.—On Camouflage." *Plebs* 28.1 (January, 1936): 41–44.

———. "The Psychology of Imperialism III.—The Empire's Appeal to the Mind." *Plebs* 28.3 (March, 1936): 57–60.

———. "The Psychology of Imperialism IV. Internationalism." *Plebs* 28.4 (April, 1936): 85–91.

———. *Spain Today: Revolution and Counterrevolution.* London: Secker & Warburg, Ltd., 1936.

*———. *An Introduction to Dialectical Materialism.* London: NCLC Publishing Society, Ltd., 1936.

*———. *Contradiction and Reality.* London: Wightman & Co., Ltd., 1939.

———. *Buddhism: Its Essence and Development.* Oxford: Bruno Cassirer, Ltd., 1951.

———. *Selected Sayings from the Perfection of Wisdom.* London: The Buddhist Society, 1955.

———. *Buddhist Wisdom Books: Containing the Diamond Sutra and the Heart Sutra.* London: Allen & Unwin, Ltd., 1958.

———. *Large Sutra on Perfect Wisdom, With the Divisions of the Abhisamayālaṅkāra.* London: Luzac & Co., Ltd., 1961.

———. *Buddhist Thought in India: Three Phases of Buddhist Philosophy.* London: Allen & Unwin Ltd., 1962.

———. "A Personal Tribute." *The Eastern Buddhist* 2.1, New Series (August, 1967): 84–85.

———. *Thirty Years of Buddhist Studies: Selected Essays.* Oxford: Bruno Cassirer, 1967.

———. *The Perfection of Wisdom in 8,000 Lines & Its Verse Summary.* San Francisco: Four Seasons Foundation, 1973 (1st ed., 1958).

———. "The Intermediary World." *The Eastern Buddhist* 7.2, New Series (October, 1974): 22–31.

———. *Further Buddhist Studies*. Oxford: Bruno Cassirer, Ltd., 1975.

*———. *Der Satz vom Widerspruch: Zur Theorie des dialektischen Materialismus*. Hamburg: Self-published, 1932 (reprint Verlag Neue Kritik, 1976).

———. *The Memoirs of a Modern Gnostic*, 3 vols. (3rd vol. unavailable, thought to be lost). Manchester: Frederick Law & Co., Ltd., 1979.

*Conze, Edward and Ellen Wilkinson. *Why Fascism?* London: Selwyn & Blount, 1934.

———. *Why War? A Handbook for Those Who Will Take Part in the Second World War*. London: NCLC Publishing Society, Ltd., 1934.

Crespi, Leo P. "Review of *Propaganda, Communication, and Public Opinion: A Comprehensive Reference Guide* by Bruce Lannes Smith, Harold D. Lasswell, and Ralph D. Casey." *The Public Opinion Quarterly* 10.1 (1946): 99–102.

Cuke.com. "Audio-Video." Accessed August 23, 2022. www.cuke.com/audio%20files/av.htm#conze

Dante. *Inferno*, trans. Lawrence Grant White. New York: Pantheon Books, 1948.

Dewey, John. "Education as Politics." *New Republic* 32 (1922): 139–141.

Dodge, Raymond. "The Psychology of Propaganda." *Religion Education* 15 (1920): 241–252.

*Doob, Leonard William. *Propaganda: Its Psychology and Technique*. New York: H. Holt and Co., 1935.

Elbrecht, Herbert. "Edward Conze: 1904–1979." http://conze.eu. Accessed August 17, 2022.

Ellul, Jacques. *Propaganda: The Formation of Men's Attitudes*, trans. Konrad Kellen and Jean Lerner. New York: Alfred A. Knopf, 1965 (1st ed. 1962, *Propagandes*).

Freud, Sigmund. *Group Psychology and the Analysis of the Ego*, trans. James Strachey. London: Hogarth Press, 1949 (1st ed. 1921, *Massenpsychologie und Ich-Analyse*).

Fromm, Erich. *Escape from Freedom*. New York: Farrar & Rinehart, Inc., 1941.

Guyer, Sara. "The Ends of Misreading: Propaganda, Democracy, Literature." In Jonathan Auerbach and Russ Castronovo, eds., *The Oxford Handbook of Propaganda Studies*. Oxford: Oxford University Press, 2013: 366–377.

Hearn, Lafcadio. *Gleanings in Buddha-Fields: Studies of Hand and Soul in the Far East*. London: Kegan Paul, Trench, Trübner & Co., Ltd., 1897.

Heine, Holger R., trans. *The Principle of Contradiction: On the Theory of Dialectical Materialism* by Edward Conze. Maryland: Lexington Books, 2016.

Herman, Edward S. and Noam Chomsky. *Manufacturing Consent: The Political Economy of the Mass Media*. New York: Pantheon Books, 1988.

Hexham, Irving. "The Moral Quest of Edward Conze." In Irving Hexham, ed., *Understanding World Religions: An Interdisciplinary Approach*. Grand Rapids: Zondervan, 2011: 213–232.

Institute for Propaganda Analysis. "We Say Au Revoir." *Propaganda Analysis: A Bulletin to Help the Intelligent Citizen Detect and Analyze Propaganda* 4.13 (1942): 1–6.

Jansen, Sue Curry. "'The World's Greatest Adventure in Advertising': Walter Lippmann's Critique of Censorship and Propaganda." In Jonathan Auerbach and Russ Castronovo, eds., *The Oxford Handbook of Propaganda Studies*. Oxford: Oxford University Press, 2013: 301–325.

Jowett, Garth S. "Propaganda and Communication: The Re-emergence of a Research Tradition." *Journal of Communication* 37.1 (1987): 97–114.

Jowett, Garth S. and Victoria O'Donnell. *Propaganda and Persuasion*, 7th ed. Los Angeles: SAGE Publications, Inc., 2019.

Khamis, Sahar, Paul B. Gold, and Katherine Vaughn. "Propaganda in Egypt and Syria's 'Cyberwars': Contexts, Actors, Tools, and Tactics." In Jonathan Auerbach and Russ

Castronovo, eds., *The Oxford Handbook of Propaganda Studies*. Oxford: Oxford University Press, 2013: 418–438.

*Lasswell, Harold D. *Propaganda Technique in the World War*. New York: Peter Smith, 1927.

*Le Bon, Gustav. *The Crowd: A Study of the Popular Mind*. New York: The Macmillan Company, 1896 (1st ed. 1895, *Psychologie des foules*).

Lippmann, Walter. *The Political Scene: An Essay on the Victory of 1918*. New York: H. Holt and Company, 1919.

———. *Public Opinion*. London: Allen & Unwin Ltd., 1922.

*Lumley, Frederick E. *The Propaganda Menace*. London: The Century Co., 1933.

Mann, Thomas. *Early Sorrow and Mario and the Magician*, trans. H. T. Lowe-Porter. London: Secker & Warburg, 1953 (1st ed. 1929, *Mario und der Zauberer*).

Marcuse, Herbert. "Review of Der Satz vom Widerspruch by Edward Conze." *Zeitschrift für Sozialforschung* 3 (1934): 266–267. Translated by Holger Heine, 2011.

Murti, T. R.V. *The Central Philosophy of Buddhism*. London: Allen & Unwin, Ltd., 1960.

Pedro-Carañana, Joan, Daniel Broudy, and Jeffery Klaehn. *The Propaganda Model Today: Filtering Perception and Awareness*. London: University of Westminster Press, 2018.

Reich, Wilhelm. *The Mass Psychology of Fascism*, trans. Vincent R. Carfagno. New York: Farrar, Strauss & Giroux, 1970 (1st ed. 1933, *Die Massenpsychologie des Faschismus*).

San Francisco Zen Center. "News." *Wind Bell: Publication of Zen Center* 12 (1973): 15–31.

Schopenhauer, Arthur. *The World as Will and Representation*, trans. E. F. J. Payne. New York: Dover Publications, Inc., 1966.

Simpson, Christopher. *Science of Coercion: Communication Research and Psychological Warfare 1945–1960*. Oxford: Oxford University Press, 1994.

Sproule, J. Michael. "Propaganda Studies in American Social Science: The Rise and Fall of the Critical Paradigm." *Quarterly Journal of Speech* 73.1 (1987): 60–78.

———. "Progressive Propaganda Critics and the Magic Bullet Myth." *Critical Studies in Mass Communication* 6.3 (1989): 225–246.

Streng, Frederick J. *Emptiness: A Study in Religious Meaning*. New York: Abingdon Press, 1967.

de Waal, Edmund. *The Hare with Amber Eyes: A Family's Century of Art and Loss*. New York: Farrar, Straus and Giroux, 2010.

Warburg, Fredric. *An Occupation for Gentlemen*. Boston: Houghton Mifflin Company, 1960.

———. *All Authors Are Equal: The Publishing Life of Fredric Warburg, 1936–1971*. London: Hutchinson & Co., 1973.

Wharton, Wallace S. "Taking the Navy to the People." *United States Naval Institute Proceedings* 49.12 (December, 1923): 2010–2021.

Wollaeger, Mark. "Propaganda and Pleasure: From Kracauer to Joyce." In Jonathan Auerbach and Russ Castronovo, eds., *The Oxford Handbook of Propaganda Studies*. Oxford: Oxford University Press, 2013: 278–297.

ACKNOWLEDGMENTS

For help of many kinds, including guidance, support, advice, and criticism, thanks to: David Chadwick, Peter Coyote, Herbert Elbrecht, Robert Finkelstein, Peter Ford, Michael Gelfond, Richard Grossinger, Neal Halfon, Travis Herb, Alexander Holzman, Arnold Kotler, Lewis Lancaster, Marc Lesser, Raoul Martinez, Elaine Maisner & Richard Jaffe, Reed Malcolm, Patrick McMahon, Joseph Parry, James I. Porter, Lynne Rienner, Mark Schenker, David Schneider, Sam Schrager, Carla Shapreau, Tori Sharpe, Jonathan Silk, Louise Steinman, Eleanor Taylor, Laurence H. Tribe, Eric Zsebenyi, and the anonymous reviewer. Most of all, profound gratitude to Frances Herb, for the power of her love and acute intelligence.

INTRODUCTION

The advent of cannon killed the feudal system;
ink will kill the modern social organization.

Napoleon[1]

What Propaganda Is

Propaganda is an attempt to extend the influence of a social group—a nation, a class, a professional or religious group, etc.—by spreading or "propagating" beliefs and practices that are current in that group. In addition, propaganda aims at maintaining unity within a social group by strengthening the bonds of emotional solidarity among its members; or, alternately, at disintegrating a rival or enemy group.

When they *do* things together, people feel most intensely that they belong together. The tribal dance is unrivalled in its propaganda effect. When they lose themselves in a rapturous crowd, people melt, as it were, into one social unity, and feel that they are parts in a greater stream of warm social life. A similar result is obtained when people sing songs together—watch the effect of community singing—or when they collectively perform ritual actions, e.g., all stand up and shout "Heil Hitler!" while raising their arms. In well-organised churches, congregations all rise and sit down together, read, sing, or recite together the same words. The revivalist urges, "Let everybody join heartily in the singing!" It is a sign of hopeless incompetence if a labour meeting is allowed to begin or to

1 Jules Bertaut, *Napoleon in His Own Words*, trans. Herbert Edward Law and Charles Lincoln Rhodes (Chicago: A. C. McClurg & Co., 1916), p. 63.

DOI: 10.4324/9781003363408-1

end without the "Internationale" or the "Red Flag."[2] The propagandist's game is as good as won if he can collect a number of people and make all of them shout the same words at the same time, or create in them a collective emotion about some symbols of group unity, like flags, fasces, or leaders. These acts and sentiments impress upon each individual the unity of the group.

Less effective is propaganda by *words*. Yet unsatisfactory as it may be, talk becomes increasingly important as a weapon of propaganda in those societies in which a number of rival groups fight for the support of the citizen, and in which the citizen expects at least the appearance of rational argument. There are two ways of propagating beliefs by words. The one tends to guide, the other to dominate. The one respects the dignity of the people, tries to put them on their feet, to develop their latent faculties and abilities, and to make them think for themselves. The other treats them as childish halfwits, as "human material," as dumb instruments of their masters. The latter is the more common. To avoid confusion, we will call the first "education," and reserve the word "propaganda" for the latter. The division between the two is, of course, not quite clear-cut. In actual practice most education contains some propaganda, and propaganda is, normally at least, slightly informative. But, on the whole, education and propaganda can be quite well treated as opposites.

Propaganda would be a poor weapon, indeed, if it had only words at its disposal—arguments and slogans, hymns and songs. Non-verbal propaganda—pictures, cartoons, flags, and symbols—is often more effective because it cannot be argued with. There is the propaganda of example and of the deed, which often carries more weight than mere verbiage. Gandhi's twenty-one-day fast in Delhi in 1924 was bound to impress the Indian peasant masses more deeply than 600,000 words in "Young India" could have done. The Mahatma's fasts and penances were anxiously marked, and quickly understood, by millions of simple villagers. That a successful politician should voluntarily deprive himself of food for weeks is so rare a spectacle that it must excite wonder and awe.

The "propaganda of the deed" had a place of honour among the weapons employed by anarchists and Russian terrorists to overthrow the existing government. The assassination of prominent persons, they believed, would reveal the weakness of the governmental machine, act as a signal for a general insurrection, create faith in the sincerity and self-sacrifice of the revolutionaries, and fascinate others into imitating their deeds. Letters of blood, they thought, were easier to decipher than letters of black ink. Kropotkin once said that one action makes more propaganda than 1,000 pamphlets.

As a last resort, big business, too, has recourse to a variety of the propaganda of action. For instance, in 1914 Rockefeller's name stank in the nostrils of his fellow citizens. His business began to suffer. Sweet words could no longer dispel the stench. The Rockefellers hired Ivy Lee. Lee proposed not merely to place before

2 *Editors: Standard songs of the socialist movement.*

the public the affairs of the corporation in the most favourable light, but to "shape the affairs of the corporation so that, when placed before the public, they would be approved."[3] In consequence mining conditions were improved, and Standard Oil started doing good deeds. In two years enormous contributions to science and charity had washed the stains off Rockefeller's name.

The propagandist has to reckon with the millions of dull people who, as Harold Lasswell puts it, are protected by their mental sluggishness from more verbal forms of propaganda. There is a type of person who, if they ever bother to go to meetings, cannot understand what the speaker is getting at. They are appealed to by silly slogans, barbaric stunts, buffoonery, and gross exhibitions which awaken them from their torpor and arouse their emotions and impulses for the time being. Those who live in drab surroundings will be impressed by a large spectacle. Parades and marches give the participants a sense of unity and importance, and arouse in the spectators a sense of universality.

Verbal propaganda is probably as old as mankind. Julius Caesar records that, preliminary to a military advance, he "caused propaganda to be spread among the tribes."[4] It was, however, only with the industrial revolution that verbal propaganda developed on a large scale. More than 40,000 pamphlets were issued during the Puritan Revolution in England, some of them selling as many as 120,000 copies each. The American colonies, during the War of Independence, maintained a propaganda bureau for Europe in Holland. The Jacobins and Napoleon spread propaganda on a large scale. It is a certain consolation that propaganda, when overdone, produces a sort of "emotional recoil." Apparently, Napoleon was the first to exhaust its possibilities; if a statement was as "false as a bulletin," it was as false as false could be.

In the 20th century the output of propaganda has, in connection with the wars, reached a new peak. For the preparation and the conduct of wars, the propagandist has become as indispensable as the engineer. The more extensive use of verbal propaganda has been rendered possible by technical innovations which have facilitated communication and have given birth to new vehicles of propaganda—newspapers, cinemas, wireless, and television. It has been rendered necessary by the growing lack of unity in the outlook of the innumerable ants that compose the modern Great Society. The authority of the rulers has, as we shall see, been undermined in many ways.[5] They often have to persuade where formerly they could command.

At the beginning of the war of 1914–1918 it became obvious that verbal propaganda is a typically democratic weapon. The generals felt that it went against

3 Quoted in L.W. Doob, *Propaganda: Its Psychology and Technique* (New York: H. Holt and Co., 1935), p. 195.

4 Will Irwin, *Propaganda and the News: or, What Makes You Think So?* (New York: Whittlesey House, 1936), p. 121.

5 See Chapter 1.3.

everything they stood for. On January 8th, 1915, General Falkenhayn, chief of the German General Staff, declared that "it was inadmissible to fight the governments of the enemy in a malicious form."[6] A leaflet which encouraged the Indian troops to revolt was suppressed.[7] On the English side, General Plumer showed his aversion to propaganda in the words: "No, that would not be fair. We have to fight the fellows."[8] Soldiers felt that the implications of modern propaganda clash with their code of honour, that propaganda is not a chivalrous weapon, and that it goes against the solidarity which continues to bind together professional warriors, although they may fight each other for the time being. In private they shook their heads at this new civilian way of "letting the mob loose."

Talking and Dancing

The chief task of propaganda, verbal and otherwise, is to create, or maintain, unity within a social group. Propaganda is, as Lasswell put it, the "hammer and anvil of social solidarity."[9] In this respect, all modern propaganda is a faint substitute for the tribal dance, and for tribal ceremonies. The size of modern groups renders it technically impossible to burn out dissent in the furnace of a common dance.

In the tempestuous rhythm of well-regulated and emotionally-overcharged tribal dances and ceremonies, the members of a primitive group melt, as it were, into unity. To take an example, A. R. Radcliffe-Brown has shown in detail how the ceremonies of the Andaman Islanders are designed to safeguard social unity.[10] In the dancing rites, "by virtue of the effects of rhythm and melody, all the members of a community are able harmoniously to cooperate and act in unity."[11] By yielding to the rhythm, the individual induces in himself the pleasure of self-surrender. Since rhythmical actions are less tiring than non-rhythmical ones, "the dancer feels that in and through the dance he obtains such an increase of his personal energy that he is able to accomplish strenuous exertions with a minimum of fatigue."[12] In addition, the dance produces a condition of warm good-fellowship in those who take part in it. When we share with others in an intense and collective pleasure, we are filled with geniality and good-will towards our companions.

By making the social unity intensely felt, the dance is a means of maintaining it. Before a fight, it creates in the individual a sense of social unity and solidarity.

6 Hans Thimme, *Weltkrieg ohne Waffen: Die Propaganda der Westmächte gegen Deutschland, ihre Wirkung und ihre Abwehr* (Berlin: Cotta, 1932), p. 36. Trans. E. C.

7 Thimme, *Weltkrieg ohne Waffen*, pp. 38–39.

8 *Editors: We are unable to identify the original source of this quotation.*

9 Harold D. Lasswell, *Propaganda Technique in the World War* (New York: Peter Smith, 1927), p. 221.

10 Alfred Reginald Radcliffe-Brown, *The Andaman Islanders: A Study in Social Anthropology* (Cambridge: Cambridge University Press, 1922). Radcliffe-Brown (p. 328) defines a ceremonial as consisting of "(1) collective actions, (2) required by custom, (3) performed on occasions of changes in the course of social life, and (4) expressing the collective sentiments relating to such social change."

11 Radcliffe-Brown, *The Andaman Islanders*, p. 249.

12 Ibid., p. 250.

During the greater part of the year, the local groups which make up the tribe are almost completely isolated from each other. Their sense of solidarity therefore tends to weaken. They meet, however, regularly at dance meetings which renew the contact, and make the unity felt by everyone. So great is the sense of solidarity generated among the small communities of the Andamanese that very little punishment is needed to keep order.

The march of industrial progress has left us with only the mutilated remnants of tribal dances and ceremonies. The incessant chatter of the modern propagandist is a feeble substitute for the communal activities of the tribe. By themselves, words have proved unable to produce that direct experience of social unity which the maintenance of society requires. For a time, industrial communities gave little opportunity for collective enthusiasm, although, in various ways, the town-dweller showed that the longing for warm fellow-feeling was not extinguished in his mind. Football matches, and other sporting events, permit many individuals to merge into one yelling crowd. Ordway Tead reports how burlesque shows did the same thing for the tenement dwellers of New England. "When the *ingénue* came down the aisle and got all the 'boys' to whistling or singing one of the popular favorites, a real and complete emotional release and satisfaction was bestowed" upon these emotionally starved and bewildered people.[13]

In more recent times, some politicians discovered that people needed this sort of experience at least as much as they need bread. In some countries, to mass people together has become a recognised device of modern statecraft. Even the rulers of Britain were surprised at the overwhelming and spontaneous response to Jubilee and Coronation. The disciplined march and the emotionally warm mass meeting are now the most effective propaganda weapons of all. The individual man and woman acquire a feeling of terrific strength when they are among a large number of people who act as one. For the time being, they incorporate into themselves the combined strength of all the others. And what is more, for a time they can merge, or lose themselves, in an impassioned and rapturous crowd. By a massed array of its forces, a "cause" binds to itself the deepest yearnings of the human soul, longings which are beyond the reach of reasoned argument.

Psychology and Propaganda

It would be a miracle if the intellectuals, always eager to find something new to write about, had overlooked a "find" like modern propaganda. In many hundreds of books, pamphlets, and articles, propaganda has been discussed from almost every conceivable angle.[14] Much information has been accumulated about the

13 Ordway Tead, *Instincts in Industry: A Study of Working-Class Psychology* (London: Constable, 1919), p. 40.

14 For an almost complete list of books published up to recently, see Harold D. Lasswell, Ralph D. Casey, and Bruce Lannes Smith, *Propaganda and Promotional Activities: An Annotated Bibliography* (Minneapolis: The University of Minnesota Press, 1935).

organisation of propaganda, and its instruments, organs, or vehicles—books, pamphlets, leaflets, newspapers, private letters, public meetings, rumours and gossip, cinema, and wireless. Others focussed attention on the various purposes for which propaganda is used, from selling toothbrushes and making more money to building empires and saving souls.

While engaged in some great social task, people like being lied to. The dresses of today look becoming, those of yesterday, often ridiculous. Similarly, the lies of today are sweet and intoxicating, the lies of yesterday repulsive like remnants of stale beer left over from the day before. After 1918, people felt that their war efforts and sacrifices had led them nowhere. They wanted to know how they had been cheated. Much of the literature on propaganda dates from that time. It was written in order to give the victim a chance to grumble, by exposing the habitual untruthfulness of verbal propaganda in the recent past.

That propaganda deceives or intends to deceive is taken for granted. Wickham Steed defines propaganda as "partial and deliberately misleading statements."[15] An anonymous genius defined it as "the art of deceiving your friends without being quite able to deceive your enemies." Arthur Ponsonby and others collected numerous instances of propagandist falsification.[16] Frederick Lumley tried to classify the fallacies of the propagandist's arguments. He noted "four major abuses of the laws of reasoning": suppression, distortion, diversion, and fabrication.[17]

Going more into detail, one studied how the methods employed vary with the social layer to which they are addressed. Intellectual lies charm intellectual people, rude and blatant lies are better reserved for popular consumption. One type of propaganda caters to the thoughtful and critical people, "who think they think," and require oceans of "facts," wrapped into subtle reasonings, before their common sense is successfully drowned. The thinking processes of the housewife, or the devotee of football pools, have to be directed on different lines.

All these studies provide useful material. They leave unanswered the question why people like to be lied to, why they put up with a mendacious press, and why they embrace the lies of today as eagerly as they reject those of the day before. It is at this point that psychology comes in. We are not passively pushed into convictions as bricks are pushed into position. If somebody wants to convince me, he requires my active cooperation. He has to make me convince myself. He has to set into motion something in me that takes up his suggestion and that is eager to

15 In Arthur Porritt, ed., *The Causes of War: Economic, Industrial, Racial, Religious, Scientific, and Political* (London: Macmillan & Co., Ltd., 1932), p. 172.

16 Arthur Ponsonby, *Falsehood in War-Time: Containing an Assortment of Lies Circulated Throughout the Nations During the Great War* (New York: E. P. Dutton & Co., 1928); Kurt Mühsam, *Wie wir belogen wurden: Die amtliche Irreführung des deutschen Volkes* (Munich: A. Langen, 1918); George Sylvester Viereck, *Spreading Germs of Hate* (New York: H. Liveright, 1930).

17 Frederick E. Lumley, *The Propaganda Menace* (London: The Century Co., 1933), pp. 116–117.

follow him.[18] We study propaganda from a psychological angle when we want to know what it is in us that takes up and welcomes the propagandist's suggestions.

Since the propagandist addresses himself to men in the mass, we have to concentrate on the mentality of men in the mass. A special branch of psychology, social psychology, has been developed for the purpose of studying the behaviour of men in the mass. Social psychology does not deal with you as an individual, but as a part of a "social group." Propaganda is a way of manipulating social groups. "A [social] group is a collection of people organised by some common appetite, instinct, caprice, interest, sentiment, or ideal."[19] The French or the Scotch, the industrial workers or the medical profession, the Church of Rome, a public meeting, or a billiard club—all these are social groups. The unity of a social group is maintained by common interests and intentions, by customs, taboos, and convictions, by ceremonies which in the case of more important groups are connected with birth, puberty, death, marriage, burial, etc.[20]

The individual has, as we shall see, ample reason to try to fit in with the stream of social life. But, when he fits in, he is usually not aware of what he is doing. He often believes that he does what he does because it is reasonable to do it. This, however, is an illusion. We do most of what we do because we are afraid to isolate ourselves from our group. Abstract reasoning has very little to do with our assent to social convictions. Primitive people are often more honest in that respect than we are. When ethnologists ask them, "Why do you do or believe this or that?" they answer, "It is our custom," or, "Because our fathers did so before us." Norman Angell somewhere tells a story which admirably illustrates this mentality among modern Americans. Smith asks Jones, "Well, Jones, what do I hear about you? You do not believe in the Monroe doctrine?" "Now, Smith, what do you think of me? Of course I believe in the Monroe doctrine. All I said was that I do not know what it means." Psychologists are often reproached for depriving us of our pride in our reasoning powers. The reproach is most vocal in quarters where there is least reason for pride.

The desire to maintain social unity is a force infinitely stronger than the flickering lamp of reason. A species tends to preserve its existence. If there is any purpose or meaning in the existence of animals and plants, it is that of perpetuating the species simply because it exists. A social group equally tends to perpetuate its coherent existence simply because it exists. Several mechanisms have been devised which increase the number of factors that are common to all members of a group, and which thus foster their unity, cooperation, mutual aid, solidarity, and loyalty.

---

18 In technical language: most suggestion involves auto-suggestion. *Editors: See "auto-suggestion," PMP, p. 161.*

19 Frederic C. Bartlett, *Psychology and the Soldier* (Cambridge: Cambridge University Press, 1927), p. 94.

20 It is usual to divide groups into "primary" and "secondary." Membership in a primary group tends to involve the total personality. Participation in a secondary group affects persons only to the degree to which they identify themselves with this particular interest.

Social heterogeneity, due to differences in class and race, is expensive, to say the least. In the USA, in the 1930s, 12,000 people were murdered each year, fifty times as many as in Great Britain. Two thirds of the crimes were committed by persons born outside the USA, or by their immediate descendants. In this country, there is one policeman to every 857 persons outside London. But there is one policeman to every 390 Londoners.

In the USA, deliberate standardisation has been employed to create a group uniformity of 100% Americans. People are made to live in the same kind of houses, read the same newspapers, see the same films, etc.

> The third generation of European immigrants seen in American public schools tends towards a uniformity of face and feature suggesting the work of a Heavenly Henry Ford. I have seen children of Italians, Swedes, and Greeks sitting side by side looking almost alike and talking exactly the same.[21]

An amazing uniformity of opinion prevails among American "men in a car." The greater the stress, the greater the need for social unity; in wartime, social inequality seriously hampers the national effort, and the propagandist has to work hard in order to make people forget the inequality of sacrifice.[22] By cutting everybody to the same pattern, one transforms a rabble into a nation.

Pride and Prejudice

Scientific discoveries are usually unwelcome, unless they vindicate themselves by bolstering up some class or race prejudice, or lead to the invention of some new toy. It is a misfortune that many developments of scientific thought compel us to think less and less of ourselves. With Copernicus, our planet lost its privileged position in the centre of the universe. In the course of subsequent astronomical research, we found our stature steadily reduced until at present we appear to be no more than, say, a colony of microscopic infusoria sitting on top of a pebble in the Atlantic Ocean.

In the 19th century, some philosophers believed that this dismal picture was offset by the splendour of the human mind which lifted man far above the rest of creation. Alas, this illusion was dispelled as soon as, from 1900 onwards, our *mind* was subjected to scientific treatment. The results went far to encourage the virtues of modesty and humility. It appeared that our destiny, that our thoughts,

21 R. J. Cruikshank in *Daily News*, April 25, 1930, quoted by Charles Duff, *This Human Nature: A History, A Commentary, An Exposition From the Earliest Times to the Present Day* (New York: J. J. Little & Ives Co., 1930), p. 352.

22 During the last war, in Germany especially, the wealthy were much better provided with food than the poor. In all countries the bodies were conscripted, but the money was not. In England it still takes the whole-time labour of 2,000,000 workers, year in year out, to produce the annual cost of the war debt.

emotions, and actions, were shaped for us to an overwhelming extent by heredity, glands, instincts, complexes, shocks, external environment, and upbringing—in short, by factors of which the high-minded were slightly ashamed, and for which they could not take much credit. "Shall the axe boast itself against him that heweth therewith? Or shall the saw magnify itself against him that shaketh it?"

Social psychology adds to the insult. Here we are expected to perform the feat of, as it were, looking down upon ourselves from a high mountain or an airplane, swarming hither and thither, each one of us not himself, but one among many. It is not easy to make friends with social groups. We do not easily contemplate with equanimity how we are forced into a passive role, how our will and choice weigh little against the impersonal social forces which push us about, how we are carried away by them, and how the reasonings which accompany "our" decisions are mostly self-deceptions. We feel that, when seen in a mass, we present a sorry spectacle. Nor are we reassured by the impersonal tone of the social psychologist who makes us feel that we do not count at all.

It has to be remembered, of course, that the social psychologist claims to describe only one side of human beings. One may, for instance, look up the "Statistical Abstract for the United Kingdom," and find that the number of suicides rose almost steadily from 4,209 in 1922 to 6,247 in 1933. A social psychologist might then, impersonally, try to account for this increase in terms of social conditions operating on the mentality of the "average person." From his angle, it does not matter whether there were 6,247 or 6,248 suicides in 1933. From an individual angle, it matters a lot if the 6,248th is myself. For the social psychologist, it does not matter whether I and my friends make up this total, or complete strangers. 6,000 suicides are an impersonal affair. Individuality exists, but in social psychology we abstract from it.

What we call a human personality is an incompletely unified collection of "selves" which all inhabit the same body.[23] It is a matter of common observation that often the behaviour of one's "public self" is very much at variance with that of one's "private self." The same person may be timid in his private, and bold in his public life. He may be intelligent and circumspect as a tradesman, but utterly empty-headed when it comes to politics. Many public men have been kind-hearted individuals, but ruthlessly bloodthirsty when it came to carrying out "the will of the people." A man may be decent and kindly when you meet him in his house or when you are in need of help. He may show common sense in his daily tasks. He may be self-assured in his family, or among his mates. But when he is thrown together with a preferably large number of heterogeneous people, he is often utterly transformed. "Every numerous assembly is a *mob*, whosoever the individuals who compose it," wrote Chesterfield.[24] Moreover, his reactions

---

23 *Editors: Cf. the Buddhist concept of the self as an impermanent assemblage of five aggregates or* skandhas.

24 Robert McMurdy, ed., *The Modern Chesterfield: A Selection of Chesterfield's Letters to his Son* (Boston: R. G. Badger, 1917), p. 199. *Editors: Philip Dormer Stanhope, Earl of Chesterfield (1694–1773) was a British statesman and intellectual.*

may be shaped by his participation in a mass, although he is not in physical contact with its members. One may act as part of a mass in a small circle. A person who dishes out the views of the *News Chronicle* or of the *Daily Mail* to his patient family does not speak only as himself. The discussions of this book deal with people only in their public capacity.

So much about the emotional resistance which the reader is bound to feel at one stage or another of our enquiry. It remains to touch slightly on three methodological points. By making a clean sweep of them here, we may avoid misunderstanding later on.

1. Any statement about the behaviour of human beings in a group allows for exceptions, for divergent individuals who do not move in the direction indicated. These exceptions do not invalidate the truth of the statement. "The English hate the Hun," "The French fear the Germans," "The working people feel oppressed," "We are still superstitious"—statements like these refer to the majority of the group concerned. The exceptions do not affect the issue and are, in most cases, of little importance for propagandist work. In our vanity, of course, we are only too apt to feel that we, personally, are one of the exceptions whenever an apparently stupid form of social behaviour is under consideration. This is rarely the case. If we suffer badly from a sense of inferiority, we will be obsessed with a desire to distinguish ourselves from the despised mass. We will resent being lumped together with the mass. It is rather foolish to despise the mass when one belongs to it.
2. It is a general rule that, wherever there is one mental trend in one direction, there is the opposite, or countertrend, also. We hate others, but we also love them. We boast, but we also deprecate ourselves. We are submissive, but we also assert ourselves. We desire security, but we also wish to take risks.[25] When discussing propaganda, we often have to emphasise one of two mental trends, but we should always bear in mind that the opposite equally exists.
3. Finally, we should add a warning that man is not all soul. Specialists usually overemphasise the importance of the factors they understand. When we talk about the influence of peoples' minds on their behaviour, we should never lose sight of the bedrock of economic factors which are at least as potent as the trends of our souls.

---

25 I have explained this rule in *The Scientific Method of Thinking* (London: Chapman & Hall, Ltd., 1935), chapters 5 to 11, and 14; *An Introduction to Dialectical Materialism* (London: NCLC Publishing Society, Ltd., 1936), chapter 3; and its applications to psychology in Henry Lyster Jameson's *An Outline of Psychology* (9th ed., completely revised by Edward Conze, Cedar Paul, and Eden Paul, London: NCLC Publishing Society, Ltd., 1938), pp. 63–64.

Survey of the Book

The bulk of Part 1 ("The Mentality of the Victim") is devoted to sentiments and modes of behaviour which result from the derangement, or blocking, of various needs or instincts. Suggestibility, hero worship, and tribal behaviour provide the most fertile soil for propagandist efforts. We further have to pay considerable attention to aggressive behaviour, and to the emotion of hatred which accompanies the blocking of any instinct or desire. In Part 2 ("The Veils Which Hide the Truth"), we discuss the problems of that self-deception which makes us want to see the real truth only when it is veiled. As a German officer in 1918 expressed in his crude Teutonic way, "Propaganda can yield good fruit only when it is so cleverly designed that one does not notice its real purpose."[26] Finally, in the conclusion, we discuss the part propaganda plays in the evolution of history and in the planning of social events, and we try to discover how deep it goes, and what kind of social transformations can be expected from it.

Starting with the clearly visible surface of our minds, we first of all deal with the more *rational* aims of which men are more or less conscious in their efforts. It will be the first, and comparatively the easiest, task of the propagandist to promise that he will further these aims, and add to the income, status, power, and security of his followers. Men, however, are not rational animals, though they were sometimes thought to be so in the 19th century. The Liberals imagined that superstition and nationalism would disappear if only shown to be unreasonable. Nothing of the kind has happened. People cling to superstition and nationalism not because it is reasonable to do so, but because it gratifies their instincts.

Human beings, whether learned or unlearned, whether rich or poor, whether sharp-witted or dull-witted, can be likened to those volcanoes which have a small cap of snow and ice on the top. Man is filled with emotions, passions, and desires, and he has got a very small bit of reason covering the top. Julian Huxley has summed up the result of fifty years of research when he wrote that, according to modern psychology, human behaviour and mental life are

> the resultants of a series of urges or drives, harnessed to a series of goals or aims, which push and pull the human being in various directions. Reason is not an impelling force, and all too rarely a guiding hand: in the majority of cases it is just engaged in finding reasons—more or less rational excuses, if you like—for the actions to which we find ourselves impelled.[27]

The emotions and passions that make up the greater part of our minds are brought into motion whenever the propagandist wants to achieve anything. The heart has

---

26 *Gute Früchte zeitigen kann nur eine Propaganda, die so geschickt angelegt ist, daß der Mann den wirklichen Zweck nicht merkt.* Thimme, *Weltkrieg ohne Waffen*, p. 267.

27 Julian Huxley, *Scientific Research and Social Needs* (London: Watts & Co., 1934), p. 189.

reasons of which reason has no knowledge. It may be useful to bring them to the knowledge of reason.

If we could make a cross-section through the human mind, we would find, immediately below the thin layer of comparatively rational convictions and strivings, a thick layer of *magical* beliefs. Men under modern conditions are no longer clearly aware of the magical character of many of their attitudes and practices. The mode of life in an industrial community does, on the whole, little to encourage the magical longings and habits of the human soul. At the end of Part 1, we study the propagandist as the successor of a long tradition of witch-doctors, in his role as a spell-binder who skilfully uses ancient magical modes of thought for his own purposes.[28]

Instincts and sentiments are almost blind. With proper guidance they can be made to drive almost any mill. Let us take, for instance, the sentiment of tenderness for animals. This sentiment can be "appealed to" for nearly any cause—for anti-German propaganda (German officials ill-treating dogs), pro-Nazi propaganda (Goering the animal lover), pro-Bolshevik propaganda (Professor Schmidt and the wounded seal near the North Pole),[29] monarchist propaganda (the respective king and almost any animal), etc. In the same way, given a floating sentiment of hatred, the propagandist can divert it to almost anything.

In this book we have very little to say about instincts in themselves.[30] Instincts become interesting to the propagandist only when they are not satisfied. If a person's instincts were satisfied—if, in other words, he had reached adaptation—he would turn a deaf ear even to the enchanting propaganda of the Sirens. But an instinct, impulse, or desire, if unsatisfied, leads to repression and discontent, and that gives the propagandist his chance.

Repression is usually the outcome of a conflict between social necessities and individual desires. When repressing, we hold back ideas and wishes from our consciousness, hold them back from ourselves and others, and force the impulse into disguise and concealment.[31] By repressing something in our mind, we do not get rid of it. Everybody is familiar with the fact that persons who repress the sex instinct fail to destroy it that way. It crops up in innumerable disguises, for instance in dreams. Freud and his school have considerably enriched our knowledge of the various substitute satisfactions in which our sex instinct seeks an outlet. Dancing

---

28 *Editors: Thirty-five years later, Conze revisits his thoughts on magic in the article "The Intermediary World" in* The Eastern Buddhist *7.2, New Series (October, 1974): 22–31.*

29 *Editors: Conze is here referring to Otto Schmidt (1891–1956), the Soviet scientist and explorer of the Arctic.*

30 Instincts have been defined as a legacy of patterns of behaviour which are ready for use, like the sex instinct. At the present stage of our knowledge, it is impossible to give an authoritative list of instincts. The current accounts give between 150 and 2.

31 "Repression" must not be confused with "suppression." I *suppress* my desire to kill my aunt when I know perfectly well that I want to kill her, but refrain from doing so. I *repress* this desire when I even convince myself that I never had any intention to kill my aunt. When I repress a desire I "disown" it.

is, of course, a fairly obvious one. There are others, so cleverly disguised that only a trained psychologist can detect them.

Psychology is to a great extent the science of substitute satisfactions. Propaganda is very largely the art of providing public substitute satisfactions for frustrated private wants. The mobilisation of instincts and emotions, however, is only one of the tasks of propaganda. Essentially dishonest, propaganda veils the results of the actions taken in response to it, whether the propagandist is aware of his interested aim or not.[32]

Argument of the Book

The argument which goes as a red thread through this book can be summed up as follows: the purpose of propaganda is to increase the sense of social unity. It aims at making up for the relative weakness of social ties within a group. In other words, propaganda succeeds in making good a deficiency in *genuine* social unity by creating a superstructure of *artificial* social unity. Genuine social unity cannot be obtained unless the members of a group are approximately equal in income, status, education, and sense of values. Wherever inequalities diminish social unity, propaganda generates artificial social bonds which bind people together by a common hatred, by a common conceit, by a common servitude to a leader, or to an "ideal."[33]

It would, however, be difficult to say anything useful about propaganda in general and in the abstract. Like any other social activity, propaganda cannot be torn out of its social context without losing its distinctive meaning. At any period, propaganda receives its chief and characteristic features from the nature of the public to which it is addressed. At the present time, propaganda must appeal to the mental needs of a vast, socially disintegrated, and oppressed population.[34] The mentality of this public is shaped by its living conditions. The salient features of its living conditions are (1) the size of its social units, (2) a high degree of social disunity, and (3) habitual oppression. Whatever we have to say about modern propaganda can be deduced from these three basic facts of our social situation.

There is first the question of *size*. In their quest for power—technical and political—men group themselves together into wider and wider units. In one way

32 Lumley's definition stresses this aspect (*The Propaganda Menace*, p. 44):

> Propaganda is promotion which is veiled in one way or another as to (1) its origin and sources, (2) the interests involved, (3) the methods employed, (4) the content spread, and (5) the results accruing to the victims—any one, any two, any three, any four, or all five.

33 An "ideal" is not always as ideal as it looks. In many cases, as we will see, "ideals" are just a cover for one's spite against oneself, or against somebody else.

34 It is difficult to find an appropriate word for the kind of social group which constitutes the "human material" of the modern propagandist. "Conglomeration" is too clumsy, "mass" too ambiguous, "mob" too contemptuous. Perhaps "indiscriminate crowd" comes closest.

or another, every one of us cooperates with a wide range of people, as a producer, as a distributor, as a consumer, as a soldier, as a citizen. But technical cooperation is compatible with a very low degree of solidarity. When I cooperate with somebody in a coffee plantation in Brazil by indirectly exchanging my money for his coffee, he remains a very remote person, and I have few if any feelings about him. In the modern nation state, the citizen has to act in unison with innumerable strangers at the behest of a remote central authority which nothing but incessant propaganda can make him first tolerate, and then even "love." To convince these strangers that they belong together requires a vast apparatus of propaganda.

For, within certain limits, it is true to say that we can fully exercise our social instincts only in small groups.[35] Fellow feeling evaporates when it has to travel a long distance to reach its object, say from Lanark to Devonshire. The sub-structure of small social groups—village, communities, clans, and even the family—is steadily being eaten away by industrial progress.

The people whose activities have to be coordinated in a modern nation-state are not only numerous, but separated from each other by considerable *inequalities*. The wealthy live apart from the poor, and between them the barriers of manners, customs, and language are impenetrable. The educated shun the uneducated. In periods of common danger and stress, sacrifices are distributed very unequally. Were it not for the propagandist, there would be no sense of solidarity in this unequal mass. Propaganda imposes a "synthetic" brotherhood upon this social chaos, and helps to render innocuous the dilution of the social sense which results from the size of the group and the inequality of its members.

Social conditions in a modern industrial country are, indeed, unfavourable to the development of the social virtues. They are directly opposed to the formation of "social cells"—i.e., small groups which allow for physical contact among its members, bring out the social instincts, give them full scope, and are the condition for man's dignity.[36] Physical contact may seem unimportant to the spiritually minded, but it is vital for the simple reason that it is difficult to love somebody

---

35 We may distinguish four "social" instincts: The desire for company; the desire to do as others do; the desire to do something with others; the desire to help others.

36 Aldous Huxley, *Ends and Means: An Enquiry into the Nature of Ideals and into the Methods Employed for their Realization* (London: Chatto & Windus, 1938), pp. 73–74:

> It is found empirically that group activities and characteristic group feeling [as distinct from mob feeling, EC] become increasingly difficult when more than about twenty or less than about five individuals are involved.... It is significant that Jesus had only twelve apostles; that the Benedictines were divided into groups of ten under a dean...; that ten is the number of individuals constituting a Communist cell. Committees of more than a dozen members are found to be unmanageably large. Eight is the perfect number for a dinner party. The most successful Quaker meetings are generally meetings at which few people are present. Educationists agree that the most satisfactory size for a class is between eight and fifteen. In armies, the smallest unit is about ten.... All evidence points clearly to the fact that there is an optimum size for groups and that this optimum is round about ten for groups meeting for social, religious or intellectual purposes, and from ten to thirty for groups engaged in manual work.

or to be intimate with somebody one has never seen. In order to reach its full maturity, our social behaviour has to be fused with our sexual and homosexual inclinations, which, even in their sublimated form, require physical contact and the physical presence of their object, and are nothing without the body. In addition, the social cell is built on a mutual give and take, and a common sense of value, or a positive attachment to positive aims. Its members must not be very unequal in either income or status. Adam after the fall could not have been more different from what he was in his original state, than the modern citizen of an industrial country is from men who live in a social cell.

It remains to say a few words about the third feature of the modern mass. Staggering inequalities cannot be maintained for any length of time without *oppression*. Although it is one of the chief tasks of modern propaganda to convince the average citizen that he is not oppressed, the propaganda would remain ineffective if it did not make use of the traits created in people by oppression. In order to remove the vague emotional associations of the word "oppression," we have to define it clearly. People are oppressed if, economically, they are hopelessly dependent on their masters; if, sociologically, they are treated as inferiors; and if, psychologically, many of their private and most of their collective actions are governed by frustration, anger, and fear. It will be admitted that this definition fits nine persons out of ten.[37]

It would be sweet to speculate on the kind of propaganda that would appeal to "dis-oppressed" masses; such speculation would, however, throw no light on propaganda as it is actually practised at the present time, and I have done my best to avoid it. At present, any effective propaganda among the masses must bear the marks of the mass mind. No mass propaganda can be successful unless it gives expression to, and fosters, hatred, fear, conceit, and deceit. It is successful to the degree that it succeeds in mobilising these mental forces for some political or social purpose.

This statement, which sums up the results of our analysis, does not condemn all propaganda. It merely states the limitations which its social context must impose upon modern mass propaganda. And it is only with this mass propaganda that we deal here, with a propaganda addressed to a promiscuous assemblage of people who are temporarily bound together by a common fear, hatred, or leader.

I distinguish "mass propaganda" sharply from two other kinds of "promotional activity" which fall outside the scope of this book. There is first a neutral kind of publicity, which makes known, without any attempt at constraining. It serves as a means of overcoming our spatial dispersion. Psychologically, a sign in a shop to the effect that "Here you can buy X's soap," which *enables* the customer to know where he can get what he wants, is a different thing from an advertisement

37 The psychology of "oppressors" falls outside the scope of this book.

which shows a girl in her bath using X's soap—thereby *inducing* people to use it. Secondly, there is the *training* which is exercised by and within social cells.[38] Small-scale training differs in many ways from large-scale *social engineering*. Within a limited circle, it can genuinely increase human cooperation.

The word "propaganda," when understood simply and etymologically as the "propagation of beliefs," is applicable to all these forms of activity. Scientific precision cannot, however, be content with the loose popular usage, which slurs over essential differences which spring from the pattern of social relations within which "promotional activity" is conducted. "Mass propaganda" can be defined as the dissemination of assertions, for which there is no first-hand evidence, among a socially disintegrated mass.

Purpose of the Book

One might wish that a book on propaganda could be written in such a way that "the facts speak for themselves." In actuality this commendable idea is incapable of fulfilment. One cannot completely paralyse one's sense of values when one discusses social activities. The author's standards of value must determine at least the purpose which he has in mind when he writes about propaganda.

Some people are interested in propaganda because, as Lasswell puts it, they are puzzled, and "probe the mysteries of propaganda with that compound of admiration and chagrin with which the victims of a new gambling trick demand to have the thing explained."[39] In this book they will, I hope, get enough entertainment for their money. Others want to learn how to make propaganda. They may find one or two useful hints. But I must say frankly that I do not share the assumption of the majority of my contemporaries, that propaganda in some hands is good, and in others bad—their own hands being the good ones. The book is written for those who want to learn how to *withstand* propaganda in all its forms, by whomever or for whatever ends it may be used.

My attitude to propaganda is based partly on facts, and partly on a philosophy of life which it will be out of place to discuss here.[40] For scientific purposes, in any case, one philosophy or hypothesis is as good as another, as long as it does not obscure the facts. And it seems probable that one can understand the inner

38 Real "education" requires a social cell. "Mass education" is a contradiction in terms. Where the word is used, it camouflages the drilling of machine minders.

39 Lasswell, *Propaganda Technique in the World War*, pp. 2–3.

40 I have explained my philosophical beliefs in *Contradiction and Reality* (London: Wightman & Co., Ltd., 1939). Readers who are interested may obtain a copy from me for 1/6 post free, or from J. M. Watkins, Cecil Court, London, W.C. 2. *Editors: Conze's pamphlet* Contradiction and Reality *is a 32-page condensation in English of his 552-page* Der Satz vom Widerspruch: Zur Theorie des dialektischen Materialismus *(Hamburg: Self-Published, 1932; reprint Verlag Neue Kritik, 1976).* Der Satz vom Widerspruch *has recently been published in English for the first time as* The Principle of Contradiction: On the Theory of Dialectical Materialism, *trans. Holger R. Heine (Maryland: Lexington Books, 2016). See Editors' Introduction, pp. xxiv–xxxii.*

workings of propaganda better when one sees all propagandist activities impartially on the same plane, than when one is hampered by partiality for one of the creeds which are promoted by propaganda.

Friends who have read this book in manuscript have told me that it made depressing reading. This cannot be helped when we study man in his state of degradation and depression. Insofar as they are susceptible to propaganda, men, in my opinion, are deficient in that habit of brotherhood which alone can confer dignity upon them, as well as happiness. One is more likely to derive uplift and optimistic views from an examination of the liver of jellyfish than from a study of propaganda.

Even though we may come to the conclusion that mass propaganda degrades all those who participate in it, we need not therefore abandon all hope of improving social conditions by collective efforts. The question is, however, whether we should choose "social cells" as the instruments of social change, or the vast conglomerations of our big towns. I believe that reformers are more likely to reach their aims by patiently building up social cells, or genuine communities, than by adding to the flood of mass propaganda. But be that as it may.

PART I

The Mentality of the Victim

1.1
OUR AIMS AND THEIR PROMISES

There was never promisse made but it was broken or kept.

Queen Elizabeth[1]

Adaptation is the one great aim of all our mental efforts. In order that we may do anything, a stimulus, or disturbance, must stir us up, either from inside or from outside our body. We then make an effort to remove the stimulus. If we succeed, we are adapted to that stimulus. But there is little reason to rejoice. Soon a new disturbance forces us to react again. Stimulation ends only when life itself ceases. As long as there is ever new stimulation, all-round adaptation cannot be achieved. "All-round adaptation" is another word for complete happiness.

In social life, men hope to attain happiness by collective efforts only in some comparatively rare periods of exaltation, which arise as a relief from despair. In such periods, a population may expect a complete reversal of all their fortunes. They hope that all their wrongs will be righted, and that the millennium is near at hand. Such "eschatological" hopes call for a special kind of propaganda, of which we find examples in the Apocalypse of St. John, in the oratory of Thomas Müntzer, and in the speeches which socialist leaders like Rosa Luxemburg and Zinoviev made in moments of decisive revolutionary importance. Normally hopes are less highly pitched, and in the long run disappointment is less profound. Under ordinary circumstances one expects no more than an improvement in some direction or other.

But whether we look forward to a wholesale or a piecemeal improvement in our conditions, in what direction do we expect that improvement to lie? The people's

1 In James Orchard Halliwell, ed., *The Private Diary of Dr. John Dee and the Catalogue of His Library of Manuscripts* (London: The Camden Society, 1842), p. 37 (entry of October 11, 1590).

DOI: 10.4324/9781003363408-3

hope determines the propagandist's promises. What then has a propagandist to promise so that his recommendations may carry weight? On the whole, it appears that the masses by their social aspirations attempt to further, or to protect, their *economic welfare* (property and income), their *status*, and their *security*. In addition to these more selfish considerations, they are often spurred on by a desire to collaborate in the realisation of some ideal value, like progress, or the Kingdom of God. We reserve the discussion of such more "ideal" aims to Part 2. In this chapter we are concerned with the more selfish and material hopes which often, more or less consciously, induce people to participate in a social, political, or religious movement. Before we can proceed to the deeper layers of the human mind, we have to evaluate the importance of economic motives, to show the decisive importance of "status," and to expose some of the contradictions which mar the ideal of "security."

Economic Motives

The majority of the world's population is engrossed in a perpetual struggle to make ends meet. In their minds considerations of economic welfare are bound to overcrowd the foreground of the stage. The propagandist naturally often appeals to economic motives, holding out the prospect either of *plunder*, or of a higher *standard of living*.

> Soldiers, you are naked and ill-fed! Government owes you much and can give you nothing.... It is my design to lead you into the most fertile plains of the world. Rich provinces and great cities will be in your power; there you will find honour, glory, and wealth.[2]

With these words Napoleon assumed command of the French army about to invade Italy. When addressing himself to a less warlike but more industrious public, the modern propagandist has found the "standard of living" to be an excellent bait. He assures us that "the standard of living has risen more than fourfold under capitalism." He tells us to impose tariffs, or to oppose Japan, so as to maintain our high "standard of living." All political parties promise—within the limits of what is "practicable"—to raise the wages of the masses, to build them better houses, to improve their health, to hand out pensions, and to make their jobs safe.[3]

---

2 Ida M. Tarbell, ed., *Napoleon's Addresses: Selections from the Proclamations, Speeches and Correspondence of Napoleon Bonaparte* (Boston: Joseph Knight Company, 1897), p. 27.

3 In industrial countries the masses now expect that their standard of living will rise continually. In agricultural countries they are glad if they can maintain a steady and stable standard of living. See M. Gandhi, quoted by Charles F. Andrews, *Mahatma Gandhi's Ideas, Including Selections from His Writings* (London: G. Allen & Unwin, Ltd., 1929), p. 188:

> There was wisdom in the sages of old having so regulated society as to limit the material conditions of the people. The rude plough of perhaps 5,000 years ago is the plough of

On the other hand, economic motives are clearly not all-powerful. If they were, there would be little room for a psychology of propaganda. The economics of propaganda would cover most of the ground. But there are at least four limits to the sway of economic interest over our minds: (1) economic self-interest and advancement occupy no more than a segment of our personality; (2) non-economic motives are often more intense than economic motives; (3) economic interests are not clearly and unmistakably defined; and (4) economic considerations are often subordinated to considerations of status.

First of all, we care for many things besides money and commodities. Sex and love, family and friendship, health and hatred, amusements and sports, and sometimes science and art, state and church, take their toll on our attention and interest. It is true that there are always some few men who pursue wealth to the exclusion of everything else. A similar obsession is found at the other end of the social scale. In their private lives, masses of the poor dare not take their minds off the interminable worry about wages. But we must not forget that if the poor are bonded together into a social movement, they seize upon it as an opportunity to forget their day-to-day cares. They then transcend the narrow selfishness of misery, and their minds are filled with daydreams about high ideals. A movement is the more idealistic the more influence the poor have over it. They expect it to be, like the cinema, a temporary escape from the horror of their surroundings.

Secondly, economic goods are not those for which we care most intensely. For some aims we are ready "to do something"; about others we get really enthusiastic; for others still, we are ready to die. Except in the extreme straits of actual and prolonged hunger, the masses are unwilling to die for the realisation of their economic aims. It is a curious fact that movements which assign a prominent place to economic motivation—I speak here about conscious motives—are beaten by those in which it occupies a subordinate place. After 1918, the socialist movement in Germany stagnated and finally collapsed. It had confined itself to a fight for an increase in wages. It was unable to mobilise the whole man. It was beaten by those who openly proclaimed that they despised economics, and who were enthusiastic about the ideal aims of saving their nation, their race, and even mankind—for a small consideration. A movement which concentrates on hard economic facts cannot stand up against hostile movements whose members have their heads in the clouds of rather intangible ideals—like the honour of their nation, the liberation of mankind, the realm of right, or democracy. In Part 2 we explain why this is so.

---

the husbandman today. Therein lies salvation. People live long under such conditions in comparative peace, much greater than Europe has enjoyed after having taken up modern activity.

Scientifically speaking, "the standard of living" is not an unambiguous economic concept. Because of its inherent vagueness, it lends itself to propagandistic distortion. As understood by many at present, it is a propagandistic fiction, evolved and spread to make an industrial civilisation more attractive and bearable.

Thirdly, men are obviously not completely governed in their actions and beliefs by economic facts and statistics. Irrational impulses and desires often prevent the majority of a population from reading the economic facts correctly. In consequence, what *is* economically beneficial is often very different from what is *believed* to be advantageous. Economically speaking, an international organisation of production and distribution would, for instance, be a quite sensible thing. Our (non-economic) tribal sentiments (see Chapter 1.6) are so strong, however, that the idea is quite impracticable at the present time.

It would be a waste of time, ink, and paper if I were to prove in detail that our minds are not impelled by neat calculations of self-interest only. Robert Louis Stevenson once remarked that "man is a creature who lives not upon bread alone, but principally by catchwords."[4] Quite a number of governments remain powerful for a long time, although they may neglect and even outrage the economic welfare of the average citizen.

The average person is not at all a neat calculating machine which weighs up each issue correctly and imperturbably in terms of wages, hours, and "standard of living." On the contrary, he is highly suggestible in this direction. A small child who falls down sometimes first looks to the mother to find out whether she hurt herself. She will cry if the mother's face or words indicate that there is a reason for crying. Otherwise she will just pull a face and carry on with her play. Adults rarely succeed in shaking off this kind of childishness.

Bewildered by the complexity of economic phenomena, the modern citizen is sometimes at a loss to foresee with any degree of certainty the effect certain measures of political economy, like the abandonment of the gold standard, is going to have on his economic welfare. He sometimes is not quite sure on which side his bread is buttered. What is more, he relies to a certain extent on the propagandist to tell him whether his bread is buttered at all. We know, of course, how many £sd[5] we are paid each week, or month. Whether we are economically contented or discontented, resigned or rebellious, depends, however, only in part on the absolute amount of £sd we receive.[6] The mental satisfaction, or dissatisfaction, as the case may be, which corresponds to a given sum of money depends also on the relative prosperity of those around us, and on the amount we expect to get

4 Robert Louis Stevenson, *Virginibus Puerisque* (New York: H. M. Caldwell Co., 1900), p. 53.

5 *Editors: Once common abbreviation for* pounds, shillings, *and* pence, *from the Latin* librae, solidi, *and* denarii.

6 Another item, which I omit in the text, deserves at least a footnote. J. A. Hobson points out the following (*Wealth and Life: A Study in Values* [London: Macmillan & Co., Ltd., 1929], p. 410):

> No worker pays due regard to the fluctuations in purchasing power of his money wages. If his weekly money wage remains unaltered he will accept with an almost stoic indifference the rising prices that reduce its commodity value. On the other hand, he will fight to the death any proposal to reduce his money wages, though prices may be falling so rapidly that he can purchase as much, or even more with the reduced sum.

under the circumstances. In order to spread economic discontent, one draws the attention of people to those of their fellow citizens who are so much better off. If, on the contrary, he wants to content us, the propagandist directs our attention to those human beings who have less than we have. In three countries at least—England, USA, and USSR—the workers are told continually that their standard of living is high as compared with that of their poorer brethren abroad. This talk soothes the pangs of poverty. In addition, propaganda can persuade the poor to blame external circumstances for their poverty. It is usual to assure them that they are better off than they would be under any other system under the circumstances. The soporific effect of such assertions should not be underestimated. Under their influence millions take the shadow of propagandist talk for the substance of economic benefit.

Seeing that the propagandist interpretation of the wage slip has, within limits, as much to do with the economic contentment of the "underdog" as the economic fact of the wage slip itself, some governments have decided to give their propagandists a freer hand by drawing a merciful veil over the economic facts. They have succeeded in obscuring the issue to such an extent that nobody can ascertain what wages are being paid. Everybody who tries to compare Russian and English wages knows that the Russian Government is a great master in this art. The Nazis were quick to copy so useful a device. All one has to do is to pay part of the wages in money, and part in services or privileges. It is impossible to add the two quantities. If, further, one creates a different price level for different categories of workers, rations some goods while selling others in the open market, and introduces a system of voluntary contributions to and deductions for various good causes, the resulting confusion is bound to give a violent headache to anyone bold enough to try to fathom the basic economic facts of the regime.

One can further add to the contentment of the poor by diverting their attention altogether from their "dirty economic interests." A systematic campaign against "materialism" and in favour of spiritual values has, for generations, helped innumerable individuals to resign themselves to conditions of poverty and squalor. In Italy and Germany, state officials have been quite candid on such matters. As Mussolini puts it in his 1932 *Doctrine of Fascism*,

> Fascism, now and always, believes in holiness and heroism; that is to say, in actions influenced by no economic motive, direct or indirect.... Fascism repudiates the conception of 'economic' happiness.... which would reduce men to the level of animals, caring for one thing only—to be fat and well-fed—and would thus degrade humanity to a purely physical existence.[7]

7 *The Political and Social Doctrine of Fascism*, trans. Jane Soames (London: Leonard and Virginia Woolf at the Hogarth Press, 1933), pp. 13–14.

Thus far Mussolini. Hitler is of the same mind. In a speech to the Nuremberg Congress in 1933, he said, "The man who, in order to be satisfied, requires nothing but eating and drinking, has never understood him who sacrifices his daily bread in order to still the thirst of his soul and the hunger of his spirit."[8] Dr. Robert Ley[9] underlines the point, writing in March, 1935 that "We could not offer the working masses any material benefits, for Germany was poor and in a state of confusion and misery. New rates of wages and similar things were out of the question." It was therefore necessary to "suppress the materialism... [and] instead, divert the gaze of the workers to the ideal values of the nation."[10]

Non-commercial motives, properly mobilised, help to stifle much of the discontent that bad material conditions might cause. Few people evaluate their position in terms of money alone. They are, for instance, glad to have work which satisfies their desire for self-expression and self-direction, their joy in congenial activity, their professional and business pride, their sense of workmanship, their feeling of proprietorship, and last but not least, the feeling that their boss cares for them. Where, on the contrary, work is restrictive, repressive, emotionally unsatisfying, apparently purposeless, uncreative and monotonous, industrial psychologists have been partly successful in rendering it mentally more satisfactory. Their conjuring tricks fall outside the scope of this book. But it is, for instance, obvious that if one convinces a worker that a new blast furnace is his property, he may be willing to put up with less pay. The "morale" of the workers will likewise improve if they can be convinced of the social value of their work. Hardships can, within limits, be interpreted as an adventure for the sake of a better future. In Japan, low wages are supplemented by the consolation of patriotism, by the feeling that in national solidarity the workers loyally contribute to the greatness of Nippon.

The attitude of the British workers to their Empire affords an example nearer home. To be sure, they may gain economically from the Empire, although at the present time they appear to pay for its defence more than they can hope to squeeze out of it. In any case, the intensity with which the vast majority of the workers cling to the Empire is out of proportion to their material gains. Many workers get quite excited about a threat to "their" rule in the Sudan, or in India, or "their" oil interests in Mexico, or "their" shipping interests in Spain, or to "our property in the Mediterranean."[11] In such attitudes they are impelled by "ideas attuned to instinctive emotions."[12] The masses are, to a great extent, bound to

---

8 Daniel Guérin, *Fascisme et grand capital* (Paris: Gallimard, 1936), p. 51.

9 *Editors: Robert Ley, a Nazi politician, led the German Labor Front from 1933 to 1945.*

10 As translated in Robert A. Brady, *The Spirit & Structure of German Fascism* (London: Gollancz, 1937), p. 143.

11 *Daily Express*, October 20, 1935.

12 P.T. Moon, *Imperialism & World Politics* (New York: The Macmillan Company, 1926), p. 67. I have discussed this question in more detail in *Plebs*, 1935–1936. *Editors: Conze is here referring to a series of four articles which appeared in the journal* The Plebs: Organ of the National Council of Labour Colleges: *"The Psychology of Imperialism" in* Plebs *27.12 (December, 1935): 280–283; "The Psychology of Imperialism II.—On Camouflage" in* Plebs *28.1 (January, 1936): 41–44; "The Psychology of*

the Empire by the *mental* satisfaction they derive from its existence. The Empire gives them something to feel superior about. When our Empire is threatened, our standing as an imperial race is at stake. It is inconceivable to yield to the threat and to give up any part of the Empire. "Such sacrifices, though they might frequently be agreeable to the interest, are always mortifying to the pride of every nation."[13] The vastness of imperial possessions and resources further allays fear and creates an illusion of powerful security. And, thirdly, the bigger an Empire, the more enemies it is likely to have. Enemies are good for the soul. They provide a useful outlet for surplus hatred, as we shall see. Such satisfactions are highly irrational indeed. They are nonetheless real.

Income and Status

Finally, in actual practice, concern for economic welfare is often subordinated to a wish for status. A person's "status" is his standing in society. The position of rank he holds in relation to others gives him the gratifying right to look down upon those below him, coupled, in most cases, however, with the uncomfortable feeling that he, in his turn, is looked down upon by others.

Property and income are often sacrificed to status, either by investing wealth in status, or by elevating social standing as compensation for a deficiency in economic emoluments.

To take an extreme case, in some so-called primitive societies property *must* be spent on status. Among North American Indian tribes (viz. the Kwakiutl), huge amounts of property sometimes accumulate in the hands of an individual, or of a family, or of a clan. The value of this property consists solely in its social prestige. One debases rivals by giving them an expensive feast (potlatch); the rivals can regain their status only by giving an equally big one.[14]

Imperialism III.—The Empire's Appeal to the Mind" in Plebs *28.3 (March, 1936): 57–60; and "The Psychology of Imperialism IV. Internationalism" in* Plebs *28.4 (April, 1936): 85–91.*

13 Adam Smith, *An Inquiry into the Nature and Causes of the Wealth of Nations*, 6th ed., vol. 2 (London: George Bell & Sons., 1896), p. 129.

14 Alexander A. Goldenweiser, *Early Civilization: An Introduction to Anthropology* (New York: Alfred A. Knopf, Inc., 1922), pp. 59–61:

> The potlatch is a feast given by an individual to another individual, or by one family or clan to another.... The feast giver presents his guests with blankets, canoes, oil and other valuables.... The more sumptuous the presents given away, the more lavish the destruction of property, the greater is the feast and the higher the esteem that accrues to the feast giver, while the rival to whom the feast is given is correspondingly debased in social status. To regain popular favor, the latter must give a feast in return.... The essence of social position among these people rests on these feasts. 'Rivals fight with property alone,' says the Kwakiutl, and the best way to humiliate a rival is to 'flatten him out' by means of a sumptuous feast.... The value of property is estimated in terms of social prestige which comes to the owner when he gives away his property.

In the modern world, too, money is often used to buy social standing. Public benefactors, like Lord Nuffield, derive considerable prestige from giving away their money. The expenditure of the middle classes is regulated to a great extent by considerations of respectability, by what the neighbours do, and by what the neighbours will say.

> The artisan's wife must get a piano because she is one of the very few in the street without one.... Weddings and funerals must have that touch of distinction which sets a final seal on the painful effort to live in what is imagined to be a good style.[15]

The piano and the car satisfy family pride and connote prosperity and distinction. The funeral gives a welcome opportunity for ostentatious display. In 1917, women in munition works often ate less to buy fancy shoes, ostrich plumes, silk stockings, and thin shirtwaists. Higher social standing may render shopgirls flat-footed, anaemic, and more anxious than girls labouring under harsher conditions in factories. The clerical classes frequently maintain the dignity of their dress only at the cost of rheumatism, chronic bronchitis, varicose veins, and early senility.[16]

Wise employers and governments discovered that it is cheaper to pay out a part of the wages and salaries not in money, but in "honour." In recent times, Germany and Russia showed that decreases in income and comfort become tolerable for a time when coupled with increases in social status. For many years after the revolution, Russian workers had to make great economic sacrifices. In their majority they continued to support the Soviet Government, because their status was raised immensely, and they could, from their privileged position, "dish" those who had been their betters. Distinctions of birth were not abolished but accentuated. Improper family descent deprived many people of bread cards, jobs, schooling, etc. Engineers felt gratified if they could procure a document which certified that they were entitled to the same treatment as a factory working man. Proletarian social origin became all-important. For those who have it, all privilege, and nearly all facilities, are reserved. "A fierce pride of birth arose—pride of proletarian birth, the more snobbish, intolerant and bellicose because it was new and self-conscious."[17]

---

15 A. J. Greenly, *Psychology as a Sales Factor*, 2nd ed. (London: Sir Isaac Pitman & Sons., Ltd., 1929), p. 184.

16 Robert Sinclair, *Metropolitan Man* (London: G. Allen & Unwin, Ltd., 1937), p. 41.

17 Eugene Lyons, *Moscow Carousel* (New York: Alfred A. Knopf, 1935), p. 83. Kosiarov, leader of the Young Communists, said to Lyons: "We are the true product of the revolution. Mother is still working in a factory. She has been at work 26 years and is a shock-brigadier." As Lyons elaborates, "He said it proudly, as in other lands a son might boast that his mother is in the Social Register."

Social Status

The question of status touches the very core of our personality. The conception we have of our own role is profoundly influenced by the attitudes our fellows adopt towards us. It is hard to go without an adequate income. It is harder to feel that one is treated as a contemptible outcast, or as a negligible inferior. It may be more exasperating to find that one counts for nothing than that one has nothing to count. At the end of the 18th century, it was the haughtiness of the noblemen which annoyed the commoners most of all. As Napoleon put it, "Vanity made the Revolution; liberty was only the pretext."[18]

So deep-seated is this worry about status, that a good many activities which appear to be prompted by a striving for the acquisition of economic goods are at bottom actuated by a desire for status. Status partly depends on wealth. In a country like England, poverty, unless compensated by titles or other advantages, brings shame, and it may mean social degradation and extinction.[19]

In a feudal society, fixed rules once and for all place the majority of the population "in that state of life to which it has pleased God to call them." One resigns oneself with comparative ease to an unalterable fate. In an industrial society, status is thrown open to competition. The idea is fostered that one has the possibility, and even the duty, to "improve oneself" by personal exertions. A low status then becomes more intolerable to self-esteem. People are more prone to worry about their status when they believe that they are largely personally responsible for it. Occasionally, of course, we may pretend that we don't "care a hang" what other people think about us. We are certain, however, to belie this lofty pose soon by the often ridiculous aspirations and tremblings of our vanity, by our craving for honour and a good reputation, by our efforts to get others to recognise in us some distinction, or something praiseworthy, by the envy and jealousy we so often feel at the successes of others which make us look small in comparison, and by the paralyzing despondency, or the boiling anger, which a sense of inferiority often calls forth. A superabundance of emotions accompanies our failures in the quest for status. To the philosopher, all these feelings must appear as a blemish, a foible, a degrading foolishness. But few people—and not always the best—are philosophers. The desire for social standing is responsible for four distinct lines of behaviour: "looking down," "looking up," "sneaking upwards," and "consoling oneself about being looked down upon."

---

18 Quoted in Gustave Le Bon, *The Psychology of Revolution*, trans. Bernard Miall (New York: G. P. Putnam's Sons, 1913 [French: *La Révolution Française et la Psychologie des Révolutions*, 1912]), p. 83.

19 At the time when the British middle classes were the most prosperous in the world, Edward Lytton Bulwer could say in *England and the English* (London: George Routledge & Sons., 1876; 1st ed., 1833), p. 38:

> We do not think them [the foreigners], as we once did, *inherently*, but *unfortunately*, guilty!—in a word, we suspect them of being *poor*! They strike us with the unprepossessing air of the shabby genteel.

It is pleasant to look down on other people. I speak from personal experience. As a son of wealthy parents, I was trained early to ignore the servants, and to look upon working people as a shabby, incompetent, spendthrift, and rebellious mob which even the insatiable charity of my aunts could not paralyze into a state of staggered gratitude. Many well-to-do people are keener on being distinct from their fellows than even on the physical comforts they enjoy. Dress, for instance, is a not particularly strenuous means of showing class.[20] The middle classes especially—subjected as they are to a twofold social pressure, from big capital and from the trade unions—are frightfully worried about their right to be better than the workers. In post-war years their political outlook has been, almost everywhere, coloured by the fear that they might "sink down into the great, grey and dreary mass of the proletariat where all have the same, i.e. nothing."[21]

As far as "looking up" is concerned, there would be no status unless the lower orders acquired the habit of knowing their place, and of looking up to their "betters." Persons who are forced into the status of an inferior are called "oppressed." The oppressed are the chief targets of propaganda. In feudal societies, submissiveness manifests itself rather crudely. A predominantly industrial society, more subtly, renders its citizens submissive, but in addition inculcates into them the conviction that they are free. The average citizen is nowadays allowed to laugh at the well-known song of the villagers:

> O let us love our occupations,
> Bless the squire and his relations,
> Live up to our daily rations,
> And always keep our proper stations.[22]

But he knows quite well that he is not the equal of his betters. In his workshop, in his office, in hospital, on poor relief, almost everywhere outside his home, he is never allowed to forget it.

A low social status is coupled with a sense of inferiority. Nobody can fail to resent being looked down upon. People become dangerous when they begin to see clearly that they are reduced to the miserable status of tributary slaves. A stable social system therefore aims at mitigating the sense of social inferiority among the

---

20 See "Man and His Clothes" in the *New Statesman*, April 27, 1935:

> It is not surprising to me to see West End shops pushing linen sports shirts in preference to the knitted variety which have had such a long run. Too many vanmen and delivery boys wore knitted shirts last year for the style to hold long with the really smart men—that is my opinion.

21 The words in inverted commas are from a German Nationalist leaflet, circulated in 1932.

22 From Dickens' *The Chimes* (1844).

lower classes. The "underdog" is encouraged either to *sneak* upwards in this social scale or to *dream* himself upwards.

The desire to sneak upwards results in snobbishness. Snobbishness can be defined as the desire to appear socially better than one in fact is, coupled with a desire to do as one's betters do. In England it is a major factor in preventing social unrest. By the very nature of their social position, the middle classes are somewhat insecure about it. They are, in consequence, more glaringly snobbish than any other class. By drinking a certain gin we somehow participate in the social distinction of the duchess who recommends it. But if the reader lives in England, what is the point in telling him about snobbishness? This social disease cripples working people, too. Some of them like to be thought middle class, who proclaim that they "ain't no workers," and prove it with blue suits and bowler hats. The Labour Party takes this feeling into account when they make a cult out of the men who go to Eton and Oxford, and who "are the young men of the type that the L. P. wants."[23] And thus they are accorded deferential treatment as middle-class saviours of the proletariat.

Political propaganda finally helps people to forget their sense of social inferiority by encouraging them to dream themselves upwards. Its suggestions make them believe that they have a higher social status than they actually have. The demagogue earns his bread by flattering the masses, and giving them something to be proud of. The nation to which the respective "underdog" belongs is naturally the "top nation." The demagogue relieves individuals of a sense of social inferiority by praising the group to which they belong, be it a nation, profession, religion, or party. He addresses his audiences as the "true patriots," the "right thinking people," the "leaders of advanced opinion." He treats them as those who are "in the know," while the followers of other creeds grope in the dark. An audience shows its intelligence and discrimination by agreeing with the speaker. In political meetings demagogues convince a collection of rather timid rabbits that they are roaring lions.

As a fine example of demagogic flattery, I give the beginning of a speech Alexander Kerensky[24] delivered shortly after the February revolution:

> Citizens, warriors, in the name of Free Russia, in the name of the Provisional Government, I, the Minister of Justice, *make you a low bow*. (Furious applause) Comrades, warriors, citizens, sailors, and officers, if you had not stood on the side of the liberated people, and if you had not helped her with your armed force, Russia would not now be a free democratic country. To all of you, honor, glory, permanent glory for all time. (Furious applause) etc. etc. etc.[25]

---

23 *Daily Herald*.

24 *Editors: Alexander Kerensky was a key figure in the Russian Revolution, overthrown by Lenin in the October Revolution.*

25 Quoted by Paul Pigors, *Leadership or Domination* (New York: Houghton Mifflin, 1935), pp. 216–217.

The mass of the people cannot afford to keep private flatterers. But in a mass democracy, everybody contributes, say, a farthing so that they all may enjoy the flatteries of the Kerenskys.

Power and Equality

The sense of inferiority has its grip on us, whether we feel inferior or whether we feel superior. It is absent only in those who live quietly in the firm equanimity of complete self-assurance. As long, however, as we are at all concerned about our relative standing as compared with that of other people, the underlying sense of inferiority drives us to act in two opposite directions at the same time. On the one side, we welcome opportunities to submit, and to lower and abase ourselves (see Chapter 1.3). Yet at the same time, we wish to lower others and to rise above them. The desire for power is little more than an attempt at overcompensating for a sense of inferiority.[26] It finds a particularly frank and brutal expression in the words of Genghis Khan: "The greatest joy is to conquer one's enemies, to pursue them, to seize their property, to see their families in tears, to ride their horses, and to possess their daughters and wives."[27]

Real power is beyond the reach of the common people, except in the narrow walls of their homes, and in their function as petty tyrants—foremen, N.C.O.s, etc. Where prominence is difficult to attain, it is sometimes loved so ardently that the demands of economic self-interest are completely forgotten. In a munitions plant during the war, a shield made of paper was given to the most productive shift. "The knowledge that they have earned a title to a scrap of paper is as proud a possession to these humble toilers for the Empire as were the laurels given to the Greek Marathon victor."[28] A woman, inspired by the bonus system, turned out 132 shells (100 being normal at the time) and had, as a result, to remain in bed on the following day. "When it was pointed out to her later that she had acted foolishly, the reply was that she knew, but she 'wasn't going to be beat.'"[29]

Political propaganda allows the poor to share vicariously in power on a large scale. A bank clerk hears with delight that the whole world "sits up and listens" when England speaks—or Germany, for that matter. When *he* speaks, nobody ever sits up and takes notice. By identifying himself with the government of his country, he experiences the thrill of being feared, respected, and obeyed. He feels like "somebody." A "nobody" feels like "somebody" when he beholds the power of

26 Since there is no desire for power without a sense of inferiority, the sons of the ruling classes of an imperial and conquering nation have to be brought up in such a way that in their youth a brutal education makes them feel inferior. Roman education was very harsh, and in England, without the public school system, there would have been fewer Empire builders.

27 *Editors: The point Conze makes here is clear, though the quotation itself is of dubious attribution.*

28 *The Manchester Guardian*, November 12, 1915.

29 Ordway Tead, *Instincts in Industry: A Study of Working-Class Psychology* (London: Constable, 1919), p. 92.

his navy, or the width of his possessions, or the fame of his national culture. Here we have one of the reasons why the "nobodies" listen uncritically to appropriate propaganda. Does it not open up a cheap way of being powerful, without the responsibility, danger, and discomfort which real power involves?

After what has been said, it would be a mistake to assume that the oppressed really desire *equality*, although their political leaders sometimes pretend that they do. It is true that in times of social unrest inferiors clamour for equality with their superiors. But then the cry for "equality" is a polite way of expressing a desire to lower one's "betters." Real equality, of everybody with everybody else, is the dream of some few privileged intellectuals. The overwhelming majority of people seem to consider the prospect of a strict and genuine equality more as a nightmare than as a shining ideal. The reason is not far to seek. Nobody would have any "status" if all stood equally high.

The idea of economic equality, and the perspective of a uniform communistic society, creates a feeling of revulsion not only in the rulers of a country, but in all those who consider themselves a little better than their neighbours. And who does not? The oppressed, taught to feel inferior towards their "betters," can restore their mental balance in no other way than by inventing some kind of superiority which raises them above others who are just a little lower in the social scale.[30] They are, therefore, usually content with some shadow of equality, like equality before the law, spiritual equality in the sight of their Maker, or political equality.

Security

Apart from the pursuit of economic welfare and status, the hope of security spurs men into collective action. *Mental* security would be the actual absence of worry, fear, and anxiety. *Social* security would be achieved when our social position contained no adequate reasons for worry, fear, and anxiety. At present, when the man in the street speaks about "security," he has in mind an absence of danger to his income, social standing, job, and health, and an exemption from "premature" danger to his life.

---

30 James Sexton, the general secretary of Britain's National Union of Dock Labourers, gives a vivid account of the caste system found at the Liverpool docks some years ago (*Sir James Sexton, Agitator: The Life Story of the Dockers' MP: An Autobiography* [London: Faber and Faber, Ltd., 1936], pp. 111–112):

> The hand busheller of grain—now displaced by the elevator—looked with scorn upon the man who did the donkey work on the quay; the grain carrier, who could easily sling a four bushel sack weighing a couple of hundredweights across his back and shoulders, and run along a swinging plank, thought himself the master workman of the ages; the stitcher of bags used in the bulk salt trade, a veritable artist in his craft, had a most colossal contempt for the man who merely handled bags filled at the salt factory, whilst the tallyman who weighed and checked the bags considered himself the best and most important of all the 'casual labourers.'

The ideal of security is most illogical and elusive. We can distinguish between *actual* and *felt* security. Paradoxically enough, it is doubtful whether the approach to actual social security increases the feeling of security. The development of medicine, hygiene, sewage systems, insurance, social services, etc. seems to have appreciably diminished the actual perils of life. The feeling of insecurity nevertheless seems to have become more and more harrowing.

The *feeling* of security, or insecurity, is the result of the equation:

$$\textit{felt security} = \frac{\textit{realised security}}{\textit{expected security}}$$

Everything which increases our expectations of security reduces our chances of safety. The farther we look ahead, the more do we widen the range of our fears. Nothing is as certain—psychologically—to defeat its own ends as the effort to establish security for a long time ahead. As Hobbes has it,

> That man, which looks too far before him in the care of future time, hath his heart all the day long gnawed on by fear of death, poverty, or other calamity; and has no repose, nor pause of his anxiety, but in sleep.[31]

A widespread propaganda had some time ago persuaded millions of our countrymen that security was directly within their reach. They were thus led to expect social security as an entitlement of civilised man. In consequence they are now, at the time of writing, swept off their feet by the apparently avoidable risks to which they are still exposed in their social lives—slumps and wars. They are far more terrified by the prospect of aerial bombardment than they would have been had they resigned themselves to the fragility of human life, and continued to realise the capriciousness of Fortune and Fate, or the inscrutability of Divine Providence.

"In one sense civilization may be characterized as an immense conspiracy to make things safe.... Thus perhaps all that human mechanism by which we meet danger, endure discomfort, bear fatigue, and do not shrink from pain, gets but little exercise and grows weak like a flabby muscle."[32] In this way the habitual expectation of material security may create a sort of hypersensitivity to danger which renders people more liable to exaggerate the formidability of the dangers that may threaten them.

31 *Leviathan* part 1, 12.5. In 1921, a report was published in South Africa which calculated that in fifty years, the European population of South Africa would rise from 2 to 4 millions, while the native population would jump to between 19 and 24 million. "A good deal of South African politics ever since has continued to turn on the fear thus heavily enforced." William M. Macmillan, *Africa Emergent: A Survey of Social, Political, and Economic Trends in British Africa* (London: Faber and Faber, Ltd., 1938), pp. 64–65.

32 Frederic C. Bartlett, *Psychology and the Soldier* (Cambridge: Cambridge University Press, 1927), pp. 170–171.

Security is so closely bound up with its opposite that its attainment is more difficult than one often thinks. It is even doubtful whether we really with all our soul wish for security. Some risk seems necessary in order to add spice to life. A person who is too cautious to risk his life can never appreciate what it is worth. The man who voluntarily exposes himself to danger gains a sense of elation and freedom which he can experience in no other way. It is one of the paradoxes of security that it can be won only by those who despise it. Nobody can take away that which we are willing to throw away. Running risks gladly fosters that indifference which is our safest, and our sole, refuge.

The excitement of risk lies in the prospect that everything may go wrong. Finding that in their daily routine they live too rarely on the edge of danger, some individuals go away to hunt wild animals, climb mountains, explore unknown districts, or drive cars and planes at a quite absurd speed. The power of the capitalist class was to a certain extent based on the fact that the capitalist was a man who could take risks, and liked doing so. As soon as the capitalists tried to eliminate the element of risk from their activities—by trusts, and all that—they began to liquidate themselves, and to pave the way for a bureaucratic state control of business. In courtship the possibility of a rebuff makes lovemaking interesting. At least in fantasy, everybody enjoys daring deeds by identifying himself with risk-takers—heroes in adventure stories, acrobats, and tamers of wild beasts in a circus, etc.

Because the human heart longs both for the salt of security and for the pepper of insecurity, a propagandist has to promise his followers both.[33] He usually combines both appeals by promising "security through insecurity." In any case, the vigour of his cause will depend on his ability to call out the inextinguishable desire for adventure, sacrifice, and even self-destruction and self-annihilation, to which human beings owe any dignity they may have.

33 The relative strength of the desire for risk, and for security, varies with social conditions, age, etc.

1.2

OUR FEARS AND THEIR SUGGESTIONS

A pilgrim, on his way to Baghdad, was overtaken by a grim figure. "Who are you?" asked the pilgrim. "I am the Plague, and I am going to Baghdad to kill a thousand people." On his return journey the pilgrim again met the Plague and he said: "Why did you tell me that you were going to kill a thousand people in Baghdad, whereas I found ten thousand of your victims in the town?" "I spoke the truth," said the Plague. "I killed but one thousand, the remainder died from fright."[1]

Anxious to obtain our support, the propagandist approaches us with all kinds of "suggestions." He tries to suggest certain convictions or *opinions*—that Mohammed is Allah's prophet, that the earth goes round the sun, that Russia is a wonderful place to live in, that Zinoviev was guilty,[2] or that the Japanese are going to win the "China incident." In connection with certain social stimuli he suggests the appropriate *emotions*—say veneration for king, flag, and bishop, or detestation and wrath for certain shirts, flags, tunes, and emblems. Finally, he may suggest a *course of action*—if you want to have peace, fight for Czechoslovakia; if you do not want to be bombed, you must pay for rearmament; if you want a better life, vote Labour!

Such suggestions make an impression partly because they contain some "truth," and partly because we expect them and delight in them. The term "suggestibility" is

1 *Editors: We are unable to determine the original source of this anecdote, though a similar version, also referring to Baghdad, appeared in an article entitled "The Witchcraft of Fear" in the* Boston Herald, *quoted in* The Christian Science Journal *7.11 (February, 1890), p. 562; as well as another version, referring instead to Cairo, in* The Penny Illustrated News *8.1 (Saturday, December 15, 1849), p. 58 and other sources.*

2 *Editors: The "Zinoviev letter," later exposed as a forgery, was published by the British* Daily Mail *four days before the 1924 UK general election. It was purportedly from Grigory Zinoviev, head of the Communist International in Moscow, and addressed to the C.P. of Great Britain. It called for interference with the British electoral process, to the detriment of the Labour Party, and thus served to benefit the Conservatives.*

DOI: 10.4324/9781003363408-4

used to describe our willingness to fall in with suggestions. Propaganda can impress only waxen minds. Its victims enjoy following. They readily swallow the miraculous pills which the chosen propagandists of their group recommend. They normally put up resistance only to those opinions and cures they have been told to resist. We must cooperate with the propagandist at least to the extent that he requires our "will to believe." The god of half-truths is not content with unwilling victims. He wishes that those who are sacrificed on his altar should not be like sheep led to the slaughter, but like sheep clamouring aloud for someone to lead them to the slaughter.

Three factors combine to give "pull" to suggestions (see pages 47–53). There is often an attempt to win over our reasoning faculty by some kind of *argumentation*. In modern times, some appearance at least of reasoning is held to be indispensable, so that we may keep our self-respect. We are persuaded that we act on the suggestions offered because they are quite reasonable. On the whole, however, the actual pulling power of suggestions owes but little to reason. In most cases, propagandist arguments are sound only on the very surface. The scientific mind finds them inconclusive at best. They carry away only those who are prejudiced in their favour.

Secondly, we often do things on suggestion because *we like doing them*. Let us suppose that three young men are together after 6 p.m. One of them suggests, "Let's have a drink." The others obey the suggestion because they like to have a drink. Instincts and desires create the motivation which is necessary for us to fall in with a suggestion. With few exceptions, suggestions must remain in touch with people's desires. The propagandist rarely commands: "You must do that." He argues, "*If* you want this, you must do that." *If* people want to drink, "Guinness is good for you" gives them an excuse for doing so. *If* people want to feed a family of five on fifty shillings a week, Rowntree's arguments for cocoa will attract them. *If* people have more hatred in them than is good for them, they will be delighted to hear that it is their duty to hate this or that enemy of mankind.

Finally, there is this elusive factor of *suggestibility*—a willingness to be led, and to surrender our will, judgement, and decision to others. We can define suggestibility as the readiness to believe, feel, and do what others want us to believe, feel, and do, chiefly or exclusively *because* others want us to believe, feel, and do it. Suggestibility is closely akin to docility and submissiveness. It is chiefly fear that makes us conform to the will of others. The public are gullible because they are frightened.

Three Kinds of Suggestion

One may distinguish three kinds of suggestion: *herd* suggestion, *prestige* suggestion, and *scare* suggestion. The suggestible person submits either to the voice of a herd of his equals, or to the prestige of a leader, or to threats. In other words, one does what one is told to do because (1) other people do it; (2) one is overawed by the prestige of authority; and (3) one is afraid of not doing it.

The advertiser employs *herd* suggestion when he claims that millions bought his product. He uses *prestige* suggestion when he shows that the best people, like actors, writers, or duchesses appreciate his product. In the first case he tries to overawe us by big numbers, in the second by big names. In addition, he often attempts to *scare* us. If we refuse to buy his product, we see ourselves threatened with body odour, lack of success, ill-health, pyorrhoea alveolaris, burglars, accidents, disasters, and almost everything else we dislike.

Herd suggestion is set into motion either by words or by actions. Relying on the strength of our social instincts, propagandists often appeal to our desire to imitate or to copy others.[3] With an almost disarming simplicity they assure us, "but everybody is doing it"; "most of our customers prefer this brand"; "there is a widespread support for this view"; "but nobody wears it like that, Madam"; "millions of your fellow citizens are going to vote for..."; "the whole civilised world condemns..."; "no intelligent (or sane) person nowadays denies..."; "all people of goodwill agree." Few notice how barren of conviction and how threadbare these "arguments" really are. The average man values sound reasoning if it is not overdone. But he does not mind unsound reasoning if it allows him to fall comfortably in with the herd, and to satisfy his wish to be like others of his own kind.

Direct experience speaks louder than words. Demonstrations, marches, processions, and mass meetings tangibly demonstrate to Henry Dubb that a vast mass of decent folk supports this or that cause, and that he is in danger of being left out if he does not join up soon.[4] The political mass meeting wins support and dispels doubts not only by disseminating information, but chiefly by showing each participant that so many people agree with the speaker, and among one another, that there seems to be something in what is being said. Those who take part in massed arrays are, as it were, immersed into a fluid of good fellowship. Outside society, the individual feels incomplete. Ecstatic joy and emotional exuberance often accompany his success in breaking down the barriers of his narrow selfhood. He feels that participation in a "cause" has heightened his stature. Since he felt

---

3 G. F. Stout, *Manual of Psychology*, 2nd ed. (London: University Correspondence College Press, 1901), Book 3, Chapter 2, p. 281:

> (1) It is easier simply to follow the current mode of procedure than to be continually striking out new lines of action for ourselves. Thus, the habit of following suit constitutes an enormous economy of time and trouble. (2) It is generally disagreeable to attract attention by singularity and to disturb others by aimless novelty. (3) We learn by experience that what others do is very often based on good reason and that deviation from it is likely to be disadvantageous. Such conditions as these lead men to form the settled habit of doing as others do, where they feel no special interest in attending to a matter for themselves and forming an independent judgment.

4 *Editors: Henry Dubb was a character in the American political humor magazine* Good Morning. *Dubb represented "that prototype of all that is humble and stupid and easily imposed upon by Capitalist magic and meaningless forms and ceremonies" (Ryan Walker, "The Origin of Henry Dubb,"* Maoriland Worker *[June 17, 1914]).*

better as one among so many, he will attribute his heightened vitality not to the mere fact that his social instincts were satisfied. Additionally, the emotional satisfaction which he gained will endear to him the particular cause with which it was associated, and will impress him with its justice and rightness.

Prestige is a quality in men and institutions which dazzles, blindfolds[5], overawes. It smashes resistance by arousing that mixture of fear and reverence which we call "awe." We readily become suggestible to persons we have invested with prestige. In an experiment performed in a lecture hall at the University of Wyoming, American scientist Edwin Emery Slosson elegantly illustrates how "prestige suggestion" works:

> I had prepared a bottle filled with distilled water carefully wrapped in cotton and packed in a box. After some other experiments I stated that I wished to see how rapidly an odor would be diffused through the air, and requested that as soon as anyone perceived the odor he should raise his hand. I then unpacked the bottle in the front of the hall, poured the water over the cotton, holding my head away during the operation and started a stop-watch. While awaiting results I explained that I was quite sure that no one in the audience had ever smelled the chemical compound which I had poured out, and expressed the hope that, while they might find the odor strong and peculiar, it would not be too disagreeable to anyone. In fifteen seconds most of the those in the front row had raised their hands, and in forty seconds the 'odor' had spread to the back of the hall, keeping a pretty regular 'wave front' as it passed on. About three-fourths of the audience claimed to perceive the smell, the obstinate minority including more men than the average of the whole. More would probably have succumbed to the suggestion, but at the end of a minute I was obliged to stop the experiment, for some on the front seats were being unpleasantly affected and were about to leave the room. No one in the audience seemed offended when it was explained that the real object of the experiment was the production of a hallucination.[6]

If a professor's prestige can induce an assembly of students to hallucinate about objects under their direct observation, the influence of "prestige suggestion" is that much greater over events that are *not* accessible to direct observation. In general the average citizen cannot observe political events directly, and the various "authorities" thus have the field all to themselves. Among their conflicting testimonies we have to choose as best we can.

---

5 "To blindfold" is the meaning of *praestringere*, the Latin word from which "prestige" is derived.

6 "A Lecture Experiment in Hallucinations," *Psychological Review* 6 (1899): 407. See also Helen Clark ("The Crowd," *Psychological Monographs* 21 [1916]: 26–36), who experimented with a more critical group of 168 students of whom only 33 smelled the non-existent odour.

Scare suggestions may be illustrated by a simple example. If in a dictatorial country the Government should decide that air raid drills are good for the public, a decree is passed, and those who refuse to obey are "re-educated" in a concentration camp. In a democratic country this method would be too crude. The public here have to be stampeded democratically into the same thing. Thus, when Hitler took Austria, almost the entire British press used this opportunity for going on a campaign of fright. Everything was tried to give the average man the "jitters." He got the impression that the end of the world was near. Lurid details of the bombing of Barcelona were used to fan the fear still further. In consequence, a large part of the public was genuinely frightened. The stock markets collapsed. Under the influence of their fears the public was ready for almost anything, for a "measure of national service," or even conscription. They were quite glad then that they were—at that time—let off so lightly with voluntary air raid precautions.[7] Within a few days, the scaremongers had achieved their purpose. A halt had to be called in view of the damage done to the stock markets.

When scared, we are ready to believe almost anything. Rumours and myths spread like wildfire, and are disseminated with great rapidity. Twelve years ago, a Communist march took place in Berlin. The middle classes were scared. I stayed with a bourgeois family, and in the evening a public prosecutor, a very educated man, told us stories of houses being plundered, buildings being burnt down, well-dressed persons being mishandled. In all cases he gave the exact time and place of the occurrence. As a matter of fact, this march passed without any incident whatever. Swayed by excessive fear, we easily believe that what we expect to happen has actually happened. Stories of White-Guardist émigrés about Russia, or of Jews about Germany, are often ridiculous in the extreme.[8] They are confirmed by fear, and they gain easy adherence among the fearful.

In wartime, atrocity stories are readily believed by civilians, partly because it eases one's conscience to know that one fights a really wicked foe. The wish thus adds to the fear. Atrocity stories are welcomed because they confirm a course of action and dispel the qualms of an uneasy conscience. German atrocities in Belgium justified the blockade. Belgian atrocities in Belgium reconciled the German mind to the execution of Belgian civilians. In wartime, social pressure disposes of most of the resistance that our reasoning faculty may offer. "Any attempt to doubt or deny even the most fantastic story has to be condemned at once as unpatriotic, if not traitorous. This allows a free field for the rapid spread of lies."[9]

---

7 *Editors: Air Raid Precautions (ARP) was an agency of the British government established in 1937, dedicated to withstanding air raids.*

8 *Editors: It should not pass unnoticed that events were soon to show Conze badly mistaken in the particulars of this assessment.*

9 Arthur Ponsonby, *Falsehood in War-Time: Containing an Assortment of Lies Circulated Throughout the Nations During the Great War* (New York: E. P. Dutton & Co., 1928), p. 26.

Suggestions and Fears

The propagandist would have to go out of business if we were the undaunted knights we fancy ourselves to be in our more rosy daydreams. His words would not frighten the fearless. He can count, however, on the presence in our minds of a vast store of fears—fear of pain, shock, mutilation, sudden loud noises, loss of support, vague fears of magical contamination and punishment, fear for one's after-life, and the fear of losing the love of one's parents or friends. We dread to lose anything we consider vital for the integrity of our personality. It may be a part of the body, or another person, like a child, whose loss would be felt by the mother as a shrinkage of her own personality. The fear of death is largely a fear of the extinction or collapse of the personality. The fear of poverty is a fear of social extinction, and of a perceived inability to assert oneself in crippling circumstances.

All the propagandist has to do is to bind these private fears to a social purpose. Herd suggestion is based on the fear of *social isolation*. It is in order to avoid the anxiety of social isolation that we usually obey the suggestions of the group to which we belong. Although it may not otherwise be pleasant to travel in a suburban railway compartment, the human mind longs for company. Congenial company confers security and comfort. Lonely persons suffer from a deep-seated anxiety and a hidden terror which they often conceal from themselves and from others. It is true that on occasion we long for privacy. On the whole, however, company is as important to us as the water we drink.

Solitary confinement brings out this anxiety in an acute form. The religion of ancient Persia had threatened the faithful with numerous hells. The blackest and worst of them was a place in which the wicked are crowded together as closely as eye and ear. They are "as numerous as the hairs in a horse's mane," but they neither see nor hear each other. Each one reflects, "I am alone." And when a man has spent only one day in this hell, he exclaims, "Are the nine thousand years not yet past after which we shall be set free?"[10] The humanitarian zeal of the 19th century succeeded in inflicting this kind of punishment on sinners already before they were dead. Soft-hearted philanthropists everywhere erected model prisons. Within the walls of each hygienic prison cell one human being sat alone in solitary confinement. Here, if anywhere, the effects of social isolation could be studied.

"To be withdrawn from his fellow-creatures was a punishment, compared to which the torture, the rack, or the stake were vulgar and inefficient." That is how the Recorder in Birmingham saw the effects of enforced solitude.[11] Soon it became obvious that nine months of solitary confinement was the most that could be safely borne. All prisoners were frightened with their solitude. Many,

10 Carl Clemen, *Religions of the World: Their Nature and Their History* (London: George G. Harrap & Co. Ltd., 1931), p. 152.

11 Reverend John Field, *Prison Discipline: The Advantages of the Separate System of Imprisonment, as Established in the New County Gaol of Reading* (London: Longman and Co., 1846), p. 112. *Editors: A "Recorder" is a judge or barrister.*

in intervals, would wail and howl fearfully. Driven to frenzy, they would often "break out" and destroy everything around them. The most elaborate precautions had to be taken to prevent suicides. Nevertheless, Henry Morselli's statistics in his book on *Suicide* prove that self-destruction was many times more frequent among convicts exposed to absolute isolation than among those confined in association prisons.[12]

Submissiveness and Intimidation

It is obvious that submission to prestige is very largely based on fear and enforced by intimidation. A class society would collapse unless the majority of people were habitually submissive. Fear cows them, keeps them in their place, and creates that acquiescing and yielding frame of mind and receptive mood which predisposes them to "take in" the propagandist's words.

Men submit willingly when placed into a position of perpetual danger. A background of intimidation induces millions to submit to a crippled life of poverty, ill-health, and boredom. The more spectacular instruments of intimidation—armies, policemen, prisons, concentration camps—are pushed into the foreground only in the rare moments of rebellion. In a well-governed and smoothly functioning society it is the dread of hunger and poverty, the fear of losing one's job, of offending charitable friends, etc. which daily commend humility and obedience to millions. Perpetual worry is the lot of the poor, and they are the most suggestible of all.

Submission based on fear alone would, however, create no more than a very unstable social unity. The emotion of fear is too closely allied with anger and suspicion. We hate those who frighten us (see Chapter 1.5). Fears may whip the "underdog" into shape, but they do not make for contentment. They are supplemented by the sentiments of *awe*, *reverence*, and *respect*, under the influence of which Jack *likes* to be a good boy. Dingiswayo, a Zulu chief, was aided in his first conquest "by having a horse and a gun, which had never before been seen by the natives and consequently made him an object of awe and admiration."[13] When the people of the Empire march in procession through the streets of London, when the might of the Navy is assembled at Spithead, the man in the street shrinks before the might of the established order of society. Pomp and splendour, court dresses, robes, uniforms, quaint wigs, golden cars, and antiquated ceremonies all cover up the weakness of the rulers. They have, on the unsophisticated adult, the same paralysing effect which the father's over-towering size had on the child. In institutions, age is taken as a sign of strength. The dignity of office is enhanced by time-honoured customs, stately ceremonies, symbols, modes of address, and reminders of an ancient lineage. Pigors tells us that the snuff boxes of the American

12 Henry Morselli, *Suicide: An Essay on Comparative Moral Statistics* (London: Kegan Paul, 1881).

13 Pigors, *Leadership or Domination*, p. 157.

Senate are kept filled even today and that custom "even now requires that all Senators' desks should be provided with sand dusters although that method of blotting letters has long been obsolete."[14] The British House of Commons is a veritable antiques shop.[15] All this is good propaganda. Ordway Tead describes the methods used by American corporations to squash the self-reliance, and to bring out the submissive tendencies, of the worker who appeals his grievances to the president of his corporation.

> The worker is taken into the president's office with its expensive and exalted atmosphere. The president presses a button and a stenographer attends upon him. The whole situation is highly artificial and calculated to induce an unreal attitude of humility, insignificance, and weakness in the mind of the employee. The result must almost inevitably be that he hastens to acquiesce in whatever decision the president announces.[16]

The propagandist furnishes his temple with all the idols of the age. He mobilises the prestige that attaches to the flag, the Bible, heroic figures like Lincoln, or to titles, superior social status, science, etc. He will insist on calling his particular brand of social theory "Scientific," or "German," or "Christian." His party will try to monopolise the flag. The candidate fought in France, regularly goes to church on Sundays, and is very interested in cricket. Although he be a Communist, an English politician will not rest until he has found some lord or duchess to put on his platform. In all these little ways the propagandist benefits from the reflected glory which radiates from established prestige.

Prestige and Self-Effacement

Without confidence and sympathy the submissiveness thus generated is but a sounding brass, or a tinkling cymbal. The propagandist's victim is cowed. But, at bottom, he remains suspicious. His "betters" have let him down too often before. In order to allay the latent or patent suspicions of his victims, the propagandist has either to efface himself, or to emphasise the bonds of brotherhood, comradeship, and sympathy which bind the leaders and the led together.

By effacing himself the propagandist allays the distrust we feel for a man who appears to have an ulterior motive. A paid advertisement warning the public against a new oil tax is far less effective than an editorial note in an "independent" paper uttering the same warning. The public distrusts those who too obviously have an axe to grind. Our newspapers continually remind us that they are "free,"

---

14 Ibid., p. 248.

15 For a nice account, see e.g. Herbert G. Wells, *The Work, Wealth, and Happiness of Mankind* (London: Heinemann, 1932).

16 Ordway Tead, *Instincts in Industry*, p. 120.

thereby implying that we can trust them since our journalists can, of course, write as they please. Many readers are put off by a paper if they know that there is a "special interest" behind it—a government, or a private company.

The propagandist is rather shy about showing his face. Businessmen and foreign governments prefer to "take the veil" when on the propaganda warpath. During the last war Captain von Rintelen's German agents were exceptionally clever when they worked through the American Trade Unions on the docks, and succeeded in holding up supplies of Allied munitions.[17] The businessman who works against public ownership or disarmament likewise conceals his identity. Frequently the public do not know with whom they are dealing. To take quite a small point, some time ago an article in the *Advertising World* gave advice to business firms about sending out questionnaires which might serve as a basis for advertising. "Put headings to your letter like 'Scientific Research Bureau,' 'Institute for Health and Welfare,' or 'School for Marketing and Research Work,' anything that gives you authority." We must reserve for Part 2 a more detailed account of propagandist secrecy.

Special precautions against suspicion have to be taken when propaganda is carried into an outside group, like capitalist propaganda among workers, or the propaganda of a government among the citizens of a foreign country. "Tribal" differences make for distrust (see Chapter 1.6). Even a half-wit is naturally inclined to assume that the enemy's interest is different from and antagonistic to his own. The enemy's propagandist will therefore try to drum into his head the conviction that, while fighting him like blazes, he has really nothing against him. A thousand voices proclaim each day that the interests of employers and employees are the same. During the last war, it turned out that the Allies, while apparently fighting against Germany, were really fighting for the German people against a common enemy, Prussian militarism. More than once have groups ceased to offer resistance because their would-be oppressors promised to "liberate" them (see Part 2).

It is natural that in questions which affect the welfare of a group the testimony of group members carries more weight than that of outsiders. It is therefore a part of the everyday routine of the propagandist to pay special attention to utterances of members of a hostile group which support his own contentions. Such evidence, while the ordinary public does not require it, deeply impresses people "who think they think." Allied propaganda, for instance, maintained that German pre-war policy was aggressive and detestable. From 1917 onwards, German liberal and socialist writers such as Prince Lichnowsky said pretty much the same thing, but they made a deeper impression on the thinking public both in England and Germany than the Allied propagandists.[18] Andrew Smith's *I was a Soviet Worker*

---

17 *Editors: Captain Franz von Rintelen was a German Intelligence officer stationed in the United States to sabotage American military cargo-ships during World War I.*

18 *Editors: Karl Max, Prince Lichnowsky was a German ambassador to Britain whose 1916 pamphlet* My Mission to London 1912–1914 *argued that poor German diplomacy in 1914 had caused the outbreak of World War I.*

did more damage to Russia's reputation as a working-class country than anything Lord Rothermere might have said.[19]

The propagandist may even drive his self-effacement to the point of non-existence. He impresses upon his victims the conviction that they hear their own voice when he speaks. Nobody likes to feel bullied. The common man, on the contrary, feels flattered if he finds that some important and much advertised personage has come all the way not to lecture him, nor to boss him about, but just to voice his (the common man's) own opinions. While hammering some strange message into the heads of the masses, many propagandists are careful to give the appearance that they are helping the masses to express themselves. They avail themselves of the wish of half-educated and bewildered people to have their opinions confirmed. If you have something new and unexpected to say, if you try to make your audience think, you disturb them. You can almost feel the anger and suspicion rising up against you. After it is over, some of the more vocal may be heard to exclaim, "I never heard such nonsense in all my life." If, on the contrary, you confine yourself to safe platitudes, if you just reel off what you are expected to say, it was a good meeting, and you may hear, "That was an excellent speaker. He said what I thought the whole time." If therefore one wishes to state a comparatively new point of view, one can appreciably weaken the resistance of the audience by leading them on to form a conclusion without affirming it expressly. In this way, when they come to the point, the hearers regard it as a confirmation of their own thoughts.

In a mass democracy it is an asset for a political leader to look like the average man. When men like Baldwin and Hitler fill the stage, they cover up for the less engaging members of the ruling class, the haughty aristocrats, the overweening generals and officials, and the profiteering bosses. In such leaders the average man recognises himself. When he obeys them, he thinks that he obeys himself. The suggestions of mediocre-looking politicians gain force because they emanate from somebody who is "one of us." Because in their habits and mentality they appear to belong to the multitude, they appear to speak in the name of the multitude. If they persuade the man in the street, he believes that he persuaded himself. The master's voice is made to sound like the people's voice. And who is not charmed by the sound of his own voice?

Prestige and Sympathy

A government builds its prestige on the apparently voluntary assent of the governed. If propaganda aims at establishing social unity, fear and prestige have to be stabilised or rounded off by *sympathy*. It is easy to have a unity of thought, feeling, and action when members of a group are more or less on a level, and when

19 *Editors: Harold Harmsworth, 1st Viscount Rothermere, a prominent British supporter of the Nazis, promoted support for Germany in the 1930s.*

there is little scope for relationships of superiority and inferiority. Friendliness and "primitive comradeship" arise spontaneously. In a class society, in which inequalities tear people asunder, propaganda has to achieve some kind of artificial unity by handing out what we might call "tokens of equality." If ever he should feel discontented with the inequalities around him, the modern citizen can console himself by remembering not only that he rules himself, but that he is the equal of his betters in political rights and before the law.

Consciousness of inequality creates a breach which, when it widens sufficiently, demoralises a group. A united group, on the contrary, is said to have *morale*. Morale arises from a sense of unity between followers and leaders. Bartlett defines morale as "obedience to authority under external circumstances which impose great strain, the source of authority being within the man, or the group, that is obedient. Morale produces a steadier, more persistent, less fluctuating type of conduct than discipline."[20] Pigors elaborates, "Morale is based on the belief of the leader in the follower, of the follower in the leader, of each in himself and of both in the cause."[21] In socially non-homogeneous mercenary armies, discipline is enforced chiefly by drill, by often excessively severe punishments, and by the prestige of the commander.[22] The organisers of a modern people's army have in addition to foster a spirit of comradeship between officers and soldiers, and among the soldiers themselves. A group has a high morale if its members believe that their leader's cause is their own. Morale requires an approximate equality of sacrifice. Men die with enthusiasm for officers who share all their hardships, eat what their men eat, and refuse to use their privileged position for sneaking extra comforts. In an industrial society, such tokens of equality as exposure to the risk of death, military service, and Arbeitsdienst[23] for all classes—and, in dictatorial countries, occasional ill-treatment of a capitalist—can, cleverly handled by the propagandist, help considerably to reconcile the "underdog."

In a class society morale is always slightly shaky. Under excessive stress, the basic inequalities of status and income become so odious that a group easily disintegrates. Workers are demoralised from their employers' point of view when they feel that the factories are not theirs anyway. A high percentage of scrap and waste is the inevitable result. A "demoralised" worker would calmly see a piece of machinery ruined because he feels that it is not his machine after all. That is why industrial psychologists in all countries take so many pains to persuade the employee of the identity of his interests with those of the employer, and why they try, by various schemes, to give him the feeling that he is a part owner of the works.

20 Bartlett, *Psychology and the Soldier*, p. 152.

21 Pigors, *Leadership of Domination*, p. 291.

22 The psychology of a drill is too complicated for an introductory volume. Discipline, incidentally, is defined as the habit of constant obedience and of strict compliance with established rules.

23 *Editors: "Labor Service."*

The morale of the German army had broken when the soldiers said, as it were, "We neither fight for our country, nor for our honour; in our stupidity we fight for our millionaires." The Allies, backed up by revolutionary socialists, confirmed the German soldier's suspicion that he was fighting just to get more wealth for his oppressors. They perpetually stressed a picture of the Kaiser and his sons with the caption, "A family which lost none of its members." These leaflets struck the German imagination so forcibly that few of them were delivered to the authorities.[24] Hunger and the unequal distribution of food increased the class antagonisms. Because the war had made the wealthy still wealthier, the common people became convinced that their masters deliberately prolonged a war which gave them such excellent opportunities to amass profits. The rulers and the ruled drifted apart, not so much because of hostile propaganda, but because of two objective facts: (1) defeat after defeat shattered the rulers' prestige and (2) the wealthier classes and many officers failed to keep up the appearance of an equality of sacrifice. The propagandist could help to bring these facts to the consciousness of the German people. He could not have invented them.

Suggestion and Argumentation

Suggestibility is increased by inexperience, ignorance, and stupidity. The mentally deficient show unlimited credulity. We have dealt with the emotional and instinctual basis of successful suggestions—the obedient and passive attitude, and the lack of self-assertiveness, self-confidence, and self-reliance. But an attitude of receptivity is not enough. Propaganda cannot break into a brain unless *reason* has fallen asleep.

Suggestions are usually backed up by some appearance of argumentation. A conflict of authorities diminishes the weight of each. The more you have to compete, the less authority you have, and the greater therefore the show of argument you need. In 1905, it was sufficient to put the one word *Bovril* on the hoardings. Now we are faced with such a superabundance of similar "health foods" that each one of them has to give a reason why it is particularly good. Under the spur of growing competition, the size of advertisements grew steadily during the last century.[25] Advertising becomes more and more expensive. We may look forward to a time when it will kill itself.

---

24 Thimme, *Weltkrieg ohne Waffen*, pp. 135–136.

25 See Greenly, *Psychology as a Sales Factor*, p. 82:

> The length of an advertisement in the *Century Magazine*, for example, is stated on an average to have been four and a half times as long in 1913 as in 1872. The last fifteen years have seen a rapid increase in the use of the full-page advertisement; indeed, it would be no exaggeration to say that it is five times as common as it was twenty years ago.

Judged by logical standards, propagandist arguments are rarely conclusive. It is well-known that, scientifically speaking, arguments from *authority* are of very doubtful value. In any case, divergent authorities would also have to be mentioned. But no propagandist would dream of doing so. Often an appearance of united authority is deemed sufficient to warrant a suggestion. "Doctors recommend it." "All army bicycles are Raleighs." The scientifically dubious assertion that "British goods are best" is backed up by the tremendous authority of patriotism. In political life we often have little to go on beyond authority. Even the "facts," since they mostly lie beyond the range of our direct experience, are vouched for only by authorities.

A propagandist is naturally tempted to ease his burden and to increase his authority by eliminating his competitors once for all. It seems doubtful, however, whether an enforced monopoly serves his best interests. The British system seems preferable where it can be applied. The political world here is split up into conflicting authorities who disagree on almost everything, and who appeal to the sporting instincts of the public by abusing each other heartily at election times. Yet as soon as they are confronted with a really vital issue, all the politicians "who matter" can be relied on to pull the same string. ARP was recommended over the wireless first by Sir Samuel Hoare, and then by the Rt. Hon. Herbert Morrison. Liberals oppose wars and are then allowed to declare them—as Fox in 1806, and Grey in 1914. Labour Ministers join Tories in war cabinets. An enforced unity is far less impressive than the apparently voluntary agreement of persons whom the public have been brought up to regard as opponents.

Arguments, Facts, and Wishes

Propagandist arguments are effective not because they are scientifically or logically valid, but because they confirm our wishes. Most of our convictions contain two factors, in that they reflect some objective facts and in that they satisfy some wish or other. The proportion of fact to wish-fulfilment is naturally not the same in all our beliefs. If I say "There is fog outside," this conviction owes most, if not everything, to the fact that there *is* fog outside. The element of wish-fulfilment is usually nil. About political questions, however, we often form opinions without being either able or willing to ascertain the objective facts. The political propagandist tends to move away from subjects which are accessible to direct experience. He prefers international politics to domestic issues, higher ideals to straight forward bread-and-butter questions, complicated and obscure economic problems to simple ones.

The gaps in our knowledge of a foreign country are filled by myths which, while they have only a tiny foundation in objective reality, are satisfactory because they make us believe what we wish to believe. Spain is quite a recent case in point. The average person is blissfully ignorant of the facts about Spain. John Smith just knows that Spain is a country in the south of Europe where some war is going on, and that it is peopled by foreigners, some of whom are good and some of whom are indescribably wicked. But although that is usually all, John Smith had somehow acquired firm convictions about the rights and wrongs of that civil war, and he knows quite well what we should do about it, and what the Spaniards should do. He cannot answer the simplest questions about the history of Spain, her geography, her industry and agriculture, her political system, and the composition of her government. In these matters John Smith is an easy prey for the propagandist. The convictions which he derives from a perusal of propagandist literature on Spain reflect objective facts as much as the story of Red Riding Hood. John Smith clings to them because they fulfil his wishes to a certain extent.[26]

This is an extreme case, but we will generally find that the good propagandist, like Hitler, will bury a molehill of truth in a mountain of lies. A propagandist who thinks he can do without the molehill overreaches himself. A propagandist who thinks he can do without the mountain disappoints. An account of social problems or of social and political events is so much more lively, alluring, and attractive when presented in a legendary or mythical form. It will fall flat unless it appeals to the desire for hero worship, self-righteous indignation, and national, racial, or class conceit. A myth or a legend can be defined as a story which is designed to satisfy these three cravings of our minds.

The victim of propaganda has little chance to assert himself where the facts are beyond his reach. It is a curious fact that lack of first-hand evidence makes for strength of conviction, and for that intolerance which drives a political movement to victory. Intolerance feeds on ignorance. We are fanatical only about unverifiable assertions. The reason is that we shout others down only when we want to over-shout our own doubts. A belief not wholly supported by first-hand evidence becomes more plausible when we can force others to share it. We thus create, or help to create, that vast number of supporters for our belief which in itself lends credence to it.

We may see a man getting red in his face when he explains the treacherous activities of somebody or other in Spain, or Russia, or Germany, or when he praises the blissful conditions or denounces the atrocious oppression of people here or there. In all this the element of first-hand evidence is usually nil. Three centuries ago people were equally firm and fanatical about religious questions. In statements about "transubstantiation," for instance, the almost complete absence of factual evidence made room for passionate assertion, and liberated the wish to verify the truth by the massacre of other people.

A bewildered Liberal who has never lived for any length of time among the Russian people, either before or after the war, may be heard to say with the utmost conviction, as if he were stating a final and self-evident axiom, "But the standard of living is higher now than it was under Tsarism." While the statement may perhaps be objectively true—I myself do not know—neither the quantity nor the quality

26 *Editors: See Conze's 1936 publication* Spain Today: Revolution and Counter-Revolution *(London: Secker & Warburg, Ltd.).*

of the research done by the Liberal in question does, by scientific standards, entitle him to be so terribly cocksure. All shades of political opinion throw up such "self-evident" though usually ambiguous,[27] meaningless,[28] or fantastic propositions which are designed to terminate rather than to clarify a discussion. Intellectually speaking, politics is rather a dull and monotonous occupation, something in the nature of a noisy competition between gramophone records.

The range of our knowledge is indeed very limited. Most of our beliefs are due to hearsay and suggestion. I do not suggest that we should talk only about what we really know. Conversation would dry up. But it seems to be desirable that we should realise the degree of confidence we can have in an opinion, and that we can distinguish between a statement we know is true, and a second-hand opinion.

Thought-Saving Devices

This leads us to our second point. To keep up an interest in politics, it is necessary for political discussion to be facilitated by the introduction of *thought-saving devices.* Thinking is not exactly a popular pastime. A few freaks think. The vast majority crave to be told what to think. They treat a conviction just like any other imperative custom. Safety lies in blind obedience. Impartial discussion of certain things like marriage, property, religion, or the fundamentals of politics is disagreeable because it shakes the props on which the security of our existence is built.

One should never try to conduct a crowd through a process of reasoning. A fair account of the pros and cons would only bewilder them. When confronted with a decision, the ordinary person comfortably reduces from the very start the possible alternatives to two—when there are, say, six. The others are at once discarded as unreasonable. As Bartlett puts it, "A man thinks only when he is faced with a genuine alternative."[29] Politicians prevent the appearance of genuine alternatives. Neither do they admit that there is another side at all, at least as far as "decent," or "civilised," or "patriotic," or "reasonable" people are concerned. Alternatives may be presented from the very start with so much contempt, hostility, and ridicule that one cannot take them quite seriously. The implicit attitude, when a particularly red herring is under consideration, is that the whole world knows, and nobody seriously contests the fact.

Propaganda discards cumbersome scientific proofs. Direct commands, passionate repetitions, slogans, "labels," and "principles" are the chief thought-saving devices employed in propaganda. In advertising, the *direct command* has an obvious value. "The well-worn phrase 'Do it now' has sold more goods than any other three words in the English language."[30] Fruit importers ordered us to "Eat more fruit."

27 As any proposition about standard of living, democracy, fascism, and such words.

28 Like the famous "survival of the fittest," the "fittest" being those who survive.

29 Bartlett, *Psychology and the Soldier*, p. 162.

30 C. C. Freer, *The Inner Side of Advertising* (New York: Van Nostrand, 1921), p. 175.

In the first six years of their campaign they could increase their imports by 78%.[31] Direct commands clearly appeal not to reason, but to the kind of suggestibility which forces the soldier to jump instantaneously to attention in response to "Shun, Orderly Officer."[32] Harry Reichenbach tells us how in a circus "it was the barker's duty to warn the customers, 'Beware of pickpockets!' and instinctively they would all put their hands to their money betraying to the keen-eyed fingermen where it was hidden."[33]

Political meetings are impatient of elaborate reasoning. If you prove your assertions you create the impression that they need proving. A speaker who heaps reason upon reason, far from carrying conviction, does on the contrary nothing but manufacture doubts. If he goes to a lot of trouble in refuting an opponent, the crowd will believe that the opponent has a case. They become uneasy, whereas they came to be cheered. Unwavering *repetition*, as Hitler assures us, is more cogent than any argument.[34] Bare assertions are best. It does not occur to the crowd to dispute them. The response of a grateful public to the assertion that "Guinness is good for you" enabled the firm to pay an extra £900,000 to the revenue department in the first year of its campaign on the increase in its British sales.

In actual practice, ideas and beliefs are spread by affirmation and are backed up by persistent and incessant repetition. What you hear on all sides cannot be entirely wrong. Tenacity of beliefs impresses the crowd. The propagandist who hangs on to a view doggedly and expresses it fiercely is taken for a sincere man. Dogmatism in tone and language, while it may repel the educated, goes to the very heart of a mass of people who have been cowed all their lives, or of those simple souls who, well aware of the extent of their ignorance and unwilling to carry on their shoulders the burdens of the entire world, desire nothing so much as to follow safely. Students of Wesley's oratory noted the decisive part played by confident repetition *ad nauseum* of certain beliefs and particular phrases.[35] Abdul Majid even attributes the success of religious scripture to its use of this proscribed literary sin: "Those very books which have been the greatest sinners in this respect have exercised the most profound and far-reaching influence on the masses—the Revealed Books of all religions."[36]

Frederick Lumley defines a *slogan* as "any brief, popularly reiterated [incitement] to immediate participation in competitive or conflicting interactions."[37]

---

31 To be sure, the command was wrapped into jocular stories, articles about the health value of fruits, etc. But it essentially remained a command.

32 *Editors: The reference is to an abbreviated command of "Attention!" addressed to the "Officer of the Day."*

33 Harry Reichenbach and David Freedman, *Phantom Fame: The Anatomy of Ballyhoo* (London: Noel Douglas, 1932), p. 46.

34 In all this, I except the readers of the *New Statesman*, and other thinking people.

35 *Editors: The reference is to John Wesley (1703–1791), the zealous orator and founder of Methodism.*

36 Abdul Majid, *The Psychology of Leadership* (London: T. F. Unwin, Ltd., 1915), p. 63.

37 Lumley, "Slogans as a Means of Social Control," *Publications of the American Sociological Society* 16, *Factors in Social Evolution* (1922): 124.

Present-day slogans are the direct successors to the battle cries of primitive times. The passionate reiteration of the name of a chief, or of some famous hero of the past, or of some sacred gathering-place of the clan brought the kettle of tribal emotions to the boiling point. Slogans, by simple affirmation, sum up a whole line of action in a concise statement. "They shall not pass"; "Make the world safe for democracy"; "Thrift is power"; "Socialism in our time"; "All power to the Soviets"; "Get Germany"; "Liberty, equality, and fraternity"; "Keep that schoolgirl complexion"; "They never vary"; "British goods are best"; "Safety first"; "America for the Americans."

Just because most slogans look quite plausible and capture assent at once, they save and prevent thought. A slogan should be so brief that the dullest wit can pick it up, and the weakest memory retain it. "Anything balanced or accurately stated would inevitably be too long."[38] In view of the receptiveness and retentiveness of the popular mind, four words are considered a good average length for a slogan. One cannot argue with slogans. They cannot be effectively criticised, no more than the battle cries of former times. They do not argue a case but drum it in. They inflame the mind, and burn out all balance and judiciousness. A slogan often injures and damages those against whom it is directed. Its first victim, however, is the reasoning power of the person who bawls it into his enemy's face.

Personified abstract words become the basis of "labels" and "principles" which obscure the facts of the case, inflame the mind, and cut short cumbersome scientific discussion of the issues involved. Annoyed by somebody's arguments, we often ignore them and hastily look for some *label* to stick on him. Once we made up our mind that he is a "Fascist," a "Stalinist," a "Trotskyite," a "Pacifist," we know where we are with him. Anything he may say is discredited from the very start. Astute democratic leaders know the desire of the masses to kowtow to abstract words. In 1920 "Americanism" was to be the issue of the election campaign. A senator was asked what Americanism was. He said that he did not know but that it was a damned good word with which to carry an election.

When bewildered by political problems, the average citizen still has his "principles" to fall back upon, principles which he regards as eternal, good for any situation, anywhere, at any time. Stuart Chase gives a list of contemporary American principles:

> Democracy is the best form of government. Governments are by nature corrupt and inefficient. A worthy man can always get a job. Pecuniary thrift is a sterling virtue. Laziness is a vice. The Constitution is a divinely inspired document. Private property is a sacred right. You can't change human nature.[39]

---

38 Dr. Henson as quoted by Greenly, *Psychology as a Sales Factor*, p. 165.

39 Stuart Chase, *The Tyranny of Words* (New York: Harcourt, Brace & Co., 1938), p. 109.

Chase explains that these principles "are not tools by which discoveries are made, for they tend to close the mind against free inquiry." Rather, the history of principles "is a succession of romantically unnecessary sacrifices of human life or comfort in their honor."[40]

Propaganda and Scientific Mentality

To conclude, the propagandist expects and fosters a mentality which is diametrically opposed to the spirit of science. The difference can be briefly summed up in the following table:[41]

Popular Mentality	*Scientific Mentality*
Unquestioning faith in creeds, codes, economic systems, and taboos in social relations.	Attitude of "questioning disbelief." Nothing is of value simply *because* it is traditional.
Emotionalised wish is the father, social habit, the mother, of the thought.	Detached and impersonal attitude.
Assurance without evidence.	To the scientist, everything must *show cause* for its right to exist.
Statements are absolutely true or absolutely false.	Shades of validity. A thing is probably so, possibly so, tentatively held in suspended judgement, possibly not so, probably not so.

If we take into account what science has actually done for people up to now—leaving out the promises for a moment—we cannot quite blame them for their reluctance to take up scientific habits. Some contend that a world run entirely along scientific lines would be a more tolerable place to live in than a world run on popular prejudice. They believe that scientists in power would put things right. In this context we had only to describe the difference between two outlooks on life—propagandist and popular, as against scientific and unpopular—without passing judgement on either. Many lectures I gave on scientific method taught me that the inhumanity and aloofness inherent in the scientific mentality repels and terrifies the man in the street. Nor does the pursuit of science, as a profession, seem to breed a superior type of man. After all, the average man has work to do. And it is just possible that too much scientific thinking might spoil him, and render him unfit for action.

40 Ibid., p. 112, quoting Thurman W. Arnold's monograph *The Symbols of Government* (New Haven: Yale University Press, 1935).

41 Adapted from W. T. Root, "The Psychology of Radicalism" (1925), quoted by Kimball Young in *Source Book for Social Psychology* (New York: A. A. Knopf, 1927), "Two Types of Radical Leadership: Emotional and Scientific," pp. 609–610.

1.3

LEADERS AND FATHERS

Adolf Hitler is a universal personality full of genius. There exists no field of human activity, one might say, of which the Leader is not a supreme master.

Wilhelm Kube[1]

The broad outlines of political propaganda are determined by the mental concomitants of oppression. Most propaganda addresses itself to the oppressed. In Chapter 1.2, we considered the submissiveness which results from their fears; in this chapter, we discuss an important outgrowth of the submissiveness of a scared population—the longing for divine or semi-divine leaders.

To the popular mind, ideals, without a personal incarnation, remain hazy, abstract, and intangible. Events without a personal hero lack the "human touch." Deprived of most of their self-confidence, the oppressed feel that they cannot shape their own destiny, either individually or collectively. They look outside themselves, hoping for some person who is free from their own shortcomings to lift them up, or at least to protect them from falling still deeper. Deprived of most of their self-respect, the oppressed find a world consisting only of their own kind rather dreary. In their craving for a leader, the masses seem to be inveterate idolaters and myth-makers.

Commanding personalities are vital to any political movement. In the absence of a spectacular leader, the League of Nations could never capture popular fancy. A committee is not half as good as a man, for purposes either of admiration or of vituperation. For centuries the Russians worshipped icons. Now the portraits and busts of Soviet leaders have supplanted the images of the saints. In all public buildings they occupy an honoured place. Eugene Lyons writes that

1 Nazi official quoted in *Manchester Guardian*, September 8, 1934.

DOI: 10.4324/9781003363408-5

during revolutionary festivals these portraits "blossom on every wall, in every shop window."[2] As a friend of his explained,

> The repetition of Stalin's features in every window, on every poster, is not just hero-worship. It's magnificent advertising technique. Stalin's face is the trademark of the big job they're putting over.... [It] is as good as an oration on the *Five Year Plan*, only better, terser, more effective.[3]

Popular discussions of social processes easily degenerate into speculations about the intentions and motives of leaders. The more curious want to know what is really in the mind and heart of Hitler, Stalin, or Mussolini. During a discussion of the policy of German imperialism, for instance, a popular meeting will automatically switch over to the more stimulating problem: "Does *Hitler* want war?" A problem remains beyond popular comprehension unless re-stated as a conflict between persons. A political crisis is seen in terms of personal drama. As Albert Guérard puts it in his admirable *Reflections on the Napoleonic Legend*, the popular imagination

> ...has no use for delicate shades, complex problems, and subtle characters. Vast and confused events, which all the forces of a culture have been preparing for generations, become in the popular mind the work of a few men. The wreckage that rides the flood most arrogantly is supposed to be guiding it. Then subordinates are absorbed into the personalities of their leaders: and One at last stands out, the sole embodiment of a Cause.... Thus it was that the great convulsion which occurred between 1789 and 1815, impersonal and multitudinous, was transformed into the background for the life drama of a single man, Napoleon.[4]

Persons are so much more interesting and familiar than ideas or objective social forces. It is as if the masses long to efface themselves out of existence when they show so little interest in their own contributions to history, and throw all the greatness—and all the blame—on a few extraordinary individuals. Heroism, for instance, is commonly transferred from the soldiers to the chief. One speaks of the heroic defender of Madrid or Verdun when one means a general who sat safely in his office.

The propagandist who wants to present his message in a mentally satisfactory form must help build the legend of a leader, but he need not invent the legend all out of his own brain. It is sufficient for him to collaborate with the longings

---

2 Lyons, *Moscow Carousel*, p. 140. *Editors: Lyons was an American journalist and a critic of the Soviet Union.*

3 Ibid., pp. 256–257.

4 Albert Léon Guérard, *Reflections on the Napoleonic Legend* (New York: Charles Scribner's Sons, 1924), p. 171.

of the popular mind, and perhaps to speed up and to guide a process which the people are all too willing to perform on their own. It is not our business here to discuss the various types of leaders we meet with in political life—demagogues, experts, heroes, bureaucrats, administrators. Nor do we propose to explain why *this* man becomes a leader instead of *that* man. In this game the success of a particular person is a gambling success.[5] In this context we have to narrow down our inquiry to one point only, in order to show how and why the popular mind exaggerates the importance of outstanding individuals.

Divine Leaders

One can, I think, make the case that only a divine leader can give abiding satisfaction. The masses who worship a leader hope to find a god. Their mind usually contains at least one man who is idealised to the extent that he is raised directly into the sky. It is easy to show that in many instances people regard a social system as incomplete unless it includes an infallible and divine leader. Painful as it may seem to the "enlightened," there can be no doubt that the majority of the world's population still looks up to some divine leader or other.

Populations with strong religious leanings are often ruled by a real god, like the Pharaohs of Egypt, or the Emperors of Rome, or as in India where peasants told Mahatma Gandhi that they were governed by a god who in actual fact was a Maharaja. Others were content to have the *son* of a god as their ruler. The Emperor of Japan is the 124th descendant of the Moon Goddess, omnipotent, and without any blemish, as the Emperor of China was the "Son of Heaven." In all Japanese schools a photograph of the Emperor stands in a cement frame on the school grounds. Teachers and pupils bow to it before and after school. During the great earthquake of 1923, teachers died trying to save these sacred images from the flames. In European countries, kings were and are thought to be specially near to God, anointed by him, ruling by his grace, by divine right, or by divine will. Theoretically the King of England can do no wrong. The King rules by the grace of God, is too sacred to be brought into any party conflict, and cannot be criticised in Parliament. His actions bear the numinous authority of religious rites.

Lenin, in the Soviet Union, "is loved and revered with all the emotion and feeling that deeply religious people accord their gods. His pictures have largely replaced the ikons, and thousands of people daily make a pilgrimage to his mausoleum."[6] The film *Three Songs About Lenin* gave us Western barbarians a faint idea

---

5 Publicity of course, can help to "build up" a man. But it has to keep in close touch with popular preconceptions. General Joffre was to be photographed. It was noticed that there were no maps on the walls. According to popular ideas, one cannot think of a general without maps. A few maps were thus placed in position for the picture and removed soon afterwards.

6 Reuben Osborn, *Freud and Marx: A Dialectical Study* (New York: Equinox Co-Operative Press, 1937), p. 269.

of his godlike stature in the popular imagination.[7] Lenin's deification was due less to a deliberate policy on the part of the Communist Party than to a spontaneous wish of the Russians themselves. In India the masses have tried to transform Mahatma Gandhi into a God, despite Gandhi's resistance to this impulse. The history of Christianity and of Communism taught him that the masses deify a prophet as a first step towards discarding the more strenuous side of his teachings. In Germany, Hitler is sometimes believed to be sent by God, although there are some doubts as to whether by the God of the Christians or that of the Teutons. On the whole, although the incense burned to tribal chiefs in modern countries has lost its distinctly religious flavour, the leader is still invested with all the qualities that belong to a God on Earth, such as Jesus Christ or the Buddha. The leaders are half-gods who can do no wrong, who can say no wrong, who know everything, who love everyone in the group equally, and whose every word is law. That is the way of modern dictators in Italy, Spain, Russia, and Germany.

Traces of the same mentality can be found even in our American sister democracy. When President Harding died in 1924, the President of the New York Board of Education wrote, "It is our duty as leaders of the school system to firmly entrench that *sanctified reverence* of our departed President."[8] This quotation from Harry Elmer Barnes' *The Twilight of Christianity* may be supplemented by another from the same source:

> The Supreme Court of the United States is regarded by the average American as a veritable collection of semi-divine sages dispensing absolute justice after the manner of the hebraic Yahweh. The suggestion...that the Judges might be human beings, swayed by their prejudices and predispositions as are other mortals, was greeted with a chorus of rage by even highly cultured Americans, who regarded such insinuations as nothing short of sacrilege.[9]

Further, a divine leader, because he is more than a mere man, easily becomes a sort of cosmic agency. Because he is divine, the major events of his life have their repercussions in nature. In some ways he can magically direct the processes of nature. In ancient Egypt this belief flourished in a rather unsophisticated form. Since the control of irrigation required a central power, the Pharaoh became, in legend, the actual source of life both to the land and to the people. He was supposed to control the Nile and to cause it to inundate the fields. A scribe of the XXth Dynasty put the following words into the mouth of the dead Pharaoh:

---

7 *Editors: Three Songs About Lenin (Три песни о Ленине) is a 1934 silent film by Russian director Dziga Vertov. It is a Soviet paean to Lenin's legacy.*

8 Quoted in Harry Elmer Barnes, *The Twilight of Christianity* (New York: The Vanguard Press, 1929), p. 54. Emphasis E. C.

9 Barnes, *The Twilight of Christianity*, p. 69.

> I have made the heaven and the earth, I have ordered the mountains and formed all that is thereon. I am he who made the water, creating the inundation....The water of the Nile riseth at [my] command; the gods know not [my] name. I make the hours and create the days; I send the festival of the New Year and form the river.[10]

When Jesus died, "the earth did quake, and the rocks rent."[11] When Napoleon reached Paris in 1814, "the chestnut trees of the Tuileries decked themselves with precocious foliage to hail his return."[12] English restraint of feeling usually avoids the more offensive forms of leader-worship prevalent in other countries. Nevertheless, rudiments of the same beliefs are current among us. The Jubilee left its mark on newborn babies[13]; the planets paid tribute to our King[14]; "an egg laid by an ordinary hen in the chicken house of a Chatham innkeeper on Jubilee day has a perfect 'J' embossed on the narrow end of it"[15]; and then, "There must be more than a mere coincidence in the fact that our uncertain weather has been uniformly favourable on State occasions to his late Majesty King George V."[16]

In industrial countries, however, the teaching of natural science has rather emasculated the belief that the leader's magical power extends to the processes of nature. But in the field of social events, the divine leader has retained his central position. The educated person of liberal convictions is usually inclined to underrate the importance of such beliefs. Instead of being studied, they are usually laughed at. Choosing his friends among persons of his own frame of mind, the educated man is inclined to overlook or to minimise the fact that in all countries, civilised or uncivilised, some form of worship of a divine leader is almost universal.

---

10 Grafton Elliot Smith, *Human History* (New York: W. W. Norton & Company, Inc., 1929), p. 301. Similar beliefs were current about the emperors of China.

11 Matthew 27:51.

12 Guérard, *Reflections on the Napoleonic Legend*, p. 96.

13 "The prize-winner at a baby show at Abbey Wood had a complete representation of the Crown of England on its back." *Daily Telegraph*, quoted in Gerald Reid Barry, *This England: The Englishman in Print* (London: G. Bles, 1933).

14 See *Daily Telegraph*, quoted in Kingsley Martin, *The Magic of Monarchy* (New York: A. A. Knopf, 1937), pp. 3–4:

> The unusual beauty and brilliance of three planets—Venus setting in the West, Mars overhead, and Jupiter mounting from the East—seemingly contributed their share with the nation's beacons to the tribute to our king. Curiously enough, they obscured their radiance with the termination of the Jubilee illuminations beneath them on Sunday night.

15 "Mayor's Nest Egg: Hen Lays a Royal Greeting" in *Daily Herald*, Friday, May 10, 1935, p. 11. Hens appear to be particularly susceptible to royal influence: "Even the local poultry is playing its part, for it appears that a Little Thurrock hen has laid an egg with an undoubted 'C' on its shell; that the letter stands for 'Coronation' will not be disputed by anyone." *Grays and Tilbury Gazette*, p. 44.

16 Letter in the *Times*.

In times of social stability, this worship takes only a mild form. In times of distress, however, people rush to a divine leader as the small child runs to the skirts of its mother in times of emergency.

Angels and Monsters

The small fry of public men and women fail to reach such heights. But once a person has caught on, the public invest him with powers and faculties he does not possess. His ability to do good, or to do harm, and the purity or the wickedness of his intentions, are exaggerated to such an extent that he is transformed into an angel or a monster.[17]

A legend, though it may have some basis in reality, is largely a free creation of the intellect. In the minds of an admiring public, a leader's prestige easily outgrows his personal existence. The discrepancy between fact and fancy is obvious to the small minority who know leaders personally. If one has an intimate acquaintance of a politician, and if one then talks about him with his admirers, he is struck by this. The semi-divine leader appears to his best advantage from the perspective of a hazy distance. Napoleon's family had no faith in him. They remained sceptical and convinced that it could not last. So were most of his direct collaborators. He was idolised by those who only knew him superficially and who saw him, as it were, in the awe-inspiring twilight of a Gothic church.

We are dazzled only by the purest lights. A politician has to keep up the appearance of a quite supernatural perfection. Association with the slightest scandal would bring out the secret hatred of his followers. Before he meets his public, he has to bury his lower self and hide his more selfish motives. The appearance of disinterested devotion to a cause is as indispensable to a politician as a black suit is to a waiter. There are enough people who suspect him to be out just for what he can get—money, power, limelight. If he should lose money by public service, nobody would remain ignorant of his sacrifice. If he should make any money, this is more his private affair. Really popular political leaders are great actors (see Chapter 2.3). They require little effort to efface their real self, in quite a number of cases because there is nothing substantial to efface.

It would be quite interesting to describe exactly by what means popular imagination adds to the stature of those who are singled out as great leaders. For reasons of space I must refer the reader again to Guérard (see page 55), who shows in detail how, perhaps partly for reasons of mental economy, popular memory blots out the contributions which collaborators, predecessors, and the masses made to Napoleon's historical achievements. Napoleon soaked in all the glory there was, and

17 Our attitude towards leaders is ambivalent. It combines love and hate, respect and rebellion, reverence and anger, a tendency to depend and a desire to break loose. Leader-hatred, though usually more latent, is an ever-present menace. The propagandist will try to divert it to the leaders of hostile groups. When the people shout "Hang the Kaiser!" they forget to kill their own king.

"he lay claim to every achievement within the Empire—even when he had merely been the fly that buzzed about the horses' ears and took credit for pulling the coach over the hill."[18] Even failures do not detract from the glory of an established reputation. If Napoleon failed in Russia, Winter and Providence were blamed. His responsibility for successes is exaggerated, his responsibility for defeats minimised. The great man's memory becomes sacred, and his detractors are brushed aside as small and piffling minds who cannot comprehend a greatness that is beyond them.

In some ways a leader initiates social changes. In most of his actions, however, he just follows the social trend. It has been said that a leader is never more compliant than in the hour of his greatest triumph. In the popular mind, however, a leader's initiative receives far more emphasis than the forces which push him along. The leader himself remains aware of his passivity when he feels that "destiny" guides him, that he is the instrument of a higher force, or that he is an agent serving God, like Cecil Rhodes.

The Leader and the Father

Of course not all of us are equally prone to lose ourselves in legends. There are some who are only lukewarm in their admiration for heroes. Others are definitely hostile and anxious to belittle current leaders, but usually in order to substitute some superman of their own, if not themselves. In any case, whatever may be said about the exceptions, the number of idolaters is so considerable that no propagandist can afford to ignore their cravings. Why then this almost irresistible desire to magnify leaders and to worship them?

To a certain extent, the tendency to magnify leaders is carried over from childhood. The masses are not content with leaders as they are. They expect to find in adult society a pattern that is familiar to them from their childhood. Because they tend to identify the leader with the father, they turn the leader into a sort of superman, as our father appeared to us when we were two years old. According to Freud, the father reappears as a god, king, chief, or dictator. Most people expect a leader who is to them what a father is, or is meant to be, to a child, as omnipotent as a father appears to the infant. In our earlier years, we get so used to having a father that later on we find it difficult to manage without one. By the very nature of things, the child is dependent on the parents, helpless without them, and, when unspoilt, grateful for their guidance. This situation produces a habit of depending upon and of clinging to others early on. The habit may persist even after the objective necessity for it has disappeared. Adults often like somebody who can "father" them. "Let me be your father" not only appeals to young people in search of a successful career; in political movements, people require somebody with whom they can enter into the emotional relationship of the father of childhood days.

18 Guérard, *Reflections on the Napoleonic Legend*, p. 262.

This emotional relationship includes a more or less latent hatred for the father. The hostility towards the authority of the old finds its social expression in modern youth movements. But in the very act of revolt against their fathers, the young acknowledge their bondage. It is just the young whose aspirations fill society with leaders. The son regains his mental equilibrium when he becomes a father himself, or when he can identify himself with a father substitute. The father-son pattern is perpetuated in youth movements. The revolting young want somebody to worship, but somebody of their own. Just as those who channel reverence for the father into leader-worship have to take care of the father-hatred, so those who rally youth in its father-hatred have to find a use for its father-love.

Many prominent leaders in history were indeed termed "father." The Pope is the "father of the fathers," "the father of all the faithful." The very word "pope" means "father," and he runs a paternal government. To many Englishmen George V appeared as a benevolent "father of his people." In a discussion with Trotskyites I was greatly puzzled by perpetual talk about "the old man"; it turned out that they meant Trotsky. Lenin enjoyed the same epithet. At the moment Russia is ruled by a real Vozhd, which is the Russian word for "leader." This leader, infallible as he is, expects also to be called "immortal," and from his predecessor the Tsar he inherited the attribute "father." This has also its amusing side. Some years ago the parachute-jumpers proudly announced to the World Congress of the Communist International that they were Stalin's "children," and in Novosibirsk and similar places Stalin was greeted as the "father" of the local football club. One could easily multiply the examples. Since the seeds of leader cults are sown in the family, we can easily understand why the cult of a leader has been backed up so frequently by laws intended to make for the sanctity of family ties.

Social Conditions

But this is not the whole story. Otherwise it would follow that at all times people who had a father tended to deify their great men. Freudians are, indeed, a little inclined to forget the concrete social circumstances under which leaders are deified. The inclination to deify is not at all so universal as we might expect from a survey of recent history. A. Moret and G. Davy, in their excellent book *From Tribe to Empire: Social Organization among Primitives and in the Ancient East*, have shown that originally, under conditions of communal property and approximate social equality, leadership and authority were diffused among the members of the tribe. At that time people could do without permanent and divine living chiefs. They governed themselves democratically by committees and assemblies. A chief took over control only temporarily, in emergency.

A deified leader arises as a *symbol* of unity only in those societies which lack *real* unity and harmony, based on equality of property and income, and on a common outlook on life. The leaders are not "the gods." They are a poor substitute for them, a way of glossing over the gods' absence. Allegiance to a divine leader is a substitute for genuine social unity. When the pressure of a social crisis drives the inhabitants of a country against each other, or when non-homogeneous populations are gathered into vast imperial units, then a social group is bound to fall to pieces unless all its members are willing to prostrate themselves before the same divine chief. Vast empires, like the Roman, British, Chinese, or Russian, have always relied on the adulation of half-gods as a means of bridging social gaps. In modern times a country turns "fascist" under the stress of crisis. In fascist countries "it is the leader who keeps together and maintains the equilibrium between the contradictory elements and groups. Therefore each fascist party has one thing at least in common—a leader."[19] It is no accident that the cult of the leader in Soviet Russia grew hand in hand with the multiplication of social inequalities. A real *socialist* revolution would abolish social inequalities and give equal rights to all working men and women, whatever their religious, philosophical, and political opinions. A socialist country will have a more effective cement of social unity than the common adulation of a divine leader can provide.

Divinity and Inferiority

Social inequality within a group is maintained by oppression. The oppressed feel inferior because they are habitually treated as inferiors. In their daily lives they are cramped and obstructed. Only in their daydreams can they express that which they cannot achieve in actual reality. We know that the poor can find some substitute satisfaction in reading about the wealth of others. Papers like *Everybody's* are full of stories about big money, big legacies, big money-makers, the ways of the wealthy, etc.[20] The poor man identifies himself with a person who has got what he feels he lacks most.

The inferiority-ridden masses long for greatness and perfection perhaps more intensely than the smug and powerful because fate has so obviously denied it to them. Perpetual intimidation has firmly put them into their place. They realise that perfection is not "for the likes of us." A divine leader is their daydream, a mirage thrown up by their dissatisfaction with their own mediocrity. On him they throw all the excellencies they sadly miss in themselves, compensating for their own inanity by admiring its absence in outstanding personalities, projecting their most intimate wishes onto the legend of a leader. Half-gods incarnate popular hatred or hope. They materialise a haunting fear or desire.

Hero worship psychologically lifts up the oppressed in quite a number of ways. The oppressed think less cheaply of themselves and their lives when they reflect that once an almost divine personality arose out of their own midst. "The knowledge that in the city is a man who invented the railroad, raises the credit of all

19 Ellen Wilkinson and Edward Conze, *Why Fascism?* (London: Selwyn & Blount, 1934), p. 75.

20 *Editors:* Everybody's *was a weekly tabloid founded in 1913 in London as* The Competitor's Journal; *it later appeared under a variety of names but was known as* Everybody's *from 1930 to its last issue in 1959.*

citizens."[21] Identification with an all-wise and trustworthy leader also helps the weak to master a difficult situation. With affection they regard him as their private property, as *their* leader, whose excellence radiates somehow upon them. His kind wisdom is their best protection. They hope and expect that he will perform miracles.

From a rational and intellectual point of view the logic of the heart is often weird and paradoxical. We have seen that the oppressed derive emotional satisfaction from a leader who is completely different from them. But it is not enough for a leader to be a model of perfection. In addition he should have some human traits which allow the average man to recognise himself in the leader, and to raise himself along with this incarnation of his wish fantasies. The Son of God is a distant and somewhat stony ideal that passes comprehension. He remains a remote and otherworldly idol unless he also becomes the Son of Man.

The average man is reconciled to the existence of a more perfect man, like Achilles, Hector, Jesus, Roland, Napoleon, Bismarck, etc., if he discovers that, after all, the venerable leader was of the same clay as his oppressed worshippers.[22] The leader's failures make his fate all the more poignant. Empathy tempers and heightens admiration. It also washes away that hateful feeling of inferiority which another man's unbounded excellence and success would arouse in jealous hearts. And then, when you are worried about your status, is it not a pleasant consolation to discover that the divine leader himself was born in a stable, at Nazareth, among the poor and despised, or that he was a worker, like you and me? The historical Buddha was the son of a king; the Buddha of legend spent many of his incarnations among the oppressed. Deep down in their hearts, the oppressed resent the high-handed methods of their betters with a futile and impotent rage. Here again, the image of a leader enables the oppressed to "let off steam." Did we not learn that our leader, too, was persecuted by the mighty of the earth—by the Pharisees, by the haughty noblemen of Europe, or by the bureaucrats and moneylenders of the Weimar Republic who threatened to drive him out with a horsewhip?

---

21 Ralph Waldo Emerson, *Representative Men: Seven Lectures* (London: John Chapman, 1850), chapter 1, "Uses of Great Men." In 1869, the *Tribune* wrote about Cornelius Vanderbilt: "In honouring him, we honour the commercial enterprise, commercial sagacity, and commercial success which make him the 'realised ideal' of more people than almost any other living American" (quoted in Pigors, *Leadership or Domination*, p. 215). In the case of Napoleon, the possibilities of identification are particularly ample. He was a self-made man, and became the idol of young men who dream of conquering the world. He was a common man on a gigantic scale, with dazzling success. He thus gave the common man a chance to worship himself, and furnished him with an excuse for his own baseness.

22 If this book should reach another edition in 20 years' time, the author will be pleased to include in this list some of our present-day half-gods, whose image in the popular imagination will no doubt have been humanised by qualities that permit a more intimate identification. *Editors: The reader can easily imagine a roster of "half-gods" whose reputations have been both burnished and tarnished during the past century.*

Few readers of the Bible can fail to find similarities between Jesus and themselves. As Buddhism spread through East Asia it propagated the doctrine that everybody is a potential Buddha. There is scarcely a village in Germany that cannot boast of some little Hitlers. Without much effort, a moustache brings them nearer their God. Though it may be difficult to copy the genius of a great man, it is comparatively easy to imitate his mannerisms. Some queer birds feel like Napoleon when they put their right hand between their coat buttons in front of their stomach. Before he switches on the wireless for a speech of his King, the English bank clerk can nowadays discuss with a patronising and amused self-importance the hesitating diction of His Majesty King George VI. "You know, my dear, what an effort it must be for him." One day, the loyal German is gratified to hear that the leader slaves day and night to make him happy. The following day, he is relieved to learn that Hitler, with his "artistic temperament," is fond of loafing about in cinemas. The two pieces of information logically contradict each other. For the legend of the leader they are both indispensable.

The theologians of the "dark ages" were extremely acute and logical minds. They elaborated one theory after another in an attempt to reconcile the divinity of Jesus Christ with his manhood. The modern propagandist loses no sleep over such metaphysical trifles. All he knows or feels is that the masses expect a leader to be completely different from his followers, and at the same time to be so much alike that they can understand and appreciate him. It is indeed important to see that in some respects the political leader, in particular, must be mediocre, either in character or in intelligence.[23] Obedient to the wish of the masses, the good propagandist at one time divinises a leader and at another humanises him. Now he raises him to the sky, and then he brings him back to the earth again. The two opposite processes both, as we showed, have their function in the mental economy of the oppressed.

---

23 In *Gifted Children: Their Nature and Nurture* (New York: The Macmillan Company, 1926, summarised in Gardner Murphy and Lois Barclay Murphy, *Experimental Social Psychology* [New York: Harper, 1931], pp. 402–403), Leta Stetter Hollingworth showed that

> children of *extraordinary* intelligence (let us say with intelligence quotient around 160) are not as apt to be leaders in a group of average children as are those who are merely 'superior' (that is, whose intelligence quotients are 125 to 135).... In other words, to be a leader in a school, it is well to be relatively clever, but not too clever.

1.4

HATRED AND AGGRESSIVENESS

The moral enthusiasm of the crowd always demands a victim.

Everett Dean Martin[1]

Propaganda should give its followers or victims something to hate or destroy. Political propaganda cannot afford to ignore the hatred, spite, cruelty, bloodthirst, and aggressiveness which are latent in our minds. If a propagandist preaches no hatred at all, his competitors will soon get the better of him. A vital and enthusiastic social movement must be "against someone." The propagandist must find some enemy whom one can hate with a good conscience. His words must give shape to daydreams of destruction. This is not a matter of his own free choice. He has to fit in with the mentality of his clients. It appears probable that frustrated masses take over a creed only on condition that it gives them something to "kick." Propaganda which gives no outlet to their aggressiveness seems to remain futile and ineffective.[2]

First of all we shall illustrate by some examples the extent to which the more successful propagandists actually appeal to hatred. We then analyse the origins and consequences of aggressiveness, and show why an appeal to aggressiveness seems indispensable to successful propaganda. Some remarks on atrocity stories wind up the chapter.[3]

---

1 Everett Dean Martin, *The Behavior of Crowds: A Psychological Study* (New York: W.W. Norton & Co., Inc., 1920), p. 112.

2 Gandhi expresses dismay at this phenomenon: "The present-day cow-protection has degenerated into a perpetual feud with the Mussulmans, whereas cow-protection means conquering Mussulmans by our love." From "Hinduism" in *Young India* (October 6, 1921), quoted in Andrews, *Mahatma Gandhi's Ideas*, p. 38.

3 A note on terminology: *Aggressiveness* is the desire to smash or destroy somebody or something. *Aggression* is the act of smashing somebody or something. *Hatred* is an emotion which accompanies

DOI: 10.4324/9781003363408-6

The Nazis

It is only in times of acute crisis that the masses take a lively interest in social and public affairs. In such periods, the "causes" which had been kept alive by some few enthusiasts get hold of the masses themselves. In such times, frustration, a chief cause of aggressiveness, is exceptionally strong. Mass movements, therefore, cannot exist unless they offer considerable outlet for collective hatred. Let us consider the familiar case of National Socialism, which was able to create a mass drive for its aims only in a time of deep crisis. Loss of employment, income, and hope among millions of Germans created those privations which call forth aggressive impulses. To "smash the system" became the common goal. Other slogans current at the time include "rather a terrible end than an endless terror," and "better for three million to die on the field of battle than to starve to death in the streets of our cities." The Nazis cashed in on the hatred and fury which conditions had created among the masses. The stormtroopers indulged in wish fantasies of a "night of the long knives" in which they would massacre their opponents.[4]

Careful propaganda fostered hatred and called it the highest virtue of which the German mind was capable. "The natural hostility of the peasant towards the Jews must be whipped up to a frenzy," ran a party instruction in March, 1931.[5] Similar examples abound[6]: "The Third Empire will treat Jews like plant lice"; "The Jew is the tape worm in the human organism and it is our duty to exterminate him"; "The Jew is the cause and beneficiary of our national slavery. He ruined our race, rotted our morals, hollowed out our way of life, and broke our strength"; the young men were singing in the streets, "When Jewish blood spurts from our knife, then all is twice as good."[7] Julius Streicher printed a series of posters in *Der Stürmer* which Mowrer describes as showing "disgusting Semites wading through seas of Christian blood, kicking a pregnant Christian woman in the abdomen, releasing snakes from a box marked 'The Talmud' upon a naked Christian woman, picking the pocket of a pilloried German workman."[8]

The Nazi mind gorges itself on aggressiveness. Göring, in order to enjoy his wedding, had two anti-fascists beheaded in the morning. That is Nazism in a nutshell. Nazi propaganda and actions, while they satisfy the sadistic instincts of their followers, tend to create fear in their opponents coupled with the hope that by inactivity they can avoid the worst.

---

chronic or abortive aggressiveness. *Cruelty* is the desire to contemplate pain being inflicted on a being capable of feeling it. *Sadism* is severely tinged aggressiveness.

4 *Editors: The reference is to Hitler's purge of Nazi party leaders on June 30, 1934.*

5 Edgar Ansel Mowrer, *Germany Puts the Clock Back* (New York: William Morrow & Co., 1933), p. 223.

6 Ibid., chapter 18: "Perish the Jew!"

7 *Editors: The original German text of the song ran,* Wenn das Judenblut vom Messer spritzt, dann geht's nochmal so gut.

8 Mowrer, *Germany Puts the Clock Back*, p. 232.

Pacifists and Others

Or take pacifist propaganda. Few things are more boring and uninspiring than a meeting devoted to the praise of the virtues of peace. But watch how pacifist audiences sit up, become eager and interested, when their attention is drawn to the enemies of peace—to the armament manufacturers, to bloodstained but stupid generals, to the fascists, or to the stockbrokers of the city of London.

This was also the experience of the League of Nations. For years it led a quiet and inoffensive existence. Then, for some months, its slogans made a nation-wide appeal. What had happened? An aggressor, Mussolini, had come to the rescue. The cause of the League of Nations suddenly became immensely popular.

In recent years antifascism has had a popular success which was denied to constructive socialist ideas. Mentally cutting the throat of Hitler or Mussolini has become, in some circles, a substitute for bullfights and cockfights. Nor must we forget the great services rendered to Russian propaganda by Austen Chamberlain,[9] Trotsky, and the worldwide bourgeoisie. In France, the Popular Front decided to have a more concrete enemy than the "capitalist system." The "two hundred families" proved an immense success.[10] It was a stroke of luck that quite a number of them had German names.

Ever since the belief in the devil, in Hell, and in the unutterable wickedness of infidels and heretics has declined, Christianity has no longer been what it was. It is the distinction of Christianity to have invented a worse Hell than any other religion. The vitality of the Church cannot survive the loss of its Hell. Many Christians become lukewarm to the faith. Formerly it was the fear of Hell which peopled Heaven.[11] Hell provided such a solid and ample basis for fantasies of cruelty. And then, the loss of their Hell deprives Christians of what was a very useful outlet for pent-up vindictiveness. The modern Christian must go without the feelings of Tertullian when he wrote,

> How shall I admire, how laugh, how rejoice, how exult, when I behold so many proud monarchs, and fancied gods, groaning in the lowest abyss of darkness; so many magistrates, who persecuted the name of the Lord, liquefying in fiercer fires than they ever kindled against the Christians; so many sage philosophers blushing in red hot flames, with their deluded scholars.[12]

9 *Editors: British statesman, half-brother of Neville Chamberlain.*

10 *Editors: The reference is to a purported group of elite families alleged to dominate the European economy and political stage from behind the scenes. In the 1930s, the term became popular as a left-wing rallying cry, and was later co-opted by the extreme right.*

11 "Nothing moves the people like the terrific. They must have hell-fire flashed before their faces, or they will not *move*." Harold Begbie, *The Life of General William Booth: The Founder of the Salvation Army*, vol. 1 (New York: The Macmillan Company, 1920), p. 210.

12 Tertullian, *De spectaculis* 30, trans. Edward Gibbon, *The History of the Decline and Fall of the Roman Empire*, vol. 2, chapter 15.

He can no longer feel with the great scholastic writer, Peter Lombard, that "the elect shall go forth...to see the torments of the impious, and seeing this they will not be afflicted with grief, but will be satiated with joy at the sight of the unutterable calamity of the impious."[13]

Kindled with religious fervour, the Christian men of the First Crusade rallied to the call of Pope Urban II: "If you must have blood, bathe your hands in the blood of the infidels."[14] The infidels responded in kind. Imad ad-Din al-Isfahani, the Muslim historian and eyewitness to the "horrible spectacle" of the battlefield of Tiberias, writes:

> I saw severed heads; dull, dead eyes; dust-covered bodies, twisted limbs; severed arms; crushed bones; gashed and bloody necks; broken thighs; feet no longer joined to the leg; bodies in two pieces; torn lips, and split foreheads. On seeing their faces strewn over the ground, and covered with blood and wounds, I recall the holy words of the *Koran*: "And the infidel shall say, what am I but dust!" Ah! what sweet odor is exhaled from this victory.[15]

The masterpiece of Allied propaganda during the last war worked on the same lines. The dangers and privations of wartime could not fail to create an atmosphere of animosity among the suffering people. If the animosity had not been led into proper channels, it might have turned citizen against citizen, or worse, the bulk of the population against their own ruling class or government. Well-bred instinct and calculating intellect alike told the allied propagandists that this eventuality had to be avoided at all costs. They could not allow the hatred to float about unattached. They had to bind it to one object and direct it against one target. A "chief monster" was invented. The Kaiser was invested with an importance which even his vanity had never suspected. He was easy to draw, and fond of bloodthirst and bombastic speeches. He came to personify the criminal tendencies of the Hun. This one man was personally responsible for all the misery of the war. One had only to rid the world of him, and all would be well again. Posters depicted his face composed of corpses, his mouth streaming with blood. As an ideal "substitute object" for aggressiveness, the Kaiser inadvertently did much for national unity in the Allied countries. Lord Ponsonby observes that the Germans were not so well-placed: "They had no chief Monster to depict as the Allies had, but only a number of not very distinguished statesmen."[16]

---

13 Peter Lombard, *Sentences* IV.50. Another prominent scholastic writer states that the elect have a reason for their joy "seeing that their enemies will be tortured." Percy Dearmer, *The Legend of Hell: An Examination of the Idea of Everlasting Punishment, With a Chapter on Apocalyptic* (London: Cassell, 1929), p. 34.

14 Charles Duff, *This Human Nature: A History, A Commentary, An Exposition From the Earliest Times to the Present Day* (New York: J. J. Little & Ives Co., 1930), p. 241.

15 Duff, *This Human Nature*, pp. 243–244.

16 Ponsonby, *Falsehood in War-Time*, pp. 168–169.

The Ideal Enemy

The ideal enemy should look powerful without being able to hit back at the individual who hates him. The devil should be "sufficiently human to be popularly execrated, and sufficiently apart and monstrous to make acute appeal to the imagination."[17] Few people are capable of hating an abstraction or an impersonal force. When things go wrong, the majority feel certain that one powerful but wicked person is responsible. A personal incarnation of all iniquity proves the most popular and attractive enemy. As a second choice the propagandist will personify a social group, like the Jews in Germany, or the "Boche" and "Hun."[18] The misdeeds of this group should be capable of pictorial representation, particularly in caricatures and cartoons. The memory of the crowd is visual rather than intellectual. Everybody in Germany knows, or believes he knows, what a Jew looks like. And if he had any illusions about Jews, the cartoons in the papers of Dr. Goebbels or Herr Streicher soon put him right.

Much popular enthusiasm in history has been expended on the hatred and removal of some personal or personified enemy of mankind, like Napoleon,[19] Abdul the Damned, the Kaiser, various Antichrists including the Pope, and various "Mad Dogs" of Europe. At present the world bristles with Antichrists and enemies of civilisation. A new war is indicated to get rid of them.

Why All This Hatred?

Man's ferocity and destructiveness are equalled only by those of the rat—although the rat still has a lot to learn. Human ferocity reaches its highest degree when it is inspired by a shining ideal. In 1097, the crusaders had conquered the tomb of the Son of God, Jesus Christ, for the glory of Christendom. When they rode through Jerusalem, their horses waded up to the ankles in the blood of the heathen, and the Jews, notorious murderers of God's Son, were locked up in their synagogue and burnt alive. At present, almost every nation in Europe is bent on some crusade or another.

It would be a mistake to say that human beings are aggressive on principle, as it were, or for the mere fun of it. It is a pernicious though widespread error to assume that aggressiveness is an "instinct," an innate tendency in us, one of the eternal springs in the clock of human nature. Observation and experiment demonstrate that aggressiveness arises as a consequence of certain well-defined conditions.[20]

---

17 George Ives, *A History of Penal Methods: Criminals, Witches, Lunatics* (New York: F.A. Stokes Company, 1914), p. 236.

18 *Editors: Both pejorative terms to describe Germans.*

19 In passing we may mention a brilliant propagandistic idea of a century ago. During the Napoleonic wars chamber pots were sent to Southern Italy from England which showed Napoleon at the bottom, his mouth wide open. That was a fine way of becoming intelligible to illiterates.

20 Seneca gives a full survey of the causes of aggressiveness in his third book, *On Anger* (*De Ira*).

People become aggressive when they encounter what they feel to be an obstacle—when, as psychologists say, they are *frustrated*. In other words, whenever they can't get, or keep, what they want. A small child explodes in anger when you hamper his movements. A dog becomes furious when you take away the bone he thought was his. If a tendency to react is first aroused and then interfered with, the result is pugnacious behaviour, often accompanied by the emotion of anger.[21]

We are, further, inclined to respond aggressively when our sense of social importance or our *pride* and *prestige* are at stake, when we are made to feel insignificant and inferior. When the English were told in 1914 that the Kaiser had spoken of their "contemptible little army," a wave of pugnacity went through the country despite the fact that the Kaiser never made this remark.[22]

A person suffering from an inferiority complex will be inclined to feel that everything conspires to frustrate him. He may overcompensate by all-round aggressiveness and a desire to dominate. Almost all those historical persons whose domineering mind led them from one act of aggression to another have felt the ceaseless sting of inferiority. This is as true of Napoleon as of Hitler or Caesar.

To humiliate a person is the best way of earning his undying hatred. In 1918 the Allies acted on that principle. Not content merely to make Germany pay reparations, they demoralised the Germans by forcing them to agree that they were guilty of the war and unworthy of colonies. The inflated sense of "honour" in Hitler's Germany is the direct and inevitable consequence of that entirely unstatesmanlike procedure, which in its turn was prompted by the hatred the Allied populations felt against Germany in 1918 and 1919, a hatred largely begotten by fear. For *fear*, aroused by the prospect of frustration, is another potent source of aggressiveness. There is even a close physiological link between fear and hate. When we are confronted with danger, the adrenal gland secretes the stress hormone "adrenaline" into the circulation. The presence of adrenaline in the bloodstream results in that curious blend of fear and anger which we experience in the face of danger.

During the last war, Archbishop Davidson of Canterbury received plenty of letters from frightened inhabitants of English towns which had been bombed by the Germans. They urged, "Let gutters run with German blood. Let us smash to pulp the German old men, women and children," and so on.[23] The best way of transforming a man into a raving beast is to frighten him out of his wits.

21 Up to a certain point, all-round frustration will increase pugnacity. "The tired man seeks a quarrel" (*Vetus dictum est a lasso rixam quaeri*, from Seneca, *De Ira*, 3.9). If a certain degree of increasing misery is reached, other factors intervene and choke pugnacity.

22 As shown by Ernest Scott, *History and Historical Problems* (London: Oxford University Press, 1925), pp. 157–158.

23 *The London Times*, June 22, 1917.

Forms of Aggressive Behaviour

We saw where we get our aggressiveness from. We now have to find out what we do with it. When in rage, people want to smash, or to kill, or to destroy that which frustrates or frightens them. In its uninhibited form, aggressiveness aims at the downright annihilation of the offending object. In a fury which is restrained neither by habits of self-control nor by considerations of expediency, a person simply smashes and annihilates that which stands in his way. We try to remove (annihilate) an annoyance by smashing it, by going away, by shutting our ears, etc. Our social environment, however, tends to inhibit, or to restrict, our aggressiveness. The outer world resists our combative tendencies. Society, in order not to be blown to pieces, has by social conventions of politeness, by laws, and by moral exhortations placed innumerable restrictions on the open and direct manifestations of aggressive desires. We are thus outwardly tamed, though our minds may remain as brutal as ever they were. A long process of education teaches us to find milder forms of expression for our aggressive impulses. If a small boy hates his younger brother, he may try to kill him in the cradle. When he becomes older, he may beat him up or throw chairs at him. When he is grown up, he will be content to intrigue against him or speak ill of him. A similar process takes place in public life. The King of England originally devastated the habitations of a felon, eradicated the woods, ploughed up the meadows, etc. Later on he was content to take, instead, the profit of the land for one year and one day.

Social restrictions either inhibit or socialise aggressiveness. In most cases, our aggressiveness is inhibited in the sense that we stop short of the total annihilation of our enemy. One no longer destroys. One only harms. Instead of killing an enemy outright, we may be content to smash our fist into his face. The more "civilised" we become, the more content we are with even less. We may merely run him down with words, jokes, or witticisms, by malicious slander or open derision. Gossip allows much latent hatred to evaporate. Over human dwellings it creates a sort of spiritual mist, which we can only feel, but not see. In other cases we daydream about how we or how somebody else will destroy or murder the person we hate. We imagine that a hated enemy may come to grief and thus be punished. When drink has loosened their tongue, employees may sometimes tell you of the most atrocious calamities which, they hope, will befall their boss, or of the terrible punishment they would inflict upon him if they could. Punishment by castration is a favourite.

When blocked, aggressiveness may also turn to a substitute object (see page 68). We are often annoyed by people who are stronger than we are. Unable to hit back, we divert the aggressiveness to another person, or even to a lifeless object. An office worker is shouted at by his boss. He feels frustrated. An aggressive impulse is set up. He would like to answer, "Mind your own business," or something to that effect. But he has to "swallow his wrath." The inhibited aggressive impulse now sticks in him, and when he comes home, he finds fault with his wife's cooking, or a chair is in the wrong place. He "vents his wrath" on his wife. She, again, may vent it on a tradesman or neighbour, or on her child. The child may soon be found pulling the tail of the cat. What the cat then does is no longer our business.

Lester Hutchinson reports how the Meerut prisoners would beat their soaked shirts "against the stone with all [their] force until [they] had beaten out both the dirt and the soap. Additional pleasure was derived by imagining the stone to be Mr. Yorke [the judge] or the jailer."[24] The Gestalt psychologist Wolfgang Köhler reports similar instances of "displacement" in chimpanzees. When he punished the young chimp Sultan, Sultan did not dare to avenge himself on Köhler. His anger could not expend itself on the object that aroused it. He thus turned to an entirely different object. Sultan would run in a fury at Chica and persecute her, "although she had absolutely nothing to do with the cause of his rage."[25] Similarly, if one of the Eskimo dogs fixed to a sledge is hit by the whip, he often bites the dog in front of him. The hostility of a crowd can also on occasion survive the loss of its object by substituting another object.

> A mob in the street, driven back from the object of its attack, will loot a store or two before it disperses. Or, bent on lynching a certain negro, it may even substitute an innocent man, if robbed of its intended victim—as, for instance, the lynching of the mayor of Omaha.[26]

It is interesting in this context that most outdoor games consist in killing something, or in kicking something about. People who have had to swallow aggressiveness become generally irritable. Many of their urges and instincts have been impeded and blocked for a long time. Any occasional object may furnish an outlet. A minor incident may cause a quite disproportionate outburst. In a sudden explosion of running amok, of cafard, or of tropical frenzy, some men beat down and destroy anything they meet. All-round frustration makes us spiteful and malicious. One may come to hate everybody.

In extreme cases of despair, we turn part of our aggressiveness against ourselves. Unable, or unwilling, to punish others, we may resort to punishing ourselves. In our self-hate we accuse ourselves of our sins. We may hate our flesh because we fear its desires. Following John Wesley's advice, we may "murder ourselves by inches."[27] When faced with a small annoyance, we sometimes bite our hands or gnaw our nails in frustrated fury. Aggressiveness turned inwards is the cause of much mental conflict and personal unhappiness.

---

24 Lester Hutchinson, *Conspiracy at Meerut* (London: G. Allen & Unwin, Ltd., 1935), p. 170.

25 Wolfgang Köhler, *The Mentality of Apes* (New York: Harcourt, Brace & Co., 1927), p. 289.

26 E. D. Martin, quoted by Young, *Source Book for Social Psychology*, p. 653. *Editors: The reference is to the race riot that occurred in Omaha during September, 1919 which resulted in the lynching of one black man and two white men, and the attempted lynching of the mayor, who had intervened.*

27 Sydney G. Dimond, *The Psychology of the Methodist Revival: An Empirical and Descriptive Study* (London: Oxford University Press, H. Milford, 1926), p. 49.

Daydreaming

We saw that we can, to a certain extent, satisfy our aggressiveness either by merely *imagining* that our enemy will be destroyed, or by kicking a *substitute* person or object. It is possible to combine the two methods and to find satisfaction in imagining other people getting hurt, or in daydreaming about other people getting kicked about. To read novels and newspapers means, psychologically, to daydream without the mental effort of making up a story. Such reading provides relief by feeding instinctual desires. "The daily press is, to the average Englishman, what the Colosseum was to the old Roman or the bull-ring is to the Spaniard: the chief thrills of life are to be found in it."[28]

Mass media (novels, newspapers, films, etc.) give us ample opportunity to indulge with a good conscience in wish fantasies of hatred and revenge, and to contemplate with enchanted equanimity all sorts of murder and destruction. A statistical table which I owe to Charles Duff illustrates the extent to which the press gives us food for aggressive thoughts. In 1928, at the time when Thomas Hardy died, Kennedy and Brown were tried for murder.[29] How many column-inches did the newspapers devote to each of these events respectively?[30]

	Murder Trial Coverage (inches)	*Thomas Hardy Obituary (inches)*
Daily Mail	336	180
Evening News	624	96
Daily Express	522	90
Evening Standard	263	150
Sunday Dispatch	152	30
Reynolds News	240	12
News of the World	312	30
The Times	352	262
Daily Telegraph	361	320

Nor do the "well-bred" wholeheartedly despise this kind of fare. The more successful writers of the last generation were apparently expected to tickle the aggressive impulses of their public. Pierre Bovet could say of Wells' scientific tales that "in each you will find detailed narratives of horrible carnage. Every grand discovery which he imagines gives him the opportunity for hecatombs."[31] George Bernard Shaw's wit never ceases to slash anything it can get hold of. Gabriele

28 Charles Duff, *A Handbook on Hanging: Being a Short Introduction to the Fine Art of Execution* (London: G. Richards and P. Sainsbury at the Cayme Press, Ltd., 1928), p. 94.

29 *Editors: The reference is to a sensational murder of a policeman in the UK in 1927, which resulted in the execution of Kennedy and Brown in 1928.*

30 Duff, *A Handbook on Hanging*, p. 95. The notable exceptions were: *Morning Post* (now defunct): 304 inches, 432 inches; *Daily News* (now defunct): 279 inches, 528 inches; *Observer*: 22 inches, 182 inches.

31 Pierre Bovet, *The Fighting Instinct* (London: G. Allen & Unwin, Ltd., 1923), p. 99.

D'Annunzio, national poet of Italy from 1900 to his death in 1938, turned out a whole string of "plays of medieval or modern incest and murders, flames and horrors."[32] His mind was in rare harmony with that of his public. At the dawn of the century he said to his Florentine barber, "I have experienced all, except the joy of killing." He wrote of the "matchless human joy" with which the victorious Italian sailors of a torpedo-boat might someday see a big enemy ship sinking "into the unfathomable gurge."[33] In one of his poems he summed up his programme of a full life. It reminds us rather of the Mongol ideal of happiness (see page 32). "Wilt thou fight? Kill? See streams of blood? Great heaps of gold? Herds of captive women? Slaves? Other, other spoils?"[34] In all countries barbarian bards help to brighten up our civilisation. Kipling, the British D'Annunzio, was particularly clever at ghastly, ugly, and sadistic stories. If a devil should leave hell and set himself up as a novelist, he could not improve on "My Son's Wife."[35] His biographer writes,

> At times Kipling seems to take a fiendish delight in morbid, bizarre and repulsive details.... As the painter of such blood scenes [he] owes his success to the fact that, while we had at that time thrust personal physical warfare almost out of our own lives, there was still enough primitive hellishness in us to leave us fascinated with the recitals of torture.[36]

The following is a survey of the forms that inhibited aggressiveness takes, from its direct expression through increasingly derivative or sublimated forms.[37]

1. *The direct infliction of cruelty.* Torturing prisoners or animals; legal punishments (blinding, castrating, boiling alive, hanging in chains, etc.); callous treatment of the helpless (paupers, animals, prisoners, aborigines, and the insane).
2. *Looking upon the infliction of cruelty.* Public executions, auto-da-fés, lynchings, bullfights, cockfights, wrestling; visits to Madame Tussauds' Chamber of Horrors, or to torturing instruments in German castles; eagerness to watch accidents; motorcyclists on a dirt track thrown off their vehicles and injured;

32 Giuseppe Antonio Borgese, *Goliath: The March of Fascism* (New York: The Viking Press, 1937), p. 101.

33 Borgese, *Goliath*, p. 96.

34 Ibid., p. 95.

35 *Editors: First published in Kipling's 1917 collection* A Diversity of Creatures.

36 Robert Thurston Hopkins, *Rudyard Kipling, A Character Study: Life, Writings and Literary Landmarks*, 3rd ed. (London: Simpkin, Marshall, Hamilton, Kent & Co., Ltd., 1921), p.112. A similar phenomenon can be observed in the cinema. A representative of the American film industry gave a survey of 620 feature pictures produced in the USA in one year (1928): 33.7% contained no villain and no crime; in 17.5% the villain was killed; in 33.8% the villain was imprisoned; in 4.4% the villain was reformed; and in 10.6% the villain was punished by the hero (Duff, *This Human Nature*, p. 379).

37 *Editors: Aim-inhibited aggressiveness is a concept of psychoanalysis introduced by Freud in* Group Psychology and the Analysis of the Ego *(1921). It refers to the quality of an instinct that only achieves incomplete satisfaction, through approximations to the behavior that would provide full satisfaction.*

circus shows in which the artists may break their necks or be torn by some wild animal.

3. *Hearing or reading about other people's calamities.* The torments of the impious in Hell; sadistic literature (*Foxe's Book of Martyrs*, including "pictures of hideous tortures, enlivened by fantastic miracles"[38]; *The pleasures of the Torture Chamber*[39], etc.); detective stories, almost invariably based on a juicy murder; newspaper accounts of horrible murders, accidents, hangings, tragic deaths, rapes, burning tragedies, fatalities and inquests, suicides and other "news in grief"; many nursery rhymes.
4. *The hatred is projected onto an aggressive god.* One splits off a part of one's aggressive self and creates a cruel God, a further excuse for cruelty in his name, because he can be conciliated only by sacrifices of blood—Jehova, Shiva (adorned with a chain of skulls), Huitzilopochtli, etc.

The reader will notice that a number of the above-mentioned channels of aggressiveness have, under the influence of *humanitarianism,* during the last two centuries gone more and more out of use in a number of European countries. One might infer that the total amount of available aggressiveness has been diminished. A closer analysis of the facts would show that this is not the case. The humanitarian ideals, and the economic system with which they are bound up, have failed to appreciably diminish the influx of aggressiveness. There is even some evidence to show that man's ferocity has increased with civilisation. Since one cannot close one outlet to aggressiveness without opening up another, aggressiveness has simply changed its direction and form. Richard Martin,[40] Schopenhauer, and Göring, all prominent animal lovers, were not distinguished by their kindness to human beings. In an industrialised country there is less brutality, but probably more cruelty and callousness. We have little reason to pat ourselves on the back for our loving-kindness. Efforts have been made to eliminate the more nauseating forms of physical cruelty. Mentalised forms of aggressiveness have become more and more preponderant, while in some European countries humanitarian sentiments are again rapidly on the decline. Fascinating as the subject is, I can give no more than these few hints in an introductory volume.

Socialised Aggressiveness

I now state briefly some of the laws which govern aggressive behaviour. First of all, *an aggressive impulse will persist until it has found an outlet.* Aggressive feelings are

---

38 William Edward Hartpole Lecky, *History of European Morals: From Augustus to Charlemagne*, 3rd ed., vol. 1 (New York: D. Appleton & Co., 1891), p. 464.

39 By John Swain (London: Noel Douglas, 1931).

40 *Editors: Colonel Richard Martin, an Irish politician, campaigned against cruelty to animals and championed the 1822 Cruel Treatment of Cattle Act, which came to be known as Martin's Act.*

dispelled only when they can be expressed freely. A peace-making ceremony of the Negritoes of the Andaman Islands is based on that principle. The ceremony takes place when two hostile groups bring their quarrel to an end. The group which has committed the last act of hostility is visited by the others. By shouting at their hosts, threatening them with gestures, or shaking them, the guests evaporate their own wrath. The hosts remain completely passive, and take care to show neither fear nor resentment at the treatment to which they have to submit. After such a ceremony all concerned feel that they have "got even" and can be friends again.

Secondly, *the satisfaction of aggressiveness brings emotional release*. During a Spanish bullfight the cruel faces of the spectators gradually come to wear a beatific smile. They look almost happy after they have gorged themselves on the sight of six bleeding and dying bulls. I am told that a good lynching has a similar effect. After Hitler's rise to power in 1933, the average German felt more cheerful than he did before, although economically speaking he did not improve himself. This cheerfulness is attributable in part to Nazi propaganda which gives him countless opportunities to "let off steam" and to relieve himself of his repressed hatred. As a medieval storyteller puts it, "Nay, when the poison is suppressed then it is all the more harmful, but when we can belch it forth we are relieved by the very act."[41] Our mental ease depends on our ability to get rid of the poison of repressed anger.

When we consider the frustrations, fears, and humiliations to which the masses are subjected, we can formulate a third law. *In a class society, the average person typically takes in more aggressiveness than he can get rid of.* Therefore his mind contains a store of unused aggressiveness which waits to be used. The comparatively harmless outlets for aggressiveness which we have mentioned are not yet sufficient. Part of the latent aggressiveness has to be *socialised*. Aggressiveness becomes an overwhelming social force when it can mobilise the social side of human nature for its own ends. Socialised aggressiveness is responsible for all the atrocities and crimes which fill our records of human history. How does it work?

In its naked selfish form, hatred is antisocial and meets with social disapproval. Society tends to keep it down.[42] The vice becomes a virtue, however, and even a duty, if hatred clothes itself in the cloak of justice and righteousness, hides behind big and high-sounding ideals, or masquerades as the desire to "do good" to others. One is indeed surprised to find how often the following situation has repeated itself: There arose an enemy of God, of humanity, of progress, and of civilisation.

---

41 Robert of Holy Island (Bishop of Durham from 1274 to 1283), quoted in George Gordon Coulton, *Life in the Middle Ages*, 2nd ed., vol. 3 (Cambridge: Cambridge University Press, 1928), p. 92.

42 It may be observed that aggressiveness is more respectable than the sex instinct, if we can believe Canon Maynard Smith (quoted in Barry, *This England*, p. 182), who said that

> as far as he could make out, the fiction of the present day was divided into books dealing with adultery and murder. He was sure they would agree that to read books on murder was by far the more healthy and laudable pursuit.

Thousands, nay millions, jumped at the chance of hating with a good conscience. They resolved to deliver mankind from its enemies. They set about to do so by a gigantic massacre and an orgy of bloodshed. After all was over, they found that a new enemy of mankind had robbed them of the fruits of their good works.

It should now be clear why hatred of an enemy is bound to loom large in the minds of the members of a vigorous social movement, and why the propagandist has to provide food for aggressive thoughts. In the course of each day, more aggressive impulses arise in people than they can discharge in the ordinary way. If I had the space, I could describe in detail the innumerable frustrations to which the average bank clerk, or factory worker, or bus driver, or housewife, are subjected all day long. The reader, however, may be familiar with them. In times of social crisis misery spreads, and growing frustration produces an increasing need for opportunities to discharge collective hatred. It would be a miracle indeed if the extra frustration and fear which the crisis brings with it did not lead to a surplus aggressiveness which eagerly seizes any ready "cause" as a means of socialising and expressing itself.

In addition, we must remember that the average man's self-complacency cannot endure the idea that he himself might be responsible for his misfortune. So he invents a devil who "got him into the mess." If things go wrong, somebody must have put them wrong. The genius of Nazi propaganda offered the despairing German plenty of devils. Jews, Communists, social democrats, Liberals, financiers, priests, Frenchmen, Englishmen, Russians, all of them were working hand in hand to keep down the hard-working, industrious, and able German. And the man who felt so insignificant when he thought of his shaky business or job could now jubilate when he contemplated the might of his enemies. He must be somebody after all. What a man am I that so many have conspired to kick me down, and yet they did not succeed! The desire to save one's self-respect in misfortune is at the root of the age-old desire for a scapegoat. It was the Jews' fault that the grand old order of the Kaiser had gone, that you were unemployed, or unsuccessful in your job, or that your shop did not flourish.

> The primitive man, overtaken by catastrophe, hunts high and low for a scapegoat and a messiah. The scapegoat is the person who got him into the mess and the messiah is the person who will get him out. History is the story of the struggle of devils and deliverers.[43]

Any plague or famine was an occasion to hunt down the offender who had caused the divine wrath. In Roman times, national misfortunes often resulted in the death of some Vestal Virgin whose unchastity was blamed. Later on, the Christians were singled out.

---

43 Lasswell, *Propaganda Technique in the World War*, p. 59.

> If the Tiber ascends to the walls, or if the Nile does not overflow the fields, if the heaven refuses its rain, if the earth quakes, if famine and pestilence desolate the lands, immediately the cry is raised, 'The Christians to the lions!'[44]

The Christians, in their turn, could scarcely blame themselves. They decided to persecute witches. Witches have gone out of fashion. Nowadays, Jews, bankers, Fascists, Trotskyites, or Bolsheviks persecute the bewildered citizen.

If the main aim of propaganda is to maintain unity within a social group, the scientific management of hatred is one of the most vital tasks of a propagandist. If they do not hate some bogeyman, the people will hate their own government, or an unpopular ally. It is perhaps preferable that they should blame it on the cat than that they should blame it on the ruling class.

Atrocity Propaganda

As a psychologist, I distrust people who love atrocity stories.[45] Their mental health, if nothing else, is suspect. In recent years, each sharp political tension has begotten its batch of atrocity stories. It is true that atrocity stories used to brighten the firesides of our ancestors. The Christian mind, nourished by the atrocity story of the Crucifixion, is perhaps specially attuned to them. When Pope Urban II, for instance, stirred up the people of Europe with the First Crusade, his speech dwelt in detail on the cruelties committed by the heathen. Nevertheless, the reader of the "Chronicles" of the Crusades will find comparatively little of that nauseating unctuousness which mars the imperialist wars and conflicts of the 20th century. In England, books on foreign countries have an assured market if they peddle one long string of atrocity stories. We need only think of Katherine Mayo's *Mother India* (1927), "a drain inspector's report," as Mahatma Gandhi called it, or Taid O'Conroy's *The Menace of Japan* (1934). The Nazis, in this as in everything else Great Britain's keenest disciples, have also made it a habit to prepare and to justify every act of suppression and aggression by a barrage of atrocity tales.

The objective value of atrocity stories is variable, though they cannot be entirely dismissed. Among those who delight in spreading them, there are some who would enthusiastically commit atrocities if they could do so, including the atrocity of war. The bulk of the stories are, however, exaggerated or invented. Even the general public does not take them seriously after they have fulfilled

44 Tertullian, *Apology*, 40: *Si Tiberis ascendit in moenia, si Nilus non ascendit in arva, si caelum stetit, si terra movit, si fames, si lues, statim: "Christianos ad leonem!" acclamatur. Editors: We are unable to identify the translator.*

45 *Editors: After emigrating from Germany in 1933, Conze taught Tutorial Classes in psychology at the University of London, remarking, "What in my first years in England I taught as 'Psychology' was largely Freud, Oedipus complex and all"* (Memoirs *1, p. 29).*

their purpose.[46] And yet, although atrocity stories are often demonstrably spurious, there remains the startling fact that they should assume such undue proportions in the public perception of social events, and that they should so greatly colour the average person's conception of political strife. Many take for the ocean of social life that which is just the foam on the wave. Few reflect why a merciful Fate should so often induce our enemies to commit atrocities just when we think of pouncing upon them.

Atrocity stories throw little if any light on social problems, yet the emotional satisfaction they give is so intense that even the most palpable absurdities are overlooked. During the last war, stories were circulated about German soldiers cutting the hands off Belgian babies, "so that," according to the *London Times* correspondent in Paris (September 2, 1914), "there shall be no more soldiers for France." Ponsonby writes,

> Everyone will remember the handless Belgian baby. It was loudly spoken of in buses and other public places, had been seen in a hospital, was now in the next parish, etc., and it was paraded, not as an isolated instance of an atrocity, but as a typical instance of a common practice.[47]

Although many claimed to have seen them walking about thus mutilated, no evidence of any such handless children was ever actually confirmed. Signor Nitti, Italian Prime Minister during the war, mentions this atrocity story in his memoirs, stating that "every case investigated proved to be a myth."[48]

Often, when in actual life we cannot get what we want, we daydream that our desires and instincts have been fulfilled, and that is better than nothing. Atrocity stories are a particularly nasty form of collective daydreaming. They are lapped up by a great part of the public with the same delight with which they formerly witnessed executions. Behind the curtain of self-righteousness, horror, and indignation, the atrocity-monger hides the lurid attraction to cruelty which lurks in his mind, and vicariously commits the very act he condemns. It is a rare virtue to face really unpleasant facts. If the public were simply repelled by atrocities, they would avoid hearing about them. Actually, a great number of people, far from shunning atrocities, seek them out, show a positive greed for them, and, in a terrified delight,

---

46 See Robert W. Desmond, *The Press and World Affairs* (London: D. Appleton-Century Co., 1937), p. 162 n. 31:

> In the Boer War, General Smuts and Louis Botha, as leaders of the Boers, were alleged to have been poisoning wells, shooting prisoners and indulging in other atrocities later ascribed to Germans by Allied propagandists in 1914–1918. Yet, after the Boer War, those gentlemen became highly respected and honored in Great Britain, even as Germany's Field Marshal von Hindenburg became honored and respected in Allied countries after the Great War.

47 Ponsonby, *Falsehood in War-Time*, p. 79.

48 Ibid., p. 81.

are positively attracted by them. Psychologically speaking, horror and fascination are the obverse and reverse of the same medal. The psychologist is not particularly impressed by the kindness of a person who cannot start the day without getting in his morning paper his quota of bombings, massacres, mutilations, outrages against women and children, and other atrocities. Similarly we will tend to distrust a clergyman who spends his time in brothels because he must fight the white slave traffic.

For a whole century, the British public has required a regular diet of incessant atrocity stories for their peace of mind.[49] They crave them as a source of vicarious satisfaction for suppressed and repressed instincts. The best atrocity propaganda has sex appeal, with schoolgirl complexion all over. The "Crucified Soldier" was a quite palatable piece of propaganda in the *London Times*, but American papers went one better: they transformed the crucified Canadian into a naked girl who was nailed to a barn-door. A play which had the blessing of President Wilson was based on this new version of an old story.[50] Stern laws, backed up by a sensitive conscience, withhold from sex-starved citizens the more amusing specimens of pornographic literature. In consequence people resort to stories about rape, preferably in front of husbands and fathers. The Bolsheviks were reported to have violated the "Women's Battalion of Death" after their surrender in 1917. "A young woman, ravished by the enemy, yields secret satisfaction to a host of vicarious ravishers on the other side of the border."[51] Some identify themselves with the rapist, others with the raped, according to sex and personal inclination.

---

49 I suppose that I must have overlooked some examples, but here is the list I have gathered of atrocities reported in British newspapers in the past century: **1835** onwards: Palmerston interferes in the domestic politics of Belgium, Portugal, Spain; various atrocities in Africa. **1849**: General Haynau suppresses Hungarian insurrection. **1857–1858**: Indian Mutiny. **1860** onwards: Various massacres of Christians by Turks. **1850–1864**: Tai-ping Rebellion. **1863**: Russian atrocities in Poland. **1870–1871**: Siege of Paris. **1875**: Turkish atrocities in Bosnia. **1876**: Turkish atrocities in Bulgaria. **1878** onwards: Zulu, Hottentot, Burmese, Afghan, and North-West Frontier atrocities. **1883–1898**: Mahdi atrocities. **1895**: Turkish atrocities in Armenia. **1899–1900**: Boxer Rebellion. **1899–1902**: Boer atrocities. **1900** onwards: Tsarist atrocities against revolutionaries and Jews. **1895–1913**: Congo atrocities. **1903** onwards: Macedonian atrocities. **1914–1918**: German atrocities. **1915–1918**: Turkish atrocities in Armenia. **1918** onwards: White Terror and Red Terror in Russia. **1919–1922**: The Black and Tans in Ireland. **1920's**: English and Indian atrocities in India, cruelty to Negroes and Jews in the USA, Japanese cruelty to prisoners, Balkan cruelties, etc. **1933** onwards: Nazi atrocities. **1934**: Spanish atrocities in Oviedo. **1935**: Italian and Abyssinian atrocities. **1936**: Japanese atrocities in China.

50 *Editors: The reference is to an anti-German atrocity story of World War I, later morphed into an account falsely attributing victimization not to a Canadian soldier but to a naked young woman in the French town of Suippes, and adapted by the American essayist and dramatist Francis Neilson. See James Hayward,* Myths & Legends of the First World War *(Stroud: The History Press, Ltd., 2002).*

51 Lasswell, *Propaganda Technique in the World War*, p. 82.

Some authors are said to embarrass their printers by using up all the available type for "I." In the harassed printing offices of some newspapers and publishers there must be by now a shortage of letters which make up the word "rape." The conquest of countries like Abyssinia, Manchuria, Austria, etc. is so much more pleasant to read about when we add the sexual flavour of the word rape.

Soviet Russia was said to violate her women by law, when, in the fantasy of her enemies, she "nationalised" them. The condition in which we find many Greek statues suggests that there is an impulse in men to mutilate women's breasts. When our Liberals learn that barbaric Nazis burn swastikas on Czech women's breasts, they veil their primitive titillation with civilised outrage. The Nazis, in their turn, delight in describing how innocent Christian girls are ravished by Jews. This "mongrel race of curs" is "driven by [its] blood and by [its] inborn abnormal sensuality to ravish non-Jewish women and girls."[52] A similar mentality leaked out in cartoons like that printed in *Ulk* in 1916, showing a burly John Bull waving a whip over a prostrate female figure labelled "Egypt."[53] In the USA and South Africa, Negroes are smeared with the imputed rape of white women, and much brutality is justified by such accusations. Behind all this we cannot help perceiving the lewd and lascivious mind of a civilised population.

A Typical Atrocity Story

In 1918, the Allied armies in France required Chinese coolie labour. In order to kindle the flame of a horrified moral indignation among the Chinese, the Allies invented the "corpse factory."[54] The story goes that the Germans, a thorough race, were using the corpses of their enemies to make them into food for swine, and into margarine for their troops. Verifiably and admittedly untrue, it nevertheless played successfully on Chinese ideas of the sacredness of the dead, ideas which to a certain extent are also our own. The mental mechanisms behind a story of this kind can best be explained by an analysis of pages 13 to 16 of the *Daily Mirror* of September 28, 1937, which contain all the salient features of a good atrocity story. The subconscious mind of the editor was apparently particularly well-attuned to the theme.

Even the most superficial observer will see at once that of these pictures, whether owing to accident or design, numbers 3, 4, 10, 11, and 12 appeal to the horror of dead bodies; 1, 3, 4, 8, and 10 to aggressiveness; 2, 7, and 9 to the sex

---

52 Mowrer, *Germany Puts the Clock Back*, p. 232, quoting from *Der Stürmer*, October, 1931.

53 *Editors: Ulk was a German satirical publication printed by Rudolf Mosse from 1872 to 1933.*

54 *Editors: In* Falsehood in War-Time, *p. 102, Ponsonby describes the "corpse factory," or* Kadaververwertungsanstalt, *as "one of the most revolting lies invented during the war, the dissemination of which throughout not only this country [England] but the world was encouraged and connived at by both the Government and the Press."*

Tuesday, September 28, 1937 THE DAILY MIRROR Page 13

KEEP IT DARK

By CASSANDRA

THERE'S no doubt that the Americans who have arrived over here mean to do business in the film world.

The place is jammed with technicians and stars who plan to give English movie-goers a good time.

I wish them all the luck in the world.

But I hope they understand what we want.

And I hope their understanding of the British mind is a little better than that of Louis B. Mayer, the Hollywood film executive, who recently said:—

"Once I had the honour of parading before his late Majesty King George V in a suit of armour, when he visited my home town in Canada—so I think I can say I understand Britishers."

* * *

Postcard

Here is a postcard that is now on sale in Devonshire.

If you will look at it closely—it is rather a poor photograph—you will see that it is a stag in the water being pursued by a hound.

There is nothing unusual in this.

But the title printed on the picture is a masterpiece of cruel irony.

It says:—

"A refreshing plunge in the Exe."

* * *

Just about a record for sheer callous glee.

* * *

Holiday Hint

One of the best holiday hints I have read for some time:—

"Do not forget to take a packet of ready-stamped envelopes and postcards. If you are sending a letter that is liable to be opened by someone to whom it is not addressed, fasten down the flap with the white of an egg. Then it cannot be steamed open."

* * *

Boy! Bring me pen, paper, ink and half a dozen new laid.

* * *

Political Notes

Political news for to-day is confined to one solitary crack from Popeye, who has somehow strayed into this column:—

Pooey to dictipators from me!

Correction

In this column on September 25 I translated "Juden sind unser ungluck" to read "Jews bring unhappiness and bad luck."

Innumerable people have written to me pointing out that the true meaning is:—

"Jews are our bad luck," or
"Jews are our misfortune."

* * *

My apologies to my readers, Jews, Germans and offended linguists.

* * *

Cynical Readers

A reader in Ceylon sends me a little advertisement from the Ceylon *Daily News*:—

"Wanted—immediately, a governess to look after six children. Christian preferred."

* * *

What a lot of cynical folks there are around. This reader grimly remarks:—

"How's this for optimism?"

BAIL IS REFUSED IN £65,000 SHARES CHARGES

IT was stated at the Mansion House, London, yesterday that £65,000 was involved in an alleged share-pushing conspiracy when four men were again remanded.

The four men were George Vivian Woods, thirty-four, of Gloucester-place, W.; Haydon Randolph Hamilton-Mowforth, forty-three; John Whitaker Campbell, forty-one, of Collingham-gardens, Kensington—all described as company directors—and Sam Rockfelt, thirty-two, a tobacconist, of Carysfort-road, Stoke Newington, London.

They were accused of conspiring with others to cheat and defraud people who might be induced to part with moneys to the Carlisle Investment Trust, Ltd., for the purchase of shares.

Bail of £2,000 was granted to Hamilton-Mowforth, Campbell and Rockfelt. The police opposed bail for Woods, saying he had failed to divulge his nationality.

Woods denied he was an alien.

Mr. Gwatkin, prosecuting: I place Hamilton-Mowforth as one of the principals and Woods as another, because soon after he became associated with the company, its circular letter was sent out to various shareholders in a gold mine asking them to consider the question of the Carlisle Trust taking part of the shares in part payment of other shares.

FIGURE 1.4.1 (1) A postcard (the small image in the left column) showing a stag being hunted, and described as "Just about a record for sheer callous glee." (2) An almost-naked woman in an advertisement for Celanese.

Source: *Daily Mirror,* September 28, 1937, p. 13. Daily Mirror/Mirrorpix.

Page 14 "THIEVES' PICNIC," latest and greatest SAINT serial by— THE DAILY MIRRO

Civilised Nations Salute the Enemy's Dead, but—

"HONOURABLE" JAPANESE USE THE BODIES FOR BAYONET PRACTICE "TO SHARPEN THEIR KNIVES"

WE give you pictures to-day of the greatest barbarians in war in the thousands of years of the human race:—

JAPANESE !

Always, civilised nations have honoured, saluted, the bodies of their gallant foes, the dead who gave life for country.

Now look at these pictures. They were taken by an English Press photographer with a hidden camera.

They show dead Chinese being used as targets for bayonet and sabre practice. Strapped upright to poles, the bodies are pierced again and again by the steel that has already taken their lives. The Japanese call it "sharpening their knives."

"Honourable" Japanese they have named themselves. They bore another name in the West for many years—"Yellow Devils of the East."

Take your choice after you've read a bit further.

\+ + +

Twelve Chinese junks were rocking peacefully on the waters near Hong Kong. The occupants were fishing.

Suddenly, a Japanese submarine appeared. The guns were manned, the fishing fleet was blown out of the water.

AND THE SUBMARINE SAILED AWAY WITHOUT TRYING TO ASSIST THE SURVIVORS STRUGGLING IN THE WATER OR CLINGING TO WRECKAGE.

"Honourable" Japanese. . . .

Held rigid by poles, the body receives a vicious bayonet thrust.

Sword Practice—Human Body for a Target

THESE SUFFER MOST IN THIS WAR

Women and children, these are the chief sufferers in the holocaust in the Far East.

Typical of such helpless victims are this old Chinese woman and her little granddaughter, injured when Japanese bombers blasted their village and now, by the irony of fate, riding in a rickshaw, privilege of the rich, for the first time in their lives.

Who W

Well, the c of her, for 300,000 Am

EVERY day when Frank B at the offices of Williar Sons, solicitors, of West Bromw to whom he was managing Madeline Elizabeth Smith, dau of the partners, used to call for a talk.

She told him all about he dolls' houses; discussed ser frocks and the furniture we so to speak.

Mr. Berks, who was over seve and gave advice with the sam seriousness that he discusse with grown-ups their lega troubles. Then Mr. Berks died

In his will he left £5 to Made line "to buy a new dolls' house."

And in the picture above is Madeline with the new dolls house.

FIGURE 1.4.2 (3) Japanese soldier (with two horns on helmet) bayonets a Chinese corpse. "Held rigid by poles, the body receives a vicious bayonet thrust." (4) "Sword Practice—Human Body for a Target." A Japanese, this time with two feathers on his helmet, sticks his sword into a person. (5) Chinese refugees (old woman with child). "These suffer most in this war." (6) Child (English) with doll's house.

Source: *Daily Mirror,* September 28, 1937, p. 14. Daily Mirror/Mirrorpix.

:PTEMBER 28, 1937 —LESLIE CHARTERIS, appears to-day on page 21. Don't miss it! Page 15

A KICK IN THE PANTS FOR CAROLE!

t Fall for This Leader of the Band?

New York didn't. They were only too glad to see the last ..ke of Annie Laura Bishop, of Tupalo, Mississippi, came ..ionnaires, who defied the police and painted the town red.

There's a right and wrong way of doing most things, including giving a lady a good kick! Not satisfied with the way Fredric March did it, and thinking he was too gentle with Carole Lombard, Director William Wellman takes a lunge at her himself just to show Fredric the proper way! And the David Selznick Technicolour film they're making in Hollywood is called "Nothing Sacred"!

Left: Let's kiss and be friends—Fredric and Carole making it up.

FIGURE 1.4.3 (7) A girl with pronounced sex appeal. "Who Wouldn't Fall for This Leader of the Band?" (8) Director William Wellman gives Carole Lombard a "good kick." (9) "Let's kiss and be friends—Frederic & Carole making it up."

Source: *Daily Mirror,* September 28, 1937, p. 15. Daily Mirror/Mirrorpix.

FIGURE 1.4.4 (10) A "Buck Ryan" cartoon strip, showing somebody using a skeleton to knock out somebody else. (11) A picture of a Hollywood costume giving the appearance of a contorted human body, with an arm growing out of the throat. (12) Popeye's girlfriend Olive Oyl terrified by a ghost.

Source: *Daily Mirror,* September 28, 1937, p. 16. Daily Mirror/Mirrorpix.

instinct; 8 to sexual aggressiveness (sadism[55]); and in 1, 3, and 4, the aggressiveness is socialised.

The obvious appeal to the sanctity of the dead is underlined by the text. We read:

> Civilised Nations Salute the Enemy's Dead, but—
> "HONOURABLE" JAPANESE USE THE BODIES FOR BAYONET PRACTICE "TO SHARPEN THEIR KNIVES"
>
> We give you pictures to-day of the greatest barbarians in war in the thousands of years of the human race:—
>
> **JAPANESE!**
>
> Always, civilised nations have honoured, saluted, the bodies of their gallant foes, the dead who gave life for country.
>
> Now look at these pictures. They were taken by an English Press photographer with a hidden camera.
>
> **They show dead Chinese being used as targets for bayonet and sabre practice. Strapped upright to poles, the bodies are pierced again and again by the steel that has already taken their lives. The Japanese call it "sharpening their knives."**
>
> "Honourable" Japanese they have named themselves. They bore another name in the West for many years—"Yellow Devils of the East."

The setting, or position, of the pictures also deserves our attention. The atrocity pictures (3 and 4) and the sex pictures (7 and 9) cannot help fusing together in the mind of the delighted readers. The resulting sentiment is sexually tinged aggressiveness. In picture 8, the sadism is appealed to openly, without even the pretext of a high ideal.

The atrocity pictures of the *Daily Mirror* evoke in their viewer a horror coupled with delight. The delight was evident, for instance, when they were shown about in a big office. Enchanted office workers exclaimed, "How horrid! Oh, let me see it again." A critic, referring to a photograph of a child torn apart by a Japanese bomb printed the week before in the *News Chronicle*, quoted an acquaintance in the *New Statesman* (October 2, 1937):

> "I couldn't sleep at night for it," said Mrs. Tomkins, the publican's wife whom I've never known to be interested in politics before. "I could just hear that little child screaming, and my husband says to me put that paper in the

55 Sadism is a normal component of the sex instinct, ferocity a normal part of the primitive and uninhibited sexual act. Freud defined sadism as "an aggressive component of the sexual instinct which has become independent and exaggerated and has been brought to the foreground by displacement." From "Three Contributions to the Theory of Sex," in *The Basic Writings of Sigmund Freud* trans. A. A. Brill (New York: Modern Library, 1938): 553–629 at 569 (1st ed. 1905, *Drei Abhandlungen zur Sexualtheorie*).

> fire and think of something else, *but I was kind of fascinated with it and kept looking at it all day long* [emphasis added].

In extreme mental states, the law of the unity of opposites manifests itself most clearly. The words "pleasure" and "pain," for instance, have a definite meaning only for intermediary states. In the shock of extreme pain or pleasure both become indistinguishable. Similarly, excessive love is ever ready to change into excessive hate, and *vice versa*. Excessive reverence lives very near blasphemy. Death and everything connected with it, as it involves the total destruction of all things that are dear to us, stimulates an excessive reaction. Dead bodies therefore both fascinate and horrify. This element of fascination accounts for the "pull" of ghost stories, which represent the dead as walking, and of many atrocity stories.

I conclude with a quotation from Thomas à Kempis, who, noting that one is better employed in self-criticism than in judging others, summed up the perils of atrocity propaganda better than anybody else: "We generally judge of persons and things as they either oppose or gratify our private views and inclinations; and, blinded by the impetuous motions of self-love, are easily led from the judgment of truth."[56]

56 Thomas à Kempis, *The Imitation of Christ* (trans. John Payne, 1785), 1.14.2.

1.5

TRIBAL SENTIMENTS

Once, beside Lake Ochrida, a mule driver gave me a lesson in politics. The Albanians, he said, are the world's greatest people, for "we conquered the earth for Alexander the Great." Since then I have tried never to forget that each people is, to itself, incomparable.

Edgar Mowrer[1]

Like so many cocks crowing on their dunghills, the citizens of the nations of Europe are engaged in an ardent boasting competition. We may as well book a seat in the theatre, and watch the more vocal competitors performing. Their efforts are both entertaining and instructive. The more so since the performers, like the band of Mickey Mouse playing the overture to *William Tell*, are conjuring a storm that will soon blow them sky high.

There is first the *Frenchman* who has learned at school that France is "the educator of the human race," and that the French are the finest soldiers in the world. No other nation has so many memorable feats to her credit. She is the "soldier of justice." She works hard, steadily, and modestly for the salvation of mankind. Unfortunately the French make their claims for the universal validity of their thought in a language which loses half its flavour in the process of translation. With inimitable charm they tell us, "Tout homme a deux pays, le sien et puis la France," and "O France idéale, tu es le Verbe du monde! Quand tu ne parle plus, le droit disparaît sur toute la surface de la terre."[2]

1 Mowrer, *Germany Puts the Clock Back*, p. 30.

2 "Everybody has two countries, his own and then France." Henri de Bornier, from *La Fille de Roland: drame en quatre actes en vers* (1875). "Oh perfect France, you are the Word of the world! When you cease to talk, Right disappears from the surface of the earth." Mme Edgar Quinet, from "La France Idéale" in *Revue Moderne*, vol. 47 (August 10, 1868), pp. 581–590.

DOI: 10.4324/9781003363408-7

We turn to the more congenial idiom of the *Briton* who does not bother very much to instruct the foreigner about his own perfections. He believes that the foreigner has heard of them before. Yet, conscious that they "are the most self-deprecating people on earth," the Britons sometimes cannot help telling each other the simple truth about themselves.[3] The more intelligent Englishman finds the most sparkling gems of nationalist thought collected each week in *Forward* or *The New Statesman*. An industrious Dutchman, G. J. Renier, shows by a random selection of quotations from newspapers that "apart from a relatively small minority, the English are convinced that they are, that they own, and that they produce, all that is best in the world."[4] London is the most brilliant and the healthiest big city in the world. England's landscape, her zoo, her Underground stations, her judicial system, her judges and juries, her secret service and police, her civil service and post office, the English home, English butlers, footmen, grooms and waiters, the produce of her home farms and gardens, the play of her girls, the British press, British cooks, the system of education, the British climate "taken all round"—they are all the best and the finest in the world.[5]

Nor is the *Teuton* hiding his light under a bushel. "Each people has its day in history, but the day of the German is the harvest of time as a whole," said Schiller.[6] As the born rulers of other nations the Germans are a "shining people of half-gods."[7] Werner Sombart, a prominent economist, found in zoology a scientific basis for German superiority. "As the German bird, the eagle, soars high above all the creatures of this earth, so the German shall feel himself elevated above all the peoples which surround him, and which he sees under him in a boundless depth."[8] Religion equally favours the German: "Germany is the center of the world and the world cannot exist without Germany.... Germany is the Kingdom of God."[9] It is well known in Germany now that the Nordic race is the noblest blossom on the human tree. The Nordics alone are capable of creating and sustaining civilisation. Liberty, loyalty, and freedom from prejudice are the main roots of the German

---

3 *Manchester Guardian*, January 16, 1930.

4 G. J. Renier, *The English: Are They Human?* (London: Unwin Brothers, Ltd., 1931), p. 44.

5 Renier gives chapter and verse for each of these claims. His book is well worth consulting. It may help to open the eyes of Englishmen to the degree to which their neighbours among the modern nations of the world—and perhaps themselves—are soaked in nationalist self-complacency. Almost any newspaper, almost any conversation about international problems and foreign countries will yield further material.

6 "Jedes Volk hat seinen Tag in der Geschichte, doch der Tag des Deutschen ist die Ernte der ganzen Zeit." Friedrich Schiller, sketches for *Deutsche Grösse*, an unfinished poem of 1797 not discovered until 1871.

7 "Ein leuchtendes Volk von Halbgöttern." Atto Ammon, *Die natürliche Auslese beim Menschen* (*Natural Selection among Humans*) (Jena: Gustav Fischer, 1893), p. 181.

8 "So wie des Deutschen Vogel, der Aar, hoch über allem Getier dieser Erde schwebt, so soll der Deutsche sich erhaben fühlen über alles Gevölk, das ihn umgibt und das er unter sich in grenzenloser Tiefe erblickt." Werner Sombart, *Händler und Helden: patriotische Besinnungen* (München: Duncker & Humblot, 1915), p. 143.

9 Franz Schauwecker, quoted in Mowrer, *Germany Puts the Clock Back*, p. 37.

nature. In 1924, enthusiastic students at Heidelberg University informed me that all great men had been Nordics and thereby Germans, including Confucius, Genghis Khan, and the rulers of the Incas. They probably did not know that in 1896, the Korean minister of education Sin Ki Sun issued a manual which contained the statement,

> How grand and glorious is the empire of China, the middle kingdom! She is the largest and richest in the world. The grandest men in the world have all come from the middle empire. Europe is too far away from the centre of civilization, which is the middle kingdom; hence Russians, Turks, English, French, Germans, and Belgians look more like little beasts than men, and their language sounds like the chirping of fowls.[10]

Until recently, the rival claims of the *Italians* received less attention. They were not backed up sufficiently by military prowess. Yet the descendants of the ancient Romans can look back on a long tradition of boasting. About 1850, Vincenzo Gioberti exclaimed, "Italians are the elect people, the exemplary people, the creative people, the Israel of the modern age."[11] In 1877, Giosuè Carducci modestly asserted, "Everything that is civil, great, and august in the world is still Roman."[12] And in 1937, Signor Mussolini hit the nail well on the head when he said,

> We have long had proof that Italians are the most intelligent people in the world. Now we know that Italians are the most courageous as well, for only a courageous people could have resisted, undaunted and unafraid, against fifty two nations.[13]

On the other hand, no amount of literacy seems to protect people against tribal sentiments. Public opinion credits scientists and philosophers with a single-minded pursuit of truth, but in actual practice, their reasoning power only too willingly gives in to tribal sentiments. A collection of tribal remarks from scientific writers would fill not only one library, but two or three.

Even Aristotle, opposing the Greeks as a race (*ethnē*) to the barbarians, naïvely reiterates the convictions of his contemporaries. In his *Politics*, he calls the barbarians "more servile in their nature than the Greeks," claims that they "have no class of

---

10 From the *Confucianist Scholar's Handbook of the Latitudes and Longitudes*, quoted in Hubert Howe Bancroft, *The New Pacific*, rev. ed. (New York: The Bancroft Company, 1912), p. 101.

11 "L'Italia è il popolo eletto, il popolo tipico, il popolo creatore, l'Israele dell' età moderna." Vincenzo Gioberti, *Il gesuita moderno* vol. 5 (Losanna, 1846/47), p. 461, quoted in Robert Michels, *Der Patriotismus: Prolegomena zu seiner soziologischen Analyse* (München: Duncker & Humblot, 1929), p. 14.

12 "E tutto che al mondo è civile, grande, augusto, egli è romano ancora." From *Delle Odi Barbare Libro I: Nell'annuale della fondazione di Roma* (1877), stanza 4, quoted in Maurice Muret's brochure, *Le nationalisme italien* (1910), p. 10.

13 Quoted in *Yorkshire Evening Post*, Wednesday, April 21, 1937, p. 9.

natural rulers," quotes with approval Euripides' dictum, "'Tis meet that Greeks should rule barbarians," and concludes that "barbarians and slaves are the same in nature."[14] He advised Alexander the Great, according to Plutarch, that "he should care for the Greeks as for his friends, but use the others like animals or plants."[15] Accustomed to frame things on a rational plane, Aristotle explains:

> The nations inhabiting the cold places and those of *Europe* are full of spirit but somewhat deficient in intelligence and skill, so that they continue comparatively free, but lacking in political organization and capacity to rule their neighbours. The people of *Asia* on the other hand are intelligent and skilful in temperament, but lack spirit, so that they are in continuous subjection and slavery. But the *Greek* race participates in both characters, just as it occupies the middle position geographically, for it is both spirited and intelligent; hence it continues to be free and to have very good political institutions, and to be capable of ruling all mankind if it attains constitutional unity.[16]

Tribal sentiments are universal and inseparable from social life. An accumulation of examples can, of course, not provide a proof of universality. Book-readers, proud of their own intelligence, may even be inclined to brush them aside as examples of exceptional stupidity. Advocates of a rational social system, whose wish fantasies cloud their field of vision, will minimise the importance of sentiments which are so serious an obstacle to their schemes for world reform. In order to get the tribal emotions into a properly scientific perspective, we have to study their origin and function. In this chapter I intend to show that their origin lies in the most basic features of social life itself, and that their function is indispensable to social life as such. In the following pages, I try to establish three propositions:

1. Feelings of tribal superiority are not attached to nations only, but to almost any social group.
2. Tribal boasting relieves the sense of inferiority of the oppressed.
3. The feeling of superiority, together with the other tribal sentiments, springs from the inevitable isolation of one social group from others.

To prevent misunderstandings, "tribal units" will include nation, race, profession, and religion, as well as abstract and correlative groups, among others. "Tribal sentiments" are those sentiments which become attached to tribal units. These include a sense of superiority (or inferiority), dread, suspicion, anger, aversion, reticence, reserve, etc.

---

14 Aristotle, *Politics* 1285a, 1252b, trans. Harris Rackham.

15 Plutarch, *De Alexandri magni fortuna aut virtute* 1.6.

16 Aristotle, *Politics* 1327b, trans. Harris Rackham. Italics E. C.

Throughout this chapter I find myself, however, faced with an almost insuperable difficulty. Tribal sentiments appear in such an innumerable variety of disguises that my examples and illustrations can cover only a tiny proportion of them. Tastes vary. A vocal and blatant affirmation of sentiments often repels, as tiresome and vulgar, those who cultivate a noble restraint of their feelings. Differences in temperament drive some into self-idolisation, others into self-complacency, others again into an inert self-satisfaction. The language used may be naïve,[17] sophisticated, statesmanlike,[18] or prophetic.[19] Well-fed people may be quite tolerant, broad-minded, and good-humoured about their tribalism. The self-assured may even arise to ironical detachment.

It also has to be borne in mind that emotions rarely achieve logical consistency. The human mind is capable of harbouring any amount of self-contradiction. When one feels like it, one may find some good in other tribes. Occasionally one may deprecate one's own. The nationalists of one country, out of hatred for internationalism, often commend the nationalists of another country for their national pride. Given proper circumstances, a feeling of superiority over the collective image of another nation may not prevent individuals from reaching some degree of understanding and friendship with individuals of another nation or tribe. Without going to the length of regarding themselves as the very best people, many members of the human race are more modestly content to think of themselves as very good people. The luxury of belonging to a top or "A-1" nation is usually reserved for the citizens of the "powers." But all these shades and variations of tribal opinion do not affect the essence of the matter. In this context we can ignore them.

I have been told that this chapter lacks conviction because it takes no account of the really intelligent people who are exempt from childish tribal sentiments. Now, whether these "intelligent people" exist or not, in propaganda they do not count for much. If they existed, they would form a small and feeble minority of disembodied spirits, hopelessly out of touch with the majority. Their impotent moanings and perpetual grumblings can be safely ignored in the practical organisation and management of society.

---

17 For example, "The voices of Englishmen are the most agreeable in the world."

18 For example, in 1892 (*The London Times*, November 17), Lord Rosebery claimed that the British Empire was "the greatest secular agency for good the world has ever seen."

19 For example, Michels (*Der Patriotismus*, p. 38, trans. E. C.) reports that the German philosopher Eucken in 1915

> made a very deep impression when he raised his finger and accused England before the court of history and of the entire world, and attributed to her the greatest guilt, and how then a priest, in front of the altar of the spirit, blessed the German people in their sacred fight for the soul of mankind.

Tribal Groups

Sentiments of tribal superiority are not only met with in connection with national groups. Participation in almost any social group, in the widest sense, can act as a basis for a pleasing sense of superiority. Most social groups are therefore automatically tribal groups. One may be proud of one's religion, profession, class, sex, sport club, family. The habit of overemphasising the values attached to any of these groups easily shades into a habit of exaggerating its relative importance in the world, and generates a more or less conscious conviction of the inferiority of those who are excluded from its excellence.[20]

Because they are so often overlooked, I want to draw special attention to the tribal feelings attached to those more abstract groups which are either very loosely organised or not organised at all, whose members are spatially dispersed and rarely act together. Because their members, however, share in some common vital distinction, such groups are particularly fertile breeding grounds for tribal sentiment. Most of them are correlative groups, like "whites vs. non-whites," "civilised people vs. primitives and savages," "decent and law-abiding people vs. criminals," "men vs. women," "the reasonable and intelligent people vs. the stupid masses," "town-dwellers vs. country yokels," "the washed vs. the unwashed." Since an individual participates in many groups at the same time, he can pile up many tribal perfections. Adding together the various groups to which he belongs, we may get such a specimen of mankind as a civilised white Presbyterian law-abiding English lawyer, male, intelligent, clean, and well-dressed. He should be purring with self-satisfaction. As his opposite we may construct a savage, dark-skinned, illiterate, and dirty "animist" woman in rags. Let us imagine her in rural Rajasthan, say in a Banswara jail. Biologically alike, the two are tribally worlds apart.

In those circles whose monotonous conversation bores the clever intellectual, the topic "oh, *women*..." (you know what they are like) and "oh, *men*..." (likewise) proves a source of inexhaustible delight. To look at the matter from one side only, men often bolster up their shaky self-confidence by dwelling complacently on the supposed inferiority of women. This sort of futile talk compensates them for the fears and humiliations which their mothers inflicted upon them, and their wives, sisters, mistresses, and the women they could not get. The more thoroughly sex is repressed, the greater the fear that one might be overwhelmed by sexual

---

20 The American social psychologist Emory S. Bogardus ("The Occupational Attitude," *Journal of Applied Sociology* 7 [1923]: 173–174) describes this "occupational egocentrism":

> A person who has enjoyed his work in a given occupation and has succeeded in it, is apt to feel that 'his' occupation or profession is the most important of all.... An anonymous writer, for example, illustrates the point when he says: "The miller thinks that the wheat grows only in order to keep his mill going."

attraction. The most abusive slander of women can therefore be found among celibates.[21] Long usage has evolved a number of stereotyped and consoling stock rationalisations: women's brains weigh less than those of men; the female mind is superficial, capricious, and uncreative; it knows neither moderation nor independence of opinion; its reasoning processes obey a special kind of inferior logic.[22] The eternal reference to the subject seems to indicate that tribal animosity between the sexes satisfies a deep-seated need.

The Drives behind Tribal Sentiments

In order to understand tribal sentiments we must find out what satisfaction people get from them. Nothing is so natural that it has no reason.[23] To a certain extent, we are pushed, as it were, into a tribal attitude by an urge in our ancestral blood. Primitive tribes are as proud of themselves as modern nations are. A tribal name of the Kiowa people of the Great Plains means "the real or principal people." The Greenland Eskimos hurt European sensibilities when they took it for granted that the Europeans had been sent to Greenland to learn virtue and good manners from the Greenlanders. "You'll soon be quite like a Greenlander" is the highest form of praise given to a European. A South American tribe, the Bakairi, uses the same word for "good" and "we"; "others" conveys the meaning "bad." This is tribal mentality in a nutshell.

But obviously the mere fact that our more primitive ancestors were talking a lot of conceited rubbish about themselves is no sufficient reason for us to do likewise.

Sharing in Glory

The greatest mental advantage of tribal sentiments is that they increase the average person's estimate of his own importance.

In a class society most people suffer from the feeling that they are of no importance, that they are "nobody in particular." They lead a drab and commonplace existence in standardised houses, on standardised food, with standardised

21 See Saint John Chrysostom, quoted in "Middle-Age Spiritualism," *The Popular Science Monthly* 16 (January, 1880), p. 358:

> What is woman but an enemy of friendship, an unavoidable punishment, a necessary evil, a natural temptation, a desirable affliction, a constantly flowing source of tears, a wicked work of nature covered with a shining varnish?

22 A fine collection of such stereotypes may be found in Stevenson's *Home Book of Quotations*, under "Woman" (entry 1: "The weaker sex, to piety more prone").

23 It goes without saying that the friction of economic interests contributes much to national and racial antagonisms. In this context, however, I have to single out the mental side of the matter.

newspapers, in monotonous and undistinguished jobs. Naturally they try to find some distinction to mark them off from other human beings. In a certain school a boy was the worst in everything, yet he appeared to be content with his insignificance. The reason for his contentment was that he cherished one secret pride—he could spit farther than any other boy in the school.

Everybody, in some way or another, tries to find compensation for a sense of inferiority. Socially most useful are those individuals who find distinction in real achievement. Others, devoid of special abilities, find other ways. One has been to school with Thomas Hardy, and nobody is allowed to forget it. Another can drink more than anybody else in the village. Another still can make the best pancakes in the country. One person gains distinction from the possession of a parrot which can whistle. Somebody else is the only person to know that the fall of the gold standard was prophesied by Daniel.

The middle classes like to have in their homes pieces of furniture, etchings or pictures, which are either considered to be "unique," or which are in some rather doubtful way associated with an historical person. This or that school tie distinguishes them from the common herd. Well-to-do circles spend much of their time looking for the "unusual." To be unusual, whether it is a novel they are reading, or the colour of their car, or a new cocktail, warrants the highest praise. For some guineas these persons are able to buy distinction in Oxford Street in the form of "distinctive" and "individual" pullovers, frocks, hats, etc.

A more common way of achieving distinction is by participating or sharing in the importance of some collective entity. Everybody identifies himself with some social group. Our vanity enjoys drinking in the prestige reflected upon us from our family, workshop, football club, city, profession, office, nation, and Empire. Some time ago, for example, there was a petty official by the name of Jones who accepted that the councillors of his town might treat him with contempt, but insisted that they should beware of slighting "His Majesty's Representative" (i.e. the same Mr. Jones). The propagandist who knows his job makes people feel that they are of great importance because they belong to a certain very important class of people, because they are Englishmen, or workers, or prosperous, or dentists, or teachers.

The achievements of this group add to our personal pride and self-assertion. We can share in the glory of a social body or institution without contributing anything in particular to it. Persons who combine the muscles of a guinea pig with the courage of a rabbit may feel elated at the idea of "our glorious navy." In Germany I noticed that just the most illiterate and dull-witted individuals were particularly fond of boasting that they belonged to the "country of Goethe, Schiller, and Kant." As Lord Bryce once observed, "The less a man has to be proud of, the more proud he will be of his colour."[24] The mere fact that a person is English may put him—in

24 James Bryce, *The American Commonwealth*, 2nd ed., vol. 2 (London: Macmillan & Co., 1889), p. 306.

his own estimation—above the remainder of mankind. An Englishman may be as mangy as he can possibly be, but he can still console himself with imperialist sentiments which provide him with foreigners and coloured people to look down upon. He belongs to a top nation, and that idea lifts him up, even if he feels that he himself is rotten and small.

Tribal sentiments thus give a man the same sort of satisfaction which he may get from keeping a dog. The whole social order seems to regard him as something that fell off a dustcart. The dog, for him, has a compensatory value when everything conspires to keep him down and humiliate him. As Yaffle, one of our few genuine political humourists, said in *Reynolds News*:

> [The unemployed man] goes home wondering why his parents made such a bloomer[25], and then he meets the dog, who looks up into his face and says: "Gosh, what a piece of work is old George! How noble in reason! How infinite in faculty! In form and moving, how admirable! In action how like an angel! In apprehension how like a god!" And he pulls himself together again and says: "Perhaps there is something in it."[26]

In other words: A person owns as an Englishman—or as a Frenchman, German, Italian, Albanian, Brazilian, Ecuadorian, just as the case may be—all the perfection and distinction he lacks as an individual. No wonder that he clings to the patriotic sentiments without which he would drop into the abyss of spiritual nothingness. No wonder that patriotism is a popular sentiment. Its fervour grows as one descends the social scale.

Tribal Isolation

To complete the picture, we have now to deal with the chief factor behind tribal sentiments, a factor inherent in social life as such: tribal isolation.

Birds of a feather flock together. Human beings tend to congregate in communities or groups of limited size. The members of one group are united by common customs, habits, ceremonies, symbols, superstitions. They are separated and, to a certain degree, isolated from those of another group not only in space, but equally as much by differences in looks, food, gestures, language, habits and customs, attitudes and ideas. Members of different groups cannot get together easily. It is challenging to feel at one's ease with someone from an utterly foreign culture. His reactions are unknown, misunderstandings abound, and even his facial expressions tell us very little. The development of commerce and travel has broken down some of this isolation, but much of it remains:

---

25 *Editors: Dated British slang for "blunder."*

26 Yaffle, "They Mustn't Keep Dogs" in *Reynolds News*, Sunday, May 23, 1937, p. 2.

The stranger within my gate,
He may be true or kind,
But he does not talk my talk—
I cannot feel his mind.
I see the face and the eyes and the mouth,
But not the soul behind.

The men of my own stock
They may do ill or well,
But they tell the lies I am wonted to,
They are used to the lies I tell.
And we do not need interpreters
When we go to buy and sell.[27]

Kipling describes here an attitude towards outsiders which is technically known as "social distance."[28] The members of different social groups remain at a distance from each other, because they tend to "keep to themselves," and to retreat or withdraw from strangers. They can act together with people "of their own kind" only at the price of acting apart from members of an out-group. An American student once remarked to me about the Japanese that "they are all right as long as they keep a good distance from you." An occasional conversation with strangers is sometimes quite stimulating. Usually, however, one avoids the intimate contact of living together with them. They are not "easy to meet" or "close to us."

In the Indian caste system social distance is standardised and flaunted openly. "The pariah may as well think of building his house in a higher-caste district as a pig may think of going to live in his master's front room."[29] All personal contact is avoided. The approach of a pariah is considered as unholy. His shadow is hated and feared. In Malabar, the lower the caste, the greater the distance that must be kept from a Brahmin. A Nayar may not approach within six paces of the Brahmin, a Palayan within ninety-six paces. Outside India, people are less systematic in this respect, but equally firm. In the first century of our era, the Jews deliberately withdrew from Gentile contamination. They went into the Ghetto. Later on, they were forced to stay there. It is still not easy for them to mix with Gentiles on equal terms.

---

27 Kipling, from "The Stranger" (first published in 1908, included in the collection *Songs from Books* [New York: Doubleday, Page & Co., 1912]), concerning the poet's visit to Canada in 1907.

28 Bogardus devised a "social distance" testing scale which stratifies members of various national, ethnic, and racial groups with respect to one's willingness to accept a level of intimacy with them, from close kinship through degrees of progressive estrangement—i.e., from tolerating marital relations to an insistence upon total exclusion. Bogardus, "Measuring Social Distances," *Journal of Applied Sociology* 9 (1925): 299–308.

29 Godfrey Edward Phillips, *The Outcastes' Hope, or: Work among the Depressed Classes in India* (London: Church Missionary Society, 1912), p. 2.

In England, all sorts of devices keep non-white people away from intimate contact—in dwelling houses, swimming pools, hotels, tennis courts, clubs, etc. In the USA, Negroes are kept apart or "in their place." The American Negro must have the impression "that he and his race were something to be kept out of sight as much as possible, as careful housekeepers manoeuver their slops."[30] We limit our relationships with members of the out-group.

> The Negro is all right in his place, as a personal servant or as a workman, but not as an equal. The Jew is all right as a rag-picker, a peddler, or a small tailor, but not as a social equal or as a member of a college fraternity.[31]

Old American families move out of districts when Italians or Slovaks move in. A Scotch saying in Canada well illustrates the close connection between tribalism and isolation: "Oh Lord, build a wall as high as heaven between the cursed Irish and thy chosen people the Scotch." It is a vicious circle. Social isolation contributes to tribal sentiments. Tribal sentiments perpetuate and increase social isolation. Nor is tribal isolation confined to national or even racial groups. We expect cooks and servants to remain in their proper place, at a proper distance. Religious groups thrive on isolation. Lecky speaks of "the numerous efforts that were made to separate the Christian community as far as possible from the society in which it existed," namely the Roman Empire.[32] While they were strong enough to do so, Roman Catholics acted in accordance with the precept of Titus 3.10, "A heretic we avoid." Heretics are excommunicated, or removed from the community,[33] excluded from the body of the Church, and not allowed to participate in prayer and rites. In the second century AD no social contact whatsoever with heretics and the excommunicated was permitted to the faithful. The orthodox Christian had to break off all relations so that he might not be dragged into the same abyss. Even in the arena, the Catholic martyrs withdrew from the Montanists lest they should be mingled with the heretics in death.[34]

Members of different professions, without actually being repelled, may keep out of each other's way by mutual boredom. Bogardus speaks of "occupational distance," which he defines as the degree of sympathetic understanding existing between the members of any two occupations.[35] The rich keep the poor out of

30 Thomas Sigismund Stribling, *Birthright* (New York: Century & Co., 1922), p. 13.

31 Young, *Social Psychology: An Analysis of Social Behavior* (New York: A. A. Knopf, 1930), p. 450.

32 Lecky, *History of European Morals*, vol. 2, p. 101.

33 *Ex-commun-icare*.

34 But Vacant, under "Hérétique," in his *Dictionnaire de théologie catholique*, vol. 6, part 2, col. 2231 (Paris: Letouzey & Ané, 1914), explains that nowadays one can tolerate the presence of heretics at our ceremonies because of grave difficulties to the contrary.

35 Bogardus' researches revealed, among other things, the fact that college students preparing for careers in teaching and the ministry "reacted against motion picture actors, vaudeville actors, and jazz musicians, on the ground that these occupations are socially detrimental." However, students

their sight. They look away from them as from an unsightly blot on an otherwise pleasing and beautiful social landscape. In the dwellings and streets of the poor they feel ill at ease, suspecting lice, filth, sudden assault, and bugs. The food of the poor evokes the associations which pork has for Muslims. In most cases, the wealthy avoid such unpleasant shocks by keeping out of the way of the poor.

Apart from everything else, strangers require us to make a special effort at re-adaptation. We like to regulate our daily lives by smooth habits. A deeply embedded habit becomes sacred. When someone else interrupts a well-established habit of mine, I feel uneasy. In sheer self-defence I socially ban those people who, for instance, in manners at table or in the drawing room, would tend to upset my habits. I feel uncomfortable in the presence of a person with manners different from those of myself. He irritates me just as an untidy person irritates a tidy one, and vice versa. On rare occasions he may seem stimulating, but then social contact usually remains superficial and is restricted to a sort of slight mutual tickling.

The Necessity of Social Isolation

It is easy to see why members of different groups should tend to isolate themselves from one another when we consider the means by which a social group maintains, against rebellious individuals, that unity, uniformity, and coherence which are so essential to its perpetuation. Those who break the taboos of the group, whose behaviour deviates from its customs, or whose opinions differ from its well-established creeds, are punished by a social disapproval which is always, more or less clearly, a means of isolating the offender. In order to make people alike to one another, one almost invariably relies on one method: to shut out, by some kind of barrier, those who are unlike. Execution, exile, and excommunication do so very effectively. Among the Sea Dayaks of North Borneo, a quarrel not infrequently leads "to the migration of the whole house with the exception of one troublesome member and his family, who are left in inglorious isolation in the old house."[36]

Sidney and Beatrice Webb quote Trade Unionist William Crawford's speech about scabs:

> It is no use playing at shuttlecock in this important portion of our social life. Either mingle with these men in the shaft, as you do in every other place, or let them be ostracised at all times and in every place. Regard them as

in commerce and dentistry reacted favourably to these performing artists, because "the occupations in question 'add zest to life.'" Occupational (tribal) cohesion and inter-occupational competition will influence our judgement on these questions. From "Occupational Distance," *Sociology and Social Research* 13, (1928): 73–81.

36 Charles Hose and William McDougall, *The Pagan Tribes of Borneo: A Description of their Physical, Moral and Intellectual Condition, with Some Discussion of their Ethnic Relations*, vol. 2 (London: Macmillan & Co., Ltd., 1912), p. 195.

> unfit companions for yourselves and your sons, and unfit husbands for your daughters. Let them be branded, as it were, with the curse of Cain, as unfit to mingle in ordinary, honest, and respectable society. Until you make up your minds to thus completely and absolutely ostracise these goats of mankind, cease to complain as to any results that may arise from their action.[37]

With a little imagination, the reader will readily see that milder forms of social disapproval, which punish the breach of minor customs, also serve to class or mark off the offender as different: by moral indignation ("I would never dream of doing such a thing in all my life"), by sneering, ridicule, and haughtiness, by being shocked, by "cutting" people, snubbing them, giving them the cold shoulder. People who laugh together at somebody else establish a social bond and feel more kindly disposed towards one another, while treating the other as a temporary outcast.

As long as he persists in his evil ways, the dissenter is "not one of us." And unless superior social status surrounds the difference with a halo of distinction, to be different is to be wrong, and different manners are bad manners.[38] Isolation sets up fear and anxiety, and a sense of guilt, sometimes covered by a thin veneer of defiance. Shut out from his group, the isolated person loses the ability to rely on its resources. "So long as he acts in conformity with tradition he can enjoy safety and happiness, because he is relying on something much greater than his own qualities of mind and body."[39] Social pressure squeezes us out into a vacuum. Few people prefer the breathtaking desolation of social isolation to the comforting warmth of good fellowship.

The same defence mechanisms which are brought into play against deviating insiders—who behave as temporary outsiders—operate, with redoubled force, against outsiders in general. A group cannot maintain its unity and thereby itself, except in comparative isolation from other groups. Intimate contact with strangers destroys our tribal selves. When we see that quite a number of people in an out-group do everything differently, and apparently "get away with it," we may easily

---

37 Sidney and Beatrice Webb, *The History of Trade Unionism* (New York: Longmans, Green & Co., 1911), p. 280 fn.

38 I can do no more than just mention a complication which results from a conflict between two tendencies: the tendency to diversify a group, connected with feelings of superiority and inferiority, and the tendency to unify it, brought about by fear of isolation. This conflict allows some individuals to get away with being different. Making use of the crowd's respect for social superiority, they convince themselves and others that their particular brand of difference is a sign of distinction. Though hostile to innovations, a crowd may make an exception when overawed by prestige. Whereas social groups are essentially conservative, the economic conditions of industrialism have, for a time, slightly checked the conservative tendencies of group life. The prospect of added comfort through scientific and technical progress has given greater social approbation to impulses of novelty, originality, and eccentricity.

39 Alfred Reginald Radcliffe-Brown, *The Andaman Islanders: A Study in Social Anthropology* (Cambridge: Cambridge University Press, 1922), p. 382.

lose faith in the "rightness" of our doings, unless a tribal sentiment of unshakeable superiority chokes our doubts. Taboos persist because few dare to break them. Intimate contact with strangers on equal terms provides encouragement and opportunity to try out whether, for instance, it is so terrible to eat ham sandwiches. Taboos prosper only in social isolation. In intimate contact with strangers, taboos lose much of their binding force because they cease to look so absolutely right. Tribal behaviour is no more ridiculous than sexual behaviour. Some people pretend to be without tribal prejudice as others deny the power of libido in their lives. They still choose their company. We cannot be in equally intimate touch with everybody all the time, however our society may be organised. As the appropriate reaction to separation and isolation, a certain amount of tribal mentality seems thus to be ineradicable.

We can now define "tribal sentiments" as those emotional attitudes towards outsiders which maintain social unity by means of group isolation. Solidarity inside a group is fortified when emotional obstacles prevent intimate contact with outsiders. The challenge of strangers to our ways of doing things is met by contempt and a boasting sense of superiority which extinguishes any desire we may have of imitating them. Aversion keeps strangers at a distance. In different historical circumstances, the aversion for outsiders takes different forms, but it always contains both fear and hatred, which may manifest themselves as hostility, antipathy, mistrust, derision, dislike, disgust, scorn, reticence, reserve, etc. In this chapter I attempted to establish that tribal sentiments form an invariable ingredient of the minds of those to whom propaganda appeals. In the next chapter I show how the propagandist manipulates this pre-existing sentiment.

1.6

NATIONALIST PROPAGANDA

> *The French call a "cabbage" a "shoe" (choux). Why don't they call it a "cabbage" when they know it is one?*
>
> *An English sailor*[1]

Rudyard Kipling, in 1915, contributed to the *Morning Post* a deeply inspiring thought: "But however the world pretends to divide itself, there are only two divisions in the world to-day—human beings and Germans."[2] When he wrote this sentence, his sentiments were shared by many Englishmen. In times of comparative international peace, such views about the national enemy seem rather exaggerated, out of place, and even a bit foolish. The nearer, however, a country approaches an armed conflict, the more will the propaganda machine endeavour to create in the citizen a state of mind similar to that of Kipling in 1915. In this chapter I propose to give the reader some idea of how it is done.

One of the reasons the propagandist of *international unity* does not make much headway is that the propagandist of *national hatred* can count on certain deep-rooted prejudices in the average mind, prejudices of which we are often not quite clearly aware. We have seen how the psychology of tribal sentiments cuts us off from and makes us feel superior to people who live outside our own social group or tribe. Here we look specifically at the effects of tribal sentiments on nationalist propaganda. The formation of strong nationalist sentiments requires three conditions: (1) a positive attachment to the nation; (2) a dislike for the ways of

1 *Editors: See* The Casket of Flowers of Literature, Wit and Sentiment 1, *New Series (Philadelphia: Atkinson & Alexander, January, 1828), p. 41. Conze cites the same quote in his* Memoirs *1, p. 12.*

2 *Morning Post,* June 22, 1915, p. 9.

DOI: 10.4324/9781003363408-8

other nations; and (3) social conditions in which a sense of nationalist superiority eases the mental conflicts of a great number of people.

Nationalists are, in most cases anyway, more conscious of their negative attitudes to outsiders than of their positive affection for their own group. Tribal hatred is psychologically more weighty than tribal love. Nothing unites a nation so much as an enemy. Lumley mentions the experience of an average American who found that "patriotism...was not so much loving one's country as hating other countries. It did not flourish in time of peace. It was always martial."[3] The "fighting spirit" is a conspicuous element in the mental make-up of patriots everywhere.

What are the stimuli that evoke negative attitudes to foreigners?[4] To judge from some ideological effusions, one might think that national differences and quarrels are a matter of abstract principles and disembodied national "souls." As a matter of fact, for the vast majority of the population, tribal sentiments centre around food, dress, customs, sexual relations, and mother tongue.[5] English people retain their national identity in almost any surroundings because they stubbornly carry along with them their ham and eggs, whisky, tennis, cricket, and manners. They are safeguarded against foreign contamination as long as their *bodily* habits remain English. Conversely, sound tribalism contains a feeling of *physical* disgust. At the height of the Spanish Civil War, Professor J. B. S. Haldane assured us that he found the presence of a supporter of Franco "physically repugnant." This is the state of mind a propagandist aims at fostering.

Food and Dress

Man must *eat* before he can think. "The way to a man's heart is through his stomach." Eating is not merely a matter of munching a quantity of calories a day. Food should be customary and tribally right. "One fat Sir Loin possesses more sublime, than all the airy castles built by rhyme."[6] In the USA the Germans stuck to lager beer, Limburger cheese, sauerkraut, and sausages. Italian emigration is followed by a regular export of Italian food. Michels tells a good story of the American Civil War: Danes fought Danes; no national feelings deterred them. One day, however, a Danish regiment conquered the tents of another contingent

3 Lumley, *The Propaganda Menace*, p. 373.

4 "A stimulus is any process inside or outside a person which disturbs the organism and 'stimulates' to bodily and mental activity." Jameson, *An Outline of Psychology* (ed. Conze, Paul, and Paul), p. 7.

5 During the war, "persecution of Germans and everything German was undertaken with zeal; Wagner was unfavourably compared to Sousa, the danger of sauerkraut was emphasized and people rooted up 'bachelors' buttons' from their gardens, as being a German national flower." Ponsonby, *Falsehood in War-Time*, p. 183. Duff takes the point further: "The war was waged even against inanimate things; we were forbidden to speak the enemy language, to read its books of philosophy, or to eat foods emanating from the culinary art of the opposing forces." *This Human Nature*, p. 58.

6 Peter Pindar, *Bozzy and Piozzi*, part 2 (Sir John).

of Danes. They found remainders of Danish national food. Struck in their inmost heart, they wept with joy and sang Danish national songs.[7]

The popular mind, in its attitude to a foreign nation, is not uninfluenced by the food which is felt to be characteristic of it. Sausages and Germans somehow belong together. To my surprise I found that war propaganda led some members of the lower-middle class in Britain to associate Germans with the smell of boiling cabbage. For Italians, the Germans and Austrians are *patatucchi*, "potato eaters." Italians themselves are "macaroni eaters." Germans are convinced that Jews feed on onions. The Hindu is shocked to hear that the Englishman devours the corpse of the sacred cow. Differences in food may even prove stronger than verbal propaganda of the idealistic kind. During the war, they were a serious obstacle to friendliness and intimacy among Allied troops.[8]

Most Englishmen contemplate with disgust the foreign habit of eating snails, rats, dogs, rainworms, etc. The mere thought of garlic repels. The Greeks were fortified in their contempt for barbarians by the discovery that they drank something like foul wine.[9] Many English people have assured me how glad they were, after a week or a weekend in France, to sit down again to a decent meal in Newhaven or Dover. When German antisemites address the populace, their arguments centre around food and sex. Unsavoury details about the way in which the Jews prepare their food go a long way to make the Jews themselves appear disgusting.

Distaste for foreign food has its basis not in the taste papillae, but in social habits. As a German proverb puts it, "The peasant refuses to eat what he does not know." In other cases it is as much a consequence as a source of tribal prejudice. Many Americans in the North have a distaste for eating from a dish handled by a Negro. (In the South this sort of skin prejudice has been weaned down by familiarity and economic necessity.) Another component of the disapproval of strange food is carried over from the days of magical thinking. For the Maoris, "there was no pollution worse than that which came from the kitchen instruments."[10] Disgust for horse flesh is magical in its origin. In heathen times, horses were

---

7 Michels, *Der Patriotismus*, pp. 78–79.

8 The Frenchman Tharaud reports, "I well remember the reprobation that the men of my regiment, who came from Charente, felt during the war for the British soldier whose nourishment was different from ours." *The Chosen People: A Short History of the Jews in Europe* (New York: Longmans, Green & Co., 1929), p. 30. Hugh Dalton found that the Italian troops who were fed in the English way found the food unbearable. "Our tea they did not fancy. The first time it was issued to them, they thought it was medicine. 'Why do the English give us *camomilia*?' they asked their officer, 'we are not ill!'" *With British Guns in Italy: A Tribute to Italian Achievement* (London: Methuen, 1919), p. 193.

9 Aeschylus, *Suppliant Women. Editors: See lines 952–3, "but you will find that the men who dwell in this land do not drink wine made from barleycorns"; i.e., some foreigners drank a sort of beer that the Greeks would have viewed as a spoiled version of their familiar wine.*

10 *Il n'y avait pas de souillure pire que celle qui provenait des instruments de cuisine.* Lucien Lévy-Bruhl, *La mentalité primitive* (Paris: Librairie Félix Alcan, 1922), p. 451. Nowadays commerce and travel have slightly mitigated such superstitions. Even in tribal times, suspicion of the stranger's food sometimes

sacrificial animals. The Church then forbade the consumption of horse flesh as a relapse into heathenism. The magical element in the fear of foreign food is still obvious in the attitude of orthodox Jews. An American teacher reports about her experience:

> Although I repeatedly tried to ascertain why the Jewish pupils were afraid to eat Gentile dishes, all one would ever say was, "Honest to God—I dassent do it." They seemed to fear some unseen, indescribable force that must do them harm did they not comply with the rituals. Some unmentionable terrible calamity would surely overcome them if they failed to abide by these dietary laws.[11]

One suspects a harmful magical effect from incorporating a strange food into oneself. Pork eaters are said to fill their bellies with impure and unclean substances. The relations between Hindus and Muslims are embittered by the Hindu's horror at the blasphemy of his cow-eating Muslim neighbour. In industrial countries, the magical connotations of repulsive food are often hidden behind rationalisations about hygiene.[12]

Eating together, when voluntary, indicates friendliness. Inter-dining is one of the essential features of the Indian caste system. In Bloomsbury, the intellectual flaunts his emancipation from tribal prejudice by assuring everybody that he loves to feast in a Chinese restaurant. I confess that I did not pass this test.

Language and Gestures

Closely linked to a man's physical appearance are his *language* and, integral to the spoken word in most countries, his *gestures*. The *positive* attachment to one's mother tongue is usually latent. The affection for one's native language manifests itself primarily when it is ill-treated, especially in oppressed and awakening nationalities, where the sacred language of the ancestors is threatened with destruction. The *negative* attitude to foreign languages is usually more in evidence. In some cases it was the funny language of the foreigner which impressed itself most upon the native. When the Greeks called foreigners "barbarians" they had in mind the characteristic syllables of their language, which sounded to them like "bar-bar." The word originally referred to persons who emitted sounds as inarticulate as those of animals, or who babbled like children. Since they appeared to speak no

---

went side by side with the desire for it. Olivier Leroy points out that some Australian aborigines died out from poisoned whiskey and arsenic cakes. *La raison primitive* (1927), p. 198.

11 Young, *Social Psychology*, p. 490.

12 The magical taboos do not always work in the same direction as our views on hygiene. The same American teacher says: "The effort to be clean about the school kitchen was almost tragic in consequences. The mere mention of soap created an uprising, marked by emphatic choruses of 'Honest to God, we dassent do it.'" Ibid., p. 489.

intelligible language, they were called *aglossoi*, "without speech." In the same way the Russians call a German *nemetsky* (neméckij), a "mute man," somebody who cannot speak Russian.

A person who speaks a foreign language bewilders. His emotional reactions remain uncertain. Obsessed by a desire for tribal isolation, the Jewish Shammaites forbade their followers to learn the language of the heathen.[13] As far as the masses are concerned, such a special ban is rarely necessary. To them the foreigners remain incomprehensible jabberers. Convinced of the inestimable superiority of their own native language, they love to chaff at some outstanding feature of a foreign language: clumsy and long-winded German, fast and voluble French, squeaky Chinese, the "chchch"-sounds in Russian, the gesticulations of many Southerners.

Folk memory is visual rather than intellectual. The foreigner, if at all possible, is summed up as a type with distinctive, special physical features: cropped hair over a fat and brutal face like the Hun, a black gorilla-like face as the Negro, or a big nose like the Japanese in communist propaganda cartoons in China. The dress of other social groups often strikes the unsophisticated as simply ridiculous or tasteless. There are those who cannot picture the Negro without an excessively gay Easter hat, or the Jew without a vulgar display of big rings on his fingers, both stereotypes which foster racial aversion. That type then easily becomes a peg for myths and legends, and a powerful lever of tribal prejudice. Thought-saving stereotypes often sum up the result in one word: Wops, Dagos, Chinks, Huns, Goyim, barbarians, foreign devils. In South Africa, the whites use "Kaffir" as a term of contempt and abuse—any low-down person is a "dirty Kaffir."

Some few features are sufficient to size up the alien: "For the Christian the Jew is an inferior person—dirty, ill-smelling, and offensive if he is from the lower economic classes, or arrogant and ostentatious if he is from the middle classes."[14] As an American sorority student puts it, "The Jews are noisy, impolite, and smelly."[15] The picture of the stranger should include at least some vague hint at unsavoury and offensive habits on his part. The gluttonous Germans are accused of eating too much. The Jews are ridiculously accused of sacrificing little children in the course of their religious ritual. An Englishman in hostile Italian opinion is a tea-drinking and pipe-smoking homosexual with protruding teeth. A reader writing to *Picture Post* about "the ghastly doctrine of Bolshevism" remarks, "Bolsheviks practice sexual immorality of such a depraved kind that the normal English mind cannot grasp it."[16]

13 *Editors: The Shammaites were followers of Shammai, a Jewish scholar of the 1st century BC who engaged in legal disputes with his more moderate contemporary Hillel.*

14 Young, *Social Psychology*, p. 488.

15 Ibid., p. 495.

16 *New Statesman*, May 27, 1939.

The Great Unwashed

All this physical repulsion generated by the foreigner is summed up in the one word "dirty." Foreigners are suspected of carrying on their bodies a strange mixture of *physical*, *magical*, and *moral* dirtiness. In primitive times, the fear of a vague "magical uncleanliness" was topmost in the mind of the patriot. James George Frazer shows that primitive tribes looked upon strangers as a source of magical danger, of baneful influences which emanate from them either involuntarily or through the deliberate practice of black magic and witchcraft.[17] Abetted by offended spirits, strangers might easily bring with them unforeseen harm—disease, treachery, the death of the king, or the general displeasure of the gods. Contact with strangers may also cause illness by magical contamination—unless people are properly fortified against them by smearing themselves with blood, for instance, they may fall ill even at the mere sight of one. Some tribes go so far as to kill strangers and even those of their own members who return from abroad, lest they be infected. In other cases the returning traveller is purified before he is allowed to mingle freely with the members of the tribe. He is subjected to ceremonies which try to exorcise all harmful influences:

> It is believed that a man who has been on a journey may have contracted some magic evil from the strangers with whom he has associated. Hence, on returning home, before he is readmitted to the society of his tribe and friends, he has to undergo certain purificatory ceremonies.... in order that all alien substances and influences may be removed.[18]

When we speak of "dirty foreigners" our attitude is still determined by the old fear of magical contamination. In recent times, however, the development of hygiene has pushed the physical aspect of foreign dirtiness more into the foreground. French lavatory accommodation is an obstacle to the *Entente Cordiale*.[19] French women are alleged to use so much perfume because they never wash. The satirist Multatuli gives an anecdote in which a Dutch skipper notices a foreign woman diving and swimming most perfectly. The skipper consoles himself, "Of course, all those foreigners can swim. They've got to wash continually because they are so dirty."[20] To the Victorian middle classes the workers were "the Great Unwashed." Some time ago I heard a story of a butcher in Smithfield who cut himself when handling a foreign turkey. The man who dressed his wound told him to be careful because foreigners have but two baths in their lives—the first the midwife's, and the second the undertaker's. The South African whites associate

---

17 James George Frazer, *Taboo and the Perils of the Soul* (London: Macmillan & Co., Ltd., 1911), chapter 3, p. 101 et seq.

18 Frazer, *Taboo and the Perils of the Soul*, pp. 111–113.

19 *Editors: The reference is to the 1904 treaty between the English and the French.*

20 Boris Brasol, *Oscar Wilde: The Man, The Artist* (London: Williams and Norgate, Ltd., 1938), p. 210.

black skin mostly with dirt. Ian MacCrone reports that several people told him, "Some natives I can touch indifferently but some seem as if they would contaminate and pollute my hand."[21] In the USA the war generation learned that what is dirty has got "germ(an)s" on it.[22]

Tribalism Breeds Tribalism

Nothing confirms the members of a group in their tribal sentiments as much as the tribal sentiments of another group. By collecting evidence for *foreign* tribalism, the propagandist nourishes the flames of *native* tribalism. He would have us believe that "the Jews" all stick together, keep to themselves, praise one another, and help each other to jobs; further, that they have little sense of moral obligation towards the Gentiles (as shown by quotations from the Talmud) and, while always denying it, show a high tribal solidarity against the Gentile. When one reads Continental nationalist newspapers one gets the impression that all peoples are nationalists except, alas, the writer's own. Before 1933 French papers held the patriotism of German socialists over that of their own, and *vice versa*. German papers never get tired of commending the English for the maxim "My country, right or wrong," and deplore the mentality of the weak-kneed "Deutsche Michel" who, alone among the citizens of the world, is deficient in patriotic zeal.

Knowing the touchiness of tribal sentiments, one will scour the foreign press for deprecatory comments about one's own country. The cocky and contemptuous remarks of foreigners are continually kept before the eyes of the public. When the *Tokyo Nichi Nichi Shimbun*, *Das Schwarze Korps*, or *Il Popolo d'Italia* speaks with contempt of England, all Englishmen should be informed at once of the contemptuous utterance. One must make the most of every affront to the honour of the country. When the average man hears for the umpteenth time that the British Lion's tail has been twisted, he is made to feel, through identification, that he is some sort of a lion himself and should behave accordingly towards his detractors. To take a particularly crude example: "The world is saying that we are yellow. They sneer at our flag! They are calling us cowards!" The stirring article under this headline from the pen of a certain Charles Wilberforce ends with the noble words, "The world is saying that the colour of the British flag is yellow. The world must learn that the colours of that flag are Red, White and Blue."[23]

The Jews owe their survival as a separate group to the excessive tribalism which lurks behind every page of the *Old Testament*. The Jews tried to isolate themselves from the Goyim—the strangers or heathens—and showed strong aversion to their customs. Under Ezra and Nehemiah, vigorous measures were proposed

---

21 Ian MacCrone, *Race Attitudes in South Africa: Historical, Experimental and Psychological Studies* (London: Oxford University Press, 1937), p. 273.

22 *Editors: Cf.* Kicking the Germ Out of Germany, *a "lost" silent film from 1918 starring Harold Lloyd.*

23 *Sunday Pictorial*, June 12, 1938.

to ensure the purity of the holy seed of Abraham. The Ammonites and Moabites "shall not enter into the congregation of the Lord forever"[24]; the aliens who lived in Palestine under Jewish rule—the seven native nations of the Promised Land—were to be destroyed.[25] Foreigners were strongly suspected of unnatural vices. Other countries were "unclean"[26] and their destruction pleased Yahweh, for the prophets of other Gods were inferior and abominable, and so were the foreigners who worshipped them. Sacred objects of foreigners were continually referred to as "abominations" and "filth."[27] Innumerable regulations of ceremonial cleanliness emphasised the foreigner's "dirtiness," and produced mutual dislike and contempt between Jew and Gentile. The Goyim were wicked, God's enemies. But one day all nations would come to Zion and learn the true religion.

This was some few thousand years ago. At present, antisemitism attributes this ancient mentality to the modern Jew. Jews who boast about their achievements, their contribution to civilisation, and who remind Englishmen that they were still savages at the time when the Temple was built are a godsend to the antisemitic propagandist. By strengthening Jewish tribalism, antisemitic propaganda furthers its own horrific goals.[28] I am sometimes terrified to see how fast things are moving in that direction. Of all the tribal prejudices, those of the antisemite may be the most offensive.

As a particularly able piece of tribal propaganda, we may next take Professor Taid O'Conroy's *The Menace of Japan*.[29] The book is that of a man genuinely shocked by the unrelieved wickedness of the "Japanese devils." He naturally dwells extensively on their *sexual iniquities*. They indulge in mixed bathing without clothes on, they practice phallus worship, the Buddhist priests indulge in sexual orgies, and the prostitutes get ten juicy, though gruesome, pages.

Of the three aspects of a foreigner's "dirtiness"—physical, magical, and moral—Professor O'Conroy focuses on the third. To mention only some few items, the Japanese are cruel and fond of bloodshed, they are habitual liars, they are cruel to animals, their army commits atrocities, they have no word for "love," and they are unkind to the poor. The women are good, but their treatment is not. The Japanese woman's tragedy "is the coarseness inherent in all the men of Nippon."[30]

But the chief burden of Professor O'Conroy's case rests on Japanese *tribalism*, from the contemplation of which he cannot get away. He heaps example upon

---

24 Deut. 23:3.

25 Deut. 7:1–6 etc.

26 Am. 7:17; Hos. 9:3 et seq.

27 See, for example, 1 Kings 11:7.

28 "Whoever lives by fighting an enemy has an interest in keeping him alive." Nietzsche, *Human, all too Human*, section 9, item 531.

29 New York: Grosset & Dunlap, 1934. A pocket edition arrived in 1938 for 6 pence. By then, 40,000 copies had been issued. G. B. Shaw said that "Professor O'Conroy is one of the most remarkable men in the world."

30 O'Conroy, *The Menace of Japan*, 111.

example to show that the Japanese are conceited, but touchy about foreign criticism; that they speak ill of Westerners, though they are appallingly ignorant of the Western world; that they dislike, insult, and abuse foreigners; and that, in short, they are an aggressive nation of fervent nationalists. Professor O'Conroy does his job well. If I may speak of my own reactions, reading about the silly nationalist prejudices of "those Japanese brutes" for a moment at least evoked and strengthened my own nationalist prejudices. Cockiness begets cockiness.

In preparation for a new World War the output of tribal literature is tremendous. How can we prevent it from getting a hold over our minds? It will help, I think, always to remember the material or economic basis of tribal propaganda. Most anti-Japanese literature, for instance, is at bottom more concerned with the £400,000,000 of British investments in China than with the unspeakable wickedness of the Japanese as such. When we train ourselves to see propaganda about national virtues and vices for what it is—a cloak for conquest, and for the defence of investments, property "rights," and the fruits of imperial robbery—we come to take it much less seriously. Psychology may also be of some use. Whenever we feel tempted to think ill of foreign people, we may disintegrate the sentiment by dispassionately decomposing it into the elements which I have tried to outline.

Positive Attachments

It is, however, desirable that all these predominantly negative tribal sentiments should be organised around a nucleus of positive attachment to the nation. Only people accustomed to abstract thinking can love their nation as such. Among the masses, love for a nation can be fostered only indirectly, by promoting affection for home and family. Positive attachments to familiar food, dialect, and local people grow up in the family. The familiar food is the food which mother cooked at home. The dialect is the mother tongue. The local people are substitutes for the family, and especially the mother.

The feeling for the home, for the local unit, for the place where we were born and brought up, is largely a matter of childhood memories. We know the people and their familiar ways, the river and the valley, that house and that tree, we love to hear that particular dialect, we remember the tower of a church, or a dog which used to bark at night. Italians call it *campanilismo*, the affection for the country round the church tower. In bigger towns, people often learn to love the quarter in which they lived as children. Sometimes people go back to die in their home town or native village. Even a positive nuisance can acquire a sentimental value. From a safe distance under a southern sky, a Londoner may feel, "I should love to be in a real nice London fog."

Affection for the native place renders nationalist sentiments more stable. Industrialism threatens to undermine it. Nationalist propaganda cannot neglect to foster local pride, and to revive the old local folkways—dances, dresses, weaving, etc.

Nationalists invariably proclaim the sanctity of the family. The family is the best breeding ground for nationalist sentiments. The protection of the family is always one of the foremost demands in a nationalist program. The destruction of the family would mean, in the words of the Nazis, "the end of all higher humanity."[31] "God, family, nation" are the dominant ideals of French nationalism.

Loyalty to the king has at its core the infantile attitude towards the father. The government of a country is represented by a man—Uncle Sam, John Bull, Jean Crapaud. The country itself, on the contrary, is represented by a woman—Columbia, Britannia, Germania, La France. In their emotional core, home and nation are ideas of mother and family. This is a commonplace of modern psychology. Leading nationalists are passionately devoted to their mothers. The Nazis proclaimed, "Home is the mother of your life; never forget that.... The idea of 'mother' and of 'being German' are eternally connected."[32] In a more aggressive mood, Dr. Goebbels wrote,

> If somebody beats your mother with a whip over her face, do you then say 'Thank you; he is also a human being'? He is not human, he is subhuman. And remember what the Jew has done to our mother Germany.[33]

When, many centuries ago, Pythagoras was asked how one should behave towards an ungrateful fatherland, he answered, "as to a mother."[34] The Church also tries to use this attachment to the mother for pulling its cart. As the Pope is the father, "the Church is our mother, we call her 'our holy mother the Church.'"[35] "The children of one common mother have one common mother tongue, one Lord, one faith, one baptism, one Church, one sacrifice, one Kingdom, one tongue."[36]

We distinguished between *tribal* and *nationalist* sentiments. Nationalist propaganda need not fear that tribal sentiments might die out so soon in the hearts of men. But there is a danger that they might be transferred to social units other than the nation. Three kinds of social groups may direct tribal sentiments away from the nation itself: *other nations*, *infranational units*, and *supranational units*.

As regards the first, a minority in each nation usually transfers its tribal sentiments to other nations. Germans imitated French ways, particularly in the 18th and 19th

---

31 *Das Ende jedes höheren Menschentums.* In Wilhelm Reich, *Massenpsychologie des Faschismus* (Kopenhagen: Verlag für Sexualpolitik, 1933), p. 95.

32 *Die Heimat ist die Mutter Deines Lebens, vergiss das nie.... Mit dem Begriff "Mutter" ist "Deutschsein" ewig verbunden.* Ibid., p. 90. Trans. E. C.

33 Joseph Goebbels and Mjölnir (illustrator), *Die verfluchten Hakenkreuzler: Etwas zum Nachdenken* (München: Verlag Frz. Eher, 1930), p. 18.

34 *Ioannis Stobæi Sententiae ex Thesauris Græcorum delectæ* (1609), p. 227.

35 John Procter, *The Catholic Creed: Or, What Do Catholics Believe?*, 2nd ed. (London: Art and Book Company, Ltd., 1901), p. 62.

36 Procter, *The Catholic Creed*, p. 255.

centuries. Chinese intellectuals developed "foreignerism," and admired Westerners as their models in everything. After the war a number of us found a spiritual home in Soviet Russia. Normally, such an attitude is confined to a small minority. It rarely endangers nationalism. On the contrary, it soon creates a violent nationalist reaction in the direction of self-reliance and freedom from foreign influence.

In Europe the citizen's exclusive attachment to the infranational units of village, county, etc. broke down only slowly. It took about 700 years to make him fully aware of the nation he belongs to. I cannot show here in any detail how the modern state managed to extend the affection for the native place to places one has never seen. The teaching of national history was an important factor, since it gave all nationals a common heritage and common memories. Equally helpful were the creation of common symbols and the development of a common language. Compulsory education did much to uproot exclusive regional patriotism. The manipulation of negative tribal sentiments also widened the social horizon. It is difficult to love Devonshire people when you are from Yorkshire, or East Prussians when you are from Württemberg. It is rather easier to hate the French, or whoever else it may be. The English unite India by obligingly acting as the common foe. A common hatred was, if not the father, at least the godfather of all modern nations.

At the present time, supranational units are the most dangerous rivals to nationalism. Classes and professions in particular are apt to form themselves into units which cut across national groups. Nationalist propaganda counteracts internationalist tendencies by revealing international organisations as a camouflage for secret national interests. International organisations, real and projected—like the League of Nations, the British Empire, the Socialist Internationals, pan-Europe, or the Churches—are all too close to one particular nation to be able to claim true universality.[37] They have all remained incomplete. In the two instances where they produced a tribal chief—the Pope and Stalin—the chief has remained closely identified with the interests of particular nations, Italy and Russia. Of 258 popes, 207 have been Italians.[38] During the Abyssinian conflict the Pope backed up Italian foreign policy. Most Roman Catholics belong to the Latin races, which serves to strengthen the reluctance of Northerners to belong to such an organisation. The nationalist propagandist does not hesitate to make the most of such facts.

---

37 In *Why Fascism?* pp.186–190, Ellen Wilkinson and I have attempted to sum up the experiences obtained from these organisations. We came to the sad conclusion that "in big decisions in which the international interest did not coincide with some important national interest, the Second International has simply not existed," and that the Third International during the last ten years "has been used almost entirely in the national interests of Russia." For a more detailed proof of these statements the reader must be referred to the book itself. In this context I speak only of "primary" international groups, and not of the "secondary." During the last seventy years, the capitalist bourgeoisie has fostered the growth of many secondary international institutions and organisations like the Red Cross, the UPU, international cartels, etc.

38 *Editors: The enumeration of popes, and their division according to nationality, varies by source; but the general proportion reported by Conze accurately reflects the figures of the time.*

Nationalism and Oppression

Nationalist sentiments are naturally most intense among the oppressed masses. Democracy and nationalism grew up together. The more the middle and working classes gained influence over politics, the more pronouncedly did politics become nationalistic. In Germany and Russia, there is no democracy in the English sense. But both the German and the Russian governments are popular governments. A general election is not the only way in which the masses can make their influence felt.

It is instructive to compare the Treaty of Versailles with the Treaty of Vienna, which in 1815 terminated the Napoleonic Wars. In both cases Europe had been devastated by a general war. In both cases the victors knew who the "aggressor" was. Yet the treaty of 1815 was mild compared to that of 1919. The Congress of Vienna carefully refrained from "punishing" France, whereas the Treaty of Versailles not only aimed at crippling Germany's strength, but at punishing and humiliating her. The "War Guilt Clause" (Article 231) did far more to embitter German nationalist sentiments than the reparations which, anyway, were paid out of foreign loans. In 1815, gentlemen and aristocrats concluded the Treaty. The Treaty of 1919 was worked out by demagogues under the pressure of bloodthirsty and vindictive masses at home. Whenever the demagogues showed some inclination towards common sense, the masses at home forced them to be more severe. One cannot say that it was propaganda which had made the masses vindictive; their aggressiveness was due to the fears and privations of the war itself. All that propaganda did was to prevent popular hatred from turning against the ruling class at home by diverting it to the enemy.

Internationalism remains alien to the working class. Internationalist ideas are carried into the working class from the outside—partly by bourgeois Liberals who for a time provided the workers with an ideology, and partly by an international, largely Jewish intelligentsia, who have no country, and who, because they feel oppressed, can throw in their lot with the oppressed workers. When Russian bolshevism became more and more *exclusively* nationalistic, the Jews among the Bolshevik leaders were liquidated.

The impact of internationalist ideas, however, never went very deep. The common interests of the workers of different countries have always been overshadowed by their national rivalries.[39] The patriot appeals of the Bolsheviks against the "white" foreign invaders won them the Russian Civil War. Nationalist pride was a powerful driving force behind the Five-Year Plans. During the last war, almost all socialist leaders came down on the side of their own country. The Popular Front governments in France and Spain never allowed anyone to doubt

39 In spite of a certain antagonism to their ruling class, the workers have many economic interests in common with them. Hendrik de Man in *The Psychology of Socialism*, trans. Eden Paul and Cedar Paul (London: G. Allen & Unwin, Ltd., 1928), pp. 304 and 324 explains this quite well. See also my *Introduction to Dialectical Materialism*, p. 42 et seq.

their patriotism. British socialists habitually divide nations into good and wicked, into peace-minded and aggressive, into guilty and innocent, into judges and felons. In cases of imperial conflicts, they rarely doubt that Britain is on the side of the angels.

On occasion, of course, the behaviour of working-class people seems to belie my thesis that they are more nationalistic than anybody else. In 1899, for instance, in the industrial centres of France, the militant workers adopted "*À bas la patrie!*"[40] as their slogan. As the subsequent history of Europe shows, those workers did not mean to decry "la France," their motherland. At that period the word "la patrie" had come to stand for everything they hated. Their bosses invariably used the word to justify their actions when they cut the workers' wages, persecuted their unions, and broke up their strikes. Under such circumstances, many workers feel that they have no stake whatever in their country. "Anti-patriotism" becomes a temporary mood.

Many of the words, phrases, and symbols with which the ruling classes conduct their nationalist propaganda repel certain working-class people, because in the army or during strikes they have come to be associated with experiences of frustration and humiliation. In consequence, such workers require a new verbal outfit for their nationalist feelings. "Left" propagandists supply it. Here in England, they assure us that we must rearm to do our duty by the Covenant, or to protect Spain or Soviet Russia, or China, or the Negroes of Africa, or anything. Some travesty of internationalism is readily accepted as the genuine article. The Trade Unions, some years ago, clamoured for "military sanctions" against Italy, so that, among other things, the Italian workers might be "liberated." Apparently the slaughter of Italian workers by British workers in the interest of their respective ruling classes was regarded as a first token of international working-class solidarity.

The tasks of socialist propaganda become quite clear when we consider the problem which confronts it. Socialist propagandists have to reckon with two conflicting trends in the minds of their followers. On the one side, conditions of oppression foster a fervent nationalism. On the other side, the same conditions make for some degree of hostility to the ruling classes, an antagonism which extends easily to the patriotic utterances of the spokesmen of the ruling class. Propaganda, to be successful among the politically minded socialist workers, must allow them to follow both these incompatible trends at the same time. This is how it is done.

It so happens that the home country of the particular socialists concerned is especially pertinent to the realisation of the socialist ideal. Thus France must be defended as the country of the original Revolution; Germany as the home of Marxism, and the country with the biggest socialist movement (at least in 1914); Russia as the citadel of the "World Revolution"; and England as the home of liberty, of democratic rights, and of the largest Free Trade Union movement in the

40 "Down with the fatherland!"

world. When Gustave Hervé, the French anti-patriot, changed his paper *Guerre Sociale* into *La Victoire*, he pleaded:

> Socialist, syndicalist and anarchist friends, you are not only the idealistic vanguard of mankind, but you are also the nerve and the conscience of the French army; the fatherland is in danger! The fatherland of the Revolution is in danger![41]

This mentality goes back far beyond 1914. We see germs of it in the manifesto of the Parti Ouvrier Francais (the French Workers' Party) in 1895 which contains sentences like these: "When the socialists cry 'Long live the International!' they are crying, 'Long live the France of Work, long live the historic mission of the French proletariat!'"[42] Or "It was France which, after having unleashed on the world the bourgeois Revolution, the indispensable prelude to the proletarian Revolution, became the great battlefield of the class struggle."[43] The French socialists thus brought their internationalist doctrines into line with the nationalist sentiments of their followers, by endowing their nation with a particularly important "mission" in the fight for working-class emancipation. The French became the elect people of the Revolution, and Paris the new revolutionary Jerusalem.

During the war, German socialists defended Germany and the small nations against the "Russian flood." Marx and Engels never concealed how proud they were that scientific socialism was a product of the German spirit. They thought it quite natural that Germans should have a preponderant influence in the First International. Later on, the German Social Democrats convinced themselves that they were the best socialists in the world.

> The German Social Democrats have a sharp eye for the faults of the socialist movements of other countries, not because of any envy, which was far from their minds, but from a secret, perhaps pitying, regret that their French, English, and Russian comrades were no German Social Democrats.[44]

---

41 *Amis socialistes, amis syndicalistes, amis anarchistes, qui n'êtes pas seulement l'avant-garde idéaliste de l'humanité, mais qui êtes encore le nerf et la conscience de l'armée française, la patrie est en danger! La patrie de la Révolution est en danger!* Gustave Hervé, "La Patrie en danger" (Friday, July 31, 1914) in *La Patrie en danger: Recueil* in extenso *des articles publiés par Gustave Hervé dans la* Guerre Sociale *du 1er juillet au 1er novembre 1914* (Paris: Bibliothèque des ouvrages documentaires, 1915), p. 37. Trans. E. C.

42 *En criant:* vive l'Internationale! *ils crient* vive la France du Travail! *vive la mission historique du prolétariat français!* Jean Jaurès, *Patriotisme et internationalisme: discours de Jean Jaurès, précédé du manifeste du conseil national du Parti Ouvrier* (Paris: au bureau du "Socialiste," 1895), pp. 4–5. Trans. E. C.

43 *C'est la France qui, après avoir déchainé sur le monde la Révolution bourgeoise, préface indispensable de la Révolution prolétarienne, a été le grand champ de bataille de la* lutte de classe. Ibid., p. 5.

44 Adolf Braun, *Die Zukunft der deutschen Sozialdemokratie: Deutsch, nicht englisch, französisch oder russisch* (Vienna: Volksbuchhandlung Ignatz Brand & Co, 1917), p. 4.

When they participated in the war, the socialists argued that Germany, the centre of the socialist movement of the entire world, must not be weakened or destroyed.

In 1847, in the *Communist Manifesto*, Marx wrote:

> The proletarian is without property; his relation to his wife and children has no longer anything in common with the bourgeois family relations; modern industrial labour, modern subjection to capital, the same in England as in France, in America as in Germany, has stripped him of every trace of national character. Law, morality, religion, are to him so many bourgeois prejudices, behind which lurk in ambush just as many bourgeois interests.[45]

This passage may describe the ideal proletarian, and the wish-fantasies of a prophet in search of suitable human material. It does not describe the British working man, who, obviously, is not "stripped of every trace of national character." Only the psychological analysis of tribalism and nationalism can explain why British, German, Russian, or Japanese workers so little resemble Marx's ideal proletarian.

45 *Der Proletarier ist eigentumslos....* (Chapter 1: Bourgeois and Proletarians, trans. Samuel Moore in cooperation with Friedrich Engels, 1888.)

1.7

MAGICAL BELIEFS AND SAVAGE SURVIVALS

> *The August girl's lucky day is Sunday, her flower the poppy, her number thirty-four, and her stone the moonstone.*
>
> *Home Notes*[1]

At a mourning ceremony in Montenegro, an English traveller met a man just back from the USA who said to her in a strong American accent, "What do you go to this damn fool business for? I won't take any part in it." According to custom, the mourners, most of whom did not know the deceased even by name, got into a frenzy, and

> yelling the death-wail, they danced furiously in front of the 'trpez' [a table on which lay a dummy of a dead man], beating their breasts and their temples with their closed fists, thus accompanying the wail with a barbaric drumming. Tears streamed from their eyes and soaked their clothes. They leaped almost a yard from the ground.

Even the American, wrote the traveller, got carried away. "Among those who had howled the most was the man from U.S.A. Local surroundings had completely broken down the thin coating of 'civilisation.' He gasped, half-ashamed to me, 'I didn't mean to do it!'"[2]

Montenegrins are not the only people who revert to ancestral forms of behaviour. A more ancient mental structure lies in all of us, concealed behind a thin

1 *Editors:* Home Notes *(1895–1958) was a popular small-format women's weekly magazine, published by Newnes and Pearson in the UK.*

2 Mary Edith Durham, *Some Tribal Origins, Laws and Customs of the Balkans* (London: G. Allen & Unwin, Ltd., 1928), pp. 218–219.

DOI: 10.4324/9781003363408-9

veneer of "reasonable" and "scientific" beliefs. Scratch the skin of a civilised European and you will find the blood of a tribal hunter. The propagandist who wishes to address modern man in his totality must pay special attention to the vestiges left in our minds from past modes of experience.

Urbanisation

Our position today, in many parts of the world, is similar to that of domesticated animals. During the last century a growing part of mankind was subjected to a severe change of environment. Men had lived for about 400,000 years in rural surroundings, collecting, hunting, and growing food. Then suddenly many millions of them were transferred into what we might roughly describe as an industrial town civilisation. The short space of one century did not quite give them an opportunity to get adapted to their new surroundings. The following table illustrates how recent and far-reaching the development of town life in Europe has been[3]:

		Towns of More Than 100,000 Inhabitants			*Towns of More Than 500,000 Inhabitants*		
Year	*Total Population of Europe*	*Number*	*Population*	*% of Total Population*	*Number*	*Population*	*% of Total Population*
1800	188,000,000	22	5,200,000	2.7	3	2,100,000	1.1
1850	265,000,000	46	12,300,000	4.7	3	4,000,000	1.5
1900	400,000,000	123	45,400,000	11.3	20	22,100,000	5.5
1930	500,000,000	271	92,700,000	18.5	44	38,500,000	7.7

The townward movement started about 1850. It gained its full momentum only from 1870 onwards. Apart from national capitals, big towns were unknown in Europe before 1850. Large towns demand an efficient system of transport which came only with the steam age. Before the advent of industrialism, big towns of over 100,000 inhabitants contained only 1–2% of the population—for instance, 1.98% in India in 1881, and 1.5% in Germany in 1800. The industrial towns of Great Britain are no more than two generations old.[4] The urban population in England

3 *Enciclopedia Italiana di Scienze, Lettere ed Arti*, vol. 34 (Rome: Istituto Giovanni Treccani, 1937), s.v. "Urbanesimo." *Editors: Such data must be viewed as imprecise. Other sources offer different numbers, but the point is clear. The formatting and translation from Italian are Conze's.*

4 For example, by population:

	1801	*1851*	*1931*
Birmingham	74,000	233,000	1,000,000
Glasgow	77,000	340,000	1,100,000
Liverpool	80,000	376,000	855,000

grew from 10% in 1800 to about 80% in 1921. In Germany in 1925, 16.7 million people (27%) lived in towns of over 100,000 inhabitants, and 8.5 million (14%) in towns of 20,000 to 100,000 inhabitants. In 1930, 42.8 million Americans lived in towns of over 50,000 inhabitants, 26.1 million in towns of over 2,500 inhabitants, and 53.8 million are still rural.

The extent of the change in environment and habits which this rapid urbanisation involves is in some ways comparable to that which the reptile faced when it went into the air, or the whale when it went from the land into the sea. The modern town-dweller is somewhat of a fish out of water. The intellectual and instinctual equipment which his ancestors acquired in many thousands of years of rural life must adapt itself to the new conditions, and it is still in the painful process of doing so.

Magic in Towns

Country people think magically. Magic in this context may be defined as an attempt to control events by means of spells (words or formulae), rituals (ceremonial actions), symbols, signs, or numbers which are laid down unalterably by social custom and tradition. Magical actions utilise occult, mysterious, and miraculous forces which can be identified by the emotional attitude we adopt towards them—e.g. fascination, or shuddering awe.

Among the hunting or peasant population of a rural society magical actions and beliefs are taken for granted. Even in towns they continue to flourish. Mascots protect motor cars and airplanes. Fortune-telling, crystal-gazing, and palm-reading number many followers. Prophetic dreams still come true. Some stones are lucky, others are not. Vast quantities of rings with birthstones were marketed only in recent years. Alexander Goldenweiser found that some half of his students at an American university wore charms.[5] During the last four years, many London papers took up astrology seriously. The great J. D. Rockefeller carried an "eagle stone" in his pocket as a charm against calamities. Many expect good luck from black cats and chimney sweeps, and bad luck from nuns and Friday the thirteenth. Magical killing and curing remain popular, though often shamefacedly disguised as medicine. Spiritualism, Theosophy, and Christian Science permit their followers to indulge in magical practices.

	1801	*1851*	*1931*
Manchester	95,000	404,000	766,000
Newcastle	37,000	90,000	283,000
Nottingham	29,000	58,000	270,000
Sheffield	?	134,000	512,000

Editors: We are unable to identify Conze's source for the data in this note.

5 *Anthropology: An Introduction to Primitive Culture* (New York: F. S. Crofts & Co., 1937), p. 212, fn. 4.

The first effect of industrial surroundings on magical beliefs is that many people become embarrassed to show their "superstitions." A mobile population, thrown together from the most diverse districts, cannot fail to observe that their various superstitions often cancel each other out. In Germany I was frightened by the sight of a black cat. Here in England I rejoice at seeing one. The comparison makes me sceptical about the value of black cats as omens. In other words, magical beliefs require some degree of tribal isolation. In any case, the town-dweller who makes any claim to enlightenment holds on to his magical beliefs only with ambivalence. They have become "superstitions." Magic has ceased to be quite respectable among those who have to pretend that they are civilised if they want to count at all. The educated or semi-educated town-dweller believes in magic only half-heartedly. His mind is divided against itself on the subject. As T. Sharper Knowlson puts it, the Anglo-Saxon is not so sure that charms work, but "with commercial instinct rather than religious feeling, he wants to get the benefit if there is one."[6]

Secondly, we observe that in towns most rural magical ceremonies and beliefs died out simply because they were connected with the production of food from the soil. Superstitions about wells naturally shrivel away when we never see a well. The towns gradually create a new set of superstitions connected with town pursuits, like motor cars, horse-racing, etc. Many customs were based on a feeling of genuine kinship which prevails in rural communities. They have proved unable to survive the disorganisation of communal life in vast towns.

As a third effect we may note that many of the old customs and ceremonies, though they brought into our lives much hidden magic, have become meaningless, or acquired a new significance. Decorating the house with greens at Christmas, originally a magical fertility rite, is now "just a pretty custom." Formerly it was good magic to use the right hand, the lucky one, for shaking hands. Now it is merely polite. Some magical customs have become a social pastime, or amusement, or material for small talk. When we throw grain, snow, paper cuttings, and sawdust at weddings, we re-enact a fertility rite without, in most cases, knowing what we do.

When the town-dweller thinks about why he performs such actions, he "rationalises" them.[7] Torn out of their magical context, they appear as isolated customs which, as far as our consciousness is concerned, have lost their magical significance. The influence of town civilisation almost instantaneously leads to rationalisation. Monica Hunter Wilson reports of the Pondos that "ritual mutilations of the body are dropped by most Christians, but some still scarify, saying...that it is 'to make the blood good.'" Those who persist in ritual killings

6 T. Sharper Knowlson, *The Origins of Popular Superstitions & Customs* (London: T. W. Laurie, Ltd., 1910), p. 157.

7 We rationalise when we explain to ourselves or to others by respectable but inadequate reasoning the actions, thoughts, and emotions which are actually prompted by instincts and impulses that are the subject of a mental conflict. For more about this see Chapter 2.1.

sometimes excuse themselves by saying that they kill "just to please the women."[8] Some of our contemporaries try to find out a rational reason for not walking under ladders. A pot of paint might fall on your head, etc. Those who observe the day of rest, or do not eat pork, nowadays back up their habits by rational instead of magical sanctions.

It is clear that the development of town life proves inimical to the conscious pursuit of magic. But the magic which disappeared from the surface of the mind was merely driven underground. Our unconscious carries a heavier load of magical attitudes than our conscious mind is aware of. The unconscious is still attuned to the magical connotations of many objects or stimuli, like the dead (see Chapter 1.4), cemeteries, kings, flags, etc. During the last century, human mentality has not changed radically. At the same time, the emergence of town conditions has made it difficult for the traditional elements of magical thought to find accommodation in the modern world, where the need for it persists as strongly as ever.

It is tempting to look upon magic as simply some nonsensical "mumbo jumbo." In some quarters magical beliefs are as unfashionable as a poor complexion. Yet whenever we adopt an air of unquestioning superiority towards convictions which are shared by millions, we are bound to be wrong. In this context it does not matter to us whether magic, judged by practical results, compares favourably with science. We need not decide what beliefs are "true" or even desirable. All that matters here is the fact that nobody can master the art of either statecraft or propaganda without realising that magical behaviour is an integral and indispensable part of human nature as we know it. People cannot live without magic and be happy.

While many forms of magical behaviour are handed down by teaching and tradition, others appear to arise spontaneously from the unexhausted layer of magical mentality in our minds. The average person who dares to think for himself, and to work out his own ideas—instead of aping the scientist—often thinks on magical lines.

In childhood magical forms of thought and behaviour arise spontaneously.[9] They are especially marked at the beginning of puberty when inner distress begins, as well as the fear of lesion to the personality by vaguely felt demoniac powers. Certain performances—eating, getting dressed, or the habits before going to sleep—may quite early turn into ceremonial rules. A habit becomes a ritual ceremony or a "rite" if it cannot be altered without disturbing or even destroying the ego, or if the order in which one action should follow the other becomes something venerable and inviolable. Before examinations and in other critical situations, children develop, often out of their own heads, ways of revealing and

8 Monica Hunter Wilson, *Reaction to Conquest: Effects of Contact with Europeans on the Pondo of South Africa* (London: Oxford University Press, 1936), p. 268.

9 Heinz Werner in *Einführung in die Entwicklungspsychologie* (Leipzig: J. A. Barth, 1926), p. 278 et seq. has collected many relevant details.

determining their fate. Young Jean-Jacques Rousseau threw stones at trees. A hit meant good luck, a miss bad luck. It is characteristic of a playful attitude to such tests that one tries and tries again until one forces a lucky omen. Mental disorders tell the same tale. Schizophrenics revert to magical behaviour, thereby suggesting that it is still latent in us.

Magic in Political Propaganda

The town-dweller has little opportunity to study magical beliefs rationally, while the countryman has little inclination to do so. On the whole, magic remains as much of a mystery to the scientific mind as science does to the magical mind. It is thus difficult to say anything definitive about many aspects of magic. It may, for instance, be possible that in some districts of the East men possess powers which are not elsewhere known.[10] But there is at least one function of magical belief which is quite clear. Bronisław Malinowski writes,

> We find magic wherever the elements of chance and accident, and the emotional play between hope and fear have a wide and extensive range. We do not find magic wherever the pursuit is certain, reliable, and well under the control of rational methods and technological processes. Further, we find magic where the element of danger is conspicuous. We do not find it wherever absolute safety eliminates any elements of foreboding.... Thus [in northwest Melanesia] the dangerous fishing of the shark, the pursuit of the uncertain *kalala* or of the *to'ulam* are smothered in magic. The equally vital, but easy and reliable method of fishing by poison has no magic whatever. In the construction of the canoe—an enterprise surrounded with technical difficulties, requiring organized labor, and leading to an ever-dangerous pursuit—the ritual is complex, deeply associated with the work, and regarded as absolutely indispensable.[11]

Superstitions are one of our eternal answers to the insecurity of life. The more we feel that our lives are controlled by unforeseeable factors, the more superstitious we are. Gamblers, hunters, actors, etc. are superstitious, as it were, by profession. A surprising number of city-dwellers are sure that some days are more lucky and propitious than others. Sailors in small boats are more particular about sailing on Fridays than those working on big liners. Nothing but the shelter of a fool-proof security could suffocate the magical trends in our minds. Magical practices may diminish anxiety by appearing to prefigure the future. If you are about to have

10 See, for example, Alexandra David-Néel, *Magic and Mystery in Tibet* (New York: C. Kendall, 1932).
11 Bronisław Malinowski, *Myth in Primitive Psychology* (New York: W. W. Norton & Co., Inc., 1926), pp. 110 and 108.

an interview whose outcome is vital but uncertain, it may console you to discover that the numbers on your bus ticket, added together, do not give thirteen.

One often hears it said that it is superstition which creates anxiety, and not the other way round. This is psychologically unsound. It is quite true that as a manifestation of anxiety, superstition may poison and destroy all peace of mind, that it may prevent the soul from having any rest. But then it does not create fear, but simply furnishes it with new objects. Fear and anxiety are the parents, not the children of a superstitious mind.

Further, as Malinowski illustrates, magical ritual renders complex cooperation possible, as in the construction of a canoe and the pursuit of game. A group of people diminish their anxiety by elaborating collective obsessional actions. A ceremony must be complete, and it must remain unchanged. Any change affects its validity, and any untoward event during a ceremony causes superstitious concern. For instance, if you divine the future by counting "one, two, three" nine times before you take up the telephone receiver or open the door, you feel that you must finish the operation, and you may feel uneasy if you get muddled up. Magical songs or texts would cease to be a firm and stable pillar to hold on to in one's anxiety, if they were altered in any detail. If they were written in Latin, they should always be recited in Latin. To change the prayer book is to court national disaster.

No substitute has been found for magical ritual, and when it disappears or decays, it leaves a vacuum to be filled with despair. In a time of social crisis, the masses are moved by insecurity, anxiety, and terror. They will continue to propitiate fate and to invite fortune, as long as mysterious powers are shaping their destiny—forces whose inner workings they can see only through a glass, darkly. The propagandist recognises that the function of magic "consists in the bridging-over of gaps and inadequacies in highly important activities not yet completely mastered by man."[12]

When the whole world is shaking underfoot, social ceremonies, like the Coronation or the Lord Mayor's Show, with their antiquated pomp, give the illusion of social stability. Time seems to stand still, and frightening change arrested. Here the anxious soul finds something to hold on to. Magical symbols like the swastika inspire faith. They act as charms to ward off adversity. King, royal family, and flag still evoke in many hearts the rather irrational magical emotions of former times. The ritual dance is replaced by the goose step. Today's successful demagogues emulate the witch doctors of old—consider Lloyd George, the spellbinder, or Adolph Hitler, a new rainmaker and miracle worker. American fraternities revive the tribal yell.

In Europe d'Annunzio did more than almost anybody else to resuscitate the collective magical soul. In Fiume he was hailed as the new tribal chief, "il Duce."[13] He introduced salutes and ceremonies which he called *sagre* (rites or

---

12 Malinowski, *Myth in Primitive Psychology* (1926), p. 110.

13 *Editors: Gabriele d'Annunzio led a self-declared "state" in the Italian city of Fiume during 1919–1920, contributing to the origin of Italian Fascism. By 1925 Mussolini had assumed for himself the infamous epithet "il Duce."*

consecrations). New yells made their appearance, like "Eya! Eya! Alala!"—yells which did not claim to convey any rational message. Black shirts, skulls, cross-bones, and other emblems abounded in Fiume. The Duce asked his followers, "To whom Italy?" In a chorus they used to reply, "A noi! A noi!" (To us! To us!). The ancestral soul enjoyed itself.

Blood Cults

Blood provides the propagandist with a potent symbol. British Empire builders assure us that "blood is thicker than water." In many countries, "purity of the blood" is held sacred. Christians spread the cheerful message that the almighty power of the blood of Jesus Christ, the son of God, has washed away our sins. Some of Wesley's converts "felt the blood of Christ running upon their arms, or going down their throat, or poured like warm water upon their breasts or heart."[14] To purify himself, the Christian drinks Christ's blood in the Communion wine.[15] Conquerors maintain that the blood of their people has sanctified the soil. The Nazis talk about "blood and iron," "blood and honour," "blood and soil," "the fight of blood and money." They "think with their blood." Some audiences delight to hear about a "bloody revolution," and about their enemies "wading in blood," and similar talk. German communists sang lustily, "Only when the bourgeoisie lies bleeding can we really be free." The Nazis prefer to see Jewish blood spurting from their knives (see p. 66). A German song with the refrain "Blut muss fliessen, Blut muss fliessen, Blut muss fliessen knüppeldick" (blood must flow, blood must flow, blood must flow thickly) is rather popular. After the last war, conversation among young men was often enlivened by the words, "Licht aus, Messer raus, Blut rühren" (lights off, knives out, stir the blood). Even in everyday life we do not treat blood like any other fluid. Gore both horrifies and fascinates. The fascination with blood may be associated with sexual sadism, and sometimes plays a role in sexual crimes which, when expounded in newspapers, are so dear to the great heart of the public. Some are so overwhelmed that they faint at the mere sight of blood.

In these cases, people react to blood not as a physiological but as a magical stimulus. The blood we know of scientifically consists of water, haemoglobin, sugar, electrolytes, lipids, proteins, etc. The propagandist may safely ignore the chemical composition of blood. The magical associations of blood dominate his attitude. When they talk about the magic of blood, people reaffirm the certainties of age-old convictions in a bewildering world. Blood is an instrument of three magical powers.

---

14 Dimond, *The Psychology of the Methodist Revival*, p. 136.

15 H. Clay Trumbull, *The Blood Covenant: A Primitive Rite and its Bearings on Scripture* (Philadelphia: J. D. Wattles, 1883), pp. 191–202, shows that when our ancestors became more squeamish, they substituted the "blood of grapes" for real blood in their rites.

First of all, blood in ancient thought is almost equivalent to "life" and "soul." When it is shed, a mysterious soul-power is lost. Its effects may be perilous. That is why many tribes dare not eat it, and Jewish custom prohibits its consumption.

Secondly, blood may give strength. For this reason the Caribs, for instance, sprinkle a baby with the father's blood to give it the father's strength. Antisemites have persistently maintained for 2,000 years that the Jews steal Christian children and use their blood to make matzos for Passover. Of course only people who themselves believe, more or less consciously, in the magical efficacy of blood can imagine that Jews act on that belief. Applied in different ways, blood is thought to cure disease and protect from epidemics. In the early Norse legends blood is regarded as a powerful means of inspiration. Creative thought itself was born when the dwarfs drank Kvasir's blood, the "mead of poetry."[16]

Blood, finally, is a powerful tie of social unity. Two lives may be united in life-long friendship by a blood covenant. Blood is mixed by drinking or perhaps by ritual handshake. The old Germans let their blood run together, blended with soil, to effect an indissoluble blood brotherhood. Among the Australians

> blood may be given also to the members of an avenging expedition; to secure unity of purpose and to exclude treachery, it may even be forcibly administered to an outsider; special meetings of reconciliation are also accompanied by blood drinking.[17]

Kinship is based on the commonality of a blood-tie, on magical participation in the same blood. This goes beyond mere physical and visible blood. As a magical force it is sacred. Blood must be atoned for by blood. Trumbull illustrates forcibly how this is sometimes taken quite literally. If the Hallenga, living in the Sudan, took a person of another tribe for blood revenge, "his throat [was] slowly cut with a razor, the blood [was] caught in a bowl" and drunk by the tribe, so that the blood, which had been lost, was now replaced again.[18]

The reader who looks back to our examples of modern blood propaganda will find no difficulty in fitting them into this magical framework.

16 Hermann Leberecht Strack, *Der Blutaberglaube in der Menschheit, Blutmorde und Blutritus: Zugleich eine Antwort auf die Herausforderung des "Osservatore Cattolico"* (Munich: C. H. Beck, 1892), p. 139.

17 James Hastings, ed., *Encyclopædia of Religion and Ethics*, vol. 2 (New York: Charles Scribner's Sons, 1910), s.v. "Blood," p. 716. See also Baldwin Spencer and F. J. Gillen, *The Native Tribes of Central Australia* (London: Macmillan and Co., Ltd., 1899), pp. 461–462.

18 Trumbull, *The Blood Covenant*, pp. 132–133. This information is reported, with some scepticism, by Swiss orientalist Johann Ludwig Burckhardt in *Travels in Nubia* (published posthumously, 1819).

A Misunderstanding Removed

During the last six years, the importance of magic in politics has been commented upon by many democratic intellectuals. While these writers have collected relevant facts, I believe that they have gone astray in the interpretation of these facts.[19]

The "primitive" gives full rein to his magical impulses. The "civilised" town-dweller struggles against them. In a primitive (i.e. agricultural) society, magic is the chief source of power over events. Only some isolated intellectuals disapproved of magic before the coming of industrialism. If, in order to keep their hold over the people, they retained magic, they reinterpreted it by linking it up with "higher" religious sentiments. In this way Christian doctors sanctified many magical symbols and ceremonies. In the big modern towns, however, the intellectuals and their hangers-on form a powerful public opinion which ridicules everybody who seriously believes, say, that a broken mirror brings bad luck. Those who calmly maintained their magical ways of thinking were considered to be of no account. They were simply "uneducated." For more than a century the common people had no means of reassuring themselves, because industrial society, which was built upon scientific principles, remained fairly stable. In recent years, however, many countries have been shaken by one deep crisis after another. Repressed citizens, ignited by demagogues, "got going," insisted on "doing their bit," and in consequence the political scene was filled with witch doctors, magical spells, symbols, and rituals. "Superstition" reasserted itself in the social field.

The liberal intellectuals were deeply shocked. It became obvious that they, the leaders of public opinion, had had very little influence indeed. They had only overshouted the common people, without converting them. To console themselves the liberal intelligentsia blamed the "reversal to barbarism" on cunning rulers. As a matter of fact, it grew out of the inclination of the common people themselves.

It is quite erroneous to say that in fascism, for instance, an ancient trend in human psychology has re-emerged. What happened as a matter of fact is that a social class has come to the top who had never parted with their magical convictions. Only the educated find it difficult to appreciate the true nature of the process. Cut off from the masses, they habitually referred to the knowledge and ideas of a small intellectual minority as the knowledge and ideas "of the age";

---

19 Leonard Woolf (*Quack, Quack!* [London: Leonard and Virginia Woolf at the Hogarth Press, 1935], p. 102):

> The rational and civilized man knows that he has no monopoly of truth or virtue and that he must be perpetually on his guard against his instinct to ascribe wickedness as well as blindness to those who do not agree with him and to turn them into scapegoats for his own mistakes and misfortunes.

We are grieved to find that Woolf's defence of "civilisation" and "reason" is written in the very spirit of self-righteous indignation which he condemns. Behind the curtain of a glimmering style we find a savage frantically beating his tomtom in front of the new idols of "science" and "civilisation."

they spoke of a "country dominated by scientific thought," or used phrases like "it is strange that in this enlightened age..." They thus deluded themselves into believing that *they* were the "age," or "the country," or "the nation." When the common man wakes up he takes a cruel revenge for having been overlooked and neglected so long by the intellectual.

One has too often exaggerated the degree to which the common man was transformed or transmuted by contact with reason and science. In many cases he acquired a superstitious veneration for the magical, mysterious, miracle-working powers of science. To be sure, he treats the motor of his car as a collection of metal, and not as an abode of spirits which have to be reconciled. But this rational attitude towards cars is more of a mechanical aptitude than evidence of a truly scientific mentality. Only a tiny minority has acquired a scientific mentality and, among other things, the spirit of tolerance which bears witness to it.

The propagandist helps us to reassert our magical attitudes. He cannot give us back the liberty of the grasslands of Africa. Instead of the veldt, he plants us in Whipsnade[20] or in some such country hamlet in which, surrounded by all the amenities of modern comfort, we can listen nostalgically to a gramophone record playing "the call of the wild." It is ridiculous to expect us to live at present as though we belonged to a purely rational society. We will become mentally ill and discontented if we try to repress our magical heritage. The propagandist fulfils a useful function when he keeps it alive. By playing upon our savage trends, he makes our civilisation more bearable.

20 *Editors: The reference is to a pastoral village in southern England, and particularly to its zoological park which opened in 1931.*

PART II

The Veils Which Hide the Truth

2.1

RATIONALISATIONS

Thus 'tis with all; their chief and constant care
Is to seem everything but what they are.

Oliver Goldsmith[1]

Discussions on modern propaganda are often sidetracked into fruitless guesswork by our inveterate desire to sit in judgement over other people. "Do you think that Dr. Goebbels is sincere?" "Did President Wilson honestly believe in his 14 points?" "Did Hitler talk with his tongue in his cheek when he said that the Czechs were a menace to Germany?" "Did Mr. Wells actually think that the last war was fought for democracy?"

Questions of this kind are sure to crop up when the victims of propaganda discuss their masters' voices. On the whole, they find little difficulty in deciding these problems. If they believe *a priori* that the propagandist in question speaks the truth, they are generally inclined to think that he is sincere. On the other hand, they are apt to regard the propagandist whom they disbelieve as either dishonest, or mad, or weak-minded.[2] "Hitler is such a fool that he quite possibly believes in his own rubbish."

I have come to the conclusion that the question of the subjective honesty of the propagandist is irrelevant to understanding propaganda itself. Generally speaking, a man who believes what he says will convince with greater ease. The deliberate liar starts with a handicap, but the absence of genuine convictions makes for greater elasticity. Scientifically speaking, the problem of the subjective honesty

1 Oliver Goldsmith, *Epilogue to "The Sister"* (1769), line 25.

2 See, for example, Albert Nesor on Hitler as *The Mad Dog of Europe* (New York: Epic Publishers, Inc., 1939).

DOI: 10.4324/9781003363408-11

of the propagandist is on a level with the child's question, "Where do the angels put their hankies?" It is fruitless to discuss it.

In human life, *unconscious lying is the rule and conscious lying the exception*. In this part of the book we will see that both the victims of mass propaganda, and the propagandists themselves, regularly practice self-deception, whether they know it or not. How could the masses be deceived for any length of time if they did not *wish* to be deceived? Very few dare admit either what they want, or what they are, or what actually exists. The propagandists take men as they are.

In Chapters 2.1, 2.3, and 2.5, I will explain how people get into the habit of deceiving themselves, and how thereby they lose the ability, and often even the desire, to distinguish truth from falsehood, and reality from illusion. Because further self-deception and dishonesty are indispensable to our mental well-being, we joyfully welcome the efforts of propaganda to envelop the facts of social strife within a thick mist of illusion (Chapters 2.2 and 2.4).

Before we deal with group mendacity (camouflage), we must first say some words about the individuals who compose the group. A person's self-deception is a simple consequence of the distinction between their conscious and unconscious mind. The greater part of our personality, being unconscious, is hidden from us. Impulses and wishes which meet with resistance or disapproval from the social environment are repressed and pushed out of sight. They nevertheless continue to exert a predominant influence over our activities. But since they are out of sight, they will naturally be missing from any account we may give, to ourselves or to others, of the way in which our activities come about.

Fifty years of psychological research have made it amply clear that the motives we believe we have usually bear only a loose connection to the forces that actually cause our thoughts, feelings, and actions. Within limits, we are now able to look behind the mask with which people, more or less unconsciously, cover their real motives.

Definitions and Examples

We say that people *rationalise* if they explain to themselves or to others by respectable though inadequate reasons those actions, thoughts, and emotions which are actually prompted by instincts and impulses that are the subject of a mental conflict. The real reason and the professed reason do not go together. The professed reason does not explain; it explains away.

To give a simple example. A wealthy person may wish to live a life of luxury. This inclination may be in conflict with the moral standards of their upbringing, and of the other people in the community. Rationalisation allows them to follow their inclinations without violating those moral standards. Some years ago, the newspapers were full of the story of a woman who had spent £1,000 on one single party. Self-glorification being at least one of her real motives, she had invited representatives of the newspapers to admire her party. One reporter did not play the game. He attacked her for squandering her money in the midst of so much poverty. A libel action was the result. The woman appeared in court. She strenuously denied that the desire for self-glorification had anything to do with the party, claimed that she preferred a simple life and disliked parties, and produced a long list of the persons who had got employment from the affair. The reason she gave is respectable, though obviously inadequate. Though she may actually believe that she had acted selflessly on behalf of the community, if she wanted simply to do good and to create employment, she might have anonymously built a house for an impoverished family.

Some people dance "for exercise," when really they enjoy dancing as a substitute satisfaction for the sex instinct. A Chinese man incredulously watched modern dancing for an hour. Then he asked his European friend, "But, they do marry these ladies?" People who have been brought up to regard the sex instinct as dirty and depraved will be disinclined to admit to themselves that they follow its promptings. In order to gratify their sexual inclinations with a good conscience, they have to rationalise them into a desire for exercise.

It will now be clear what we mean by rationalisation. The surface of our minds is one vast tissue of rationalisations. We have the father who goes to the circus "to take the boy," or the woman who goes to lectures and concerts because she loves the lecturer or conductor, though she pretends to be enthusiastic about the subject or the music. An enumeration of all possible rationalisations would fill a new *Ulysses*.

Contrary to popular belief, psychology does *not* claim that the disreputable reason is always the real one, and that nobody can ever do anything from reputable motives. The reputable motives are not completely invented. In most cases, motives are mixed, partly wholesome and partly not so much. The first will then be emphasised, and the second minimised, or blotted out completely.

A rich woman's charitable work among the poor in the slums may be partly prompted by a concern for the poor, and a sincere desire to help them. But that is rarely the whole story. In addition, the work may give her a sense of superiority, or something to talk about, or relieve her bad conscience, or give her a domineering position, or if she is single or without children, give her something to mother, or make her feel virtuous, or give her a feeling of power from being able to interfere in the lives of others.[3] But she will be far less willing and ready to admit these more "selfish" motives to herself—however much they may leak through in her actual behaviour—than the more "unselfish" ones.

By extending the meaning of the word, we say that we rationalise not only our instincts and motives, but also our failures and convictions. A person who is unsuccessful is apt to rationalise his failure, and to find excuses which shift the responsibility away from him. The task was too hard, there was this obstacle and

3 These motives are taken from a questionnaire I circulated among slum-dwellers in the East End of London.

that obstacle, he was ill and not at his best—and so it goes in a desire to minimise personal responsibility.

Our convictions, thoughts, and beliefs depend largely on temperament, upbringing, and education. But few people are fully aware of these factors. Usually we evade the real reason for our convictions because it makes us look less reasonable. A person adheres say to a religion, or believes that the Earth came from the Sun, "because the doctrine is true." Obviously the apparent reason is that he *believes* in the truth of that particular doctrine. But why? Has he weighed all the evidence for and against? Very rarely so. The real reason is that persons in authority taught this doctrine, and that his parents adhered to it. Otherwise it would be difficult to explain the geographical distribution of religions.

The one true religion is a bit too often the particular one into which we were born. Lord Melbourne, with commendable honesty, said openly that he would adhere to the Church of England *because* it was the Church of his ancestors. Two thousand years before Lord Melbourne's time, the pontifex Cotta remarked, "No one's utterances, be he learned or unlearned, shall ever move me from those convictions with regard to the worship of the immortal gods that I have inherited from our forefathers."[4] Our attitude towards parents and authority, however, is not all adoring love. In some cases hatred predominates. Rebellious sons and daughters can be seen to take up a doctrine enthusiastically in order to spite their parents. It is almost impossible for us to adopt an intimate conviction without reference to the views of persons we like or dislike. Our wish to be like the people we like, and unlike the people we dislike, usually counts for more in the choice of our convictions than the "universally acceptable" reasons on which they seem to rest.

Although this account is endorsed by almost all psychologists as a mere commonplace, the public receives it with some reluctance. They usually wonder how we can be sure of the real, unconscious reason for an action. Yet though our true nature is hidden, it will peep out and betray itself at one time or another. Psychology offers techniques for probing into the unconscious, and for discovering what lies below the surface of the mind. The analysis of dreams, chance actions, free associations, etc. furnishes ample material. Psychology, as understood by psychoanalysts, deals almost exclusively with the technique of tearing off the disguises by which we cloak our intentions from ourselves even as successfully as from others. In this context, we have to take all this for granted.

Why Do We Deceive Ourselves?

Normally people are unaware of the origin and real nature of the mental forces which are responsible for their conduct. This is only another way of saying that normally people are not psychologists. Similarly a man who falls out of a window

4 Cicero, *De Natura Deorum* 3.5, trans. Francis Brooks (1896).

is in most cases unaware of the exact nature of the force which causes him to fall. But while one does not specially mind being told that the centre of the earth attracts a falling body, one resists an attempt on the part of psychologists to uncover one's real motives. Rationalisation goes deeper than mere ignorance. It implies *unwillingness* to see oneself. The practising analyst has the experience, over and over again, that his patients waste much of their money and of his time on vain attempts to keep up appearances. It is one thing to admit that other people's explanations are rationalisations. It is another, a very different thing, to be thoroughly honest with oneself about oneself, and about the beliefs one is so fond of.[5]

Why, then, is the ordinary man so frightened at the idea of divesting himself of his rationalisations? Why does he resort to hypocrisy, dissimulation, and even to open lying in order to preserve them? The answer to this question will give us the key to the propagandist's success.

Isolated examples can show no more than that men occasionally deceive themselves. In order to realise why self-deception is more natural to us than unconditional sincerity, we must consider what we would have to give up if we were willing to be strictly honest with ourselves. In actual practice we have to choose between an attempt to satisfy our *narcissism* and sentiment of *self-regard* on the one side, and a desire for truthfulness and honesty on the other. On the whole, human beings care far less for truth than for self-respect and the respect of others.

Narcissism is derived from the sex instinct. A narcissist, in the widest sense, is a person who lovingly contemplates his own perfections. He splits his personality, and the self is reflected in itself, as in a mirror.[6] Narcissistic behaviour arises when the sex instinct is turned on our own body, as its object. It is normal in certain phases of childhood, and may lead to auto-eroticism, when the child discovers its own body as a source of erotic pleasure. In its sexual form, narcissistic self-contemplation normally persists in adults to an attenuated degree. In pathological cases, the narcissist is so much absorbed in his self-love that he loves himself too much to spare any love for anyone else.

In its clearly sexual form, narcissistic behaviour is accompanied by sexual excitement, as when a girl experiences sexual pleasure when kissing her own hand, looking at her naked body in a mirror, or kissing her own image. Some people require constant admiration from their spouse or lover. They are able to love only insofar as the beloved mirrors their own perfections.

Usually, however, the greater part of narcissistic energies is desexualised. A normal man is as proud of the size of his brain as he is of the length of his penis. We are captivated by desexualised narcissism when we "pat ourselves on the back,"

5 It is, however, remarkable how much our willingness to have an insight into the rationalisation of others is influenced by our opinions about whether their actions are objectively "good" or not. An English Protestant of 1939 will far more easily see the basic sadism in the mind of an Inquisitor than in that of, say, Florence Nightingale.

6 Narcissus was a Greek youth who fell in love with his own reflection in the water.

or "stroke ourselves" (as they say in France) for being so good at something which is not immediately connected with sex life. Sexual narcissism makes us admire the beauty, strength, and sex appeal of our body. The familiar processes of repression and sublimation drain a part of the sexual energy away from directly sexual channels. Narcissistic admiration is extended to any part of the personality which may seem admirable.

According to William McDougall, the sentiment of *self-regard* arises when assertion of self is coupled with contemplation of self.[7] A faulty perspective almost forces us to over-value anything which is so close to our self that we can imagine that it "belongs" to it. When I reflect myself in myself, or in others, I treat that which belongs to me almost invariably as dearer to me than that which belongs to others. A halo of affection surrounds what is "mine"—my body, my mind, my family, my friends, my material possessions, my country, etc.[8] A mother easily deceives herself about the qualities of her child, because it is "her" child, and a man or a woman about those of his or her lover. "*My* father is taller than your father, because *my* father is as tall as the sky." How can it be different if we want to assert ourselves? And how different everything would seem to be if we were to efface ourselves![9]

In other words, as long as I divide the things and objects of the world into "mine" and "not mine," I see myself in a biased and distorted way. I and my own qualities and possessions take up much more space in my field of vision than they occupy in actual reality. A man may therefore have to choose between self-deception and social usefulness. For if he purifies his mind of ideas of "mine" and "not mine," of likes and dislikes, of love and hate, if he abandons self-assertion and self-affection, the inner logic of his fight against self-deception destroys the basis of social life as we know it. Without the incentives of narcissism and self-assertion,

---

7 William McDougall, *An Outline of Psychology* (London: Methuen & Co., Ltd., 1923), p. 426 et seq. In this context I must push aside the problems of *negative* self-regard. In certain moods, of course, people may not estimate themselves higher, but lower than they are. Melancholics generally under-estimate themselves. An analysis of their state of mind shows that they do so out of a variant form of narcissistic self-regard. The main point here is that we almost invariably find in psychology, social and individual, that things are different from what they appear to be. Psychology teaches us to be mistrustful, and not to accept a person's assertions about himself at their face value. People are very unreliable witnesses as to themselves. We do not judge an individual on the basis of his own opinion of himself. Why should we make an exception with ourselves?

8 Things can acquire dignity from the mere fact that they belong to us. Stendhal wrote about the art critic Étienne-Jean Delécluse: "When he buys for 36 francs a dozen handkerchiefs in a shop round the corner, two hours later he believes that his handkerchiefs are a rarity, and that for no price could one find similar ones in Paris." I have to be rather brief here on a difficult subject. It may help readers to consult in conjunction with these pages the admirable chapter on the "self" in William James, *Principles of Psychology*, vol. 1 (New York: Henry Holt & Co., 1890).

9 We are so used to seeing the world from the angle of self-assertion, that it may be difficult to imagine what the world would look like if one tried not to assert oneself. The *Shinjin-no-mei* of Seng-t'san gives a most illuminating description. It can be consulted in D. T. Suzuki, *Manual of Zen Buddhism* (Kyoto: Eastern Buddhist Society, 1935), pp. 91–97.

the fields would remain untilled, the factories would close, procreation would cease, and man would disappear from the face of the Earth. But, as we said before, a species tends to preserve its existence. If there is any purpose or meaning in the existence of animals and plants, it is that of perpetuating the species simply because it exists (see page 7).

All these factors—blindness towards the unconscious, narcissism, self-flattery, self-assertion, self-regard—combine to obscure man's true and real self.[10] In its stead he throws up some Fata Morgana, some more or less pleasing image of himself, which he mistakes for reality. But even the blindest sometimes realise that what they appear to be is very different from what they really are. It happens to everyone that he does something, or wants to do something, that is incongruous with the idealised picture he has constructed of himself. His self-respect is threatened. He either suppresses his "evil wish" or, if he does what he likes to do, he covers it up from himself (and others) by rationalising it. In moments when we feel uncertain about ourselves, a rationalisation reassures us that we did not betray the goodness in us. Rationalisations indicate a mental conflict in those who generate them. Somebody in a bus is torn between his social conscience and the desire to save his fare of a penny (mental conflict). Now, supposing that he contrives not to pay his fare, he may come to the rescue of his antisocial desires by some excuse like, "Oh, I do not want to embarrass the conductor," or "This company makes too much money anyhow" (rationalisations). In other words: first one does what one likes to do. Not content with this, one still wants to believe that one did what one should have done.

Broadly speaking, it gives people pleasure to torture others. It is beatitude to torture them from higher motives—to give them a chance to show fortitude, and save their souls; or to protect the greatness of one's country and the homes of widows and orphans, etc. Sometimes even the blindest are forced to cast a furtive glance at the thieves' den of their unconscious. Rationalising allows them to look away rapidly, and to avoid recognition of their unconscious and irrational urges. Labouring under the delusion that he is a rational animal, man tries to find a reasonable motive for his actions, and to work out a consistent and not too unflattering theory of himself. Anxious to appear better than they are and to conform to the moral standards accepted in their society, the majority of people quite innocently justify, to themselves and to others, "selfish" actions by a pretence of disinterest and self-denial.

Covered with a comfortable cloak of rationalisations, one appears to live up tolerably well to a pleasing image of oneself. But while our effort to live up to this image is due to narcissism and self-assertion, we owe the ideal image itself to *social pressure*. We cannot live all alone in splendid isolation. Outside its social setting, the self is a lump of shivering protoplasm. Even our narcissism, self-centred as it may

10 It is not necessary here for me to explain what that "true and real self" really is. All we are concerned with in this context is the distorting effect of the factors mentioned.

seem, demands gratification through receiving the attention and consideration of others. Social pressure makes us conform to social standards, because we are threatened with the anxieties of social isolation and in need of receiving love. In order that we might be loved by others, we feel an obligation to justify ourselves as individuals to society even in our own conscience.[11] Only in quite unusual cases does anybody maintain his self-respect in the face of universal condemnation by society. Conversely, it is difficult to enjoy the praise of others unless one believes that one deserves it, and therefore one will be apt to rationalise antisocial impulses even to oneself.

We can now understand why people cannot give up their self-deception without giving up themselves. How can we expect reason and scientific analysis to prevail against the distorting effect of all the weighty and vigorous forces which are inherent in social life, and which compel us to deceive ourselves? The light from the tiny lamp of reason has as much chance to penetrate the thick mists of self-deception as a dry leaf has to stand up against a gale. A psychologist cannot hope to be popular if he attempts to free his clients of their rationalisations. The shattering of rationalisations—as soon as it is more than a mere parlour game, and becomes serious—is resented as a blow to self-respect. For, in most cases, self-respect is almost entirely built up on rationalisations. A man who is being stripped of his rationalisations may feel like a middle-aged sedentary businessman, whose good figure was held in shape by his tailor and an abdominal belt, were he to reveal his stark nakedness to his assembled shareholders. My experiences as a practising psychologist are unambiguous on the point. If you try to give value for your patient's money and discuss his rationalisations with him, he feels his self-respect shrink. For a time at least he will hate you because you do not think highly enough of him, and also because you show him that he is an accomplished "liar." To apply this cathartic method to persons who are an object of hero worship means to conjure up a storm. Your patient will think, and sometimes he will tell you, that you are a diffident, disrespectful, deprecatory, supercilious, pusillanimous, and suspicious person. By uncovering rationalisations, and putting "higher motives" into their subordinate place, the psychologist appears to lower human nature, and to disparage human greatness and goodness.

We have now seen why human beings, as individuals, are bent on deceiving themselves, and we can proceed to consider some of the facts concerning the role of self-deception in social life.

11 It has been said that the shams of social convention are another impediment to our sight of reality, and they increase still further the gulf between what we appear to be, and what we are. "Cursed be the social lies that warp us from the living truth" (Tennyson). Courtesy demands that we wear a mask. Politeness is an institution for mutual flattery. But our vision of ourselves is seriously influenced by the flattery of others. It is further essential to social success that we should acquire the talent of lying in a way which cannot be readily detected. As Karl Menninger expresses it, strict honesty would soon land us in prison, or in a lunatic asylum. In genuine moral indignation people would show us the door.

2.2
CAMOUFLAGE

The nation which lets its duty get on the opposite side to its interest is lost.
George Bernard Shaw[1]

We speak of "camouflage" if and when the members of a social group rationalise about a common activity or purpose.[2] In warfare, tanks, guns, and ships are disguised by obscuring their outline with splashes of various colours; smokescreens are also used. Camouflage in propaganda is one of the most powerful and effective weapons in the struggle among nations, classes, and other social groups. Half of the work of a propagandist is to suitably conceal the aims of his social group.

The Germans speak of "Tarnung." The word refers to the Siegfried Saga, where it is recorded how Siegfried made himself invisible by his magic hood or "tarn-cap." Similarly "camouflage" renders objects invisible and unrecognisable. None of these words quite brings out the psychological point that in camouflage a thing does not appear only as what it is not, but as the very opposite of what it is.

First I want to lay before the reader some of the facts of camouflage. We allow ourselves to be deceived only when it is in our interest. We therefore see quite easily through the camouflage of alien and especially of hostile groups. The Japanese propagandist impresses the British public neither forcefully nor favourably when he talks about lifting up the Chinese, and cooperating with them for their common prosperity and well-being, by making war on them and bombing Chinese towns. "One stops to wonder whether his ideas of the use of language

1 George Bernard Shaw, *The Man of Destiny* (New York: Brentano's, 1913), p. 82.

2 The word is relatively new to the English language. It appears to have come into use only in 1917. The *Daily Mail* of May 25, 1917, explains it: "The act of hiding anything from your enemy is termed 'camouflage.'" Also in French the word is new, referring to mimicry or mimic acting.

DOI: 10.4324/9781003363408-12

have anything in common with our own."[3] On the other hand, "sermons from Great Britain in particular sound to them [the Japanese] like warnings from a reformed burglar living in comfort on his swag."[4]

In the following pages I try to survey the chief types of camouflage. The reader will probably enthusiastically assent to my diagnosis in some cases. Other instances, which concern his own camouflage, may appear less well-chosen. In moments of scientific detachment we should, nevertheless, be capable of seeing our own camouflage and that of others on the same level. Only then will we get from the analysis of camouflage more than a feeling of triumph at a devastating cleverness which enables us to detect, and to look down upon, other peoples' self-deceptions. We must bear in mind all the time the following questions: Why do people require camouflage? Why and how are they deceived? Why will they continue to cling to their own camouflage even though they have seen the baselessness of analogous views held by other groups? Primitive tribes used to employ rainmakers. We only feel comfortable when we have our heads in the clouds, and so we employ in the propagandist a cloud-maker, so that we may never go without clouds to stick our heads in.

Camouflage and Empire-Building

Two thousand years ago the territories around the Black Sea were ruled by a great king by the name of Mithridates. This king came into conflict with the Roman Empire. He summed up his experiences with the Roman imperialists in the words: "There is one ever-recurring cause why the Romans have wars with all nations, peoples, and kings, and that is their boundless greed for power and wealth."[5]

To the Romans themselves, however, the matter did not appear in this light. Whenever they expanded their empire, they pretended to be impelled not by selfish reasons, but by a disinterested and self-denying impulse to do good to others. Whenever they had conquered a country, they bled it white. But whenever they attacked a country, they denied that the motive of plunder entered into their considerations. They pretended to make war for such unselfish reasons as the desire to help and protect some weak friends and allies, and to carry good

3 *The Round Table: A Quarterly Review of the Politics of the British Commonwealth*, December, 1937, p. 19. See also (ibid.):

> They have a habit, which saddens their friends and infuriates their adversaries, of defending themselves and reproving others in terms so devoid of meaning as to give the impression that, having really nothing to say, they are merely emitting a smokescreen.

The context shows that the author has the Japanese in mind.

4 Ibid., p. 21.

5 Sallust, *Historiae* 4.67. *Editors: We are unable to identify the source of this particular translation, although Conze himself had quoted the same translation several years prior in his 1936 article "The Psychology of Imperialism II" (see pp. 26–27 n. 12).*

government, law, and justice into the conquered territories whose inhabitants were "so manifestly unfit to govern themselves." Nobody admired their "magnanimity" more than they did themselves. It became second nature to Roman statesmen, orators, and historians to dwell lovingly on their "inveterate habit of giving more than they took," on their "neglect of their own interests," and on "the clemency and righteousness for which they [the Romans] claimed to be renowned among the nations."[6] Obviously, the enormous profits they got from their Empire were looked upon as a casual by-product of their virtue. "The Senate of the Roman people has always been of such a clemency and compassion that nobody ever did in vain ask for its help."[7]

The Enemy Is "Liberated"

What was perhaps the most brilliant piece of Roman imperialist propaganda deserves to be set out in some detail. Driven by a high admiration for Greek culture, the Roman consul Flamininus in 200 BC invaded Greece, spreading the news that he intended to liberate the Greeks from their Macedonian oppressors. According to Plutarch, the Greeks were persuaded "that the Romans were come to wage war, not upon the Greeks, but upon the Macedonians in behalf of the Greeks."[8] Many Greeks took the promise at its face value. When in 196 BC the freedom of Greece was proclaimed at the Isthmian games, "A shout of joy arose, so incredibly loud that it reached the sea.... All were eager to spring forward and greet and hail the saviour and champion of Greece."[9] In actual fact, of course, the Greeks were now a subject people. The Romans, occupied by many wars at that time, only waited until they had their hands free.[10] Fifty years later they felt strong enough to drop even the pretence of Greek freedom, and Greece openly became a Roman province.

---

6 Sallust, *Historiae* 1.55.

7 Sallust, *Catilina* 34.1. Similarly, Pericles said of the Athenians, "We alone are in the habit of serving others not from a consideration of our profit, but in order to secure a noble freeness of trust." Thucydides 2.40.

8 Plutarch, *Flamininus* 5.6, trans. Bernadotte Perrin.

9 Ibid., 10.5.

10 There were many reasons why it was clearly in the interest of the Senate not to subject the Greeks outright. All ancient and modern historians agree on that point. Only by detaching the Greeks from the Macedonian King could a lengthy war be avoided (Plutarch, op. cit., 2.4). A lengthy war would have led to an alliance of all their formidable enemies, and the Romans would have been in great difficulties (ibid., 9.7-8). The Romans also pre-empted a march by Antiochus, a king in Asia Minor, who wanted to make war on Greece under the same pretext of offering the Greeks their freedom. As Plutarch puts it, "The Greeks did not want to be set free by Antiochus, for they were free already" (ibid., 15.1). Further, by "setting free" the Greeks in Asia Minor, Roman magnanimity also struck a blow at Antiochus, who claimed the Greek cities of Asia Minor as his possessions. (See John B. Bury *et al.*, eds., *The Cambridge Ancient History*, vol. 8 [New York: Macmillan, 1930], p. 179 et seq.)

How far were the participants of this struggle "taken in" by the camouflage? There are three parties to be considered: the Roman Senate, the Consul Flamininus, and the Greeks. The Senate clearly used this propaganda as a deliberate calculation. Most of its members at the time still had little respect for Greek culture. They regarded the Greeks as akin to chattering monkeys, and used the high opinion the Greeks had of themselves to undermine them. From what we know about Flamininus, it is just possible that his role as liberator of Greece went to his head, and that he felt quite sincerely that he was doing good.[11] Those who doubt whether a responsible person in his senses can be taken in by this childish kind of camouflage should remember President Wilson. It is always desirable that propaganda should be carried out by people who more or less believe in what they say.

As to the Greeks, they were divided into three sections. The more sober were not deceived. They asked their fellows

> whether they were glad to have a fetter now which was smoother than the one they had worn before, but heavier; and whether they admired Titus [Flamininus] as a benefactor because he had unshackled the foot of Greece and put a collar round her neck.[12]

Others, however, as we saw, swallowed the Roman bait. Why did they believe such transparent nonsense as that the Romans came as their disinterested saviours? Partly because they were so infatuated with themselves that they thought it quite natural that the Roman barbarians should have succumbed to the splendour of the Greek name. A third section could not make up their minds. In any case, the morale of the Greeks was severely undermined. If a bully approaches and it is just possible that he may mean well, our reason easily persuades itself that he does mean well, because it would be so convenient if he did. If he assures his wavering victims that his intentions are beneficial, he provides a good excuse for all those who fear a desperate struggle. A last hope is not easily relinquished. Many Greeks believed in what they desperately wished to be true, perhaps only half-heartedly, but strongly enough to paralyse their resistance. It is true that the deception did not work long. "Disloyalty" cropped up as soon as the Greeks understood what had happened, but by then it was too late.

---

11 See, for instance, Plutarch, op. cit., 1.2:

> Since he was covetous of honour and fame, he desired that his noblest and greatest achievements should be the result of his own efforts, and he took more pleasure in those who wanted to receive kindness than in those who were able to bestow it, considering that the former were objects upon which he would exercise his virtue, while the latter were his rivals, so to speak, in the struggle for fame.

12 Plutarch, op. cit., 10.2.

The device, although extremely clumsy, has its uses. Imperialists never get tired of liberating foreigners.

Some Occasions on which Propagandists Camouflaged Conquest by the Promise of Liberation:[13]

1519 and after: The Spaniards invade Mexico for the good of the Mexicans, and in order to liberate them from Montezuma's oppression.

1789 and after: The French Revolutionary troops start to liberate German populations from their feudal rulers, as a first step towards plundering them.

ca. 1850 and after: The Tsars become keen on liberating the Slavs of the Balkans, for the actual purpose of disintegrating the Ottoman Empire and reaching Constantinople. Panslavist propaganda covers up the tracks of their advance to the Mediterranean.

1911: The Italian Government frees the Tripolitan Arabs from Turkish oppression. "To be sure the Arabs did not care to be freed, but that was a matter of little or no importance: they *had* to be 'freed' willynilly."[14]

1914 and after: T. E. Lawrence liberates the Arabs; Ludendorff liberates the Polish Jews; in preparation for the Treaty of Versailles, the Germans are rescued from the Kaiser.

1934 and 1935: Before coming to liberate the non-Amharic subject races in addition to many slaves, the Italians circulate maps which show that the greater part of Abyssinia was only conquered by the Negus during the last fifty years.

1935: The Japanese soon join in the orgy of liberations. A number of Indians are led to expect their liberation from the Japanese, who have also managed to convince some Maoris of New Zealand of their liberating mission. Major-General Tada, Commander of the Japanese Garrison in Northern China, publishes a pamphlet called *The Basic Conception of China*: "The international situation...may be regarded as the beginning of a racial war for the emancipation of the coloured people who form the greater part of the human inhabitants of the world from the enslaving oppression by the whites."[15]

1933 to present: Following the rise of the Nazi Party, Leftists rave about their desire to liberate the Germans from Hitler, the Italians from Mussolini, and the Japanese from the Mikado, by either starving them into submission, or bombing them out of existence. Meanwhile Red imperialism threatens to liberate the whole world, and Hitler contemplates retaliation. Disturbed by

---

13 For reasons of space I omit the numerous occasions on which the British have "liberated" people by incorporating them into the British Empire.

14 Vilfredo Pareto, *The Mind and Society: A Treatise on General Sociology*, vol. 3, trans. Andrew Bongiorno and Arthur Livingston (New York: Dover Publications, 1935), p. 1152, §1708.

15 Issued in *Manchuria Daily News*, October 2–4, 1935.

the observation that the Russian, French, and English people moan under the yoke of Jewish oppression, he may send his troops to set them free.

British Camouflage

This sort of disinterested attitude is affected best just by those Empire-building nations who prosper most. This is a serious problem and we must try to understand why that should be so. To hide one's true intentions and to conceal one's true motives is, in fact, an indispensable element of the imperialist game. Who can, in this connection, fail to think of the excuses brought forth during the last war?

No intelligent person any longer doubts that it was an imperialist war. On the side of Britain, the following material interests were involved: Germany's threat to India by the Baghdad railway; German naval rearmament; German goods driving English goods from the world's markets; and, finally, Germany's threat to the Belgian coast. But the statesmen of the British Empire drew a veil of unselfish motives over these material interests, and the masses of the Empire fell for their deceit. They marched to "defend poor little Belgium," to "make the world safe for democracy," to "defeat German militarism," to "safeguard the sanctity of treaties," and to "establish peace on earth."

Who now, twenty years later, in full view of all the results of the last war, does not fully agree with the words which John Bright spoke in 1878:

> It is a painful and terrible thing to think how easy it is to stir up a nation to war. Take up any decent history of this country, from the time of William III until now—for two centuries, or nearly so—and you will find that wars are always supported by a class of arguments which, after the war is over, the people find were arguments they should not have listened to.[16]

Every historian must be struck by the regularity with which this sort of thing goes on throughout the entire history of imperialism. The sauce with which wars are served up varies with the fashion of the time. But "unselfishness" and "idealism" are invariably the sauce's main ingredients.

We take our illustrations from the history of British imperialism because it is more familiar and the details require less explanation. When the British imperialists fought against Napoleon, they did so for "the deliverance of Europe." In the end, the deliverance of Europe amounted to delivering it into the hands of Metternich. Forty years later, the Crimean War was fought in order to check an expansion by Russia into those Asiatic territories which Britain had reserved for herself. But Richard Cobden noted in a speech at the time that the real question had been

---

16 "Danger of War with Russia," Birmingham, January 13, 1878. Quoted in John Bright, *Selected Speeches of the Rt. Hon. John Bright M. P. On Public Questions* (London: J. M. Dent and Co., 1907), p. 169.

"very much mixed up with magniloquent phraseology." He reports that people "spoke of our duties to mankind and to the whole world," talked about their intention "to protect the liberties of all Europe and of the civilised world," and, in the best style of their Roman predecessors, pretended to fight "for the defence of our ancient ally [Turkey]."[17] The radical *Morning Advertiser*, clamouring for war, argued in 1854:

> Has the British bosom ceased to throb in response to the claims of humanity? Has justice ceased to occupy her throne in the English heart? Has the national honour—that which used to be the glory of every Englishman in every part of the world—lost its hold on the minds of the people of these realms? It is impossible. Englishmen can never sink to that lowest depth of degradation. Let, then, the country arise, as one man, and take the national affairs into its own hands. Let the imbecile men, the minions of Russia, constituting the Cabinet, be swept by a storm of popular indignation from their official places, and men be appointed in their stead, who will vindicate the national character, afford effective aid to Turkey, and frustrate the plans of the Czar to achieve an universal empire in Europe.[18]

Is this not almost exactly the language used in recent times by the opponents of Chamberlain's foreign policy?

Examples of Camouflage in the Class War

Nor is camouflage lacking in the class war, or in the conflicts of social groups other than nations. Aristotle and Cicero assure us that it is useful (*sympherei*) for the slave that he is a slave. For it is useful for the body that it should serve the soul, and in general it is useful for the lower to serve the higher. The vanquished in war were enslaved for their own good, so that they could be tamed and humanised.

In modern times, the fight between capitalists and workers calls forth much camouflage. The real object of the fight is the distribution of the spoils of production. Each side tries to get as large a share of the national income as possible—the one in rent, interest, and profit, the other in wages and social services. But partly in order to demoralise their opponents, partly in order to get the good conscience which comes from being inspired by an ideal purpose, and partly in order to influence the wavering middle classes, both sides pour out a torrent of high-sounding propaganda. This propaganda aims at proving that it is in the interest of the opponent, and in the interests of society in general, that profits—or wages—should be high. For many years the capitalists proved that only by low wages can

---

17 December 22, 1854. Quoted in *Hansard's Parliamentary Debates: Third Series, Commencing with the Accession of William IV*, vol. 136 (London: Cornelius Buck, 1855), p. 804.

18 *The Morning Advertiser*, Monday, January 2, 1854, p. 4.

an economic crisis be avoided. The Trade Unions prove, on the contrary, that only a policy of high wages can steer us clear of a slump.

It is a matter of common observation that a group of people who want something frequently pretend not to want it for themselves, but for the sake of some social group or of some high-sounding ideal. In quite a number of countries, abortion and birth control are illegal, and the targets of vigorous propaganda. The argument is usually cloaked in moral terms when the real concern is for a supply of cheap workers and plenty of soldiers. The better classes thus compensate for their own lack of fertility.

If capitalists want tariffs or subsidies from the government, they claim to desire these privileges, not for themselves and for their own profit, but for their workers, for the good of Britain, and in order to relieve unemployment. The interests of politicians and ruling classes always somehow coincide with the interests of the country.

The capitalists never fail to say how much they are concerned about the welfare of the worker. Measures hostile to the worker are represented as being in the worker's own interest. Bourgeois economists incessantly repeat the following argument for lower wages: the worker is interested that the demand for his work should be great; the more capital, the more demand for his services. The worker should therefore be interested, more than anything else, in the increase of profit and the growth of capital. At the same time, the eight-hour work-day was claimed to be contrary to his welfare on the grounds that it took away his liberty to work more. In this case, "liberty" is just another word for "economic bondage," and "freedom of contract" masks the power to exploit. The worker was supposed to cherish the freedom to work twelve to sixteen hours a day, but he obviously had no inclination to be liberated for the chance of working a shorter day, and of finding some leisure.

The opponents of the measure to reduce the work-day for children to ten hours argued that shortening it meant a diminution of production with a reduction in wages. Foreign competitors would rob Britain of her markets, wages were therefore bound to fall, and the workers would be the first to suffer. The abolition of child labour would be contrary to the interest of the worker who did not know what to do at home with the unoccupied boys who were compelled by law to be idle.[19] In 1884 it was written in the *Zentralverband deutscher Industrieller*,

> It seems more reasonable to allow the children to do agreeable work, and to let them earn something, than to hand them over to idleness and brutalisation [Verwilderung]. A law which completely forbids children to work at school age would prolong worry and distress in many working-class families, and would bring down the standard of living. Under these circumstances

19 "The prohibition or limitation of the work of children and adolescents did not commend itself to the parents of those forbidden to work." Bernard Miall, trans., *New Chapters of Bismarck's Autobiography* (London: Hodder and Stoughton, 1920), p. 106.

> the protected children would, further, suffer in their bodily development more from insufficient nourishment than from working in factories.[20]

In 1903, the same organisation pointed out triumphantly that the growing criminality among young workers was due to the decrease in the number of those who worked in factories.[21] Recent discussions on the school-leaving age in the countryside have also given rise to specious arguments of this kind. The psychologist wants to know why people take the trouble to invent them.

We may conclude with an example from South Africa. The Hon. Oswald Pirow, South African Minister of Justice, opposed the limitation of flogging to juveniles only. He said that the limitation

> was not in the natives' best interest. No matter how they might gloss it over, the fact remained that throughout South Africa corporal punishment was inflicted by farmers upon natives. The natives themselves accepted the practice, which might almost be regarded as a traditional one, and generally speaking [!] had no objection to it.[22]

The Germans lost their colonies for saying pretty much the same thing. These are the devious ways of camouflage.

The Chief Types of Camouflage:

A. The material interests of one's particular social group are camouflaged by:
   1. A magnanimous concern for the interests of the enemy; for his standard of living; for his political liberation; for the salvation of his soul by spreading one's religion to him.[23] One deserves his gratitude for giving him good and efficient government.[24] One eradicates his foul habits of idleness and sloth, and impresses him with the dignity of labour.

---

20 Quoted in Heinrich Herkner, *Die Arbeiterfrage: Arbeiterfrage und Sozialreform*, 8th ed., vol. 1 (Berlin: Vereinigung wissenschaftlicher Verleger, 1922), p. 432. Trans. E. C.

21 Herkner, vol. 2, p. 333.

22 Quoted in Leonard Barnes, *The Duty of Empire* (London: V. Gollancz Ltd., 1935), p. 259.

23 Bellarmin writes in his *Controversies*: "It is beneficial to the obstinate heretics that they are taken away from this life, for the longer they live the more errors they think out; they pervert more people, and acquire more damnation for themselves" (John Dalberg-Acton, *The History of Freedom and Other Essays* [London: Macmillan & Co., Ltd., 1907], p. 216). Trans. E. C.

24 P. T. Moon (*Imperialism and World Politics*, p. 68) speaks of "an aggressive sort of altruism, which gratifies our innate pride." Charles Evans Hughes, Secretary of State of the USA said in his Bar Association Address in August, 1923 about the imperialist policy of his government, "We are aiming not to exploit, but to aid; not to subvert, but to help in laying the foundations for sound, stable, and independent government." Moon, op. cit., p. 407. "It is in ancient Chinese chronicles that we find wars of conquest politely described as excursions to spread righteousness among ignorant peoples, or to bring barbarians under the influence of a beniger culture." *The Round Table: A Quarterly Review of the Politics of the British Commonwealth* 109 (December, 1937), p. 23.

2. The *ideal* interests of one's own group—e.g. honour, Kultur.
3 A concern for the more or less ideal interests of a group larger than the camouflaging group; the interests of mankind in general; European civilisation versus Asiatic bolshevism; civilisation pure and simple;[25] religion;[26] the Nordic race; the protection of weak allies; the suppression of the traffic in slaves; the defeat of world menaces like Prussian militarism; upholding the sanctity of treaties and international institutions;[27] the deliverance of Europe from Napoleon. The strength and prosperity of the Empire makes for world peace; persons, or groups, who are hostile to us are clearly the enemies of Truth, Morality, Liberty, etc.; this war is a "battle for the soul of the world."[28]
4. A concern for the will of personal Godheads—e.g., Athena, Jehovah, or Jesus Christ. "God wants it."
5. A concern for abstract ideal interests of mankind in general, or for abstract nouns: Peace; Peace and Order; Efficiency; Progress; Science; Truth; Democracy; Humanity; Mankind; Nature; the Rights of Man; the Greatest Happiness of the Greatest Number; Reason; Justice; Welfare; the Goal of Mankind; Goodness; Freedom; Liberty; Equality; Fraternity; Solidarity; Civilisation; Religion (instead of God); Christianity (instead of Christ); the Freedom of the Small Nations; International Law; the Brotherhood of Man; the Dignity of Man; Duty; the Well-Being of Man; Stability; Collective Security.

B. An objectionable material interest is camouflaged by reference to a more respectable material interest:
   1. A desire for plunder is framed as a desire for "vital interests."

---

25 Barnes, *The Duty of Empire*, p. 87:

> To rob and exploit the 'lesser breeds' too weak for self-defence against machine guns and high explosives, to disintegrate their distinctive cultures, to pull down their traditional livelihoods, to conscript them as protesting or bewildered auxiliaries of industrialism—all this came to be seen not as a chaotic fury of looting [which is what it in fact was], but as a beneficent process of tidying up a disorderly world, of spreading the salt of civilisation more evenly over the earth and of sweeping the scum of barbarism away into inconspicuous corners.

26 Lasswell, *Propaganda Technique in the World War*, p. 73, points out that "the churches of practically every description can be relied upon to bless a popular war, and to see in it an opportunity for the triumph of whatever godly design they choose to further."

27 Prophetically, Lasswell wrote in 1927 (ibid., p. 67):

> International organizations are still so weak that at least one other war could be fought on the pretext of strengthening them. Should the existing League stigmatize any group of nations, there is no question that this group would be the target of a very dangerous idealistic propaganda.

28 Liberal opinion is especially amenable to the argument that the enemy is an obstacle to a "better world order."

2. A desire for expansion is framed as a desire for "historical rights."

C. Unpleasant social facts are hidden from sight by "emotional curtains." See Chapter 2.4.

Some Remarks about Different Types of Camouflage

The contents of camouflage vary with time and place. It would be fascinating to do a psychological study of fashions in mental dress, but such a study would add too much to the bulk of this book, and so we must be content with some few remarks.

Different nations and classes have different tastes in camouflage. "Democracy" is hardly less attractive to the English than the "Nordic race" is to the Germans. The warrior class speaks of "honour," the merchant prefers "vital interests." The greater the influence of the military in a country, the more often will her statesmen hide her material interests behind honour.[29] If warriors and merchants share the government of the state, both appeals will he combined.[30]

In some ages, further, men are carried away by their *religious* zeal, while in others *science* seems to offer more plausible excuses. The early English freebooters were renowned for their piety and for their hatred for the "enemies of God, otherwise called papists." They were zealous in the defence of their religion, "God's own cause," and ever ready to glorify God for increasing their wealth.[31] The civil wars of the 17th century were rife with the religious camouflage known as "cant."[32] Later, the well-known hymn "How Sweet the Name of Jesus Sounds" was composed by a slave trader while he waited for a new cargo of slaves. For the Russian masses, Constantinople did not represent a desirable outlet to the sea, but

---

29 "The whole nation must learn to understand that the maintenance of the national existence can only be achieved by the maintenance of the national honour." This remark of Gerhard von Scharnhorst is very popular again in Germany just now. *Editors: We are unable to identify the original source of this quotation. The translation is most probably Conze's own.*

30 *Koelnische Zeitung*, June 17, 1936 (quoted in *Germany Tells the World: An Account of Four Years of Nazi Foreign Policy, March 1933-March 1937* [London: The Union of Democratic Control, 1937], p. 12):

> The regaining of the German colonies is for Germany a question not of prestige but of honour, justice and economic necessity. No people in the world which has the slightest respect for itself will let itself be deprived of legally acquired possessions on account of assertions based on slanderous disparagement of its recognised achievements.

"For us the colonial question is not a matter of imperialism, but of food supply.... The colonial demand is comprised for us today in two words: bread and honour." From a speech of General Ritter von Epp on June 18, 1935, reported in the *The Times*, London, June 19, 1935.

31 The quotations are from Philip Gosse, *Sir John Hawkins* (London: John Lane the Bodley Head Ltd., 1930), pp. 112, 174–176. *Editors: "freebooters" are pirates.*

32 Joseph Addison writes in *The Freeholder* (1716) of "that cant and hypocrisy, which had taken possession of the people's minds in the times of the great rebellion." The word is presumably derived from the Latin "cantus," singing, song, chant.

the seat of the Ecumenical Patriarch of the Orthodox Church. Naturally, in those circles in which the worship of science has replaced that of God, an aggressive and expansionist policy will be justified as a scientific necessity, or as a means of enforcing the will of a group which is inspired by the high ideals of science and reason.

There is one difference, however, which requires some explanation. Many groups veil their interests by a respect for personal Gods. Others prefer to invoke impersonal or abstract nouns (see page 148). The simple-minded crusader is moved by the conviction that "God wants it." The wishes of Athena or Jehovah sanctified raiding expeditions on neighbouring tribes. For thousands of years the majority of mankind remained content with their personal gods. During the last three centuries, during the bourgeois period, however, abstract nouns have come into fashion in the more industrialised countries.

Abstract nouns seem to owe their vogue to the influence of book-learning. The illiterate worship personal Gods. Personifications of abstract entities bestow their blessings upon the conduct of people who are under the influence of book-lore. The extension of elementary education has brought about a considerable increase in the number of people who derive rules of conduct from books. They are the true worshippers of abstract nouns. They think themselves "advanced," as compared with the backward people who do not regularly read books, periodicals, pamphlets, etc. Many of them have lost in common sense what they have gained in literacy. They have learned just enough about politics to take it seriously, and just not enough to look through it. Here in England, from 1936 onwards, it has been noticeable that advanced book-readers on the Left are eager to wash out in a new bloodbath the insults done to the abstract nouns of democracy, civilisation, and progress. The less-literate members of the Co-operative Women's Guild have kept their heads, and see what war would mean to them in terms of actual reality.

In any case, it makes only a slight difference to people's *conduct* whether they invoke abstract nouns or personal gods. And what is more, in the minds of many, the abstract nouns remain personified. They are almost indistinguishable from personal gods. Liberty has her statues, and bestows her blessings upon us like any goddess. The fight between democracy and fascism is just another fight between St. George and the Dragon.

2.3

THE NECESSITY OF SELF-DECEPTION

Didn't I play my part well?

Augustus Caesar, an hour before he died[1]

In the course of Chapter 2.2 it has become clear that camouflage is a widespread device of propaganda. This chapter accounts for the existence of camouflage, and describes the state of mind which its acceptance implies. After discussing the nature of camouflage, I show that self-deception and duplicity are rendered semi-conscious by a *split* in the personality. I want to demonstrate that camouflage is not the outcome of the deliberate and consciously-lying duplicity of crooked and scheming minds, but the involuntary result of the social conditions in which mass propaganda is generated.

The Nature of Camouflage

Camouflage, or social self-deception, roughly speaking consists in overemphasising the importance of ideal interests and of unselfish motives.[2] No psychologist could claim that such interests and motives are unreal. No historian that they are without

1 Suetonius, *Divus Augustus* 99.

2 See Pareto, *The Mind and Society*, vol. 4, p. 1314, §1884:

> The majority of men merely desire to reconcile their own advantage with the residues of sociality [social instincts]; realize their own happiness while seeming to strive for the happiness of others; cloak their self-seeking under mantles of religion, ethics, patriotism, humanitarianism, party loyalty, and so on; work for material satisfactions while seeming to be working only for ideals.... The market is glutted with theories manufactured by theologians, moralists, social writers, and other people of the kind, who keep their counters covered with an article so greatly in demand, and so are able to attain their own advantage while seeming only to be in quest of the sublime.

DOI: 10.4324/9781003363408-13

some effect.[3] Psychologically, most actions result from a weirdly mixed collection of motives, selfish and unselfish. But when the members of a group look at themselves, their more disinterested motives shine brightest in their souls. In well-trained minds they receive most of the emphasis. Particularly in times of social enthusiasm, material interests and selfish motives appear relatively insignificant under the towering shadow of higher ideals. The average man prefers to see the material interests of his group through the mist of high-sounding ideological talk.[4] Only a foolish propagandist appeals openly to naked self-interest. It is wiser to bury it under a heap of ideals, so that it is just perceptible still. Only a few people would risk their skins for material interests, especially if, as is usually the case, the bulk of the benefit is reaped by others. When inflamed by ideal motives, they count their own personal safety for nothing. Rapacity, to be sure, was one of the chief motives that brought the Spaniards to Peru. But, as a good psychologist, in a moment of danger Pizarro told his men, "In the greatest extremity God ever fights for his own; doubt not he will humble the pride of the heathen, and bring him to the knowledge of the true faith, the great end and object of the conquest."[5]

The propagandist who states, without disguise, the material self-interest of his group, "gives the game away." Nobody benefits from such honesty except the group's enemies. Sir William Joynson-Hicks' injudicious remarks on Britain's purpose in India made him the most popular and most widely quoted British statesman in Indian nationalist circles.[6] Such ill-designed frankness of expression is left to third-rank statesmen. It is inconceivable in the mouths of Lord Baldwin, Mr. Gladstone, or the Earl of Beaconsfield.

In a well-tempered mind material interests and selfish motives are removed out of sight. The extent to which they are blotted out, however, varies considerably. Some professional ideologues may be so ignorant of economics, and so intoxicated with their idealistic talk, that they are completely blind to any material group interests behind it. At the other end of the scale, there are coolly calculating

---

3 As a result of Spanish colonisation, the native population of Peru was reduced from several millions in 1532 to 600,000 at the end of the 18th century. But the survivors were Christians.

4 Some people deny that they have selfish interests at all. In my book *The Scientific Method of Thinking* I have tried to show that they almost invariably do. (The material interest of a social group is defined as an interest in the acquisition of goods and status.)

5 William H. Prescott, *History of the Conquest of Peru* (London: J. M. Dent & Sons, Ltd., 1921; 1st ed. 1847), p. 230.

6 *Daily News*, October 17, 1925:

> We did not conquer India for the benefit of the Indians. I know that it is said in missionary meetings that we have conquered India to raise the level of the Indians. That is cant. We conquered India as an outlet for the goods of Great Britain. We conquered India by the sword and by the sword we shall hold it. (Shame!) Call it shame if you like. I am stating facts. I am interested in missionary work of a kind, but I am not such a hypocrite as to say we hold India for the benefit of the Indians. We hold it as the finest outlet for British goods in general, and for Lancashire cotton goods in particular.

statesmen and businessmen who realise quite clearly the material interests involved, and who use idealistic talk only as eyewash for the public. The attitude of the common man varies greatly with the issue involved. When, for instance, the occasion demands great sacrifices from the masses of a modern country, it is preferable from the propagandist's point of view not to emphasise material gains. During the last war, the *Evening News* and other popular papers held strenuously to the view that to state the material aims of the war would be treacherous pro-Germanism. Indeed in most cases the poor have less to gain materially from battles between nations than the wealthy. In 1917, the Germans foolishly proclaimed their material aim for the war: a grand scheme of commercial expansion. This disclosure considerably weakened German morale. The average man thought, "What are Belgium and Briey to us? And why prolong the war for Courland?" The material aims for the war, once stated, appeared scarcely as worthy of sacrifice as the Goddess of Democracy for whom the Allies fought.

Propaganda has therefore to be more vocal about higher ideals, the less the group to which it is addressed has to gain materially from the struggle on hand. In addition, a population which has been trained to exalt unselfish and virtuous behaviour will always be uncomfortable except in the dense cloud of idealistic pretexts. Camouflage is a tribute which selfishness pays to unselfishness. It arises when material interests are felt to be sordid and discreditable, and are therefore hidden from sight. People easily learn to pretend when they are forced to live up to inaccessible moral standards. This is why Christianity has done so much to increase the human capacity for duplicity and hypocrisy.[7] The vigour of his denunciations of the Pharisees shows that Jesus here recognised a deadly enemy. Hypocrisy spreads where public opinion demands the appearance of a particular excess of virtue. It flourishes where we have been taught to regard the basic drives and urges of our nature as degraded, and where we are therefore happy only when we can act on higher principles.

Those who are imbued with a strong moral sense of right and wrong therefore often stress their ideal motives to the exclusion of their material interests. As a French schoolbook charmingly puts it, "The colonies are very useful to the commerce and industry of France, but a noble country like France thinks not of monetary gains."[8] Or, as *The Times* wrote on November 11, 1920 about the Great War,

> They felt that this was for their all; not for greatness, not even for safety, but for those high ideals of the race... Not hatred or passion, greed or ambition,

7 In many respects "hypocrisy" is akin to rationalisation. Hypocrisy is defined as a simulation or pretence of virtue. The *New Testament* is full of terse descriptions of hypocrites who outwardly appear righteous unto men, but within are full of iniquity. They are "like unto whited sepulchres which indeed appear beautiful outward, but are within full of dead men's bones, and of all uncleanliness." (Matthew 23:27, King James Version.)

8 Quoted by Mark Starr, *Lies and Hate in Education* (London: Hogarth Press, 1929), p. 103.

> moved our people. It was duty, and duty only, that bade them draw the sword.[9]

In the same vein, Mr. Lloyd George said on November 10, 1914 that the war was fought "from motives of purest chivalry, to defend the weak."[10]

Soon, however, a propagandist finds that it is too strenuous to stand on the one leg of idealism alone. In a spirit of muddled duplicity, he and his clients try to have it both ways. They conceal their material interests while at the same time casting furtive glances at it. During the Boer War many people denied that Britain was fighting for the Transvaal gold. Yet they were dimly aware of the fact that some gold and diamonds were found in the district. It is somewhat like the attitude of a man who puts a cosmetic lint on his eczema, assuring himself afterwards that there is no eczema at all. This kind of duplicity has, indeed, to be observed to be believed.

Sometimes we get the appearance of a squint-eyed outlook on life. The following remark of Pizarro's secretary deserves to be read twice:

> It being evident that the colonists could not support themselves without the services of the Indians, the ecclesiastics and the leaders of the expedition all agreed that a *repartimiento* of the natives would serve the cause of religion, and tend greatly to their spiritual welfare, since they would thus have the opportunity of being initiated in the true faith.[11]

At the bottom of camouflage we can discern a mental conflict in connection with the "sacro-egoism" of the group. One feels that many group actions cannot be squared with the high morality the group professes to have.[12] It is therefore necessary to justify, by some highly moral and ideal purpose, actions which involve the oppression and exploitation of other human beings. The conflict is completely

---

9 On other occasions, *The Times* of course coolly acknowledges the material background of the last war (see, for example, March 8, 1915 or July 31, 1920).

10 David Lloyd George, *The Great Crusade: Extracts from Speeches Delivered During the War* (New York: George H. Doran Company, 1918), p. 290.

11 Prescott, *History of the Conquest of Peru*, p. 218. An article in the *Evangelical Magazine and Missionary Chronicle* (London: Thomas Ward and Co., January, 1840, vol. 18, p. 96, cited by James Francis Horrabin in his pamphlet "How Empires Grow" [London: NCLC Publishing Society, Ltd., 1935], p. 27), is headed "Desire of the Samoan Chiefs for English Hardware." "The Gospel," says the earnest writer,

> not only supplies the means of spiritual renovation, and opens the way to eternal happiness, but is likewise eminently favourable to the cause of social improvement.... Numbers of the natives now display uncommon eagerness to obtain articles of British manufacture.

12 One might say that in its actions the social group expresses a *conscience*. This conscience may have no social purpose which transcends its existence, but insofar as the individuals within the group have a conscience, they rationalise their group actions.

solved—for a time—if the group members discover that by lucky accident, their ideal considerations push them in exactly the same direction in which their material interests would have pulled them.[13]

In whichever way the conflict between the aggressive actions of a group and the social conscience of its members may be resolved, in practically all cases the ideal interests are more subordinate than they appear to be. History shows that if an ideal interest should be in conflict with a vital material interest, the ideal interest is always beaten. In order to maintain our self-respect and the appearance of consistency, we usually do not explicitly abandon the ideal interest. We either forget about it, or reinterpret it in such a way that it fits in with the material purpose.

To give an example. George Lansbury's attitude on war is clearly the only possible expression of the socialist ideal of the brotherhood of man, and of the solidarity of the workers of different countries. Yet the followers of Lansbury are a tiny, barely tolerated minority within the working-class movement. The material interests of the workers proved stronger than the socialist ideal. The Empire is threatened. To say the least, its break-up would dislocate industries. The standard of living would fall, at least for the time being. The Trade Union movement aims at higher wages and better working conditions, and both its leaders and members are therefore willing to defend the Empire against its enemies. But the socialist phraseology is not simply given up. It is "reinterpreted." The "fight for democracy against fascism" can camouflage the defence of the British Empire because the enemies of that Empire happen to be fascist countries.

In 1916 Colonel House said to President Wilson, "The more I see of the dealings of governments among themselves, the more I am impressed with the utter selfishness of their outlook."[14] Ideal motives without material backing are

---

13 "While England thus undertakes duties which will surely add to the rapid progress of civilisation, she confers no small benefits upon herself; for, by such a course she secures the safety of India and the East." *The Morning Post* on the Treaty of Berlin, July 13, 1878. In a message to Congress on April 11, 1898, President McKinley announced an intervention in Cuba "in the name of humanity, in the name of civilisation, in behalf of the endangered American interests." The latter amounted to $85 million invested in mines, railways, and plantations, and to a yearly trade with Cuba of $96 million.

In a speech of May 14, 1888, Joseph Chamberlain said, "The abandonment of those duties [to annex the gold fields of the Transvaal] would be as fatal to our material prosperity as it would be discreditable to our national character, and our national honour." Quoted by J. L. Garvin, *The Life of Joseph Chamberlain*, vol. 2 (London: Macmillan & Co., Ltd., 1933), p. 465. The leading article of *The Times*, August 5, 1914 read,

> We are drawing the sword in the same cause for which we drew it against Philip II, against Louis XIV, and against Napoleon. It is the cause of right and honour, but it is also the cause of our own vital and immediate interests.

14 *The Intimate Papers of Colonel House: Arranged as a Narrative by Charles Seymour* (Boston: Houghton Mifflin Company, 1926), p. 285.

indulged in by social groups only in comparatively small matters, like relief of distress abroad, etc. In most cases, a group's generosity is of the kind we described in Chapter 2.2 in connection with Flamininus' treatment of Greece. We can also see how misleading the idealistic talk usually is when we consider that the actual outcome of our political activities is in most cases very different from the result we intended to achieve. The attempt to suppress militarism by war has enormously strengthened militarism. The propaganda for communism in Russia led to the establishment of a ruthless state capitalism. Here in England the political propagandist for socialism was astonished to find that as a result of his well-meant propaganda he got governments which, far from being socialist, simply carried on the administration of a capitalist empire in the traditional ways.

To repeat, I do not think that disinterested idealism counts for absolutely nothing in the actions of a group, but it is no more than the glittering foam on the surface of a wave. When deceived by camouflage, we believe that it is the force which moves the wave.

Unconscious Duplicity

Camouflage appears to many, after they have looked through it, as a tissue of deliberate lies by which individuals or groups try to procure some advantage. It is impossible to understand the role of camouflage in propaganda as long as one believes that it is based on a conscious and reasoned dishonesty. A few individuals, it is true, act in bad faith when they disseminate camouflage. But they are exceptional.

Some authors flatter the perspicacity of their readers by picturing people as cynics. Bernard Shaw's Undershaft, an arms industrialist, says in *Major Barbara*,

> When I want anything to keep my dividends up you will discover that my want is a national need.... And in return you shall have the support and applause of my newspapers, and the delight of imagining that you are a great statesman.[15]

An armaments manufacturer is unlikely to speak like this. It is tempting to assume that the hypocrite knows that he is one. But it does not follow, because *we* can look through *him*, that *he* can look through *himself*. Few people have either enough insight or sufficient motive to look through themselves.

On the whole, it is only through complete disappointment with life that some people turn into cynical, self-conscious hypocrites. Most people are not completely disappointed. They retain a certain amount of faith in humanity, and in themselves. Conscious hypocrisy is thus comparatively rare. Contrary to popular

15 George Bernard Shaw, *John Bull's Other Island and Major Barbara* (New York: Brentano's, 1907), p. 280.

belief, few people are capable of permanently pretending to have certain views and moral standards, while being conscious all the time of their utter lack of belief in them. The majority of self-deceivers are quite honest in their hypocrisy, although they are not quite sincere personalities. Pretending has become so much part of their nature that they do it without any effort, and without the consciousness of being hypocritical.

The moral indignation which so many upholders of the British Empire felt against Italian imperialism, and its attempt to conquer Abyssinia, was quite honest and deeply felt. They were not conscious of any hypocrisy when morally condemning just the sort of action upon which their own greatness had been built. Yet rarely has a case better fitted the classical definition of the Bible: "Thou hypocrite, first cast out the beam out of thine own eye; and then shalt thou see clearly to cast out the mote out of thy brother's eye."[16] The trouble is that one has a blind spot for the beam in one's own eye.

Lies... and Lies

We use the word "lying" for that form of deception which involves a certain amount of mental effort, which does not deceive the liar himself, and which involves a conscious intention to deceive others. While blatant deliberate lies can be recognised clearly as such, many degrees of consciousness may accompany the act of lying. On closer inspection, we therefore find a spectrum of lying, from the unconscious to the relatively conscious. It is impossible to draw a sharp dividing line between rationalisation and exaggeration on the one side, and lying and hypocrisy on the other. Through sheer force of habit, lying and hypocrisy can become second nature, and may require little or no mental effort. One may learn to feel quite at home in an atmosphere of lies, and one may not notice them any more than one notices one's furniture.

It would be futile to ask whether twilight is day or night. It is neither, or both. Our minds usually are in a state of twilight. They are neither quite luminous nor are they quite dark. We are never quite honest, nor are we ever quite dishonest.[17]

It remains to explain how unconscious lying becomes possible and plausible, and secondly, why a belief in camouflage is bound to arise in the circumstances in which mass propaganda is effective. In order to clarify these two vital problems, I want to establish the following three propositions:

1. The situation in which people are massed together in collective action or emotion renders self-deception unconscious, and breeds a half-hearted though tenacious commitment to it (see below: *The Symptoms, The Purpose*, pp. 159–161).

---

16 Matthew 7:5 (King James Version).

17 "Very rarely do men manage to be altogether rascals or altogether upright." Machiavelli, *Discourses on Livy* 1.27. Quoted in Pareto, *The Mind and Society*, vol. 3, p. 1149, §1704.

   a. The mere fact that they act as members of a mass increases their suggestibility, creates a split in their minds, and brings out their "hysterical" tendencies. During "mass hysteria" duplicity remains unnoticed (see below: *Hysterical Duality, Hysterical Duplicity, Mass Hysteria*, pp. 161–164).
   b. Oppression works in the same direction as mass hysteria. It accustoms the oppressed to lying and to concealing their state of mind (see below: *Oppression*, pp. 164–165).
2. These same conditions also make room for camouflage. Anxiety, fear, and terror lead to a flight from reality. One forgets the unpleasant reality, and replaces it with a more pleasing dream world (see below: *Flight from Reality*, pp. 165–167).
3. The contents of camouflage are created by collective narcissism and by collective self-assertion (see below: *Collective Narcissism*, p. 167).

In the remainder of this chapter I will try to substantiate these three propositions. I first state the conditions under which self-deception can arise. The self could not deceive itself about itself if the personality were not split into at least two parts. It is necessary that a person should be divided into two nearly "watertight" compartments. The events in each compartment are controlled by a separate "self." The one self does not know what the other does. It is therefore easily deceived about the other's actions, intentions, and emotions. Such a duality of selves, or a "dual control" of the personality, is a necessary condition for unconscious duplicity. It often happens that one self controls the greater part of the personality, yielding only a small part to the other self. The latter is then called a "subsidiary self."

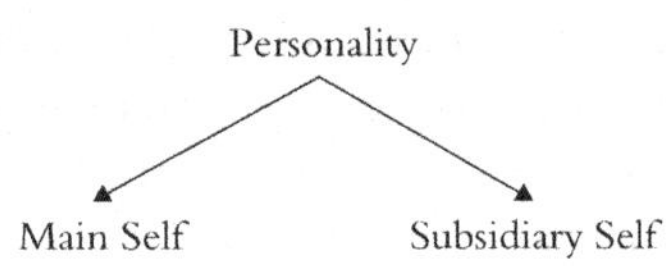

Usually we regard ourselves as being, as it were, "all of one piece." It may therefore appear strange that our personality should fall apart so much that self-deception becomes possible. Such a "dissociation" or splitting of the personality is, however, the chief feature of a mental disorder known as "hysteria."[18] Not that it is confined exclusively to hysterical patients. The mentally disordered are not in a class apart from other people. We are all of us mildly insane. Everybody has more or less a tendency towards most of the mental disorders. When we act collectively, our hysterical tendencies are strengthened.

18 The man in the street may think that a hysteric is somebody who screams. As a matter of fact, hysterical convulsions are rare. Theatrical in their setting and exhibition, they attract undue attention. *Editors: At the time Conze was writing, "hysteria" was a standard term for what is now viewed to be a wide range of psychological disorders. It is an antiquated term with misogynist roots.*

The human mind is rarely completely united and integrated.[19] While repression and dissociation may be different processes, they are closely akin. An incestuous or murderous wish, for instance, which is repressed, is thereby cut off or dissociated from the conscious personality. This kind of dissociation is therefore a normal process which is going on all the time. Mentally disordered persons show an inclination to act in a pronounced and extreme way. Many mental traits of the "normal" person are, as it were, written in large letters in the minds of the insane. They are thus more clearly visible. In this way, a consideration of hysteria can help us to decipher some of the more illegible characters in which the story of our minds is written.[20]

The Symptoms

A brief survey of the symptoms of hysteria, followed by an explanation of their purpose, will now reveal unconscious duplicity as the natural result of a split personality.

The hysteric may lose control over a part of his mind. His memory contents for a whole period of his life may be "alienated." In a state of amnesia, he forgets everything that happened to him in this period. Also striking are disturbances in the bodily functions.[21] Many organic troubles baffle the medical practitioner because they have no adequate or sufficient organic cause. Almost any part of the body can be split off from the rest of the personality, and can function, as it were, on its own. In this way, the action of a terrified mind may paralyse an arm, disturb breathing or digestion, create blisters or eczema on the skin, and pains in the limbs,

---

19 To give a quite simple example, sometimes while we are saying something, we feel that "at the back of our minds" another stream of thought is taking place.

20 Hysterical duplicity is also easier to understand than "normal" duplicity because its admission provokes less emotional resistance. I thought, for instance, for a long time that a "Christian businessman" was a good example of "normal" duplicity. Here we have a man who is subjected to the contradictory demands of Business and the Gospel. On Sundays he believes exactly the opposite of what he believes and does on weekdays. This man is rarely a conscious hypocrite. He has built in his mind two watertight compartments. The one contains his religious convictions, the other his business interests. To a disapproving outsider the duality of this personality might appear, wrongly, as conscious duplicity, but the fact of "dual control" seems to be beyond doubt. My teaching experience, however, has taught me that the inconsistency of the Christian businessman's behaviour could easily be explained away by rationalisations of one kind or another, and that the example does not convince those who admire Christian businessmen. The same holds good of Barnes' remark (*The Duty of Empire*, p. 67) that

> the faith of the so-called democratic governments of our time may be fairly summarised by saying that humanitarianism is a good image to pay lip homage to on the day of rest, but not a sound guide of action throughout the week.

Convinced "democratic imperialists" would not admit this.

21 One speaks of "conversion hysteria" because a mental trend is "converted to," or finds expression in, a bodily symptom. *Editors: "conversion hysteria" is now referred to as "conversion disorder."*

abdomen, or head. Sense organs may lose their sensation. "An interesting phenomenon is pseudocyesis [false pregnancy] in sterile married women following a lapse in the menses. The abdomen and breasts increase in size, colostrum appears and there is morning vomiting."[22]

The Purpose

These bodily symptoms always serve a more or less unconscious purpose, which determines the type of disability. Modification of the body has enabled the person to solve a conflict, to fulfil a wish. In consequence, hysterics show little sign of distress. On the contrary, they adopt an attitude of indifference. French doctors call it *la belle indifférence*. The disease is a means of escape from a disastrous situation when there is no other way out.

If a particular sense or organ is essential to an activity which one finds intolerable, this very sense or organ is the most likely to be affected. The disability then serves a clear purpose: it renders the person incapable of carrying on with this intolerable activity. Asthma, pains, or lack of sensation in the thighs and pelvis may protect a woman from sexual intercourse with her husband. In wartime, a hysterical symptom may help a soldier to escape from his present work, "as when a sniper goes blind or suffers a one-sided paralysis, or a look-out man gets a twisted neck, or an interpreter goes dumb, or a hydrophone-listener becomes deaf."[23]

Hysterical symptoms may also follow an accident, with an eye towards compensation. Menninger reports the case of an electrician who received a shock from a switch.[24] The man formed the theory that a current of several thousand volts went through his left leg and paralysed a nerve in it. In consequence he could not move his leg and had no sensation in it. He was unable to work, and demanded compensation of $50,000. Menninger argues that his injury was physiologically impossible. If a nerve had been injured, the limb should have been inert and limp, and the muscles should have atrophied. Neither was the case.

> On the other hand, however, it would be inaccurate to say that the man's symptoms were assumed. His pain and his paralysis and his disability were very real to him.... The hysterical patient is fooling himself just as much as he is fooling anyone else; in fact, he fools himself first and last and fools the rest of us in between times. He isn't faking consciously; he is faking unconsciously.[25]

---

22 Morris Braude, *The Principles and Practice of Clinical Psychiatry* (Philadelphia: P. Blakiston's Son & Co., 1937), p. 292. In such cases the abdomen is distended by gas which gives the impression of a growing child.

23 Bartlett, *Psychology and the Soldier*, p.186.

24 Karl Menninger, *The Human Mind* (Garden City: Garden City Publishing Company, Inc., 1930), pp. 132–134.

25 Menninger, *The Human Mind*, p. 133.

Frightened by a shock, he conjures up all the possibilities. His hysteria fulfils a purpose: he can escape from an arduous and uncongenial job while still receiving compensation. In this case the man got $3,500, and a few months later he was reported to be perfectly well.[26]

Hysterical Duality

It is now easy to see that hysterical symptoms are due to a split in the personality. Under the stress of acute mental conflict the patient discovers that he is unable, say, to move his arm. But he wants to. One part of him strives to move the limb while another part prevents him from doing so. The mind, split, is at loggerheads with itself, as the activity of the dissociated part runs on side-by-side with that of the rest of the personality. A subsidiary self, detached from the personality, or isolated from it, in the sense that the conscious self has no control over it, renders the functional limb non-functional. A part of the personality plays a trick on the rest.[27]

Hysterical dissociation is usually preceded by a process of "auto-suggestion." In his anxiety, the hysterical person convinces himself that an accident is bound to have certain painful consequences. In due course his unconscious produces those consequences. A period of time usually elapses between the trauma—say, an accident—and the onset of symptoms. Henderson and Gillespie point out that "evidently the latent period is filled with ruminations."[28]

We experience a degree of auto-suggestion when we get sick from reading about a disease in a medical book, or in an encyclopædia. In exceptional cases, the power of the self to suggest something to itself proves to be almost unlimited. Some time ago, a man was found dead in Munich. Near his body lay a bottle of distilled water, labelled "Poison." The man had wanted to commit suicide. He drank the water in the belief that it was poison. The autopsy showed that he died from heart failure. It has often astonished observers of primitive societies and races that natives who are told by a medicine man that they will die at a certain hour

---

26 Similar cases abound in wartime. A soldier had a slight flesh wound in the upper right arm. He formed the idea that a nerve had been hurt, and that he could not move the thumb or the two first fingers. A person of that disposition is not of sufficient military value to be sent back to the slaughter.

27 The activity of a subsidiary self is particularly striking in those cases when persons act as if their body was guided or possessed by another personality. Automatic writing is an example. See Oliver Spurgeon English and Gerald H. G. Pearson, *Common Neuroses of Children and Adults* (New York: W. W. Norton & Company, Inc., 1937), p. 214:

> The writer may or may not be aware of what is going on and what is written is a surprise to the patient as well as to others, since the content often consists of forgotten events or foreign languages learned earlier and lost to memory, and possibly of material and experiences that are entirely unrecognizable. The hand seems to be guided by a personality other than the patient's.

28 D. K. Henderson and R. D. Gillespie, *A Text-Book of Psychiatry for Students and Practitioners*, 4th ed. (Oxford: Oxford University Press, 1936), p. 463.

rarely fail to do so. Others die after discovering by accident that they have eaten taboo food unwittingly. They convince themselves that they should die, that all the circumstances point to their death. They are killed by their belief in the efficacy of magic just as the man in Munich died because he believed in the efficacy of the poison he did not take.

To sum up, under the stress of anxiety, fear, or terror, the personality may split into two. This split is often accompanied by delusions about the functioning of bodily organs. The patient sufficiently believes in these delusions for the working of the organs to be deranged. At the same time, and this is our next and final point, there is evidence to show that only a part of his personality participates in the delusion, so that his whole attitude gives the appearance of duplicity.

Hysterical Duplicity

In hysteria human duplicity reaches its peak. Hysterics are ill because they want to be ill, while at the same time they may resent being ill, and apparently do everything to get better. A hysterically blind person cannot see because he will not see. But at the same time he may be profoundly disturbed at his inability to see. The patient does not simulate illness. He is really and genuinely ill. At the same time, he cheats himself when he believes that he is organically ill. His illness is due to mental conflict. He conjured it up in an attempt to defend himself against instinctual desires which threaten to break through.

Simple scientific tests can demonstrate that the patient takes up his symptoms only half-heartedly. Taking, for instance, the unconscious duplicity of an hysterically deaf person, we may observe that "an hysterical patient with a one-sided deafness behaves as a normal person during conversation, while one with unilateral disturbance due to organic origin always uses the normal ear more readily."[29] Further, the hysteric will "reflexively contract the orbicularis palpebrarum when a motor horn—for instance—is blown at the distance of six feet. This never happens in organic deafness."[30] In hysterical visual troubles,

> The pupils react normally, and the hysterically blind person does not collide with objects. The blind eye may be tested by covering the good eye with an opaque or an unusually powerful lens and the blind eye with a plain glass and asking the patient to read. If he does so he has shown the true nature of his symptom.[31]

29 Braude, *The Principles and Practice of Clinical Psychiatry*, p. 291.

30 Ibid., p. 305.

31 English and Pearson, *Common Neuroses of Children and Adults*, p. 229.

Generally, in hysterical convulsions, "the patient chooses a spot or falls in such a way as not to hurt himself."[32] He does not wholeheartedly abandon himself to his convulsions.

Who but a poet could hope to describe adequately that twilight in which the hysteric moves? We meet with the same kind of twilight in the fantastic lies which children do not take quite seriously. Children who "pretend" or "make believe" dwell in an ill-defined borderland between truth and falsehood, between reality and fantasy. The attitude of the adult to social humbug is often similar to the child's self-deception in play. He "drinks it in," and enjoys it, although at the bottom of his heart he knows that it is not quite true.

Mass Hysteria

When a social group exhibits hysterical traits, we may speak of "mass hysteria." Men's minds are transformed by contact with a frightened mass. They are seized by an anxiety to which, like the hysterics, they react by splitting their personalities. Anxiety weakens a man's self-reliance. As a member of an anxious mass he loses control over part of his mind under the influence of suggestion. It is a well-known fact that collective action and emotion heighten the suggestibility of everybody involved. The intimate connection between suggestibility and hysterical behaviour is also attested by numerous observations. Conversion hysterias are rife among the members of disciplined groups who are trained in passive obedience—in armies, convents, and sometimes in mills and offices. When we analyse suggestibility, we see that its connection with hysteria is not a fortuitous one. Acceptance of suggestion involves the formation of a subsidiary self.

When I act on suggestion, an outside personality controls a part of my activities. To take up a former example (see page 37): when I walk along the street and somebody suggests, "Let's have a drink," the direction of my activity is deflected if I take up that suggestion. The intruder can, however, direct my actions only on condition that I accept his suggestion as my own. The foreign will is temporarily incorporated into my own personality, and acts as a subsidiary self. Anxiety weakens resistance to an outside influence. One doubts oneself, and is susceptible to abandoning oneself to a stranger. But the impact of the stranger must not be felt as something that pushes from the outside. Otherwise suggestion would not always involve a component of auto-suggestion. The situation is thus the same in suggestible as in hysterical minds. In both cases we are "beside ourselves."

Camouflage, like hysterical deception, also serves a purpose and fulfils a wish. It is my contention that, if you can deceive yourself about the condition of your body, as the hysteric does, it is not surprising that you should genuinely deceive yourself about the real motives of your collective actions.

---

32 Ibid., p. 212.

Mass hysteria is the breeding ground for camouflage, or for a system of delusions about the workings of the group. Whereas the individual hysteric suggests to himself an imaginary disability, however, group members usually suggest to each other a largely imaginary perfection.

Oppression

The propensity to self-deception—which situations fraught with anxiety are bound to create—is further strengthened by oppression. Oppression makes for insincerity. Snobbishness, to begin with a minor point, obviously makes the snob insincere. Somebody who constantly pretends that he is better than his neighbours will end up genuinely thinking that he is.

The oppressed, further, must inhibit all their natural reactions and conceal their resentment and longing in a submissive attitude, as if behind a curtain. They begin to lie out of necessity. The oppressor thus often deplores the "insincerity" of Indians, Negroes, or Jews, for example. It seems plain that nobody would be inclined to lie into anybody's face if he could smash his fist into it, but unlike the straightforward and blunt middle-class Anglo-Saxon, the slave has to hide his true mind, and attempt by cunning to outwit his master.

Plato speaks of the "tense and bitter shrewdness" of the slave:

> Slavery has dwarfed and twisted his growth and robbed him of his free spirit, driving him into devious ways, threatening him with fears and dangers which the tenderness of youth could not face with truth and honesty; so, turning from the first to lies and the requital of wrong with wrong, warped and stunted, he passes from youth to manhood with no soundness in him and turns out, in the end, a man of formidable intellect—as he imagines.[33]

Walter Francis White, leader of the NAACP, an American civil-rights organisation, depicts a Negro explaining how artfully his race has accommodated itself to the weaknesses of its masters:

> Just use your eyes and see how Negroes fool white folks all the time. Take, for instance, old Will Hutchinson who works for Mr. Baird. Will cuts all sorts of monkey-shines around Baird, laughs like an idiot, and wheedles old Baird out of anything he's got. Baird gives it to him and then tells his friends about "his good nigger Will" and boasts that Will is one "darky" he really knows. Then Will goes home and laughs at the fool he's made of Baird by acting like a fool.... And there are Negroes all over the South doing the same thing every day![34]

33 Plato, *Theaetetus* 173 a-b, trans. Francis MacDonald Cornford (*Plato's Theory of Knowledge: The Theaetetus and the Sophist of Plato* [London: Kegan Paul, Trench, Trübner & Co., Ltd., 1935]).

34 Walter Francis White, *The Fire in the Flint* (New York: Alfred A. Knopf, Inc., 1924), pp. 130–131.

It is clear that old Will Hutchinson's triumph must rather warp his soul. The "free" wage-workers of Europe also bear the marks of slave mentality, and all the difference there may be is one of degree. Slave mentality is the same at all times and in all places.

The personality of the oppressed is split. They dare not show what they feel inwardly. The fear of their masters sets up a habit of lying, untruthfulness, and duplicity. At the same time, of course, the urge to flee from reality is particularly marked among the oppressed. The habit of lying to oneself and to others, and of running away from reality, in due course makes self-deception unconscious. Habit gradually renders an action, as we all know, unconscious and effortless. Francis Bacon in his *History of the Reign of King Henry VII* describes an impostor of whom

> it was generally believed...that he was indeed duke Richard. Nay, himself, with long and continual counterfeiting, and with oft telling a lie, was turned by habit almost into the thing he seemed to be; and from a liar to a believer.[35]

Flight from Reality

Two trends, or streams, of thought go on alongside one another in each one of us—the one guided by a respect and concern for objective reality, the other inspired by a desire to escape from reality. One part of the personality tries to keep in touch with the world as it is; another tries to get away from it. When people are terrified or disappointed by reality, the impulse to rush away from it is strengthened considerably. We indulge in daydreams all the time. The terrified and disappointed may find their dream world so much more interesting, satisfying, and important that it overshadows the real world.[36] Our dream world is the result of what we wish to be. Children often indulge in pure wishful thinking which recognises no outside interference nor any responsibility to reality. Terror can throw an adult back into a childish neglect of reality and into a state of mind in which he is inclined to see as real that which he wishes to be real.

Flight from reality involves two processes. On the one side, we are inclined to push out of sight that which we dislike. Many dislike the world so much that they try to dodge it almost entirely. The ordinary tendency to forget about

35 J. Rawson Lumby, ed., *Bacon's History of the Reign of King Henry VII* (Cambridge: Cambridge University Press, 1892), p. 111.

36 In some cases, under the influence of strong repressed wishes, the dream world acquires its own organisation and logic, gets mixed up with the real world, and replaces it for hours on end. For Balzac, for instance, the characters in his novels (the dream world) could be so real that he would mix them up with people in his actual social environment.

unpleasant, distressing, and painful incidents can, in hysterics, develop into amnesia for large stretches of the patient's experience.[37] A whole period of life, sometimes covering many years, is completely forgotten. Some patients, showing evidence of unconscious duplicity, have enough insight into their state of mind to feel that their loss of memory serves as a protection against the dreaded consequences of past actions. Often patients are certain that the memory of their past life would bring back some awful sorrow or tragedy, and they shrink from the prospect.[38]

Forgetting is only one side of the process which enables us to shirk reality. It has to be supplemented by another process which replaces the forgotten events and incidents with wish fantasies. We frequently meet people who live in a world of their own making, and shut out everything that might cause discomfort. It is quite a normal thing for people to remould a painful incident in the past until they cut a good figure. They "chew over" their behaviour on that occasion until it looks more praiseworthy, interesting, romantic, or subtle than it really was. They gradually come to believe in this reconstructed account of the incident with the same earnestness and duplicity with which the hysteric believes in his symptoms.

Under the influence of anxiety people become unable to bear themselves and continually run away from things as they are. They become constitutionally insincere. False or crooked personalities, they are fundamentally incapable of either facing or speaking the truth. Even under the most favourable circumstances, human memory is unreliable. Fiction and reality fuse together. Many careful experiments on the value of testimony have borne this out. It is amazing how gossip can distort an initial fact. The insincere can rely on the congenital treachery of their memory to distort and falsify events automatically, and to act as a sieve for unpleasant facts. In the end, the insincere risk losing their footing in reality.

---

37 McDougall (*An Outline of Abnormal Psychology* [London: Methuen & Co., Ltd., 1926], p. 235) shows the close connection between amnesia and the physical symptoms of hysteria:

> Without unduly straining the sense of the words, it may be said that every dissociation is an amnesia. When, for example, the hypnotic patient cannot move a limb, or relax a contracted set of muscles, it may be said that he has forgotten how to execute the task, forgotten how to move the limb, how to relax the muscles. And, if he cannot see with one eye, or cannot see a particular object, or cannot sense an anaesthetic limb, it may be said that he has forgotten how to achieve these perceptual activities.

38 Bror Gadelius (*Human Mentality in the Light of Psychiatric Experience: an Outline of General Psychiatry* [Copenhagen: Levin & Munksgaard, 1933], p. 263) reports of one of his patients:

> He said that he had now come to the conclusion that the best thing would be not to try any longer to remember the past: perhaps he would then come to know about some trouble or other of which he would rather be ignorant. He also said of his own accord that he might perhaps have lost his memory owing to something disagreeable having happened.

Nothing serves so well as terror or acute distress to sweep the masses into a social movement. We cannot be surprised that under such circumstances they should flee from reality into a dream world of their own. They are as tenacious in holding on to their camouflage as the hysteric, and also as sincere. Rendered hysterical by mass contact, the average man offers little resistance to an interpretation of social events in which he cuts a good figure. He sees himself in a new role which flatters his desire for self-aggrandisement. As a saviour of mankind and as a guardian of its most sacred ideals, he transcends the sordidness and drabness of his daily life.

Collective Narcissism

In collective actions, the two forces of narcissism and self-assertion, which we found at the root of individual rationalisation, gain in strength. It is a simple fact of observation (as we saw in Chapters 1.5 and 1.6) that collective narcissism is even less self-critical than private narcissism. If the German soul reflects itself in the German soul, it reveals itself as a bright diamond without any stains. Mass camouflage is likewise less self-critical than individual rationalisation. We would laugh at a man who told us that he drank beer in order to save democracy. He might, of course, rationalise that a high percentage of the price of his beer goes to the government; that the government spends the money on battleships; and that these battleships defend democracy. But we would remain rather sceptical. The camouflage in which millions believe is even more crude, intellectually speaking. One easily believes that he is defending democracy when he is actually defending the empire.

There is no check on collective narcissism. The individual who bases his narcissistic feelings on private and personal perfections ought to show some reserve in the expression of his conceit. Otherwise, he might hurt the sensibilities of his fellow narcissists. When, on the other hand, a whole crowd of people assert their collective narcissism by dwelling lovingly on some common perfection, they confirm each other in their conviction of superiority by mutual suggestion. Those who disagree with them do not matter, because they are tribal outsiders.[39]

Actors and Demagogues

A crowd is rarely complete without a crowd-leader, a demagogue. The most successful and popular demagogue should have the hysterical features of the crowd-mind to a marked degree. In other words, he should be a good actor.

---

39 If we had space to go further into the psychopathology of social life, we could show that such a self-centred group attitude leads to collective paranoia, delusions of grandeur ("the world looks to Britain for a lead," etc.), and persecution mania (the Germans with respect to the Jews).

Acting and hysterical behaviour are akin in many ways. Hysterics are theatrical, exhibitionist, and "showy." They desire to impress and to gain sympathy. Some patients are cured only when the doctor refuses to take any notice of their complaints. And to be an actor, one need not be employed by a theatre. Acting has become second nature in those persons who habitually take up a pose, make a show of what is not there, and react in an ostentatious and affected way. The very word "hypocrisy" originally denoted the attitude of an actor in a theatre. In keeping with this derivation of the word, the *New Testament* also says of hypocrites that they do good works only in order to be seen by the people.[40]

In the process of acting, the personality is split. Mr. Smith, for the time being, becomes Macbeth. Smith has to identify himself with the person he plays. While he impersonates Macbeth, the real Smith is at least somewhat pushed into the background. In many cases, however, Smith is not entirely submerged. He may be Macbeth only on the very surface, like those actors who perform mechanically and without feeling. Diderot spoke of "clockwork actors." In Hollywood, I am told, they are deliberately made into mere automata.

In other cases Smith is blotted out more completely. For the time being the actor himself is more or less taken in by the illusion. Actors do not always simulate. They often feel genuinely. They believe themselves transformed, to a certain extent, into the character they represent. When Dr. Johnson asked actor John Philip Kemble whether he was transformed in such a way, he answered truthfully, "Not quite." These words describe well the typical attitude of hysterical duplicity.

When he was acting, Forbes Robertson noticed that his mind fell into two strata: "One stratum, the part, the creature I am for the time; the other, that part of my mind which circumstances and the surroundings compel me to give up to all things coming under the head of mechanical execution."[41] Actress Fanny Kemble described this multiple activity as "the sort of double process which the mind carries on at once, the combined operation of one's faculties, so to speak, in diametrically opposite directions."[42] Sometimes actors split themselves into more than two strata:

> One of them may be agonising with Othello, while another is criticising his every tone and gesture, a third restraining him from strangling Iago in good earnest, and a fourth wondering whether the play will be over in time to let him catch his last train.[43]

---

40 Greek *hypokrinomai* means "to act in a theatre." See Matthew 6:5: "And when thou prayest, thou shalt not be as the hypocrites are: for they love to pray standing in the synagogues and in the corners of the streets, that they may be seen of men" (King James Version).

41 Quoted by William Archer, *Masks or Faces? A Study in the Psychology of Acting* (London: Longmans, Green, and Co., 1888), p. 155.

42 Archer, *Masks or Faces?*, p. 151.

43 Ibid., p. 150.

Total absorption in the act is rare. But, to a measure, actors are "beside themselves."[44]

Both kinds of actors also go on the political stage. Some demagogues are clockwork actors. If you meet them over a drink after a speech, they will cynically disown everything they have just said. Others, however, impress the scientific mind more painfully because they will stick in private to what they said in public, at least as long as the crowd-emotion persists in their minds—and that may be always. The more effective demagogues are those who do not observe themselves critically, and who thus lose their heads while acting, being carried away by the role they are playing.

The ex-Kaiser was a great orator, and immensely popular in Germany for many years. He was a consummate actor. On his second visit to Turkey and Palestine, he sought to become "all things to all men."[45] J. Holland Rose writes that "at Jerusalem [the Kaiser] figured as the Christian knight-errant but at Damascus [less than 150 miles away] as the champion of the Moslem creed."[46] For the Kaiser, a new uniform meant a new personality. For the time being, he actually became what he impersonated. Those who are inclined to regard demagogues as scheming villains who lead honest people astray overlook the fact that through his hysterical constitution the typical demagogue is more a part than a leader of the crowd.

44 Fleckno described Richard Burbage as a "delightful Proteus, so wholly transforming himself into his parts, and putting off himself with his clothes, as he never (not so much as in the tyring-house) assumed himself again until the play was done" (ibid., p. 145).

45 Thomas Ashcroft, *An Outline of Modern Imperialism: Plebs Textbooks Number Two* (London: The Plebs League, 1922), p. 29.

46 J. Holland Rose, *The Development of the European Nations: 1870–1914*, vol. 2 (London: G. P. Putnam's Sons, 1916), p. 327.

2.4

EMOTIONAL CURTAINS

Qui nescit dissimulare, nescit regnare.

Justus Lipsius[1]

It is an old-established procedure to disguise awkward facts by giving them new names. This is an important device of political window-dressing. "It is one of the most essential functions of a statesman to christen with popular, or at least neutral, names things which the masses detest under their old names."[2] The two Napoleons were masters in this art, which, however, did not die with them.

The "Cheka," the name for the Soviet secret police, was changed into the "OGPU," and then, after that name was too discredited, it found shelter behind the inoffensive "Commissariat for home affairs" (*Narkomvnudel*). The "workhouse" and the "infirmary" have been replaced by "institutions" and "hospitals." The "insane poor" have become "rate-aided patients." "Protectionists" became "Tariff Reformers," and even "Empire Free Traders." "Distressed areas" lost most of their distress when they were called "Special Areas." London Tories seek to hide their reactionary aims by calling themselves "Municipal Reformers."

The death penalty in Russia goes by the humanitarian name of "supreme measure of social defence." In all countries, a massacre of rebellious poor is called "restoring law and order." Civilised imperialist nations have long ceased to annex "colonies." Instead, they establish "protectorates" (from 1800 onwards) and "mandates" (since 1918). Machiavelli informs us that, when the Romans reduced

1 *Editors: "He who does not know how to dissimulate does not know how to rule." The phrase is of uncertain origin, and has also been attributed to King Louis XI.*

2 Gustav Le Bon, *Psychologie des foules* (Paris: Felix Alcan, 1895), p. 88. Trans. E. C.

DOI: 10.4324/9781003363408-14

the Latin tribes into a state of utter dependence, they all the while pretended to treat them as "allies."[3]

Some American detective agencies dropped the word "detective" from their titles. They call themselves "industrial service bureaux," "corporation auxiliaries," "efficiency companies," and "personnel relations counsellors." In the vassal "Native States" of the British Raj, European advisers are called "European Residents." Forced labour is often called "indentured labour." The British Empire has ceased to exist. It is now the "British Commonwealth of Nations." The free part of the Empire, in the perspective of many, becomes its most important part, although its population is insignificant compared with that of the colonial Empire.

Words Which Prettify

A century ago, Jeremy Bentham gave a list of words which prettify things that are indefensible under their proper names. He noted that "persecution" became "zeal," and "adultery" became "gallantry," while "social order" was a cloak for "tyranny." He further mentions the "fallacy of allegorical idols," as when one says "Church" instead of "churchmen," "Law" instead of "lawyers," "Government" instead of "members of the government."

> As to the real persons so occupied, if they were presented in their proper character, whether collectively or individually, they would appear clothed in their real qualities, good and bad together. But, as presented by means of this contrivance, they are decked out in all their good and acceptable qualities, divested of all their bad and unacceptable ones.[4]

One substitutes for the persons "the name of some fictitious entity, to whom by customary language, and thence opinion, the attribute of excellence has been attached."[5]

The propagandist may mask himself as a "Public Relations Officer." Northcliffe's propaganda offices were known as the "British War Mission," and the propaganda department of the American Army as the "Psychologic Subsection." "War" is camouflaged in the respectable garb of "defence." War ministers in many European countries are "Ministers of Defence." "Collective security" and "sanctions" are some very recent additions to the list of words which mean war without saying so.

To invent innocuous words is only one way of hiding the unpleasant. I propose to use the term "emotional curtains" for all these devices which help to hide the ugly facts of social life.

---

3 *Political Discourses* 2.13.

4 *The Book of Fallacies: From Unfinished Papers of Jeremy Bentham* (London: J. & H. L. Hunt, 1824), pp. 222–259.

5 Ibid.

Concealing the Bad Side

The propagandist hides the terror and squalor of war behind pomp and show, smart military uniforms, displays, music, glitter, and behind talk about heroism, good fellowship, etc.

> The humorous magazines and books help to banter away the realities of battle and they profit from the impulse to turn one's head away from a spectacle which, if completely realized, might well prove unbearable. A Bruce Bairnsfather is worth at least an Army Corps.[6]

The aspect of romance is kept alive by tales of individual adventure. The stark brutality and ineffectual suffering of war are counterbalanced by the thrill of military religion and its trappings, "fine feathers, sacramental words, colourful rites, deep-seated and religious patriotism, clean buttons and pipe clay, hymns of hate and anthems of arrogance."[7]

The Slaves' Day Off

Political institutions as such have the effect of veiling the facts of social life. The British Parliamentary system, for instance, is based on the pretence that the two parties have really serious differences. As long as we are content to play that game, we are allowed to express ourselves freely—because our views are of no great consequence. Politics includes the art of creating in the citizen the illusion that he is free, and that his rulers are well-meaning and fairly disinterested. There is no point in making the slaves feel their servitude.[8] The political institutions of Great Britain carefully foster in the oppressed the illusion that they are free. Each year, the slaves of ancient Rome had one day off. During the "Saturnalia" they became—ceremoniously—the masters. In England, similarly, every two or three years the wage slave becomes a citizen, is humbly asked for his considered opinion on a number of issues he has neither time nor inclination to study carefully, is told that he is the master, is allowed to ride in a car, etc. Parliament is, indeed, quite an effective facade for the powerful to hide behind.

Military conquest of colonies easily leads to native insurrections, because the conquered people may consider themselves enslaved. It was therefore often considered wise to conceal the conquest. For instance, one could leave the native ruler on his throne with all the show of power, "but a resident general, supported by a more or less visible army of occupation, was placed by his side to advise and

---

6 Lasswell, *Propaganda Technique in the World War*, p. 98. *Editors: Bruce Bairnsfather (1887–1959) was a British cartoonist.*

7 Frank P. Crozier, *The Men I Killed* (London: Michael Joseph, Ltd., 1937), p. 191.

8 "The more cunningly it [oppression] is disguised and concealed, the less dishonourable it will seem." Machiavelli, *Political Discourses* 2.13 (trans. Ellis Farneworth, 1762).

to guide him on the way to progress."[9] Or one enslaves the native ruler financially by loans which he invariably squanders, so that the wealth of his country has to be pawned to guarantee the interest. The Japanese camouflage their rule in Manchukuo and North China, and keep up decorum, by establishing local Chinese governments and using the authority of the Emperor Pu Yi. Similarly, the British middle classes, from the 17th century onwards, could assert their power much more peacefully because they allowed the feudal owners to save their faces by retaining the majesty of the king and innumerable feudal forms, phrases, and symbols.

Conceding the Shadow

The best way of keeping power is to concede its shadow to others. A person too obviously in power excites all sorts of unfavourable emotions. He is envied, and is held responsible when things go wrong. Truly powerful people therefore usually hide themselves, if they are wise. As Augustus said of himself, "After ending the civil wars, I restored to the Senate and the Roman people the powers that I had received by universal consent.... Whereafter, though above all others in honours, I have held no greater powers than my colleagues."[10]

The personnel of the ruling class are bound to efface their real character in public. Rulers should seem to lack personal ambition and personal whims. The welfare of their people should seem everything to them. They should appear to sacrifice themselves, as it were. The ruler's human weakness and his self-interests should appear to vanish when he is invested with a sacred authority by the holy vial. Millionaires hide what Aldous Huxley describes as their vulture-like rapacity, their avarice, their swinish gluttony, their vanity and cruelty, behind a generosity which is excellent propaganda and makes us forget the sins of the Carnegies and Rockefellers. There is quite a vast literature which encourages emulation of millionaires, and attributes their success to patience, industry, truthfulness, self-control, strength of character, thrift, idealism, kindness, and Christian and human virtues. While it would be unfair to say that the exceptionally wealthy are entirely devoid of virtues of this kind, one is apt to hush over other traits which are less amiable and meritorious. In this way the ambitious members of the lower middle class get a somewhat distorted view of their masters.

Finally I may mention that newspapers camouflage their capitalist ownership, and the class structure of society, by denouncing some foreign enemy, or by stirring up some artificial political dissension with their brother capitalists. And the British Empire, of course, is covered from sight by "emotional curtains" of quite exceptional thickness. The curtains are renewed on Empire Day each year. They are washed almost daily. The Empire is represented as a source of universal

9 Francis Delaisi, *Political Myths and Economic Realities* (London: N. Douglas, 1927), p. 261.
10 From the *Res Gestae Divi Augusti*, quoted in Pareto, *The Mind and Society*, vol. 1, p. 158, §233.

justice and benevolence. Its watchwords are freedom, justice, and peace. It is the nucleus of an international peace system. Barnes points out that, for instance, Lord Lothian in his picture of the Empire completely leaves out "any reference to the all-important creditor-debtor relation in Empire affairs."[11] A thick crust of benevolent loving-kindness hides from the sight of the average man the oppression on which the Empire is built, and the indignities to which its coloured subjects—and not only they—are subjected.

Our minds, indeed, are not made to give an accurate photograph of the realities of social life. In consequence we like to live in a fool's paradise. The propagandist is far more successful in keeping us away from the tree of knowledge than old Jehovah with his crude Prussian methods.

Why "Emotional Curtains"?

Emotional curtains are an indispensable device of mass propaganda because they meet the mental needs of the majority of the population. For most of us, life would be intolerable if we saw it as it is, and if our mental perspective emphasised its distasteful features as much as its gratifying ones. The public are ready to accept the honeyed words of the propagandist because they wish to keep distressing facts out of sight. Very few people, indeed, are capable of facing unwelcome facts. Those who constantly refer to "hard facts" are the worst humbugs of all.

Quite apart from propaganda, in their private lives most people shrink from the use of words which call up disagreeable associations. Both primitive and civilised, both polite and impolite society refrain from mentioning offensive objects and actions. "Euphemism" is the scientific term for it.[12] We speak in euphemisms when we use "a mild or vague or periphrastic [roundabout] expression as a substitute for blunt precision or disagreeable truth."[13] If a term denotes something unpleasant or taboo, it is replaced by a euphemistic term.[14] There are hundreds of euphemisms for death[15], disease, deformity, sex, the processes of digestion, and domestic troubles.

It is common practice to shut one's eyes to unpalatable facts, to pass over them, to minimise their importance, to prettify them, to push them into the background, or to "shove them into a corner." People often conceal their age and are not

11 *The Duty of Empire*, p. 92.

12 From Ancient Greek *eu* (well) and *phēmi* (I speak).

13 Henry Watson Fowler, *A Dictionary of Modern English Usage* (London: Oxford University Press, 1926), s.v. "Euphemism."

14 The reader will find many excellent examples in Archibald Lyall's *It Isn't Done: or, The Future of Taboo among the British Islanders* (London: Kegan Paul, Trench, Trübner & Co., Ltd., 1930).

15 For example, "to pass away," "to breathe one's last," "sleeping," "resting," "to leave the world behind," "to go home," "not to look at the sun again," "not to be here," "to go away," "to return to one's fathers," "to recover." One also speaks of "the defunct" and "the dear lost." The word "cemetery" comes from the Ancient Greek *koimētērion* (place of rest).

gladly reminded of it. A student of mine had to fill in her age on a form. She first wrote 22, and then corrected the figure to 32. When they see a corpse, people are inclined to look away. As subjects of conversation, the disheartening aspects of life shock the "nice people," and frighten the others. Buddhists recommend meditations on death, corpses, illness, etc., in order that a true perspective on life should be attained. Those aspects of reality which are usually blotted out should thus, they hope, emerge on their own.

Flight from displeasing reality is partly inspired by concern for *narcissistic self-love*, and chiefly by *fear*, coupled with a desire to protect the personality from ideas which threaten its integrity. A leper's narcissism would be wounded should leprosy be mentioned in his presence. A fat person requires "outsize garments." The mentioning of menstruation may hurt the feelings of women who do not want to admit that they are incapacitated. In Chapter 2.5, I intend to show that the overwhelming majority of people cannot live joyfully without adopting some kind of ostrich attitude to life. Whether or not propaganda can do without "emotional curtains" will depend on the nature, strength, and urgency of the fear which we try to avoid by drawing a merciful veil over the more fearful aspects of reality. The fear which produces "emotional curtains" is partly magical, partly acquired by identification, and partly morally tinged with a sense of guilt.

The primitive fear of *magical contagion* is not yet extinct. Primitive populations formed the idea that, by looking at something unpleasant, or by mentioning some danger, one establishes with it a contact that may lead to some form of contagion.[16] To use words of ill-omen brings near the dangerous beings to whom they refer. Death, for instance, is either personified, or regarded as the work of evil spirits who have an objection to their names being mentioned. In either case, everything connected with death is ill-omened. The word alone would draw dangerous attention to him who spoke it, or there might be some contagion through uttering the name of death. By mentioning ill-omened words, the referent itself may be produced. Rudiments of this old fear still persist when we say, "Talk of the devil, and you will see his horns"; "Speak of the wolf and you will see his tail." Or, as I was told, it is bad form to say, "Don't go and kill yourself," because by referring to the action one might help to bring it about.

Instead of words which bring danger, primitive people use words of good omen. In this way they hope to flatter and conciliate the beings thus named. The Slavs called fever "aunt" or "godmother," in order to make her friendly. The Teutons called disease "the good" or "the blessed." The cobra is addressed respectfully as "the good snake" or "the good lord." The Greeks, afraid of the Erinyes, spirits of vengeance, called them Eumenides, or "the benevolent."

16 The magical attitude is well set out by J. A. MacCulloch, s.v. "Euphemism" in James Hastings, ed., *Encyclopædia of Religion and Ethics*, vol. 5 (New York: Charles Scriber's Sons, 1912).

The same fear of contagion seizes the citizen of the modern world when he sees one of his fellow creatures who is blind or badly crippled. The magical connotations of that fear are, however, no longer quite explicit. Magical contagion has become simple *identification*. Somebody's experience of shock or mutilation which enters into the orbit of our attention makes us feel, more or less consciously, that the same contingency might befall us, too. It threatens to shake our always precarious sense of security. We feel uneasy, uncomfortable, or even terrified. We protect ourselves by looking away.

Stammerers, stutterers, squint-eyed, and deformed persons are shunned partly because in some mysterious way contact may mean contagion. A working-class woman in Wandsworth assured me that her child would get cancer from merely looking at a relative who suffered from that disease. A hysterical constitution greatly facilitates the process of identification. Pierre Janet reports cases of girls who, after looking at an epileptic fit and proceeding to think about it, later had attacks which roughly reproduced what they had seen.[17]

Because we compare ourselves with the afflicted person, and often put ourselves in his place, a *sense of guilt* is often evoked by contact with him—through sight or word. Some feel that they did nothing to deserve being better off than their ill-fated fellow man, but that, on the contrary, they richly deserve to be punished and pushed into the same misery, and that there is really nothing to protect them against a similar fate. Acute mental distress is avoided by shutting out the unpleasant experience. Others, in an aggressive mood, delight at the sight of suffering, or rejoice at being so much better off. The rejoicing soon develops into a sense of shame and guilt at their own callousness. We also have to bear in mind that our "social conscience" is never quite extinct. Those who are better off are always apt to blame themselves for the misery of others. They therefore create a picture of the social world in which misery is either minimised or justified. "Nobody need go without food in England." "Everybody can find work if he only wants to." "Beggars are simply lazy, and often they are quite wealthy. Didn't you see the case in the papers recently...?" "The poor would be better off if they didn't drink so much." Malthus improved the digestion and the appetite of the middle classes by demonstrating that misery was the fault of the miserable. The more "genteel" classes maintain a cheerful outlook on life by placing a ban on the mentioning of the offensive and awkward features of social life. But, whether genteel or vulgar, most of us become false persons because we are too frightened to face reality as it is.

17 Pierre Janet, *Les Névroses* (Paris: Ernest Flammarion, 1917), p. 332.

2.5

THE VITALITY OF CAMOUFLAGE

It is their own mind that creates illusions—
Is this not the greatest of all self-contradictions?

Seng-t'san[1]

To renounce camouflage would be to go against the most deep-seated inclinations of our mind. It would amount to a spiritual hara-kiri. Without saying so in as many words, most people would think that truth, veracity, and honesty are not worth these instinctive sacrifices. Reason has thus little power to dispel camouflage. Camouflage is obviously deterred neither by self-contradiction nor by contradiction of the facts. People are rarely intelligent or instructed enough to look through their own camouflage. What is more decisive, they have no motive to do so.

In this chapter I first illustrate how easily camouflage survives a conflict with the requirements of logical consistency. I then show that it is usually belied by reality. Finally I discuss the fusion between camouflage and tribalism which is characteristic of modern propaganda.

Camouflage, Logical Thought, and Reality

In order to show that camouflage and logical thought have little "affinity"—to use a chemical term—it will be best to begin with an innocuous example which is unlikely to stir up emotional resistance. The example is drawn from Pareto.

In 1913, the Montenegrins had conquered Scutari, a small port in Albania. Certain European powers sent warships to blockade Montenegro and captured

1 From the *Shinjin-no-mei*, quoted in D.T. Suzuki, *Manual of Zen Buddhism*.

DOI: 10.4324/9781003363408-15

the king's private yacht. The British Foreign Secretary "declared that Montenegro could not be permitted to occupy Scutari because the population was not of the same race, did not speak the same language, did not have the same religion." A *communiqué* issued by the Russian government said similarly:

> Furthermore the population of Scutari is in the majority Albanian and that city is the see of a Catholic bishopric. It must, in this connexion, also not be overlooked that the Montenegrins have never been able to assimilate several thousands of Catholic or Mussulman Albanians who have settled on the frontiers of Montenegro.[2]

Pareto inquires whether a country has the "right" to occupy another country "when the latter presents those differences."[3] Substitute Russia for Montenegro and Poland for Albania, and the validity of the argument will of course not be altered. Russia is Orthodox, Poland is Catholic. Russia has never managed to assimilate the Poles. But though the reasoning is identical, the conclusions are different: Montenegro does not have the "right" to occupy Scutari. Russia has the "right" to occupy Poland.

One year after this comparatively harmless incident, the Great War broke out. From the very start, each government took shelter behind a smoke screen. It did not matter that the smoke screen was often rather transparent, as long as it was there. In 1914, Bethmann Hollweg[4] rallied the Germanic peoples against the Slavs. If he had been consistent with the above argument concerning the permissible basis for invasion, he might as well have rallied them against Austria, Germany's ally. On the other side, Serbian and Tsarist troops fought together to "make the world safe for democracy." Why should they have bothered to argue with each other in the face of a common enemy and an ideal worth dying for?

Nor do rationalisations used in the conflict between classes either reach or require a high standard of rationality. Propagandists are not afraid of the most blatant self-contradictions. The workers, for instance, are told that, because they are poor, they are "at bottom" much better off than the capitalists. Wealth is made to appear as a matter of little importance, a troublesome burden at its best. And what purpose do such arguments serve? They are used to combat measures which might slow up the accumulation of capital and wealth. One is reminded of the people who tell Hitler that there is no point in returning the German colonies, and that he should fight to keep them—because, as you know, colonies are no good, and of no use to anybody.

---

2 Pareto, *The Mind and Society*, vol. III, p. 1124, §1689.

3 Ibid.

4 *Editors: Theobald von Bethmann Hollweg (1856–1921) was Chancellor of the German Empire from 1909 to 1917.*

If we test any ideological concept—like the "Nordic race" or "Progress"—by comparing it with the facts to which it refers, we find that the facts do not bear it out, do not confirm it, do not lead cogently to it.[5] Most Englishmen would enthusiastically agree about the "Nordic race." Ideology derives its plausibility from arbitrary judgements of value which can neither be proved nor disproved, and which are just a matter of opinion. Just that which, scientifically speaking, constitutes the weakest spot of a doctrine—like the assertion of the superiority of the "Nordics" or of the "civilised"—is the very basis of its popular support.

Quite apart from that, however, a very simple test allows us to decide whether a view is borne out by reality or not. You apply your view, try it out, and see what happens. If you do that, allowing the facts to speak for themselves, and your result is what you expected it to be, perhaps the facts were on your side. If it is not, the facts certainly contradicted your view.

Camouflage is almost invariably belied by the course of events. In retrospect, high ideals seem just to be pretexts which act like signposts on the road, always "pointing a way they never go." It is tiresome to remind people that practically none of the slogans of the Great War was confirmed by subsequent events. British statesmen insisted, "Our direct and selfish interests are small.... We are not fighting a war of conquest.... We have no desire to add to our Imperial burdens either in area or in responsibility."[6] As a result, 1,415,929 square miles were added to the British Empire—in a fit of absent-mindedness, it must be said. Militarism has not been crushed. It is far stronger than before 1914. Indeed the fight against it strengthened it enormously. The world has rarely been as unsafe for democracy as it is now. Dictatorship after dictatorship has sprung up as a direct consequence of the last war. And as to the ending of war, well, the less said, the better.

In the past, the members of most social and political movements were only imperfectly aware of what they actually did. We almost invariably observe a divergence between what they did and what they thought they did. Cromwell's followers sincerely desired to establish the Kingdom of God on Earth. As a matter of fact, they laid the foundations for something very different: for England's industrial development and the transfer of political power from the feudal landowners to businessmen and merchants. Storm Jameson's *The Decline of Merry England* forcibly brings out the discrepancy between word and deed in Puritan England. Referring to the French Revolution, Guérard says, "The bourgeois never wanted Liberty, Equality or Fraternity: what they wanted was order, the protection of property, and the suppression of all privileges except their own."[7] And we may add Georges Sorel's reflection: "One may readily see that actual

5 "Ideology" is the Marxist term for what we call "camouflage." Marxists consider as ideological "all those ideas which veil to the members of social groups the real motive powers which move them to think and to act as they do" (Engels, *Letter to Mehring*, July 14, 1893; trans. E. C.). A detailed account of the Marxist theory can be found in Conze, *Der Satz vom Widerspruch*, pp. 321–360.

6 Ponsonby, *Falsehood in War-Time*, p. 165.

7 Guérard, *Reflections on the Napoleonic Legend*, p. 205.

developments in the Revolution in no way resembled the enchanted pictures that had enthralled its first converts. But could the Revolution have triumphed without such pictures?"[8]

Dr. Goebbels and the "Myth"

Though they may have their heads in the clouds, the common people often have their feet on the earth. Common sense, and the vestiges of rational thought, remain the deadly enemies of propaganda. Since propaganda has come to be pursued scientifically, the propagandist has systematically undertaken to discredit them, thus weakening his victim's resistance. In Germany, for instance, the development of the theory of "myth" has done much to clear the path for Dr. Goebbels, and to dislocate German men and women from their firm position on the solid earth. It must be remembered that the German propagandist lacks one of the advantages of his English colleague. English people are so unsystematic that some contradiction between theory and practice is not half as bad as in Germany, where consistency counts as a virtue. It must therefore be a relief for Germans to hear that in history it is not "objective truth" that matters, but a "tribal myth." Even though the myth be untrue in the sense that it does not correspond to objective facts, it is an ennobling force, far superior to rational or scientific truth.

In Germany the myth-theory attained the rank of a "philosophy of state." Alfred Rosenberg is its official protagonist. He expounded it in *The Myth of the Twentieth Century*.[9] Without going into the antecedents of his theory, I propose to give a short survey of its more salient features.

According to Rosenberg, a myth is a complex of ideas which moves the masses to great actions. Christianity was a myth. The French and Russian Revolutions each created a myth. The German soul finds itself through the creation of myths.[10] The standards of truth we apply to a scientific statement happily do not apply to

8 Georges Sorel, *Réflexions sur la violence* (Paris: Marcel Rivière et Cie., 1908), p. 83: *On peut reconnaître facilement que les vrais développements de la Révolution ne ressemblent nullement aux tableaux enchanteurs qui avaient enthousiasmé ses premiers adeptes; mais sans ces tableaux la Révolution aurait-elle pu vaincre?* Trans. E. C.

9 Alfred Rosenberg, *Der Mythus des zwanzigsten Jahrhunderts* (München: Hoheneichen-Verlag, 1934; 1st ed. 1930). *Editors: Rosenberg was editor of the Nazi newspaper* Völkischer Beobachter.

10 We cannot expect enemies of rational thought to be clear and concise writers. Rosenberg expresses his thoughts in the following way (p. 685, trans. E. C.):

> It is a mythical memory if today the figure of the Saxon Duke Vidukind appears as great and as cognate with Martin Luther and Bismarck. It is the deepest wisdom and a new mythical experience of immemorial (uralten) truth, if we place Meister Hildebrand near Meister Eckhart and Frederic the Unique. We reach the ultimate possible limit of extension of our soul when the myth of Baldur and Siegfried appears as the same in kind with the essence of the German soldier of 1914, and the recently regained world of the Edda now, after the collapse of the old Gods, means also for us the rebirth of Deutschtum from the chaos of today.

the myth. A scientific statement claims to be universally true. A myth cannot be measured by universal truth at all. Its validity is essentially confined to one social group. Baldur and Frederic the Unique obviously leave the French unmoved, and also the Arabs, or the Chinese. Nor does it matter how far mythical statements correspond with reality. We know nothing about reality as it is. The one and eternal absolute truth is beyond our reach. The "truth" of the myth can therefore not be gauged by reference to reality. We have to consult the centre of our racial soul. A myth is worth believing in when it works, is effective and fruitful in developing the life of the race. It has a value because it creates more life, because it enriches the soul, makes us grow in accordance with the specific values of the Nordic soul and helps us to express our inmost (racial) self freely. The myth is not a logical system, but a "surging of the soul."[11] It can neither be proved, nor can it be refuted. It is asserted and confessed. "The new myth which today fights for an expression among us cannot be refuted at all. It will make its way, and *create* facts."[12] The myth proves its life and reality by the willingness of people to die for it. The Christian myth therefore is dead. Nobody is willing to die for the cross any longer.

The mythical vision of life can be represented in many ways. It may find expression in a mythical story, or in fairy tales, or in religion, art, philosophy, politics. The myth has a symbol—the cross, the red flag, the swastika. Millions are changed when they come into contact with that symbol. The two million Germans who fell in the last war did not die for anything real. They died for a myth, for that myth of blood and soil, of race and Ego, of nation and personality, of blood and honour, which always constituted the essence of Germanic being. "The field-grey German people's army (1914–18) was proof of the myth-forming willingness to sacrifice [mythenbildende Opferbereitschaft]." The soldiers were "martyrs of a new living myth [Lebensmythus]."[13]

No theory could be more convenient for the propagandist, giving his work new scope and setting free all his potentialities. Common sense, his deadliest enemy and most serious obstacle, is ruled out of court. Propagandistic assertions are placed beyond the reach of rational criticism. Opponents are discredited by the mere fact that they are opponents. Why object to errors and illusions? They can be true in the mythical sense, when they increase our creative power. Rosenberg reminds us that wrong hypotheses have proved very fruitful in the investigation of nature. Although they were wrong, they enabled us to make new discoveries. In any case, once objective reality and facts have ceased to warrant respect, there is nothing to disprove propaganda—except stark hunger and the fear of death.

11 *Ein Fluten der Seele*. Rosenberg, *Der Mythus des zwanzigsten Jahrhunderts*, p. 695.

12 Ibid., p. 700. Trans. E. C.

13 Ibid., p. 701. Trans. E. C.

Camouflage and Tribalism

Everybody knows that a great deal of the talk which accompanies the social struggle is untrue, insincere, and deceptive. Both the philosopher and the average person can easily agree about the existence of camouflage.[14] Their respective opinions about the line which divides camouflage from truth are, however, bound to be miles apart. The average person goes by his tribal sentiments. He decides that his own tribal views are true, and those of other tribes transparently false and patently ridiculous. The philosopher who is by definition devoid of tribal prejudices does not quite know where he is. Unable to see any objective difference between the opinions of his own tribe and those of others, he will discard them both. He may torture his soul in the vain search for something that is not tainted by self-deception. If, in ruthless veracity, he likes to follow a proposition to its remote and ultimate consequences—and again, by definition, he should—he will end up by adopting the Buddhist position according to which the whole world is a product of self-deception.[15] It is, I think, the vague, and perhaps instinctive, perception of the rather frightening abyss of nothingness into which the philosophical interpretation of camouflage is bound to land us, which accounts for the strong emotional resistance to an impartial—non-tribal—discussion of camouflage. People resist because they see one of their cherished beliefs after another discarded as camouflage. They complain that they are left with nothing. Why, they ask, debunk everything that gives colour to our lives and raises us beyond ourselves? The philosophical interpretation of camouflage is therefore confined to a tiny minority of self-centred theoreticians. Its weight in social life is negligible, outside Tibet.

The absence of class and national prejudice takes the "kick" out of life. It smacks too much of disillusioned scepticism to ever become popular among the more useful members of society whose attitude to camouflage is determined by a fusion between camouflage and tribalism.[16] The camouflage of outsiders is treated with utter contempt. It is impatiently brushed aside. On March 27, 1875, the *Morning Post*, fearing Russia's threat to India, wrote about her policy in Central Asia:

14 When I speak here of a "philosopher," I do not mean somebody who acts as an official apologist for some political regime. A philosopher, in the old sense, is a man who is the friend of wisdom. In actual reality, the friendship is not always reciprocated. In this context, that is irrelevant. I refer to the philosophical attitude, regardless of whether anybody ever realises it more than approximately.

15 Among modern philosophers, Nietzsche saw how complete truthfulness would lead him to a world in which everything is false: "The truthful ends up by grasping that he always lies." "How can you know how much falsehood I still need in order that again and again I may be able to afford the luxury of my truthfulness?" "Who knows himself is his own executioner! [*Selbstkenner! Selbsthenker!*]" *Gesammelte Werke* (München: Musarion Verlag, 1920) vol. 14, p. 230; vol. 21, p. 127; vol. 20, p. 200. Trans. E. C. The menace of nihilism (in the philosophical sense) kept his mind in a state of perpetual restlessness.

16 One may apply to a philosopher the words of an American writer used in connection with Machiavelli: "Incapable of self-deception, he was equally incapable of faith." Ralph Roeder, *The Man of the Renaissance* (London: George Routledge & Sons, Ltd., 1934), p. 106.

> We have always contended that the 'civilising' theory is a mere blind. In view of the execution of a policy highly menacing to our interests, it was a duty to speak out plainly and to call a spade a spade.

In view of the execution of a policy highly menacing to our interests…!

As long as a tribe is intact, the overwhelming majority of its members understand no language but their own, and are deaf to any but their own tribal sounds. Mankind can be likened to bats who are distributed over the caves of a vast mountain, each cave being segregated from the others. But this takes no account of the earthquakes which sometimes demolish the walls of a cave and reconfigure tribal organisation. Tribes often disintegrate. While they are disintegrating, their members may become receptive to the camouflage of outsiders. It is therefore necessary to perpetually ridicule and, if possible, unmask the camouflage of outsiders, not merely in order to protect one's own flock, but also in the hope that the criticism may be taken up by the outsiders.

This does not, however, happen too frequently. To mention an example, the Bolsheviks scored a victory in 1917 when they published the "secret treaties."[17] They seriously embarrassed the Allied statesmen when they revealed that these treaties contained "the division of Persia, the robbery of China and of Turkey, the division of Austria, the separation of East Prussia, and of the German colonies." The treaties revealed the real purpose of a war which was fought for the redistribution of large portions of the world. All the "disinterested champions of democracy" had secured considerable territorial gains. The Bolsheviks could thus convince the wavering soldiers that the Kerensky Government was not fighting for the defence of Russia, as it claimed, but for the "secret treaties of an outspoken robberish content," treaties which "ally Russia to the English-French robbery capital." In Great Britain, the Labour Movement was seriously disconcerted by the duplicity of the Allied Governments. One should, however, not exaggerate the extent of the Bolshevik success. Many English people, especially the lower middle classes, have never heard of the "secret treaties." The thick skin of their tribalism prevents the poisonous germ from leaking through to their bloodstream.

What Is Behind It?

In a popularised form, the theory of camouflage has become one of the chief weapons of propaganda. The propagandist has always solved the problem of honesty and dishonesty by loudly proclaiming that he is honest, and his opponents dishonest. The Marxist theory of *ideology*, in particular, has profoundly influenced

17 *Editors: The following quotations refer to the "Constantinople Agreement" of 1915 and other like documents, though we are unable to identify their particular source. The translations appear to be Conze's own.*

the tactics of propagandists all over the world.[18] Marx claimed that throughout history men had deceived themselves about the real motives of their actions. His materialist conception of history at last tore off the veil of false pretences with which men used to cover their actions. And as long as they were ignorant of the real forces behind their actions, they were the slaves of these forces, and not the masters.

For Marx and his followers, this theory was a first-class fighting instrument. Marx assumed that the proletariat was exempt from self-deception. Because the working class have a "scientific" conception of social life, they alone can control society. Marx developed the line taken by the rationalists of the 18th century, for whom the opponent is full of prejudice, while they themselves are unprejudiced and clear-minded scientists. He improved, however, upon this rather naïve attitude by showing that the prejudice of the other fellow is due not only to stupidity, but to verifiable economic and material interests. The Marxist theory of ideology is meant to be a weapon of propaganda, useful to disintegrate the position of the enemy, on whom distrust and suspicion are concentrated.

The influence of this doctrine has been immense. The enemies of Marxism soon turned it against Marxism itself. Bolshevism, for the Nazis, is a world conspiracy of the Jews against European culture. Marxism, and the welfare of the working class, are but a pretext for international Jewry in their attempt to rule the world. To others, Communism is a cover behind which Russia promotes her imperial interests. In 1922, A. L. Galéot made a detailed analysis of revolutionary movements. He contended that they were, at bottom, motivated by a desire for theft and the acquisition of material goods. "But because altruistic sentiments can hope for a better reception, the revolutionary theory is inclined to give them a very prominent place in revolutionary constructions—a top position, on the surface."[19] The stage of politics is filled with honest brokers who accuse each other of share pushing.

The bewildered citizen soon enters into the spirit of the new game. Whenever a new social event startles his imagination, he wants to know who is "behind" it. Some see everywhere the hidden hand of Moscow, or the Freemasons, or the Roman Catholic Church. When Hitler became known in England, there was at once a demand for "the men behind Hitler." Thyssen, the capitalists, and the

---

18 According to Engels (*Letter to Franz Mehring* [London, July 14, 1893], trans. Dona Torr, *Karl Marx and Friedrich Engels: Correspondence, 1846–1895* [London: M. Lawrence, 1934]),

> Ideology is a process accomplished by the so-called thinker consciously, it is true, but with a false consciousness. The real motive forces impelling him remain unknown to him; otherwise it simply would not be an ideological process. Hence he imagines false or seeming motive forces.

19 A. L. Galéot, *La Psychologie révolutionnaire* (Paris: Nouvelle Librairie Nationale, 1922), p. 97. Trans. E. C.

generals filled the bill for the time being.[20] When Franco began to puzzle the British mind, it came as a revelation that a real live millionaire was behind him—a man called Juan March. When later on it transpired that persons so well-known as Hitler and Mussolini were behind Franco, the mystery was finally cleared up, and public curiosity satisfied. As Nazi propagandist Eugen Hadamovsky puts it,

> There is no leading politician who does not appear in hostile propaganda as a complete idiot [Trottel], coward, and subaltern autocrat who, devoid of any intelligence, is guided by secret forces from behind. Lenin, in bourgeois pamphlets, appeared as a sick criminal, Hitler in proletarian propaganda as an executioner and savage despot [Wüterich], Mussolini as a bloody tyrant. Caricature, distortion, one-sidedness, appear to belong to the essence of propaganda.[21]

Herr Hadamovsky should know.

It is the first rule of good propaganda that its aims should not be obvious. When the masses express suspicion about what lies "behind" a social movement, they are instinctively recognising that the surface of that movement is deceptive. That is perhaps a step forward.

---

20 *Editors: The reference is to the major German steelworks company founded by August Thyssen in 1891.*

21 Eugen Hadamovsky, *Propaganda und nationale Macht: Die Organisation der öffentlichen Meinung für die nationale Politik* (Oldenburg: Gerhard Stalling, 1933), p. 18. Trans. E. C. *Editors: Hadamovsky's* Propaganda und nationale Macht *is the only book-length Nazi treatment of the principles of propaganda. The book is dedicated "to the master of political propaganda, Dr. Joseph Goebbels, under whose brilliant leadership the neglected weapon of German politics became a creative art" (trans. Randall Bytwerk,* Propaganda and National Power: The Organization of Public Opinion for National Politics *by Eugen Hadamovsky, 2007,* German Propaganda Archive, https://research.calvin.edu/german-propaganda-archive/hadamovsky.htm, accessed August 17, 2022).

CONCLUSION

The Limitations of Propaganda

His overthrow heap'd happiness upon him;
For then, and not till then, he felt himself,
And found the blessedness of being little.

Shakespeare's Griffith about Cardinal Wolsey, Henry VIII, IV.2

In conclusion, we try to define the place of propaganda in modern society, and to decide how deep it goes, and what power it has to sway our minds and to effect social change.

Animated by a kind of professional tribalism, most professions and occupations seem more weighty and important to those who follow them than they really are. This inclination to overestimate their importance in the scheme of things can be observed in professions as wide apart as sailors, manual workers, doctors, lawyers, clergymen, philosophers, and lyrical poets. We cannot then be surprised to find that propagandists rate themselves very highly. Sir Campbell Stuart and Lord Northcliffe believed that propaganda had decided the last war. For reasons of their own, Ludendorff and his followers took up the same thesis which seemed to exonerate the military leadership of the German army.[1]

It is obvious, on the other hand, that one cannot simply talk people into anything. Propaganda is likely to meet with insuperable resistance unless its audience is predisposed to it by material interests, social conditions, group tradition, and

1 *Editors: Sir Campbell Stewart and Alfred Harmsworth, First Viscount Northcliffe, were prominent propagandists for Great Britain during the First World War (and in the case of Stewart, also during the Second). Erich Ludendorff was Quartermaster General of the German army during the First World War.*

DOI: 10.4324/9781003363408-16

mental make-up.[2] It is possible that the gullibility of the public has no limit in questions which bear no direct relation to their practical needs. In matters more pertinent to self-interest, however, propagandistic assertions can, like germs, rarely infect us unless we are susceptible to their influence.

Certain facts can also be stronger than propaganda. No amount of advertising can break down resistance to a definitely inferior product. This is true at least of all those products which have an ascertainable effect or use-value. The restraining influence of an ascertainable use-value is absent in the case of many patent medicines, for example. As long as the advertiser considers the mental needs of his clients, he has the field all to himself. But as far as kitchen utensils are concerned, the common sense of the housewife is not easily led astray by propaganda for any length of time. "The ordinary man or woman who goes shopping has a fundamental core of common sense which no amount of 'blarney' is likely to disturb very seriously."[3] The quality of goods must, in the long run, justify the purchase. The sense of value cannot be completely paralysed.

It is, of course, more difficult to detect the quality of a policy than that of a shoe cream. One might, for instance, be tempted to substantiate the assertion that material interests, first-hand experience, and common sense are serious checks on political propaganda, by citing the discrepancy in the 1936 American presidential election between the opinions of newspaper readers and the wishes of the electorate at large. Of the major American newspapers (those with 50,000 readers and over), a poll indicated that 14.3 million readers supported Landon, 7 million supported Roosevelt, and 1.7 million were neutral. In the election itself, 25 million persons voted for Roosevelt, and 15 million for Landon. It seems that only followers of Roosevelt can regard this as an example of the triumph of common sense. Another interpretation is equally possible. The propaganda of the printed word may have been beaten by Roosevelt's "propaganda of deeds." The enormous sums which the Roosevelt administration had spent on relief may have carried more weight than the arguments of his opponents. These two explanations for Roosevelt's victory—the triumph of common sense on the one hand, and the triumph of his propaganda on the other—will seem alike only to those who are unwittingly persuaded by that propaganda.

A combination of material interests and group tradition seems to account for the comparative failure of Lloyd George's propaganda among British workers during the last war. Although the British government possessed an almost complete monopoly over the instruments of propaganda, they could not destroy the British workers' latent hunger for peace. When the Labour Party voted in August,

2 I personally believe that the material interests of the people are the rock on which in the long run all propaganda breaks itself. This is only true, however, if the term "material interests" is taken in a highly special and technical sense, as I have explained in *The Scientific Method of Thinking*.

3 Greenly, *Psychology as a Sales Factor*, p. 206.

1917 on the question of attending the anti-war Stockholm Conference, a majority by a margin of 1.3 million voted to attend (1.8 million for and 0.5 million against).[4]

Propaganda and Objective Facts

I found it rather hard to give examples for the rule that successful propaganda requires the support of common sense and objective facts. Each time I discovered that I had mistaken my own sense for "common sense," and my own opinions for "hard facts."The following examples are, I hope, relatively independent of my own personal predilections.

A propaganda of discontent seems to need an objective basis in fact. Bantu agitators are fond of saying: "When the first white man came to you, he had the Bible and you had the land; but now you have the Bible, and he has the land." A phrase like this does not invent a grievance; rather it neatly conveys a grievance which many already feel. The formulation of the grievance is the first step towards organising the aggrieved. A serious grievance cannot be manufactured by propaganda. The agitators would be laughed at if the land had not in actual fact been taken away.[5]

During wartime, in the long run, the treatment of soldiers, their food, the behaviour of officers, and success or defeat in battle are stronger than verbal propaganda. The experiences of the last war are conclusive in that respect. The efforts of propagandists were unable to disintegrate any but demoralised troops. A wave of Austrian leaflets preceded the Italian defeat at Caporetto in 1917. But the brutal inefficiency of the Cadorna administration had already broken the ground for the Austrian propaganda.[6] In 1918, Allied propaganda undermined the morale of the Austro-Hungarian army. The propaganda attack was begun in 1917. By May of that year, results began to make themselves felt in desertions.[7] But the discontent was already there. Propaganda added boldness to discontent by lending it a voice, and backing it up by the promise of powerful help.

Propaganda helped to destroy the morale of both the German and the Russian troops. Again, it pushed down a crumbling mountain. Allied propaganda started in 1915. Before spring 1917 it had made no appreciable impression on the German troops. About that time, objective facts began to support it.[8] In the battles of Verdun and the Somme, the Allied troops had an overwhelming material advantage. In addition, the news of hunger at home had a demoralising effect.

4 Paul Kellogg and Arthur Gleason, *British Labor and the War: Reconstructors for a New World* (New York: Boni and Liveright, 1919), p. 12.

5 For some of the facts, see Isaac Schapera, *Western Civilization and the Natives of South Africa* (London: George Routledge & Sons, Ltd., 1934).

6 *Editors: Luigi Cadorna was the Chief of Staff of the Italian Army from 1914 to 1917.*

7 Thimme, *Weltkrieg ohne Waffen*, p. 22.

8 George Bruntz, "Allied Propaganda and the Collapse of German Morale in 1918," *The Public Opinion Quarterly* 2.1 (January, 1938): 67.

The real propaganda wave started only in summer 1918. There was little promise of success as long as the German people hoped for an early and victorious end of the war after the spring offensive of 1918. But after this offensive had come to a standstill in June and July 1918, the German troops were seized by despair. By August apathy and hopelessness reigned supreme. Nearly a million German soldiers refused to fight during the last months of the war. Instead, they moved about behind the lines. Defeat had become attractive. In this prevailing mood, arguments against militarism etc. were taken up as excuses which justified the desire to see the war ended at any price. One believed the Allied promises and arguments because one wanted to. They afforded welcome and handy rationalisations for a course of action desired independently of them (recall the Roman imperialist propaganda discussed in Chapter 2.2). Bartlett points out that

> thus fully formulated suggestions are acted upon without criticism only when they chime in with tendencies in the actor which are awake and ready to burst into action. Suggestion by submissiveness, as we may call it, is bound to break down if the command conveyed runs counter to the fundamental tendencies of the persons to whom it is given.[9]

A successful leader's unbroken prestige is only heightened by the attacks of an enemy. The Allied propagandists respected the German commanders as long as their prestige was secure. Their attacks on Hindenburg and Ludendorff began only after the retreat of 1918. It is further noteworthy that there was a substantial element of unsuspected truth behind the ideological offensive of the Allies. They fought for "democracy." The development of the war automatically increased the social weight of the common people. It was a people's war in which everything came more and more to depend on the fighters and workers. General Groener saw this when he remarked in 1917 that "a democratic wave goes through the world."[10] While *parliamentary* democracy has suffered in the aftermath of the war, the influence of the masses has increased steadily in the so-called "dictatorial" countries. Dr. Goebbels bore a somewhat ungraceful testimony to it when he said that the government "must recognise the opinions of the people if their opinions are justified."[11]

The last war thus revealed not only the importance of propaganda, but also its relative unimportance. Propaganda worked against the defeated only after four years. It never succeeded against the victors. German propaganda failed in India, Egypt, Ireland, and Morocco. The collapse of the French army in April, 1917 was due to German guns, and to incompetent leadership on the part of the French command. It owed practically nothing to German propaganda. The morale

9 Bartlett, *Psychology and the Soldier*, p. 135.

10 *Editors: We are unable to identify the original source of this quotation.*

11 *Frankfurter Zeitung*, March 25, 1934. Trans. E. C.

of troops must first of all be shaken by events. Only then are the propagandist manifestations of the enemy greeted with the feeling that they are quite right.

In some ways the mentality of the victim of propaganda resembles that of a hysterical patient. In both cases a more or less unfounded conviction serves a certain purpose, and as long as it does, the person clings to it. Hysteria can be cured by persuasion, hypnotism, or by counter-suggestion, but only on condition that the disease has ceased to be a source of emotional satisfaction. Once their interest in the symptom has disappeared, many patients shake it off easily. The *Journal of the American Medical Association* reported that of 2,500 shell-shock cases awaiting transportation back to the USA in 1918, 2,100 recovered within a day or two of the armistice.[12] The remainder had to be helped by suggestion. If nothing is in the way of a person's cure but a conviction that he cannot be cured, suggestion can help him over that final difficulty. Shell-shock cases could be cured by suggestion only if the person were not required to go back to the trenches. If he had to, he either resisted suggestion powerfully, or, if it succeeded for the time being, he had a relapse before he reached the trenches. It is practically impossible to cure a hysterical patient as long as he resists the cure because he does not want to part with his illness.

Russian propagandists seem to have drawn the lesson. An Austrian friend of mine told me on his recent return from Russia that the Russians had decided, in the event of war with Germany, not to initiate a propaganda campaign among the Germans at once. It would be a sheer waste of effort until the propaganda had a basis in fact. The Germans would become sober only after they had been kicked hard. First one would have to reply by brutality to their brutality. Then, after the German people had acquired ample experience of the more unpleasant aspects of a war, the Russian propaganda could hope to find responsive ears. The Russian Bolsheviks had first-hand experience of this mechanism in 1917. For months, as long as the outcome of the war against Germany remained in question, the average Russian was inclined to believe that Lenin was a German spy. The Bolsheviks gained the ear of the masses only after several big battles had been lost, and the peasants streamed back into their villages. Only then did indignation about the "secret treaties" (see page 183) oust the indignation about Lenin's venality and bad faith.

It would be interesting to calculate mathematically the point at which privations and social stress break the morale of a group. Any government would pay a fortune for the formula. At the present stage of our knowledge we can, however, say no more than that it is usually unsafe for a propagandist to disregard objective facts of which his clients have a first-hand experience.

12 Volume 79, number 11, 1922, p. 913.

Second-Hand Facts

Our political judgement depends, however, to a great extent on those "second-hand" facts about which we are almost entirely at the mercy of the various organs of the propaganda machine. The average man has access to information about the relative strength of armies, the designs of statesmen, or the social conditions of foreign countries only under quite exceptional circumstances. Second-hand facts can be suppressed, or rebuilt, almost at will. The poetical imagination of the propagandist suffers restraint only on the rare occasions when competitors can speak with an authority equal to his own. Usually dissenters are believed only by a small minority within a social group. If inside one group two contradictory propaganda machines, each one invested with equal prestige, both inform the public on second-hand facts, the group is disrupted, and a civil war becomes necessary. A monopoly of "information" is established by force, or in other cases is based on tacit consent.

Some of the books which I mentioned in the *Introduction* have collected many examples to show that the success of propaganda is not hampered by an utter lack of veracity in all those assertions which are warranted by second-hand information. According to Lasswell there are only two limits to what can be "put over." First, propaganda should be in keeping with unconcealable events until its end is attained. One should, for instance, not promise victory for a definite date, but ultimate success, since nothing can happen "to disprove this proposition before the attainment or the total eclipse of all hope of attaining the political objective."[13] Further, one should avoid self-contradiction to the same public in the same context. One can tell the Catholics that a war is a great Catholic crusade, and the Protestants that it is a great Protestant crusade. But one should not mix the two appeals when addressing a mixed audience.

As far as the shaping of social events, or even their evaluation, is concerned, the influence of pure and disinterested reason is of course negligible. For practical reasons it would be worthwhile finding out how far rational instruction renders us capable of withstanding propaganda. There exists only one such experimental study so far—and it is not very conclusive—in which William W. Biddle studied the resistance to propaganda among 350 high-school students.[14] The test went something like this:

1. The students read "high-powered propaganda" about domestic issues within the USA, and about relations between the USA and Europe ("Atlantic relations").
2. For three weeks they studied pamphlets about the techniques of propaganda.

---

13 Lasswell, *Propaganda Technique in the World War*, p. 208.

14 William W. Biddle, *Propaganda and Education* (New York: Teacher's College, Columbia University, 1932), p. 43 et seq. *Editors: See Editors' Introduction, pp. xxxvii–xxxviii.*

3. Two weeks later, they read propaganda material which dealt with relations between the USA and China, Japan, and the Philippines ("Pacific relations").

Susceptibility to "Pacific relations" propaganda was then measured, and compared with the susceptibility which the students had shown to the propaganda about "Atlantic relations." In most cases the students' resistance had increased considerably. The most gullible persons had, on the whole, improved more than the others. Those who consciously recognised the material as propaganda had improved most of all.

Biddle seems to have attached no importance to the fact that his students lived on the Atlantic coast, and that therefore their prejudices might be less vigorous about "Pacific relations" than about "Atlantic relations." I nevertheless mention his study, because it may show a way forward to those who want to use education to diminish the effects of propaganda on the minds of those who have leisure and inclination to reason.

The Achievements of Propaganda

As a source of information, propaganda could be dispensed with. Its function must lie elsewhere, as a unifying and stabilising force in heterogeneous and unstable societies. Propaganda pulls together the efforts of many individuals and reduces the dead weight of dissenters. It adds considerably to the fighting power of a group, and is a potent instrument for organising a common effort. Propaganda gives the group members the drive of a good conscience by convincing them that their purpose coincides with the welfare of a wider group (nation, humanity, etc.). On the other hand, the ability of propaganda to penetrate to the tribal foe is negligible, except when a long series of failures have stricken the enemy with social disintegration.

The stabilising effect of propaganda is largely the result of its considerable amusement value. As an inexpensive circus, political propaganda adds to the zest of life. During the great economic crisis following the last war, many Germans could no longer afford to go to the cinema. They found cheaper diversion by joining the Nazis or similar organisations. Politics counteracts boredom and gives the impression that something is being done, that things are moving forward. The monotony of a standardised life creates a desire for novelty, an appetite for fresh surprises, a desire for the unfamiliar. The old proverb that "everyone has a penny for a new alehouse" applies very much to modern politics.

In some ways propagandists are public benefactors. They help to put people's minds at rest. They explain why things go wrong. They have an easy way to put them right. They make the existing state of society seem more satisfactory. They look after the magical longings, the tribal, aggressive, and submissive desires of the soul. They confer status, and give the feeling that life is worthwhile.

A revolutionary socialist, on reading this, objected that it was not at all good for people to be satisfied, because then they desire no change. Dissatisfaction, however, is not in itself conducive to beneficial change, unless people as a mass know what kind of society they want to build up. If they do not know that, their discontent only gets them a more repressive form of government.

Rational Propaganda

Finally, it is difficult to resist the temptation to discuss the question whether mass propaganda can aid progress in the direction of a rational society. The answer will depend entirely on what we mean by a "rational" society. There will be room for mass propaganda in our scheme of things if we believe that the growth of political liberties and an increase in the "standard of living" will gradually bring about a rational society. The improvement of housing conditions can be assisted by propagandist indignation. Educational facilities can be increased in response to propaganda.

Similarly, we will expect a great deal from propaganda if we believe that in some moments of revolutionary intoxication a "rational" political party can induce the masses to shake off their oppressors once and for all. The "rational" party members can then, after the conquest of power, educate the rest of the population. Since, in their kindness, they will "disoppress" (liberate) the masses, these will gradually lose the irrational ideas which they owed to oppression, and all will be well. This attractive scheme does not explain what makes the party members so exceptionally rational that they will disoppress the masses.

On the other hand, if we believe that a rational society cannot be achieved before the majority of people have become rational, mass propaganda is not likely to bring us nearer to our goal. It seeks, as we have shown, to further irrational emotions, and one expects it to throw a veil of lies over events, and to enable its addicts to vegetate in the twilight of self-deception. In all these questions we have not yet found a standard which allows us to decide where the truth really lies. On one point, however, I think agreement is already possible now.

It would be a great relief for all of us if the scope of our social instincts could be increased. "All that isolates damns; all that associates, saves."[15] These words sum up the gist of what psychologists know about mental hygiene. Mental disorders can be cured only by satisfactory social relations. "Fellowship is heaven, and lack of fellowship is hell: fellowship is life, and lack of fellowship is death," as William Morris put it.[16] The fact that the present social and economic system undermines the feeling of fellowship among human beings is an important item in the case against it. A rational society would be one in which the material, economic,

15 Newton Arvin, *Hawthorne* (Boston: Little, Brown & Co., 1929), p. 59.

16 William Morris, *A Dream of John Ball and A King's Lesson* (London: Reeves & Turner, 1888), p. 29.

and social conditions create a social order in which we actually *like* to love our neighbour.

If, in order to be successful, mass propaganda has to take people as they are, it is not likely to genuinely develop our social instincts. As we have seen, propaganda increases the unity within a group by simultaneously driving one group against another and preaching aversion to outsiders. It achieves social unity by fostering servility, hatred, conceit, and fear. I do not, however, regard this as a decisive argument against the ability of propagandists to improve the world. In this book I do not set myself the ungrateful task of telling people *what they should do*. All I intended was to explain *what they actually do* when they make propaganda among the masses.

AFTERWORD

I am so pleased to be asked to contribute an afterword to this book for a number of reasons. First, it is dedicated to my old friend and dharma brother, the late Dr. Alexander Tribe, with whom I was ordained as a Buddhist priest. A psychiatrist by training and profession, Al was one of the most self-effacing prodigies I have ever met—wry and soft-spoken, with a penetrating gaze from which nothing escaped notice. Whenever I gave a dharma talk and his hand appeared at chest height, requesting permission to speak, a sinking feeling blossomed in my gut as I tried to anticipate the flaw or oversight in my presentation he was about to point out. He died tragically early and before his public reputation could catch up with the respect and affection tendered to him by his peers.

Second, Al's older brother, Laurence Tribe, is well-known to inveterate analysts of current events as an authority who is perhaps first among equals in American constitutional law. His opinion is often sought to filter the muddy water of contemporary events as it occludes the wisdom of our constitution. "Larry" and I met at Al's and my ordination, and as someone who served in government for eight years and dedicated a large portion of my life to social change, I was thrilled to meet such a formidable authority on judicial politics. I then discovered that we were born on the same day, and using our shared birthdate as my entrée to pepper him with occasional questions, we have maintained a correspondence ever since. The fact that my contribution will share the geography of this book with both Tribe brothers is a source of tremendous satisfaction to me.

Finally, when I began my study and practice of Buddhism at San Francisco Zen Center in 1974, Edward Conze was the first author I read, after our founding teacher Suzuki Roshi's book, *Zen Mind, Beginner's Mind*. Conze's *Buddhist Wisdom Books, A Short History of Buddhism*, and *Buddhism: Its Essence and Development* formed the substrate of my intellectual grounding in Buddhism, comparable to the way meditation and formal practice grounded my body. I had little idea who he was, though two good friends at the time, namely the poets Gary Snyder and Philip Whalen, both of whom were important mentors for my developing commitment to Buddhism, commended Conze to me as a very smart fellow who had written clearly and intelligently about Buddhism.

Forty-eight years later, invited to contribute an afterword to this edition of *The Psychology of Mass Propaganda*, edited by Richard and Nathan Levine (full disclosure, Rick was an early Zen Center friend), I am shocked to discover the correspondences between Conze's life and my own. I now appreciate his work with a new and quickened sympathy. A few words of explanation are in order.

I grew up in the 1940s and 1950s, born the year the Japanese attacked Pearl Harbor. At that time, the ink was hardly dry on Conze's original composition of this book. Some members of my mother's family were communists and socialists—fervently anti-Nazi champions of working people, serving them as teachers and labor organizers. It might be necessary to remind younger readers who have grown up in our culture, in which any analysis of socialism and communism is consigned to obscurity as taboos, that both of these political theories and practices were (and remain) constitutionally protected, legal pursuits.

Such niceties were ignored after World War II ended and American elites understood that we would be competing with Russia for the world's material resources, and the hearts and minds of its population. They amassed their forces and began concerted propaganda campaigns attributing every variety of evil to those who even suggested that alternatives to capitalism might be discussed. Senator Joseph McCarthy led public witch-hunts in the form of congressional hearings in which those he accused of being Communists, sympathizers, or "pinkos" were hauled in and threatened with loss of livelihood (literally) unless they informed on "fellow travelers." During America's 1940s and 1950s, Communists inhabited the terrain currently reserved for "terrorists," "drug-smugglers," and "immigrants." During this period I witnessed adults in my living room, desperate and sometimes in tears, fearful for their families' safety as government propaganda described them as enemies of the people and transformed neighbors into judges and persecutors. By the time I was ten or eleven, I was so indignant at the lies being told about my family that I stopped saluting the flag.

Consequently, it was a shock to discover that Edward Conze had grown up in pre-Nazi Germany and was a dedicated and militant communist in his youth. I understood his support for ANTIFA (Anti-Fascist Action, a term current at that time) as similar to the commitments of my own family—political expressions of compassion. Conze was clear-eyed about the similarities between Nazi propaganda and Russian propaganda, but in a world where those were apparently the only choices, especially for a young German, he made his peace with the Russians, until, as my own family would experience it, Stalin rendered such tolerance unfeasible.

Life in a family like mine predisposed me to social action. Due to complex circumstances beyond the scope of this brief essay, I was, between the ages of about 2 and 14, raised by a black family. My mother had suffered what was then described as a nervous breakdown and was unable to care for my sister and me. My aunt sent her beloved housekeeper, an eighteen-year-old girl named Susie Howard, to live with us. Susie's humor, self-confidence, and moral certainty caused us to transfer our loyalties to her and her boyfriend (later her husband) Ozzie Nelson as if we were starved pups and they were bowls of kibble. Their friends filled our kitchen every day, lighting it up with conversation, laughter, wisdom, and high-spirits while the radio played Jazz. It was as if light had returned to our house, and we remained close until I buried her last year.

It was through listening to Ozzie and Sue and their friends Jules, Violet, and John Ellerbee year after year that I learned to recognize the unearned privileges bestowed on white folks in America. My loyalty to them and my resentment of that persecution eventually led me to participate in the Civil Rights movement and to support Adlai Stevenson for president, canvassing my neighborhood on his behalf. After college, nuclear testing and the war in Vietnam collared my attention, until a group of friends in the small agitprop theater I had joined, the San Francisco Mime Troupe, realized that racism and war were virtually preordained byproducts of an economy and culture organized around profit and private property. We left the theater, organized a group known as the Diggers, and applied ourselves to the challenge of imagining an alternative culture and making it real by acting it out, which we did by providing free food and free medical care, and establishing free stores and communal housing in San Francisco.

Millions of young people likewise created similar institutions, organic food markets, alternative medical practices, the women's movement, the environmental movement, alternative spiritual practices—Daoism, Hinduism, Yoga, Tai-Chi, Chi-Gung, and what, after a decade of license, indulgence, high-hopes, and way too many drugs, finally captured my loyalty—Zen Buddhism.

By 1974, the Sixties were over. My father had died below broke, leaving my mother destitute, and me at thirty without his support which he had always promised would be sufficient to allow me to "teach at a great school, and still afford good fly-rods and suits." That appeared to be the scope of his plans for my future, all the while urging me to "forget about money, I'll take care of the money."

The last of a long series of communes I lived in had broken badly when my personal family's farm, where we'd been living after my father's death, was seized for debt. My daughter's mother had fled, leaving me a single parent. Growing children began demanding more order and stability than our "Do Your Thing" culture could afford them, and disputes and rancor forced many new parents to address their problems as nuclear families rather than continue the often chaotic conditions of our communes. Everything I had dedicated myself to for nearly a decade had failed and I was in rough shape. In light of that, perhaps the reader can imagine the shock I felt, fifty years later, when I read this passage Conze had written about the period when he was about the same age:

> ...the bottom had fallen out of what I then thought was my world. My political faith had collapsed...my marriage had failed, my job seemed distinctly bleak, I had even begun consulting psychoanalysts, and there seemed nothing left that I could live for... At 35, in the middle of my life I had, as Dante would have it, 'lost my way in the middle of a dark wood'. All my previous beliefs had collapsed and lay around me shattered to pieces.

Professor Conze's confession was an epiphany. It gave me a feeling of intimacy with him, and I suddenly saw his journey as parallel to my own.

One day, when I was troubled by a cantankerous and willful student, I quipped to a friend, "the problem with Buddhism is that it has people in it." One finds the same challenge in politics, business, social organizations, and religion. It is the central problem that stymies the best-laid plans and most impeccably designed human systems. Each being who emerges from Emptiness is the frayed tip of a long braid of tangled desires and karma from the infinite past. Millennia of repetitions have insured that each infant arrives as the perfect gift-wrapping for a *potpourri* of greed, hatred, and delusion. This may sound harsh, but any parent can testify to how willful, self-involved, and demanding infants can be; how vehement when they encounter (and then learn) "no!" And yet, that very same infant can mature to become the Dalai Lama, Martin Luther King Jr., Wangari Maathai, or Vandana Shiva. The commitment of time and practice required for such transformation may be initiated by a moment's insight. But that insight, or awakening, requires a lifetime of practice to establish an enduring foundation for ethical behavior.

Without attempting to psychoanalyze Professor Conze, there is much to be said for the total disintegration of one's hopes and belief systems as an expedient to understanding the Buddhist philosophy of Emptiness and Impermanence. Often misunderstood by non-Buddhists, Emptiness is neither "nothingness" nor a void. It is a logical derivative of understanding that all phenomena depend on one another. Simply put, because humans would not exist without oxygen, water, microbes in the soil which produce our food, pollinating insects, etc., it is clear that the "self," as we conceive it, does not exist as an entity separate from the rest of Creation. There is no organ corresponding to it in the body. It has no color, shape, or location. No physicality beyond awareness itself.

Yet, because we have a word for it—"self," "me," "I"—as with tree, dog, baby, or dolphin, we are beguiled into reifying it as an object which appears to stand alone in the universe. This is the central delusion of humankind. It's not that we *don't* exist—Buddha never answered the question as to whether "the self" existed or not. It's that we don't exist in the way we think we do. Meditation is an antidote to this delusion. It is the practice by which we can relax the ego, and with some practice allow our awareness to either drop below or stand alongside our personality for a few moments to perceive "things as it is"—Suzuki Roshi's favorite meme to describe the unity of multiplicities which is our universe.

At some point, I imagine Professor Conze realizing, as Buddha did, that the solutions to the human problems he (and I) once sought would probably not be solved by mass-oriented systems. Change happens one person at a time. Propagandists are, as he points out, clever, but each and every person on earth possesses *Buddha-nature*, the inherent formless wisdom that most closely resembles wilderness. Buddha's first disciple, Kondanna, awoke merely by hearing Buddha's teaching, and went on his own way. It did not require years of study and effort, because he was already spiritually ripe. Others must struggle patiently to overcome their ignorance and delusion. (Sign me in there.) Obviously, Buddhism had been an interest of Conze's for some time, but something precipitated his shift from the political to the personal, and my own experience suggests that it may have been his perception that unceasing practice is required to meaningfully change oneself.

And yet, his gift of this manuscript to Rick Levine, his obvious fondness for it, and his belief in its utility is, to me, evidence of his permanent concern for "all-beings" and his refusal to settle for a merely "personal" salvation. A similar impulse is what drove the Buddha himself to teach, despite his fears that perhaps what he had learned was too subtle for most to make use of. It is what compelled me. It was what compelled Al Tribe, and I daresay compels his brother, to remain amidst the world's suffering and do whatever we can.

An ancient Japanese Zen master named Fuketsu described a *koan* about picking up a speck of dust. "Picking up a speck of dust" stands for doing anything—building a temple, fighting for world peace, saving the whales. If you don't pick it up, nothing happens, and Fuketsu observes that some people are able to sit idly by and watch others suffer without becoming motivated to help them.

"But if we feel we must act," he cautions us, "remember that when we pick up the speck of dust, we pick up the entire world with it—all its good and all its evil. For every good we accomplish we will also be accomplishing multiple 'bads.'" It is as unavoidable as it is unintentional, and for this reason Fuketsu cautions us to move delicately and provisionally; checking, time and again, and being poised and ready to change course in an instant. However, we who are compelled to do something, who pick up the speck of dust, are doing what we can to be of help, all the while knowing that however hard we try, we will have regrets.

With sincere gratitude to all teachers and to Rick and Nathan Levine for bringing this manuscript into the light of day.

A deep bow,

Hosho Peter Coyote

BIBLIOGRAPHY

Ammon, Otto. *Die natürliche Auslese beim Menschen*. Jena: Gustav Fischer, 1893.

Andrews, Charles F. *Mahatma Gandhi's Ideas, Including Selections from His Writings*. London: G. Allen & Unwin, Ltd., 1929.

Archer, William. *Masks or Faces? A Study in the Psychology of Acting*. London: Longmans, Green, and Co., 1888.

Arnold, Thurman W. *The Symbols of Government*. New Haven: Yale University Press, 1935.

Arvin, Newton. *Hawthorne*. Boston: Little, Brown & Co., 1929.

Ashcroft, Thomas. *An Outline of Modern Imperialism: Plebs Textbooks Number Two*. London: The Plebs League, 1922.

Bancroft, Hubert Howe. *The New Pacific*, rev. ed. New York: The Bancroft Company, 1912.

Barnes, Harry Elmer. *The Twilight of Christianity*. New York: The Vanguard Press, 1929.

Barnes, Leonard. *The Duty of Empire*. London: V. Gollancz Ltd., 1935.

Barry, Gerald Reid. *This England: The Englishman in Print*. London: G. Bles, 1933.

Bartlett, Frederic C. *Psychology and the Soldier*. Cambridge: Cambridge University Press, 1927.

Begbie, Harold. *The Life of General William Booth: The Founder of the Salvation Army*, 2 vols. New York: The Macmillan Company, 1920.

Bentham, Jeremy. *The Book of Fallacies: From Unfinished Papers of Jeremy Bentham*. London: J. & H. L. Hunt, 1824.

Bertaut, Jules. *Napoleon in His Own Words*, trans. Herbert Edward Law and Charles Lincoln Rhodes. Chicago: A. C. McClurg & Co., 1916.

Biddle, William W. "A Psychological Definition of Propaganda." *The Journal of Abnormal and Social Psychology* 26.3 (October, 1931): 283–295.

Bogardus, Emory S. "The Occupational Attitude." *Journal of Applied Sociology* 7 (1923): 171–177.

———. "Measuring Social Distances." *Journal of Applied Sociology* 9 (1925): 299–308.

———. "Occupational Distance." *Sociology and Social Research* 13 (1928): 73–81.

Borgese, Giuseppe Antonio. *Goliath: The March of Fascism*. New York: The Viking Press, 1937.

Bovet, Pierre. *The Fighting Instinct*. London: G. Allen & Unwin, Ltd., 1923.

Brady, Robert A. *The Spirit & Structure of German Fascism*. London: Gollancz, 1937.

Brasol, Boris. *Oscar Wilde: The Man, the Artist*. London: Williams and Norgate, Ltd., 1938.

Braude, Morris. *The Principles and Practice of Clinical Psychiatry*. Philadelphia: P. Blakiston's Son & Co., 1937.

Braun, Adolf. *Die Zukunft der deutschen Sozialdemokratie: Deutsch, nicht englisch, französisch oder russisch*. Vienna: Volksbuchhandlung Ignatz Brand & Co, 1917.

Bright, John. *Selected Speeches of the Rt. Hon. John Bright M. P. on Public Questions*. London: J. M. Dent and Co., 1907.

Bruntz, George. "Allied Propaganda and the Collapse of German Morale in 1918." *The Public Opinion Quarterly* 2.1 (January, 1938): 61–76.

Bryce, James. *The American Commonwealth*, 2nd ed., 2 vols. London: Macmillan & Co., Ltd., 1889.

Bulwer, Edward Lytton. *England and the English*. London: George Routledge & Sons, 1876 (1st ed. 1833).

Bury, John B., Stanley A. Cook, Frank E. Adcock, Martin P. Charlesworth, Norman H. Baynes, and Charles T. Seltman, eds. *The Cambridge Ancient History*, 12 vols. New York: The Macmillan Company, 1923–1939.

Chase, Stuart. *The Tyranny of Words*. New York: Harcourt, Brace & Co., 1938.

Clark, Helen. "The Crowd." *Psychological Monographs* 21 (1916): 26–36.

Clemen, Carl. *Religions of the World: Their Nature and Their History*. London: George G. Harrap & Co. Ltd., 1931.

Conze, Edward. *The Scientific Method of Thinking*. London: Chapman & Hall, Ltd., 1935.

———. *An Introduction to Dialectical Materialism*. London: NCLC Publishing Society, Ltd., 1936.

———. *Contradiction and Reality*. London: Wightman & Co., Ltd., 1939.

———. *Der Satz vom Widerspruch: Zur Theorie des dialektischen Materialismus*. Hamburg: Self-Published, 1932; reprint Verlag Neue Kritik, 1976.

Conze, Edward and Ellen Wilkinson. *Why Fascism?* London: Selwyn & Blount, 1934.

Cornford, Francis MacDonald. *Plato's Theory of Knowledge: The Theaetetus and the Sophist of Plato*. London: Kegan Paul, Trench, Trübner & Co., Ltd., 1935.

Coulton, George Gordon. *Life in the Middle Ages*, 2nd ed., 4 vols. Cambridge: Cambridge University Press, 1928–30.

Crozier, Frank P. *The Men I Killed*. London: Michael Joseph, Ltd., 1937.

Dalberg-Acton, John. *The History of Freedom and Other Essays*. London: Macmillan & Co., Ltd., 1907.

Dalton, Hugh. *With British Guns in Italy: A Tribute to Italian Achievement*. London: Methuen, 1919.

Dante. *The Divine Comedy*, trans. Lawrence Grant White. New York: Pantheon Books, 1948.

David-Néel, Alexandra. *Magic and Mystery in Tibet*. New York: C. Kendall, 1932.

Dearmer, Percy. *The Legend of Hell: An Examination of the Idea of Everlasting Punishment, With a Chapter on Apocalyptic*. London: Cassell, 1929.

Delaisi, Francis. *Political Myths and Economic Realities*. London: N. Douglas, 1927.

Desmond, Robert W. *The Press and World Affairs*. London: D. Appleton-Century Co., 1937.

Dimond, Sydney G. *The Psychology of the Methodist Revival: An Empirical and Descriptive Study*. London: Oxford University Press, H. Milford, 1926.

Doob, Leonard William. *Propaganda: Its Psychology and Technique*. New York: H. Holt and Co., 1935.

Duff, Charles. *A Handbook on Hanging: Being a Short Introduction to the Fine Art of Execution*. London: G. Richards and P. Sainsbury at the Cayme Press, Ltd., 1928.

———. *This Human Nature: A History, a Commentary, an Exposition from the Earliest Times to the Present Day*. New York: J. J. Little & Ives Co., 1930.

Durham, Mary Edith. *Some Tribal Origins, Laws and Customs of the Balkans*. London: G. Allen & Unwin, Ltd., 1928.

Emerson, Ralph Waldo. *Representative Men: Seven Lectures*. London: John Chapman, 1850.

English, Oliver Spurgeon and Gerald H. G. Pearson. *Common Neuroses of Children and Adults*. New York: W. W. Norton & Company, Inc., 1937.

Field, John. *Prison Discipline: The Advantages of the Separate System of Imprisonment, as Established in the New County Gaol of Reading*. London: Longman and Co., 1846.

Fowler, Henry Watson. *A Dictionary of Modern English Usage*. London: Oxford University Press, 1926.

Frazer, James George. *Taboo and the Perils of the Soul*. London: Macmillan & Co., Ltd., 1911.

Freer, Cyril C. *The Inner Side of Advertising*. New York: Van Nostrand, 1921.

Freud, Sigmund. "Three Contributions to the Theory of Sex." In *The Basic Writings of Sigmund Freud*, trans. A. A. Brill (New York: Modern Library, 1938): 553–629 (1st ed. 1905, *Drei Abhandlungen zur Sexualtheorie*).

Gadelius, Bror. *Human Mentality in the Light of Psychiatric Experience: An Outline of General Psychiatry*. Copenhagen: Levin & Munksgaard, 1933.

Galéot, A. L. *La Psychologie révolutionnaire*. Paris: Nouvelle Librairie Nationale, 1922.

Garvin, James L. *The Life of Joseph Chamberlain*, 6 vols. London: Macmillan & Co., Ltd., 1932–1969.

Gentile, Giovanni and Calogero Tumminelli, eds. *Enciclopedia Italiana di Scienze, Lettere ed Arti*, 36 vols. Rome: Istituto Giovanni Treccani, 1929–1937.

George, David Lloyd. *The Great Crusade: Extracts from Speeches Delivered during the War*. New York: George H. Doran Company, 1918.

Germany Tells the World: An Account of Four Years of Nazi Foreign Policy, March 1933–March 1937. London: The Union of Democratic Control, 1937.

Goebbels, Joseph and Mjölnir. *Die verfluchten Hakenkreuzler: Etwas zum Nachdenken*. München: Verlag Frz. Eher, 1930.

Goldenweiser, Alexander A. *Early Civilization: An Introduction to Anthropology*. New York: Alfred A. Knopf, Inc., 1922.

———. *Anthropology: An Introduction to Primitive Culture*. New York: F. S. Crofts & Co., 1937.

Greenly, A. J. *Psychology as a Sales Factor*, 2nd ed. London: Sir Isaac Pitman & Sons., Ltd., 1929.

Guérard, Albert Léon. *Reflections on the Napoleonic Legend*. New York: Charles Scribner's Sons, 1924.

Guérin, Daniel. *Fascisme et grand capital*. Paris: Gallimard, 1936.

Hadamovsky, Eugen. *Propaganda und nationale Macht: Die Organisation der öffentlichen Meinung für die nationale Politik*. Oldenburg: Gerhard Stalling, 1933.

Halliwell, James Orchard, ed. *The Private Diary of Dr. John Dee and the Catalogue of His Library of Manuscripts*. London: The Camden Society, 1842.

Hansard's Parliamentary Debates: Third Series, Commencing with the Accession of William IV, vol. 136. London: Cornelius Buck, 1855.

Hastings, James, ed. *Encyclopædia of Religion and Ethics*, 12 vols. New York: Charles Scribner's Sons, 1908–1921.

Henderson, David K. and Robert D. Gillespie. *A Text-Book of Psychiatry for Students and Practitioners*, 4th ed. Oxford: Oxford University Press, 1936.

Herkner, Heinrich. *Die Arbeiterfrage: Arbeiterfrage und Sozialreform*, 8th ed., 2 vols. Berlin: Vereinigung wissenschaftlicher Verleger, 1922.

Hervé, Gustave. *La Patrie en danger: Recueil* in extenso *des articles publiés par Gustave Hervé dans la* Guerre Sociale *du 1er juillet au 1er novembre 1914*. Paris: Bibliothèque des ouvrages documentaires, 1915.

Hexham, Irving. *Understanding World Religions: An Interdisciplinary Approach*. Zondervan, 2011.

Hobson, John Atkinson. *Wealth and Life: A Study in Values*. London: Macmillan & Co., Ltd., 1929.

Hollingworth, Leta Stetter. *Gifted Children: Their Nature and Nurture*. New York: The Macmillan Company, 1926.

Hopkins, Robert Thurston. *Rudyard Kipling, a Character Study: Life, Writings and Literary Landmarks*, 3rd ed. London: Simpkin, Marshall, Hamilton, Kent & Co., Ltd., 1921.

Horrabin, James Francis. *How Empires Grow*. London: NCLC Publishing Society, Ltd., 1935.

Hose, Charles and William McDougall, *The Pagan Tribes of Borneo: A Description of Their Physical, Moral and Intellectual Condition, with Some Discussion of Their Ethnic Relations*, 2 vols. London: Macmillan & Co., Ltd., 1912.

Hutchinson, Lester. *Conspiracy at Meerut*. London: G. Allen & Unwin, Ltd., 1935.

Huxley, Aldous. *Ends and Means: An Enquiry into the Nature of Ideals and into the Methods Employed for Their Realization*. London: Chatto & Windus, 1938.

Huxley, Julian. *Scientific Research and Social Needs*. London: Watts & Co., 1934.

Irwin, Will. *Propaganda and the News: or, What Makes You Think So?* New York: Whittlesey House, 1936.

Ives, George. *A History of Penal Methods: Criminals, Witches, Lunatics*. New York: F. A. Stokes Company, 1914.

James, William. *Principles of Psychology*, 2 vols. New York: Henry Holt & Co., 1890.

Jameson, Henry Lyster. *An Outline of Psychology: "Plebs" Outline Number One*, 9th ed., completely revised by Edward Conze, Eden Paul, and Cedar Paul. London: NCLC Publishing Society, Ltd., 1938.

Jameson, Storm. *The Decline of Merry England*. Indianapolis: The Bobbs-Merrill Co., 1930.

Janet, Pierre. *Les Névroses*. Paris: Ernest Flammarion, 1917.

Jaurès, Jean. *Patriotisme et internationalisme: discours de Jean Jaurès, précédé du manifeste du conseil national du Parti Ouvrier*. Paris: au bureau du "Socialiste," 1895.

Kellogg, Paul and Arthur Gleason. *British Labor and the War: Reconstructors for a New World*. New York: Boni and Liveright, 1919.

Kipling, Rudyard. *Songs from Books*. New York: Doubleday, Page & Co., 1912.

Knowlson, Sharper T. *The Origins of Popular Superstitions & Customs*. London: T. W. Laurie, Ltd., 1910.

Köhler, Wolfgang. *The Mentality of Apes*. New York: Harcourt, Brace & Co., 1927.

Lasswell, Harold D. *Propaganda Technique in the World War*. New York: Peter Smith, 1927.

Lasswell, Harold D., Ralph D. Casey, and Bruce Lannes Smith. *Propaganda and Promotional Activities: An Annotated Bibliography*. Minneapolis: The University of Minnesota Press, 1935.

Le Bon, Gustav. *Psychologie des foules*. Paris: Felix Alcan, 1895.

———. *The Psychology of Revolution*, trans. Bernard Miall. New York: G. P. Putnam's Sons, 1913. (French: *La Révolution Française et la Psychologie des Révolutions*, 1912.)

Lecky, William Edward Hartpole. *History of European Morals: From Augustus to Charlemagne*, 3rd ed., 2 vols. New York: D. Appleton & Co., 1891.

Lévy-Bruhl, Lucien. *La mentalité primitive*. Paris: Librairie Félix Alcan, 1922.

Lumby, Rawson J., ed. *Bacon's History of the Reign of King Henry VII*. Cambridge: Cambridge University Press, 1892.

Lumley, Frederick E. "Slogans as a Means of Social Control." *Publications of the American Sociological Society* 16, *Factors in Social Evolution* (1922): 121–134.

———. *The Propaganda Menace*. London: The Century Co., 1933.

Lyall, Archibald. *It Isn't Done: Or, the Future of Taboo among the British Islanders*. London: Kegan Paul, Trench, Trübner & Co., Ltd., 1930.

Lyons, Eugene. *Moscow Carousel*. New York: Alfred A. Knopf, 1935.

MacCrone, Ian. *Race Attitudes in South Africa: Historical, Experimental and Psychological Studies*. London: Oxford University Press, 1937.

MacCulloch, J. A. "Euphemism." James Hastings, ed., *Encyclopædia of Religion and Ethics*, vol. 5. New York: Charles Scribner's Sons, 1912. pp. 585–588.

Macmillan, William M. *Africa Emergent: A Survey of Social, Political, and Economic Trends in British Africa*. London: Faber and Faber, Ltd., 1938.

Majid, Abdul. *The Psychology of Leadership*. London: T. F. Unwin, Ltd., 1915.

Malinowski, Bronisław. *Myth in Primitive Psychology*. New York: W. W. Norton & Co., Inc., 1926.

de Man, Hendrik. *The Psychology of Socialism*, trans. Eden Paul and Cedar Paul. London: G. Allen & Unwin, Ltd., 1928.

Martin, Everett Dean. *The Behavior of Crowds: A Psychological Study*. New York: W. W. Norton & Co., Inc., 1920.

Martin, Kingsley. *The Magic of Monarchy*. New York: A. A. Knopf, 1937.

McDougall, William. *An Outline of Psychology*. London: Methuen & Co., Ltd., 1923.

———. *An Outline of Abnormal Psychology*. London: Methuen & Co., Ltd., 1926.

McMurdy, Robert, ed. *The Modern Chesterfield: A Selection of Chesterfield's Letters to His Son*. Boston: R. G. Badger, 1917.

Menninger, Karl. *The Human Mind*. Garden City: Garden City Publishing Company, Inc., 1930.

Miall, Bernard, trans. *New Chapters of Bismarck's Autobiography*. London: Hodder and Stoughton, 1920.

Michels, Robert. *Der Patriotismus: Prolegomena zu seiner soziologischen Analyse*. München: Duncker & Humblot, 1929.

Moon, Parker T. *Imperialism & World Politics*. New York: The Macmillan Company, 1926.

Moret, Alexandre and Georges Davy. *From Tribe to Empire: Social Organization among Primitives and in the Ancient East*. New York: A. A. Knopf, 1926.

Morris, William. *A Dream of John Ball and A King's Lesson*. London: Reeves & Turner, 1888.

Morselli, Henry. *Suicide: An Essay on Comparative Moral Statistics*. London: Kegan Paul, 1881.

Mowrer, Edgar Ansel. *Germany Puts the Clock Back*. New York: William Morrow & Co., 1933.

Mühsam, Kurt. *Wie wir belogen wurden: Die amtliche Irreführung des deutschen Volkes*. Munich: A. Langen, 1918.

Murphy, Gardner and Lois Barclay Murphy. *Experimental Social Psychology*. New York: Harper, 1931.

Mussolini, Benito. *The Political and Social Doctrine of Fascism*, trans. Jane Soames. London: Leonard and Virginia Woolf at the Hogarth Press, 1933.

Nesor, Albert. *The Mad Dog of Europe*. New York: Epic Publishers, Inc., 1939.

Nietzsche, Friedrich. *Gesammelte Werke*, 23 vols. München: Musarion Verlag, 1920–1929.

O'Conroy, Taid. *The Menace of Japan*. New York: Grosset & Dunlap, 1934.

Osborn, Reuben. *Freud and Marx: A Dialectical Study*. New York: Equinox Co-Operative Press, 1937.

Pareto, Vilfredo. *The Mind and Society: A Treatise on General Sociology*, 4 vols., trans. Andrew Bongiorno and Arthur Livingston. New York: Dover Publications, 1935.

Phillips, Godfrey Edward. *The Outcastes' Hope, or: Work among the Depressed Classes in India*. London: Church Missionary Society, 1912.

Pigors, Paul. *Leadership or Domination*. New York: Houghton Mifflin, 1935.

Ponsonby, Arthur. *Falsehood in War-Time: Containing an Assortment of Lies Circulated Throughout the Nations During the Great War*. New York: E. P. Dutton & Co., 1928.

Porritt, Arthur, ed. *The Causes of War: Economic, Industrial, Racial, Religious, Scientific, and Political*. London: Macmillan & Co., Ltd., 1932.

Prescott, William H. *History of the Conquest of Peru*. London: J. M. Dent & Sons, Ltd., 1921 (1st ed. 1847).

Procter, John. *The Catholic Creed: Or, What Do Catholics Believe?* 2nd ed. London: Art and Book Company, Ltd., 1901.

Radcliffe-Brown, Alfred Reginald. *The Andaman Islanders: A Study in Social Anthropology*. Cambridge: Cambridge University Press, 1922.

Reich, Wilhelm. *Massenpsychologie des Faschismus*. Kopenhagen: Verlag für Sexualpolitik, 1933.

Reichenbach, Harry and David Freedman. *Phantom Fame: The Anatomy of Ballyhoo*. London: Noel Douglas, 1932.

Renier, Gustaaf J. *The English: Are They Human?* London: Unwin Brothers, Ltd., 1931.

Roeder, Ralph. *The Man of the Renaissance*. London: George Routledge & Sons, Ltd., 1934.

Rosenberg, Alfred. *Der Mythus des zwanzigsten Jahrhunderts*. München: Hoheneichen-Verlag, 1934 (1st ed. 1930).

Schapera, Isaac. *Western Civilization and the Natives of South Africa*. London: George Routledge & Sons, Ltd., 1934.

Scott, Ernest. *History and Historical Problems*. London: Oxford University Press, 1925.

Sexton, James. *Sir James Sexton, Agitator: The Life Story of the Dockers' MP: An Autobiography*. London: Faber and Faber, Ltd., 1936.

Shaw, George Bernard. *John Bull's Other Island and Major Barbara*. New York: Brentano's, 1907.

———. *The Man of Destiny*. New York: Brentano's, 1913.

Sinclair, Robert. *Metropolitan Man*. London: G. Allen & Unwin, Ltd., 1937.

Slosson, Edwin Emery. "A Lecture Experiment in Hallucinations." *Psychological Review* 6 (1899): 407–408.

Smith, Adam. *An Inquiry into the Nature and Causes of the Wealth of Nations*, 6th ed., 2 vols. London: George Bell & Sons., 1896.

Smith, Grafton Elliot. *Human History*. New York: W. W. Norton & Co., Inc., 1929.

Sombart, Werner. *Händler und Helden: patriotische Besinnungen*. München: Duncker & Humblot, 1915.

Sorel, Georges. *Réflexions sur la violence*. Paris: Marcel Rivière et Cie., 1908.

Spencer, Baldwin and Francis J. Gillen. *The Native Tribes of Central Australia*. London: Macmillan and Co., Ltd., 1899.

Starr, Mark. *Lies and Hate in Education*. London: Hogarth Press, 1929.

Stevenson, Burton Edgbert. *The Home Book of Quotations: Classical and Modern*. New York: Dodd, Mead & Co., 1934.

Stevenson, Robert Louis. *Virginibus Puerisque*. New York: H. M. Caldwell Co., 1900.

Stout, George F. *Manual of Psychology*, 2nd ed. London: University Correspondence College Press, 1901.

Strack, Hermann Leberecht. *Der Blutaberglaube in der Menschheit, Blutmorde und Blutritus: Zugleich eine Antwort auf die Herausforderung des "Osservatore Cattolico."* Munich: C. H. Beck, 1892.

Stribling, Thomas Sigismund. *Birthright.* New York: Century & Co., 1922.

Suzuki, Daisetz T. *Manual of Zen Buddhism.* Kyoto: Eastern Buddhist Society, 1935.

Swain, John. *The Pleasures of the Torture Chamber.* London: Noel Douglas, 1931.

Tarbell, Ida M. ed. *Napoleon's Addresses: Selections from the Proclamations, Speeches and Correspondence of Napoleon Bonaparte.* Boston: Joseph Knight Company, 1897.

Tead, Ordway. *Instincts in Industry: A Study of Working-Class Psychology.* London: Constable, 1919.

Tharaud, Jérôme. *The Chosen People: A Short History of the Jews in Europe.* New York: Longmans, Green & Co., 1929.

Thimme, Hans. *Weltkrieg ohne Waffen: Die Propaganda der Westmächte gegen Deutschland, ihre Wirkung und ihre Abwehr.* Berlin: Cotta, 1932.

Torr, Dona. *Karl Marx and Friedrich Engels: Correspondence, 1846–1895.* London: M. Lawrence, 1934.

Trumbull, Clay H. *The Blood Covenant: A Primitive Rite and Its Bearings on Scripture.* Philadelphia: J. D. Wattles, 1883.

Vacant, Alfred, Eugène Mangenot, and Émile Amann, eds. *Dictionnaire de théologie catholique, contenant l'exposé des doctrines de la théologie catholique, leurs preuves et leur histoire*, 15 vols. Paris: Letouzey & Ané, 1899–1950.

Viereck, George Sylvester. *Spreading Germs of Hate.* New York: H. Liveright, 1930.

Webb, Sydney and Beatrice Webb. *The History of Trade Unionism.* New York: Longmans, Green & Co., 1911.

Wells, Herbert G. *The Work, Wealth, and Happiness of Mankind.* London: Heinemann, 1932.

Werner, Heinz. *Einführung in die Entwicklungspsychologie.* Leipzig: J. A. Barth, 1926.

White, Walter Francis. *The Fire in the Flint.* New York: Alfred A. Knopf, Inc., 1924.

Wilson, Monica Hunter. *Reaction to Conquest: Effects of Contact with Europeans on the Pondo of South Africa.* London: Oxford University Press, 1936.

Woolf, Leonard. *Quack, Quack!* London: Leonard and Virginia Woolf at the Hogarth Press, 1935.

Youmans, Edward L. and William J. Youmans, eds. "Middle-Age Spiritualism." *The Popular Science Monthly* 16 (January, 1880): 354–362.

Young, Kimball. *Source Book for Social Psychology.* New York: A. A. Knopf, 1927.

———. *Social Psychology: An Analysis of Social Behavior.* New York: A. A. Knopf, 1930.

INDEX

Made in the USA
Monee, IL
07 January 2024

51356730R00149